ENDING THE LAST COLD WAR

To My Parents, Choon Hayong Lee and Gum Ye Park

Ending the Last Cold War
Korean Arms Control and Security in Northeast Asia

SUK JUNG LEE
The Army of the Republic of Korea

Ashgate
Aldershot • Brookfield USA • Singapore • Sydney

© Suk Jung Lee 1997

All rights reserved. No part of this publication may be reproduced, stored in a retrieval system, or transmitted in any form or by any means, electronic, mechanical, photocopying, recording, or otherwise without the prior permission of the publishers.

Published by

Ashgate Publishing Limited
Gower House
Croft Road
Aldershot
Hants GU11 3HR
England

Ashgate Publishing Company
Old Post Road
Brookfield
Vermont 05036
USA

JZ
5645
.L44
1997

British Library Cataloguing in Publication Data
Lee, Suk Jung
　Ending the last Cold War : Korean arms control and security
　in Northeast Asia
　1.Arms control - Korea 2.Korea (North) - Foreign relations
　- Korea (South) 3.Korea (South) - Foreign relations - Korea (North)
　I.Title
　327.1'74'09519

Library of Congress Cataloging-in-Publication Data
Lee, Suk Jung.
　Ending the last Cold War : Korean arms control and security in
　Northeast Asia / Suk Jung Lee.
　　　p. cm.
　Includes bibliographical references.
　ISBN 1-85521-795-3
　　1. Arms control--Korea. 2. National security--East Asia.
　I. Title.
　JX1974.L525　1997
　327.1'74'09049--dc21

96-39517
CIP

ISBN 1 85521 795 3

Printed in Great Britain by Antony Rowe Ltd, Chippenham, Wiltshire.

Contents

Preface		vii
Acknowledgements		ix
Abbreviations		xi

Part I: Introduction

1. Background to the Application of European Arms Control Techniques to the Korean Peninsula — 3
2. Review of the Debates on Arms Control — 9

Part II: Arms Control Experiences in Europe

3. The CSCE Process and CBMs in Europe — 29
4. The Arms Reduction Negotiations: MBFR and CFE — 58
5. The FRG's Arms Control Policies as a Divided State — 88

Part III: Arms Control in Northeast Asia

6. The Application of the European Arms Control Model to Northeast Asia — 123
7. Regional Stability and Korean Arms Control — 167

Part IV: Korean Arms Control and the Application of the European Model

8. The North-South Arms Control Negotiations — 205
9. The Application of the European Arms Control Model to Korea — 233
10. Conclusion — 278

Select Bibliography — 293

Preface

In the past forty years arms control has become a central activity of international relations, playing a critical role in underpinning the balance of power. In Europe, arms control was used effectively to stabilise and defuse the military competition between NATO and the Warsaw Pact.

In north-east Asia by contrast there has been no significant arms control and the Korean Peninsula has remained locked in a tense military confrontation reminiscent of the Cold War. Yet there are many parallels between the Korean situation and the situation which prevailed in Europe and especially Germany during the period of Cold War and detente. Moreover, the death of North Korea's Kim Il Sung, and the conclusion of the agreement on nuclear facilities between North Korea and the United States in 1994 has begun to break the diplomatic log-jam which prevented effective arms control negotiations between the North and South for over forty years.

Ending the Last Cold War examines the security situation on the Korean Peninsula and assesses the potential for using arms control to reduce tension and enhance confidence between the two Koreas and with their regional neighbours and allies. The book looks first at the European experience and the lessons that can be drawn from it before going on to examine the Korean situation and applying the European model to it. It also addresses the particular points of German arms control policies as a divided state and Germany's position on the front-line of the European Cold War theatre with a view to considering its relevance to the Korean situation. The third part of the book explores the regional environment with respect to Korean arms control and the regional arms control mechanisms for the management of the high level of regional forces and potential conflicts between the rival powers in north-east Asia. Finally the book examines the potential conditions and the most promising avenues for the application of the European arms control measures to the Korean Peninsula and thereby attempts to provide a suitable theoretical frameworks for Korean arms control on the basis of the regional and the Korean security situation.

Acknowledgements

I would like to express special thanks to the Army of the Republic of Korea which provided me with the opportunity to study at the University of Aberdeen through financial support during my studies. I am particularly grateful to Pil Sup Lee, the former Chairman of the Joint Chiefs of Staff, and ROK Army Lieutenant-Generals Dong Shin Kim and Yong Ok Park, who have given spiritual support and encouragement for my research. No words can express my debt to them. I would also like to extend my appreciation to Major-General In Jong Kim for providing me with special attention and to Professor Ho Jae Lee, Dean of the University of Korea and Dr Young Koo Cha of the ROK Army who have both inspired so much of this work and for their gift of academic knowledge.

I am deeply indebted to Dr. Michael Sheehan at the University of Aberdeen. He has given me much time, invaluable assistance and critical commentaries to guide this work along. Without his distinctive help, this book would be incomplete in terms of analysis and conceptualization. I would like to thank Dr. Clive Archer and Mr. James H. Wyllie in the Department of Politics and International Relations, for their generous help during the research.

My thanks are due also to Lieutenant Colonel Ei Myung Lee of the ROK Army who has sent a numerous materials related to Korean arms control, and to the personal help of Trevor Armstrong and librarian Catharina McCurdy at the University of Aberdeen.

Finally, and importantly, I would like to record the dedicated efforts of my family. I am grateful to Eun Hee Ahn, who has endured hardship as a wife, devoted mother and teacher of two lovely daughters, Bom and Saem. The completion of this research was possible thanks to the morning prayers by my parents in my homeland. I dedicate this book to my parents, and my family.

Abbreviations

ACDA	Arms Control and Disarmament Agency
ACVs	Armoured Combat Vehicles
ASEAN	Association of Southeast Asian Nations
ATTU	Atlantic-to-the-Urals
BMA	Baikal-Amur Railway
BW	Biological Weapons
CBMs	Confidence-Building Measures
CDE	Conference on Disarmament in Europe
CDU/CSU	Christian Democratic Union/Christian Social Union
CIS	Commonwealth of Independent States
CFE	Conventional Forces in Europe
CNEAS	Conference on North-east Asian Security
CSBMs	Confidence-and Security-Building Measures
CSCA	Conference on Security and Cooperation in Asia
CSCE	Conference on Security and Cooperation in Europe
DMZ	Demilitarized Zone
DPRK	Democratic People's Republic of Korea
FDP	Free Democratic Party
FEBA	Forward Edge of the Battle Area
FIP	Five Year Force Improvement(South Korea)
FRG	Federal Republic of Germany
GCD	General and Complete Disarmament
GDR	German Democratic Republic
GNP	Gross National Product
HLTF	High Level Task Force
IAEA	International Atomic Energy Agency
IISS	International Institute for Strategic Studies
IMEMO	Institute of World Economy and International Relations
INF	Intermediate Nuclear Force(s)
JCS	Joint Chiefs of Staff
JSA	Joint Security Area
JMSDF	Japanese Maritime Self-Defence Force
KIDA	Korean Institute for Defence Analysis
MBFR	Mutual and Balanced Force Reduction

MAC	Military Armistice Commission (Korea)
MBT	Main Battle Tank
MDL	Military Demarcation Line
MOD	Ministry of Defence
NATO	North Atlantic Treaty Organization
NCND	Neither Confirm Nor Deny
NNS	Neutral and Non-aligned States
NPT	Non-Proliferation Treaty
NTM	National Technical Means
OSI	On-Site Inspection
PLA	People's Liberation Army (China)
POMCUS (NATO)	Pre-Positioned Overseas Materials Configured in Unit Sets
PRC	People's Republic of China
PTBT	Partial Test Ban Treaty
ROK	Republic of Korea
SALT	Strategic Arms Limitations Talks
SAARC	South Asian Association for Regional Cooperation
SCM	Security Consultative Meeting (ROK-US)
SED	Socialist Unity Party (GDR)
SPD	Social Democratic Party
SLOC	Sea Lanes of Communication
TLEs	Treaty-Limited Equipments
T/S	Team Spirit (exercise, ROK-US)
TVD	Theatre of Military Operation (Soviet)
USFK	US Forces in Korea
VCC	Verification and Control Commission
WTO	Warsaw Treaty Organization

Part I
Introduction

1. Background to the Application of European Arms Control Techniques to the Korean Peninsula

The history of modern European arms control began with the emergence of the Cold War. Europe was the centre of the political and military confrontation between East and West during the Cold War. The sharp ideological antagonism between them resulted in the creation of the collective defence systems of NATO and the Warsaw Pact. The strategic parity in nuclear weapons which gradually emerged between East and West encouraged the two blocs to emphasise defence using conventional forces. Conventional arms thereby became the dominating factor in the security of Europe during of the Cold War, notwithstanding the importance of nuclear weapons to NATO doctrine.

Although the arms build-up made the two blocs ostensibly more secure, it resulted also in increasing the fear of war in Europe. Apprehension grew as the scope and speed of the destruction implicit in the modern armament inventories were recognized. A major conventional war between the two blocs, even if it somehow failed to escalate into nuclear war, was seen as a potential catastrophe beyond that of the fifty millions killed in the Second World War.

The political antagonism deriving from the confrontation of ideology was a principal determinant of the arms race between East and West. Therefore the primary solution to the military problem had to involve the reforming of political relations. East and West recognised each other as de facto political entities divided by differences of ideology and pursued 'detente' or 'status quo' on the principle of co-existence. However, this co-existence was based upon high levels of military strength designed to deter or withstand an attack from the other side. Both Cold War alliances placed overwhelming priority upon their own military capabilities as a means to deter aggression by the other side. In the absence of trust which characterised the Cold War period, neither was willing to countenance large-scale disarmament as a solution to the security threat posed by the other side. Therefore, faced with the difficulty of disarmament, arms control was seen as an alternative for the management of the enormous military forces of both sides. The manner of management of conventional forces was similar to that of the nuclear arms control, being mainly focussed upon prevention of misunderstanding which might lead to accidental war.

The military forces created by the confrontation of ideology would be permanent as long as the ideological hostility between the two sides continued. Indeed the efforts to conclude arms reduction did not succeed until the communist Eastern bloc collapsed.

Thus the military problem in Europe was a reflection of the East-West political confrontation. But, conversely, the significant improvement of political relations between them could not be expected without the solution of the military problem arising from the risk of war and the arms race. The arms control negotiations aimed at overcoming the military problem led in time to political security cooperation. This became a symbol of the East-West detente and operated as a means of political reconciliation during the Cold War. Consequently 'detente' and 'arms control' became closely linked in the political imagination. East and West developed a common view that emphasised the importance of arms control talks as a process, as much as any expected negotiating outcome. The arms control forums became a means of maintaining an active, persistent relationship at times of tension and further, a means of signalling shifts on broader political questions.[1]

A first step towards political security cooperation was the creation of the Conference on Security and Cooperation in Europe (CSCE) in 1975. The CSCE declared the principle of the non-use of force in Europe. The political and security problems between East and West in Europe were dealt with within the CSCE. The crucial contribution of the CSCE was in the introduction of confidence building measures as a security measure. The CBMs were the best model for the build-up of confidence and the limitation on military forces in the area where the military confrontation was tense. Through the applications of CBMs, the European theatre was stabilized, preventing a return to the crisis characteristic of the pre-detente confrontation. The transparency of the East-West forces through the application of the CBMs limited the possibility of military action by regulating military activities and consequently reduced the advantages from military superiority. Thus the CBMs were seen as a crucial basis for production of the CFE Treaty in 1990. The CFE Treaty was an epoch-making event which eliminated the legacy of the Cold War. It reduced the risk of full-scale war in Europe through the maintenance of military forces at low levels and various arms control mechanisms.

One of the most successful results of European arms control was to prevent the eruption of "Hot War" from the Cold War tensions. The

European arms control procedure represents a realistic theory for war prevention, and of the build-up of confidence between hostile countries. Arms control, originating from the Cold War, was seen as a most successful moderator of the confrontation between capitalism and communism. The European arms control model remains a very important, precious legacy for the build-up of confidence, and as a vehicle of detente, crisis management, prevention of war and finally arms reduction between hostile military alliances or countries. Therefore it would provide a useful arms control model which could be extended to other regions sharing similar security concerns to those characteristic of Europe in the late Cold War period.

Perhaps the most neglected area of postwar international security is the application of arms control for the prevention of conventional war outside of Europe. While Europe experienced few local wars or conflicts during the Cold War, most regions outside of Europe suffered a number of wars of high cost, to the extent that the levels of death and destruction are equivalent to those of World War II. Analysts found that more than 1,000 conflicts had occurred in the postwar period leaving about 70 millions dead.[2]

It is now time for rethinking the problem of conventional arms control at the global level. The efforts towards conventional arms control being concentrated in Europe were understandable in the context of prevention of full-scale war between East and West. It was also seen as a formula applicable only for a European security situation. The prolonged arms control talks in Europe might not have encouraged the other regions to consider the European model. Rather most arms control concerns outside of Europe have been focussed on the issue of controlling flows of sophisticated weapons to conflict-ridden regions by external powers. However, such efforts have failed to produce satisfactory results because of commercial profits from the sale of weapons, and the involvement of external powers' own intertwined interests. The control of arms transfers was a temporary expedient during or after the war rather than a method for the prevention of war.

Now however, the success of European arms control could give a strong incentive to the other regions. The Asian region in particular can be next in line for the application of the successful experiences of Europe. The region has been highest in the frequency of war and in the figures for men killed in the postwar conventional conflicts throughout the world.[3] In particular the Korean Peninsula in Northeast Asia is a suitable case for the application of European experience. North and South Korea have still legally remained in a cease-fire by the 1953 Armistice Agreement of the Korean War. Since then there have been a number of incidents arising from military provocations by North Korea. These prompted serious crises which on occasion brought the two Korean regimes to the verge of war. More recently North Korean attempts to possess nuclear weapons have heightened the sense of crisis on the Korean Peninsula.

The Korean Peninsula was seen as a sub-regional system within the international ideological bipolar security system. The division of Korea was a product of ideological division in the world. The Korean war, though it was limited and local, was the first ideological international war conducted in the framework of the bipolar system. From 1945 onwards, North and South Korea were central poles of the Cold War alliance systems in Northeast Asia, the Soviet Union-North Korea-China vs the United States-South Korea.

Regardless of the collapse of the international Cold War system, the regional powers in Northeast Asia continue their defence build-up in contrast with the international trend of arms reduction. North and South Korea still continue the old formula of ideological confrontation, Capitalism vs Communism. The arms race between them has remained in high gear in a mutually distorted threat perception. The array of about 1.5 million heavily armed troops along the Demilitarized Zone (DMZ) keeps alive the risk of a Second Korean War. Thus the Korean Peninsula remains burdened with residual regional manifestations of the Cold War. However the subsequent watershed events in Europe such as the collapse of Eastern and Soviet communist regimes, German unification and the CFE Treaty are stimulating North and South Korea to throw away a remnant of the military confrontation of the Cold War. Although, as will be discussed later, they have also reinforced North Korean suspicion of an arms control process which might contribute to the collapse of communism in North Korea. Most of all, the unification of Germany, which had lived in the shadow of the Cold War like Korea, has encouraged Koreans that what seemed to be unthinkable, unification, was a real possibility. Moreover the change in regional security situations also pushes the two Korean states to move toward arms control. The Soviet Union and China normalized their relations in the mid-1980's and moved towards massive arms reduction along their common border with the conclusion of a border treaty. The arms control between them was made in the aftermath of European arms control and followed a European model with the introduction of CBMs.

The framework of the alliance systems between the two Korean states and the major powers surrounding them in the days of the Cold War is changing at a high speed. South Korea is developing a friendly relationship with Russia and China through economic cooperation after establishing full diplomatic relations with them. North Korea is also sending the US and Japan signals for the ending of antagonistic relations, most dramatically through the conclusion of the US-DPRK nuclear agreement in 1994. Such developments towards reciprocal recognitions resemble the European detente situation in the early 1970s which led to the opening of arms control talks between East and West and the reconciliation between the two German states.

Figure 1-1 The Framework of European Conventional Arms Control

Political and Ideological Divisions
|
Political - Status quo - territorial
|
Detente
|
Political Security Cooperation
|
Confidence Build-up
|
CSCE - Political CBMs - Military CBMs - MBFR--->CFE
|
Crisis Management
|
Common Security Interest
|
Threat at low level
|
Defensive Force Posture------>Secure Stability

The ideological confrontation and high military tension constitute the basic rationale for the application of the European arms control model to the Korean Peninsula as a regional test case in the development of its universal applicability. With these external and internal environments for forming a new security structure, the most important background in linking European arms control with Korean arms control derives from the two Korean states' pursuit of European-style arms control dialogue. A series of arms control talks between them began in the early 1990s. In December 1991, they concluded an agreement covering reconciliation and provisions for realizing mutual non-aggression and arms control. The agreement follows the European experiences in arms control.

The attempt to apply European arms control to the Korean Peninsula begins with the design of an analytical framework which can be used in analysis as a generalized, hypothetical description based upon an analogy. The assumption is that European experience can be copied and patterned to suit Korea.

Given the particularity and complexity of European security and the evolution of arms control talks over a long period, it may be very difficult to generalize the entire European arms control process as a model for a code of conduct among states. However, the series of arms control procedures that stabilized the European theatre and finally led to arms reduction can be used as an empirical example. In this respect the European arms control process provides a suitable theoretical framework and many valuable lessons for Korean arms control in terms of political conditions, institutional arrangements, negotiating techniques, technical problems and the utility of specific measures, etc. Korean arms control will be explored in the framework of these European arms control mechanisms.

NOTES

1. Lawrence Freedman, "Arms Control: Thirty Years On", *Daedalus*, Vol 120 (1991) p. 72.
2. Catherine M. Kelleher, "Conventional War in the Postwar International System", in David Carlton and Carlo Schaerf, *Perspectives on the Arms Race* (London: Macmillan Press Ltd, 1989), p. 103.
3. For statistics on casualties and conflict frequency, Ibid. p. 105. see also Kalevi J. Holsti, *Peace and War: Armed Conflicts and International Order 1648-1989* (Cambridge: Cambridge University Press, 1991), pp. 306-334.

2. Review of the Debates on Arms Control

The Concept and Purpose of Arms Control

Arms control, as a body of thought, developed from the late 1950s onwards as a realistic alternative to the obvious failure of classical disarmament. There were many reasons why the traditional disarmament approach lost its appeal to the major powers, but one important reason was the development of nuclear weapons, which made the issue of verifying agreements a critical one. The trust between East and West necessary to make disarmament possible in these new circumstances was simply not present during the Cold War. The actual use of nuclear weapons was seriously considered in some conflicts. Such a possibility appeared during the Korean war. The United States threatened a nuclear attack against the People's Republic of China (PRC) because of its involvement in the Korean War. The possibility of using tactical nuclear weapons was also considered as a way of countering Chinese 'human wave tactics' and acknowledging the pressure to end the protracted Korean War.[1] The escalation of the Cold War thus made urgent the need to develop arms control theories for war prevention. The bipolar system, which started with the nuclear age, generated many situations likely to lead the two superpowers to nuclear war. The risk of nuclear war culminated in the Cuban Missile Crisis. Because of such crises, the control of nuclear weapons became more urgent than their abolition. Scholars were urged to study ways to avoid nuclear war. A policy of temporary security insurance was needed until political conditions changed and disarmament took place. Herman Kahn and Anthony Weiner reflected the view most commonly held by the vast majority of those who wrote on the subject of arms control:

> The purpose of arms control is ... to improve the inherent stability of the situation, decrease the occasions or the approximate cause of war within this system, and decrease the destructiveness and other disutilities of any wars that actually occur.[2]

As well as Herman Kahn and Anthony Weiner, Schelling and Halperin also referred to the common aim of reducing the likelihood of war, its scope and the violence involved if it occurs.[3] They also emphasised military cooperation between potential enemies not only to avoid accidental war but to minimize the danger of accident, false alarm, unauthorized action or misunderstanding, that might lead to war.[4] Their intention was well shown as follows:

> Arms control can be thought of as an effort, by some kind of reciprocity or cooperation with our potential enemies, to minimize, to offset, to compensate or to deflate some of these characteristics of modern weapons and military expectations.[5]

By emphasizing cooperation with the enemy the arms control approach emphasised diplomatic negotiations not unilateral actions. It was argued that communication provided the way to eliminate the possibility of pre-emptive war.

Unlike disarmament proponents arms controllers rejected the argument that the existence of weapons is a cause of war.[6] They believed that there is no simple cause and effect relationship between the possession of weapons and the outbreak of war.[7] The arms control approach also declared that political conflicts, which are created by political differences, lead to war. The way to prevent war, according to this view, was not to begin by disarming, but to concentrate upon overcoming the political antagonism. Therefore arms control need not necessarily mean the reduction of weapons. Under certain circumstances to effectively prevent war the arms control approach prefers to increase weaponry rather than to decrease it.

Arms controllers have not sought the abolition of weapons but rather have put forward methods to live with them. In the past they believed that the deterrence of war was only guaranteed by a balance of power and numerically that high balances were more stabilizing than balances at low levels. Since small forces were more vulnerable to marginal advantages on each side, the strategic balance at low levels was seen as destabilizing. As a result strategic stability in nuclear weapons for example was maintained at force levels which were higher even than those called for by 'assured destruction' requirements.[8]

But the meaning of arms control evolved steadily away from its original idea. The development of military technology led to the adoption of an insurance policy regarding nuclear weapons in the 'triad approach' where a variety of weapons would be carried by manned bombers, ground and submarine-launched ballistic missiles. Furthermore, this trend emphasised quantity rather than quality and needed a certain of number of weapons over and above the theoretical minimum due to the possibility of misfires, malfunctions and inaccuracy. Accordingly, the concept of arms control changed to acquire an essentially political rather than strategic consideration. The most notable new objective from the mid-1970s onwards was the pursuit of reductions as a primary objective.[9] The simple public goal of the fewer nuclear weapons on each side the better encouraged effort towards freezing numbers and looking toward reduction. As Thomas C. Schelling noted arms control negotiations have seen the shift of interest from the character of weapon to their numbers.[10]

The definition of arms control has evolved with development of weapon systems, narrowing the scope of control. Arms controllers have been much more concerned with new generation weapon systems than old generation ones. Time and technology entail new controls and methods. The ideas of arms controllers and policy-makers have always lagged behind military technology.

The control of nuclear weapons is mainly connected with international or superpower security. On the other hand the control of conventional weapons is directly related to regional or national security. National security is the ultimate value of national existence and is traditionally pursued largely through armament policy. This policy includes not only the amount and kind of weapons and forces in being but also the development, and utility of such forces. Donald G. Brennan defined "arms control as a cooperative or multilateral approach to armament policy which involved adjusting at least some armament capabilities and uses to those actually desirable in the light of the intention, actions and adjusted capabilities of the other nations."[11] He also demonstrated the further clarification of the concept of arms control by including the possibility of constraints on armaments that may or may not entail a reduction of forces. This concept does not require that the cooperation involved be explicit or that it go into detail in a formal agreement.

Similarly Robert R. Bowie also emphasized that "cooperation and agreement" are very important for arms control. A representative definition was that:

> The concept of "arms control" includes any agreement among several powers to regulate some aspects of their military capabilities or potential. The arrangement may apply to location, amount, readiness, types of military forces, weapon, or facilities. ... They presuppose some form of cooperation or joint action among several participants regarding their military programs.[12]

Brennan and Bowie cover comprehensively almost all the military elements required for conventional arms control. But their definitions did not specifically define the partners for cooperation, that is, potential enemies. Schelling and Halperin emphasised this crucial point Their definition of arms control was:

> all the military cooperation between potential enemies in the interest of reducing the likelihood of war, its scope and violence if it occurs and political and economic costs of being prepared for it'. The essential feature is the recognition of common interests, of the possibility of reciprocation with regard to their military establishments.[13]

However, the definition was formulated with nuclear weapons rather than conventional weapons' in mind.

The above indications also left out another important point. National security depends not only on net military capability, but on perception of threat. The greater the threat perceived, the stronger is the desire to acquire greater military power in order to deter aggression against oneself. Threat perception is a function of a potential adversary's capabilities and intentions.[14] Arms control, therefore, must affect subjective perceptions as well as objective factors if it is to enhance national security. It attempts to influence the intentions of an adversary as well as his capabilities. Nation states always tend to see the armed forces and actions of their opponents as targeted directly at themselves. The best way to change their threat perception is to eliminate or reduce the forces and weapons which pose particular threats. In more general terms, agreements which preclude the attainment of 'superiority' or prevent the development of gross imbalance in military capabilities would ease fear and reduce concern.

Conventional arms control in Europe has both political and military objectives. From the beginning of MBFR arms control negotiations have been regarded as a function of political security which improves political relations between East and West.[15] The military confrontation between NATO and the Warsaw Pact was caused by the political competition. Since political objectives determine the outbreak of a conflict, no potential stability could be expected without striking at the roots of the problem itself. The European multilateral arms control negotiations have contributed to building up political stability by codifying the status quo between NATO and the Warsaw Pact through measures commonly undertaken by both adversaries.

The basic objective of conventional arms control in Europe was to strengthen stability. Laurinda L. Rohn suggests the following definition of conventional stability;

conventional stability exists when there is a balance of conventional capabilities such that both sides believe that (1) neither side can launch a successful attack against the other, and (2) either side can successfully repel any attack launched by the other.[16]

This definition suggests two facets of conventional stability; "offensive conventional stability" and "defensive conventional stability." Ruhl enlarges the conventional stability to military stability and political stability. The military stability achieved by a balance of force enhances political stability.[17] The establishment of a stable and secure balance of armed forces is a crucial element in creating overall stability in the relationship between nations or military blocs.

NATO defined stability in its Brussels Declaration of 1986 as the "elimination of the capability for surprise attack or for the initiation of large-scale offensive action." It meant in practice the pursuit of lower levels of conventional armaments and the elimination of disparities prejudicial to stability and security, with priority given to eliminating the capability to launch surprise attacks or initiate large-scale offensive actions.[18] The above represents the overall position on objectives and methods of the conventional arms control talks from MBFR to CFE.

The control of conventional forces is largely divided into two types, the "structural" and "operational" approaches. The structural approach aims at the change of the present military system, while the operational aims to maintain the status quo. The objective of the former is to establish a permanent security system and the latter is to create a temporary security system prior to the former. The first focus in Europe was to establish a balance and stability in the conventional forces between the East and the West at lower, or at least equal, levels. The primary concern was to decrease the size of the two blocs' forces in order to build a stabilized balance.

The Eastern Bloc consistently maintained larger conventional forces than NATO. This superiority in numbers extended from manpower through all items of equipment. In Central Europe NATO forces were outnumbered by 1:1.22 in manpower, and between 2:1 to 3:1 in all major items of equipment. NATO also worried about less tangible factors; the powerful forward deployment of Soviet firepower and the mission of Warsaw Pact forces, in the event of war, to initiate offensive action, and to achieve surprise and rapid breakthrough to NATO's rear area. The elimination of the invasion capability of the Warsaw Pact forces was the primary objective of NATO. This objective was extended from the mere numerical parity of troops and weapons to the limitation of disposition, organization, logistics, command and control capability etc.[19] Therefore stability included both what the forces retained and what they cut. Even in its narrower, military sense stability has several dimensions. It not only relates to ratios of forces or firepower, or of forces to space, but also to the dynamics of the arms race and to crisis behaviour. Above all, it bears on the offence/defence dichotomy in the sense that stability requires defensive options to be more effective and viable than offensive ones.[20]

On the other hand the operational approach, the main instrument of which is CSBMs, is to lessen the possibility of sudden aggression. Western Europe has been very influenced by the capability and possibility of a Soviet and East European surprise large-scale attack. Such perception has been generalized from experience of the Eastern bloc's past military behaviour; rapid deployment of the Chinese army in the Korean War of 1950s, and the swiftness of the USSR in executing a large scale intervention against Hungary in 1956, Czechoslovakia in 1968 and Afghanistan in 1979. From these precedents Western Europe was very concerned with maintaining sufficient warning time and limiting the speed with which the Warsaw Pact could mobilize and reinforce its forward-based forces.[21]

The West's first priority before attaining a balance by reduction was to regulate the activities of military forces: to forecast action in advance; to notify exercises; or concentrations of troops in excess of various thresholds, by inviting observers to such activities and permitting on-site inspections of questionable activities. These kind of suggestions directly addressed NATO's security problems.

This provided NATO with leverage to address WTO invasion capabilities and to pursue measures which would prolong the time needed for Soviet units to reach full war strength, and help NATO prepare for attack and strategic reinforcement.[22] In the race of unequal reinforcements, according to West German MOD calculations, the Pact could deploy 48 fully operational divisions within 24 hours after orders, while NATO would need five days to deploy 30 divisions in the defence. After four or five days, the Eastern strength would amount to 68 divisions, while NATO would need 14 days to augment its effectives from 30 to 36 divisions.[23]

In general the negotiations on conventional arms control directly reflect the security problems in the European case. As Johan Holst mentioned, arms control measures may be viewed either from the perspective of accomplishing defence policy goals or as a means of furthering wider security policy objectives with no mutual exclusion of other objectives. Therefore it should be thought of as elements of a new structure in defence.[24]

Spin-offs of Arms Control

Arms control negotiations produce other benefits unrelated to their eventual outcome. They have sometimes been employed to achieve a variety of additional objectives rather than simply arms control. In the early 1970s MBFR was not initiated as a means for reducing the mutual armed forces, but was in part designed to defeat the proposals for unilateral reduction of US troops in Europe by Senator Mansfield. MBFR provided a useful formula to overcome domestic pressure for unilateral reduction, and it created good opportunities to encourage NATO countries to increase their share of the defence burden, because the US unilateral proposal was the result of economic burdens caused by the need to defend Europe. The Soviet Union accepted NATO's proposal in return for getting the CSCE, in spite of favouring the conventional forces of the Warsaw Pact in Central Europe. She tried to achieve the additional objective of enhancing political influence rather than military objectives through MBFR.

Arms control negotiations had above all contributed to enhance alliance cohesion. They led to greater exchange of information and could even produce, within each military pact, a rational reassessment of military requirements, goals and strategies. East-West arms control processes were conducted as an exercise, not only in mutual education and exchange of information, but in self-education and self-information.[25]

Moreover, arms control might generally have important impacts on the political area as well as the military-strategic relationship. The military actor has generally influenced the form of political relationship even though it is performed as a means of political mission. Visible changes in the military relationship are addressed prior to political change and are a precondition of the political normalization between hostile countries. For example in Germany, both sides proclaimed the non-use of military power as a mean of unification before they cemented the political relationship. The core accomplishment of the CSCE was basically in both sides refraining from the threat or use of force and the inviolability of frontiers. In advance of normalization with the Soviet Union, China also required the elimination of three military obstacles by unilateral action: complete withdrawal of Soviet troops from Afghanistan, withdrawal of Vietnamese troops strongly supported by the Soviets in Cambodia and reduction of Soviet troops from the Soviet-Chinese border. Thus some degree of cooperation and changes in the field of arms may be suggested by the need for some apparent political changes. Because of this, if the habit of mutual beneficial cooperation could develop in the field of armament policy, then this habit of cooperation might spill over into other areas and act as a catalyst for the solution of political problems.[26]

This may produce the feed-back circulation, "Input-Output", that is, 'that the achievement of modest arms reduction programs would facilitate the achievement of some political solutions, which in turn would facilitate further measures of armament cooperation.[27] Thus the careful design and use of mechanisms for adjustment and enforcement in arms control programs may lead to an increased dependence on peaceful and orderly means of resolving conflicting national problems between countries.

Conventional arms control in Europe was concerned with a political linkage approach. MBFR was employed as an instrument for political changes between East and West. The linkage with political objectives was shown by Johan Holst. He demonstrated that traditional objectives of reducing pre-emptive instability and saving money are inadequate as a normative guide for policy-making in regard to force limitation in Europe. Arms control was regarded as a political process for the reconstruction of Europe;

> Arms Control measures should be understood as elements which contribute to the preconditions for and facilitates the control of a process aiming at political reconstruction and normalization in Europe. Arms control measures should not be assessed separately from their impact on the political process ... They should be assessed also with reference to the goal of erecting new structures.[28]

But the question arises as to whether arms control negotiations have directly promoted the political changes in the Eastern European states and have been used to further interests in other realms such as human rights and economic changes. Kiron K. Skinner pointed out that arms control which was linked with political factors had not contributed to a broader improvement in relations as was shown with relation to the Soviet Union and the United States after the SALT II Agreement.[29] This is a crucial question as far as the possibility of adapting the model for Korea is concerned, since North and South Korea view the value of such a linkage very differently. And unlike the WTO states, North Korea can already see the impact this linkage had on the European example and therefore react to its implications for Korea.

The arms control negotiations between East and West were long and complicated processes that took account of many factors in a broader sense. There is therefore little evidence to suggest that they have directly influenced the political and economic changes, but the West linked arms control with political issues. It is noticeable that there was indirect military conflict between the West and the Soviet Union, but neither employed direct military action in Europe after the beginning of negotiations. The arms control negotiations such as CSCE, MBFR and CFE provided them with a number of contacts and cooperation for the prevention of war.[30]

Conventional arms control negotiations were proclaimed as an example of detente and superpower rapprochement. Therefore it became difficult for the West and the East to abandon the talks without sending unfortunate signals to Europe.[31] They were more interested in the talks as a symbol of detente due to the multilateral character of the talks, rather than in reaching an agreement. The political role of the MBFR encouraged them to continue the talks even when they were conspicuously unsuccessful.

The Conditions and Obstacles of Arms Control

Arms control can be conducted only when governments want it and are agreed on its terms. Political will is central to the exercise of arms control. Successful arms control is contingent on finding ways to manage the political obstacles. Quincy Wright noted that if governments are not given an equivalent in political guarantees of security, or if they are not assured of a substitute method of security, or of changes, states would not reduce armaments.[32] A sense of security has been the most important condition for arms control if states' security is not guaranteed against the threat of the adversary. It has become conventional wisdom that arms control considerations should be taken into account in shaping defence policy and programmes.

The question arises as to when arms control is undertaken by governments as a political behaviour. The historical record suggests that arms control seems to be possible only between nations which have already reached some form of political accommodation. Until now successful disarmament treaties have always been accompanied by political arrangements which are believed by the parties to augment their political security or to settle their outstanding political problems. As an example, the MBFR negotiations were proposed after the signing of the Federal Republic of Germany (FRG)-Soviet and FRG-Polish treaties on renunciation of force in August and December of 1970 and after the opening of the CSCE in Helsinki in July of 1973. This arms control negotiation was preceded by settling the frontier questions arising out of the results of World War II and including the renunciation of the use of force.

In fact, where there exists political tension of a certain degree, some kinds of arms control appear out of the question. Nations which are deeply suspicious of each other have little desire to rely on arms control as an instrument of their national security. Conversely, if relations improve beyond a certain point, then arms control negotiations are unnecessary. Rather nations may depend upon unilateral reduction. Philip Towle suggested that "it is only in the intermediate band of relationships that arms control or stabilizing are worthwhile and effective".[33] Arms control may sometimes lead to more cordial relations between the signatories of an agreement but some minimum "cooperative spirit" is necessary before negotiation. Joseph Kruzel examined eight cases in an analysis of the relation between political accommodation and arms control in agreements. The results suggested seven cases were made between nations in a "wariness-weariness" syndrome. Only one case was an accord negotiated between two states whose relationship could be described as genuinely antagonistic.[34] He found that the Rush-Bagot Agreement was concluded at a time when relations between the United States and Great Britain were tense, while other agreements were all concluded between nations whose relationship may not have been cordial, but at least involved no inordinate level of antagonism.[35]

West and East maintained very cautious attitudes towards arms reduction agreement during the period of the MBFR talks. The relations were not effectively cordial. Their main concerns were concentrated on the design of CBMs which could prevent preemptive war or accidental war by misunderstanding. On the other hand, the weariness of the long Cold War confrontation led the blocs to seek CFE talks as an alternative to MBFR. Consequently the CFE treaty was concluded during the endgame of the cold war.

The other important condition for arms control is to strive for common security or interest, that is 'security together with and not against', an adversary. This factor is most essential in developing and solidifying it. Negotiations usually succeed only when a proposal has a shared interest. The concept was described by Thee as follows,

> States can no longer seek security at each other's expense; it can be attained only through cooperative undertakings ... Even ideological opponents and political rivals have a shared interest in survival. There must be partnership in the struggle against war itself. The search for arms control and disarmament is the pursuit of common gains, not unilateral advantages.[36]

Most negotiators have attempted to gain advantages relative to the other party, or to leave gaps that either side could expect to fill by new armaments which would provide a temporary advantage. But agreements are usually sustained only when they are perceived as having equal interest measures. For example in negotiations at the Washington Conference of 1922, all attempts to press for unequal limitations in auxiliary ships proved unsuccessful. For the United States and Great Britain the limitation was 500,000 tons, for Japan, 300,000 tons. The inequality of 5:5:3 ratio so wounded the pride of Japan that it refused to continue the agreement after 1936.

The best motive for arms control is the termination of a war. This has sometimes led to compulsory disarmament of the defeated power, as of Prussia in 1807 and Germany in 1919 and 1945. Such disarmament, however, has usually been of short duration because the victors were divided or lethargic in imposing it and the vanquished have been anxious for revenge, as was Germany in the 1930s, or because the victors have desired to re-arm the vanquished against a new enemy, even though the vanquished at first wished to retain the economic and political advantages of its disarmament, as in the case of Germany and Japan in the 1950s.[37]

Finally a very significant condition for successful arms control is the agreement of the military. Responsible for the defence of the nation, military leaders tend to prefer physical weapons to metaphysical agreements, though the military is not blind to the benefits of it.[38] They have a basic perception that the security mission committed to them is successfully carried out by sufficient armaments. Because of this, arms control policy operates under the influence of the military services. For example, in 1921 the General Board of the US navy insisted that the United States expand its naval ship-building programme to use as a bargaining chip in forthcoming negotiations.

Arms control is an effort to intervene in the defence policy process, to constrain certain kinds of weapons, options and practices for the larger good of national security. Therefore, the military is generally negative about having any agreements for unilateral reduction for which it is not compensated. Governments essentially need military support for agreements because the military program is directly affected. For example, particularly, in the domestic politics of the United States, the military has a powerful voice not only in the policy formulation process but in the ratification process.[39] When President Kennedy desired a comprehensive test ban, he had to settle for the limited test ban of 1963 because he could not persuade the Joint Chiefs of Staff (JCS) to support the comprehensive treaty.[40] As a result Kennedy only got the Partial Test Ban Treaty, which prohibited atmospheric nuclear testing. In return, he promised to continue testing including the maintenance of all testing laboratories.

Arms control is sometimes confronted with severe critics. Such criticism is not limited to the practice of arms control but extended to the theory itself.[41] This results from the fact that the record of arms control from 1959 to 1987 did not produce successful results for so great an input of attention, time and energy. It means there are limits to what arms control can accomplish. The limitations are largely divided into two categories, structural and negotiable factors. Of structural factors one characteristic obstacle derives from the divergent security requirement. It is consequent upon military tradition and strategic doctrine. Moreover, each side's troops are differently organized, equipped and trained. Since the armed forces of each country rely on their own special 'mix' of armament and men, any restriction of a particular weapon or the number of men has different impacts on each of them.[42] For example, traditionally, the Soviet Union had preponderantly a special concern with maintaining sufficient quantities of arms to compensate for the gap of quality. In contrast with this, the United States preserved its capabilities in quality based on advanced technology.

In the basic strategic doctrine NATO regarded tactical nuclear forces as partially offsetting the Warsaw Pact conventional superiority, as a deterrent to the exercise of that superiority, and as a link with strategic nuclear forces which could enhance the credibility of the strategic deterrent. Thus NATO was largely interested in arms control measures which would disproportionately reduce Warsaw Pact forces and specially Soviet armed forces in Eastern Europe. On the other hand the Warsaw Pact regarded NATO nuclear forces as a primary threat and their early employment as inevitable, if not deliberate. Its own tactical nuclear forces were intended to retaliate to a NATO nuclear strike and to pave the way for operations by Pact tank, mechanized and airborne divisions.[43]

The other obstacle to arms control derives from those objectives concerning national security and alliance systems. As a result there have been differences with regard to the implications of the arms control process, in particular, between military blocs. During negotiations over Europe, Socialist Eastern Europe pursued this process as a mechanism for easing the confrontation and for loosening of NATO bloc ties, providing additional assurances against the use of forces and improving relations with Western Europe. In contrast Western Europe feared arms control negotiations might serve to divide the allies, by playing upon the fear of some and the eagerness of others for detente and disarmament.[44]

In the final analysis of structural-internal factors, one principal obstacle to arms control derives from the difficulty of trying to control constantly changing modern weapons technology through the device of negotiated diplomatic agreement. Military technology is sometimes developed through competition with the enemy in the same field. Military experts psychologically tend to overestimate the capabilities of the enemy and to discount their own force potentiality.[45] Such structural factors may be the most serious obstacles to arms control. They exist as physical obstructions before arrival at the negotiation table. In fact the obstacles cannot be overcome without negotiations. Therefore arms control negotiations need to bargain a number of the asymmetries. The understanding of obstacles in the negotiations process is of central importance in order to get an agreement.

One of the major difficulties arises from the issue of verification. It is one of the most complex and sensitive issues of the arms control agenda and is related to the credibility of mutual data in the negotiations and subsequent compliance with an agreement. The Western insistence, and the Eastern resistance, on verification issues became a habitual element of the debate during conventional arms talks and an important impasse of negotiations. US presidents have repeatedly emphasized a firm policy of no arms control without the necessary verification measures. A further indication of its importance was demonstrated by a formal Congressional resolution in 1977 that adequate verification of compliance should be an indispensable part of any international arms control agreements.[46] The difficulty of reaching a compromise on verification was derived from the broad question of the over-all role of inspection and intelligence. The inspection provided for within the agreement, together with other means of observation and surveillance, played a broader and more dynamic role than detecting violations. This can partly be used to get sensitive information and military preparation outside the agreement, in addition to the particular objects and activities that they are intended to monitor. The possibilities are noted in Schelling as follows:

> The information obtained by the formal inspection system will be channelled into the regular intelligence collating and evaluating procedure and treated as a piece of data of some, but not complete reliability.[47]

Some agreements, through a reliance upon rapidly improving NTM of verification to some extent managed to circumvent the extremely sensitive issue of on-site inspection. Dependence on the NTM may not be enough to monitor the activities of conventional forces. The eye-witness by OSI is a final method to confirm information from the NTM and to offer in practical terms evidence of the breaking of an agreement through cooperation with potential enemies. The stubborn adherence to a position either for or against on-site inspection continued to serve on occasion, as a tactic to avoid serious negotiations concerning substantive measures to curb arms.[48] Thus, the verification problems were a difficult subject which negotiating partners could not easily accommodate.

The other important obstacle in the negotiation process came from divergent negotiating styles of the US and the Soviet Union which played a leading role in conventional arms control negotiations in Europe. The US traditionally stressed technical measures such as verification, data or prevention of surprise attack. From the US point of view "detail" was vital to arms control. On the other hand the Soviet Union displayed a greater awareness of the political implications of arms control negotiation, as opposed to the emphasis upon finding technical solutions. The Soviet Union was very reluctant to discuss detailed information concerning its own military forces. With respect to negotiating tactics it traditionally displayed a willingness to make public proposals for disarmament to influence public opinion. In fact such Soviet negotiation styles existed during the MBFR era before the advent of Mikhail Gorbachev.[49] However, the negotiating styles of the two sides changed over time and became more convergent. In its final five years the proposals of the Soviet Union were convergent with those of the US-detailed and technical solutions. Such convergence contributed to the conclusion of the CFE treaty.

Conclusion

The fruits of arms control may be meagre in comparison with the enthusiastic effort and period of time spent on them. Thus Joseph Kruzel noted that the historical records prove that arms control is neither an unbounded blessing nor an unmitigated disaster.[50] Arms control has been condemned by contrasting it to a preferred ideal situation of superior agreements rather than with the more likely alternative of no arms control agreements at all.[51]

Much of the criticism was due to the confusion between arms control and disarmament. As noted earlier the concept of arms control is not simply abolition of weapons, in marked contrast to disarmament. Initially the criticism of conventional arms control in the early 1980s arose from the failure of the prolonged MBFR talks and the failure to arrive at any formal agreements. The methods of arms control have contributed to some extent in limiting the arms race, to an increase of stability and to a further decreases in the possibility of a major war, between the East and the West. Therefore it may be true that its original objective was attained because a new great power war did not occur after its introduction.

Arms control does not end by concluding formal treaties but is an enduring-process. An example of this occurs in the following reference of Joseph Kruzel:

> Arms control is an attempt, in a imperfect world, to establish guide-lines for behaviour and rules of engagement between adversary nations. Occasionally the effort involves formal negotiations aimed at producing treaties, but more generally it is an intellectual effort to anticipate and avoid the most dangerous aspect of a military competition".[52]

Ken Booth underlines arms control as a continuation of strategy in the business of politics among nations, rather than ideals or imperatives; "disarmament is a continuation of strategy by a reduction of military means and arms control is a continuation of strategy by a mutual restraint on military means".[53] Most military behaviour is a reflection of politics. For example, the countries which do not have severe political conflict with neighbours will not have any threat perception and need of military power. Consequently it can logically be argued that arms control is essentially achieved as a political consideration rather than a solely military one and it cannot be isolated from political realities.

In general the greater the threat perceived, the stronger is the motivation to enhance military capability in order to protect oneself from the adversary's attack. Threat perception is made from an adversary's 'capability and intention'. The efforts towards conventional arms control in Europe have been pursued until the present in the direction of controlling the two elements, the former to physically equalize the imbalance, the latter to establish credibility.

Conventional arms control has to consider the many factors composing military capabilities, which include manpower, equipment, foreign troop stationing, training and geographical factors etc. Because of these factors it was very difficult to artificially balance the tangible number of armed forces, bearing in mind the many asymmetrical elements.

The other part of conventional arms control has been to establish the various Confidence Building Measures which could be concluded between the East and the West by offering "common interests". If neither side desired to attack the other, as both claimed, then both were obliged to demonstrate a military openness and a greater willingness to concede. The military openness has contributed to developing military and political credibility by eliminating gradually any misperception.

Arms control has to be pursued as a part of national security policy. "Its purpose is to produce security for states by pursuing cooperative efforts with potential adversaries, even while unilateral force improvements are being under taken as a complementary route to national security."[54] When a military build up is needed to decrease the military gap, more economic effort is required. In the absence of serious efforts to negotiate arms control, the public tends to fear the arms race. And then the administration encounters greater difficulty in acquiring national consensus for defence programs. The administration can exploit arms control as a means to draw support from the people. Therefore, Hedley Bull places arms control, military strategy and armament policy in the same category as goals directed towards national security because arms control attempts to advance the special military interests of one nation and restrict the interests of its opponent.[55]

Political detente is the crucial pre-condition for arms control. Detente becomes possible when a war ends or a further military build up is not needed. Arms control negotiations were begun in the detente period with MBFR, which was proposed simultaneously with the beginning of CSCE, which declared the status quo of Europe as did earlier agreements between the United States and the Soviet Union, such as the Hot Line, and Partial Nuclear Test Ban Treaty of 1963. These became the stepping-stones to 'peaceful coexistence'. Arms control is urgently required when tension escalates and where military confrontation between potential enemies continues. Political detente leads to political stability and further cooperation with the enemy. These invite arms control.

NOTES

1. The United States considered the use of nuclear weapons during the Korean War. For this, see Roger Dingman, "Atomic Diplomacy during the Korean War" and Rosemary J. Foot, "Nuclear Coercion and the Ending of the Korean Conflict", *International Security*, Vol. 13, No. 3 (Winter, 1988/89), pp. 50-111.
2. Herman Kahn and Anthony Weiner, "Technological Innovation and the Future of Strategic Warfare," *Astronautics and Aeronautics* (December, 1967), p. 28.
3. Thomas C. Schelling and Morton H. Halperin, *Strategy and Arms Control* (New York: A Pergamon-Brasseys Classic, 1961), p. 2.
4. Ibid., p. 142.
5. Ibid., p. 3.
6. Philip J. Noel Baker, *Disarmament* (London: Carland Publishing, 1972), p. 17. He pointed out that 'policy follows armaments, rather than that armaments follow policy'.

7. Paul Diehl, "Arms Race and Escalation: A Closer Look", *Journal of Peace Research*, Vol.20, No.3, 1983, pp. 205-12. He claimed in the survey of major wars that during the years 1816-1970 only one fourth of the disputes preceded *by* mutual military build-ups resulted in war, while ten of thirteen wars occurred in the absence of joint arms increases by the dispute participants.
8. Michael Sheehan, *Arms Control: Theory and Practice* (New York & London: Basil Blackwell, 1988), p. 28.
9. Ibid., p. 29.
10. Thomas C. Schelling, "What went wrong with arms control?", *Foreign Affairs*, Vol.64, No.2, Winter 1985-86, p. 221.
11. Donald G. Brennan, "Setting and Goals", in Donald G. Brennan (ed.), *Arms Control, Disarmament and National Security*, (Brazilier, New York, 1966), p.30.
12. Robert R. Bowie, "Basic Requirements of Arms Control", in Brennan (ed.), *Arms Control and Disarmament*, p. 43.
13. Schelling, *Strategy and Arms Control*, p. 2.
14. Sheehan, *Arms Control*, p. 43.
15. Christoph Bertram, "Mutual Force Reductions in Europe: The Political Aspects", *Adelphi Paper*, No. 84, London, 11SS (1972), pp. 9-13.
16. Laurinda L. Rohn, *Conventional Force Reductions in Europe: A New Approach to Balance, Stability and Arms Control* (The RAND Corporation: R 3732-USDP/AF, 1990), p. 7.
17. Lothar Ruhl, "An Increased Emphasis on Conventional Defence: A European View", in Uwe Nerlich & James A Thomson (eds), *Conventional Arms Control and European Security* (London: Westview Press, 1988), p. 38.
18. Tomas J. Hirschfeld, "Arms Control in Europe and Now the Conventional Stability Talks", *Arms Control Today*, Vol.18, No.2, (March 1988,) p. 14.
19. Manfred Worner, "Conventional Arms Control and Security Policy", in Nerlich and Thomson *Conventional Arms Control and European Security*, p. 105.
20. Klaus Wittmann, "Challenges of Conventional Arms Control ", *Adelphi Paper*, 239 (London: IISS, Summer, 1989) p. 30.
21. John R. Galvin, "Some Thoughts on Conventional Arms Control", *Survival*, March/April, Vol.31, No.2, (1989), p. 103.
22. Wittmann, op. cit., p. 36.
23 Ibid., p. 12.
24. Johan J. Holst, "Arms Control and European Political Process", *Survival*, Vol. XV. No. 5. (September/October, 1973), p. 283.
25. Bertram, op. cit., p. 25.
26. Sheehan, *Arms Control*, p. 12.
27. Brennan, op. cit., p. 41.
28. Holst. op. cit., p. 283.
29. Albert Carnesale, "Learning From Experience with Arms Control", A final Report submitted to the U.S Arms Control and Disarmament Agency, (Washington D.C. 1985). p. 151.
30. Richard Cobden and John Bright would have contended that the more contact there was between states and peoples at all levels, the less chance there would be of frictions and suspicions leading to war. Philip Towle, *Arms Control and East -West Relations* (New York: St. Martin's Press, 1983), p.36.
31. Michael Sheehan, "A More Inane Congress: Twelve Years of MBFR", *Arms Control* , Vol. 6, No. 2, (Sept., 1985,) p. 151.

32. Quincy Wright, "Conditions for Successful Disarmament", in Marek Thee (ed.), *Armaments, Arms Control and Disarmament* (the UNESCO Press, 1981), p. 90.
33. Towle, op. cit., p. 2.
34. Joseph John Kruzel, *The Preconditions and Consequence of Arms Control Agreements* (Harvard University: Ph.D thesis, Microfilm, 1975), pp.364-365.
35. Ibid.
36. Marek Thee, "The Concept of Common Security", in Marek Thee (ed.), *Armaments and Disarmament: SIPRI Findings* (Oxford University Press, 1986), p. 210.
37 Wright, op. cit., p. 87.
38 Joseph, Kruzel, "From Rush-Bagot to Start: The Lessons of Arms Control", *Orbis*, Vol. 30 No. 1, (Spring 1986), p. 205.
39. Steven E Miller, "Politics over Promises the Domestic impediments to Arms Control", *International Security*, Vol.8, No.4, (Spring, 1986), p.81.
40. Ibid., p. 204.
41. Sheehan, *Arms Control*, p. 39.
42. Bowie, op. cit., p. 48.
43. Joseph I. Coffey, *Arms Control and European Security: A guide to East-West Negotiations* (New York: Praeger Publisher, 1977), p. 55.
44. Ibid., p. 57.
45. Herbert York, "Military Technology and National Security", *Scientific American*, Vol. 221, No. 2 (August, 1969), p. 27.
46. William F. Rowell, *Arms Control Verification: A Guide to Policy Issues for the 1980s* (Cambridge: Ballinger Publishing Company, 1986), p. 2.
47. Schelling, Strategy and Arms Control, p. 93.
48. April Carter, *Success and Failure in Arms Control Negotiations* (SIPRI: Oxford University Press, 1989), p. 26.
49. For detailed reference, See R. Ranger, "MBFR: Political or Technical Arms Control?", *World Today*, Vol. 30, No. 1 (October 1974), p. 411. He argued that this contrast extended to the content of the talks. The West was pursuing technical measures to reduce WTO ability to launch a surprise attack, whereas the Soviet Union was looking to symbolic cuts and recognition of the status quo in Europe.
50. Kruzel, *From Rush Bagot-Start*, p. 215.
51. Sheehan, *Arms Control*, p. 40.
52. Kruzel, *From Rush Bagot-Start*, p. 216.
53. John Baylis and Ken Booth (eds), *Contemporary Strategy I* (London: Croom Helm, 1987), p. 140.
54. Sheehan, *Arms Control*, p. 152.
55. Hedley Bull, *The Control of the Arms Race* (London: The Institute for Strategic Studies, 1961), p. 206. Schelling and Halperin also emphasise that the aim of arms control and the aim of national strategy should be the same, *Strategy and Arms Control*, p. 142.

Part II
Arms Control Experiences in Europe

3. The CSCE Process and CBMs in Europe

CSCE and Arms Control

The CSCE (Conference on Security and Cooperation in Europe, which became OSCE, The Organisation for Security and Cooperation in Europe in 1995) played a crucial role in maintaining peace and stability in Europe prior to the collapse of the WTO. In contrast to the military collective security systems of NATO and WTO, the CSCE contributed to the maintenance of security of Europe without any formal structure. In fact it can be defined as a mechanism for dealing with security by political means or approaches.

The CSCE was not originally an arms control conference. However, the forum devised a number of measures which can maintain stability politically and reduce the risks of war militarily. Therefore it has had an indispensable connection with arms control forums. Since the early 1970s the CSCE and arms control talks have been politically and militarily bound together. There has also been an important, though informal link between CSCE and the negotiations on conventional force reductions in Europe, as was noted at the beginning of the process in the early 1970s.

> Seeking separate discussions of CSCE and MBFR is a tactical matter, not a substantial one. The substantive issues of CSCE and MBFR are intertwined. If CSCE should turn out ostensibly to be a success and MBFR should fail, the result would cast serious doubt on the success of CSCE.[1]

The two forums have been very important vehicles which helped to bring political and military stability in Europe. Along with the arms control talks the CSCE "helped to pave the way for the continuing evolution toward a move genuine, less military-based security structure.[2]

The CSCE's significance is that it offered a decisive foundation for conventional arms control negotiations. The forum created an atmosphere conducive to arms control negotiations. Further the 1975 Helsinki Final Act codified comprehensively the rules of conduct of European countries in relation to their own security by concluding international agreements on political problems such as frontiers, renunciation of force-use, and compromises for coexistence. It was the first general agreement on the frontiers of states throughout Europe since the Versailles' treaty of 1919. As a result the Final Act of Helsinki was not only an alternative to a World War II peace treaty, but was also a guide-line for maintaining the status quo between East and West in Europe.

The Soviet Union was eager to develop the idea of a European security conference in the early 1970s. One of the Soviet objectives was to obtain international recognition of the communist regimes and the territorial status quo in Eastern Europe. It was also keen to preserve the extended frontiers of the Soviet Union itself that had resulted from the wartime annexation of the Baltic states and parts of Finland, Poland, Czechoslovakia, and Romania.[3] This argument is supported by the fact that the Soviet Union strove for the CSCE despite the bilateral agreements being completed between FRG-Soviet Union, FRG-Poland, FRG-GDR, and FRG-Czechoslovakia. In fact the legitimacy of the states of Eastern Europe and the status of the postwar frontiers had been previously established by the Ostpolitik agreements of 1970-73. Therefore there was no urgent need for a general European security conference. The effect and the purpose of the CSCE was firmly to underpin the geographical status quo in Europe.[4]

The Soviets also saw the CSCE as offering them a useful mechanism for influencing Western Europe and separating it politically from the United States. From the Rapacki Plan of 1958, which suggested "control machinery," to the Budapest Appeal of 1969, which foresaw the European conference leading to a "durable system of European security," the Soviets clearly had in mind a permanent security mechanism of some kind.[5] However, the Final Act acknowledged the legitimate interests of the United States and Canada in European Security. This helped cement rather than fragment North American and West European relations and further developed the influence of the United States on the Continent.

Conversely, the Western countries had different objectives from those of the Soviet Union in the CSCE. The West sought to obtain more open relations between East and West, advocating the free movement of persons, information, ideas, and broader contacts between peoples. The West also hoped to build a status quo that would be an acceptable one for both sides, allowing for peaceful evolution, in the belief that security is built on mutual understanding and confidence. Therefore the position of the West focussed on the "Human Rights" issue and greater openness in relations between peoples, as well as governments. Within the scope of the CSCE itself, the West accepted the existing frontiers in Europe while defending the principle of possible peaceful change. As a result the CSCE implicitly or explicitly helped to sustain developments, which led to a crucial transformation of the postwar evolution of Europe.

The CSCE was intended to recognize the political and territorial status quo in order to affirm the national independence and sovereignty of all European countries. It thus functioned as a problem-solving forum by defining the legitimate rights of countries and removing the sources of disputes between East and West or individual countries. The emphasis on non-aggression and the renunciation of the use of force as an instrument of national policy contributed to political stability and laid the foundation for arms control negotiations in Europe.

The CSCE was crucially concerned with the solution of the "German Question". The Four occupying Powers had no formal peace treaty with Germany after the war. In the absence of such an treaty, Germany - as opposed to the FRG and GDR - had remained a conquered nation since the signing of an unconditional surrender at Berlin in 1945. The arrangements amongst the four powers were based on this unconditional surrender and the rights of conquest that it implied; second, on agreements reached amongst themselves at Yalta and Potsdam; and third, on practices that had grown up since the beginning of the occupation.[6] However, the FRG and GDR were in reality independent states. Therefore, the four-power rights and responsibilities on Germany needed to be renewed and formally confirmed through some treaty or conference between European countries. The strong emphasis on the "Germany question" in the CSCE was clearly demonstrated by the Soviet pamphlet called "Helsinki: Ten Years Later, Report of the Soviet Committee for security and cooperation in Europe" (Moscow: Editions du Progress, 1985). In this publication the USSR affirmed that in its view Helsinki was "the logical prolongation of Yalta and Potsdam".[7]

In fact, the potential threat from the FRG was a crucial reason why the Soviets persistently proposed the CSCE. Initial efforts toward a European security conference date back to 1954, the year when negotiations were underway to complete the treaty that would bring West Germany into NATO.[8] The 1966 Bucharest Declaration of the Warsaw Pact ultimately proposed arms control and the permanent division of Germany. This document listed four basic preconditions on the German Question necessary for a security conference in Europe: the recognition of existing frontiers and of two German states, the reduction of the armed forces and a ban on possession of nuclear weapons.[9] Thus, the higher priority of the Soviets in the CSCE was to render the division of Germany irreversible so that a united, hostile German nation could never again threaten the Soviet Union. This was to be done through agreement on the "immutability" of postwar frontiers. The Soviets made no bones about their main objective during the negotiations, referring implicitly to the permanent division of Germany as the "key to European Security". [10]

CBMs have operated as multilateral security measures in Europe. The military aspect of the CSCE may nevertheless have played a very important role in advancing European arms control. In the Final Act, with regard to arms control the participating states of the CSCE declared that "they take into account considerations relevant to efforts aimed at lessening tension and promoting disarmament which are designed to complement political detente in Europe and to strengthen their security". The first step for tension reduction and political detente starts with the principle of refraining from the threat or use of force. The Helsinki and Stockholm Conferences declared a general prohibition over the use of force. The Conferences codified the principle of refraining from the threat or use of force against the territorial integrity or political independence of any state. This political commitment was intended and assumed to be a general requirement, not a specific requirement of a particular CBM. "CBMs were designed to give military expression to the general political principle, although they could neither substitute for non-use of force nor survive long without it."[11]

The military issues within the CSCE were different from 'classical' arms control which deals with the basic military questions of weaponry and force levels. The military CBMs focussed on devising measures for reducing the risks of war. Consequently the CBMs have been limited to the "military status quo" which confirmed the political and territorial status quo without touching very sensitive issues such as "balance or reduction." It had no impact on the military structure of NATO and WTO, but dealt with the security of the whole of Europe including the non-bloc area.

However, the broad application of CBMs to the sphere of the military forces of the two blocs with the participation of non-bloc members helped the United States and the USSR to share an interest in limiting the arms control content of the CSCE. In the early period neither was keen on treating central arms control issues in an all-European forum. The United States supported the confidence building measures for reasons of allied solidarity rather than for anticipated military or arms control benefits. Its main concerns were non-military issues such economic cooperation and human rights. Like the United States, the Soviet Union also wanted no concrete military negotiations in the CSCE. It treated the CBMs only in political generalities, as part of the confirmation of the status quo that CSCE was supposed to produce.[12] The CSCE negotiations however helped to formulate the habit of cooperation between the West and the East. The long deadlock of the MBFR talks helped turn their concern to CBMs. The idea of CBMs was viewed as the most appropriate approach for pursuing common interests between East and West without damaging their security. However the different approaches of the East and West remained one of the main obstacles to the elaboration of effective military CBMs for Europe. NATO argued that effective military-technical measures should constitute the core of any comprehensive-confidence-building regime with reliable cooperative means of verification. On the other hand, WTO felt that military technical measures could not substitute for the absence of political confidence. Instead the concept of CBMs in the broader political-military context was believed to solve the security problems of Europe.[13]

At first, the military content of the CSCE was limited to a few modest confidence-building measures, designed to reduce the uncertainties stemming from large-scale military activities. However, the CSCE's responsibilities to the military grew steadily. Its follow-up meetings advanced the other aspect of arms control which the two blocs did not deal with. For example, the 1986 Stockholm Conference produced Confidence and Security-Building Measures (CSBMs) in the area extending from the Atlantic to the Urals. This forum was concluded with an accord providing for development of notification and accompanied by original verification provisions. Further, the 1990 Vienna agreement on CSBMs was a principal step toward upgrading the security of Europe and saw the institutionalization of the CSCE process. Such institutionalization retains the possibility for devising real military CBMs which can contribute to the establishment of a new security regime for Europe after the end of the Cold War.

The Conceptual framework of CBMs

There is no clear-cut definition of "Confidence Building Measures" or even what constitutes them. However, the concept of CBMs was basically centred on Western perspectives and efforts towards European security. A large part of European military activities was traditionally shrouded in secrecy and this legacy gave rise to uncertainty and tension. Therefore, prior to reductions of military forces, very urgent work was needed to reduce tension and further to prevent unintended war, surprise attack or political intimidation. A number of military cooperation measures, which could support these objectives, emerged in the context of European security. The conceptualization of CBMs took place under different perspectives of West and East.[14]

Western approaches to CBMs were narrower, and more technically oriented. The Western conceptual perspectives can be defined from the terms that NATO employed in the official documents; 'predictability', 'transparency', 'openness', 'rationality', stabilization', 'verification', and 'miscalculation'. In fact such terminologies reflect its bias for "speculative concepts" and theoretical models which are attractive, but only loosely related to political and military facts of life.[15] On the other hand the Eastern approaches expressed broadly political concepts. These emphasised such terms as 'strengthening of peace and security', 'shaping political-logical foundation', 'non-use of force', 'military detente', 'curbing of the arms race' and 'reduction of the threat of wars'. The guiding idea was to link CBMs with political realities.[16] In relation to the European security situation, the general concept of CBMs saw a big difference between the Helsinki Final Act and the Stockholm Agreement. The Helsinki Final Act, which represented the basis of CBMs theory, declared that;

> CBMs should contribute "to reducing the dangers of armed conflict and of misunderstanding or miscalculation of military activities which could give rise to apprehension particularly in a situation where the participating states lack clear and timely information about the nature of such activities.[17]

In fact the approach of the Final Act to CBMs was heavily influenced by the experience of the Soviet invasion of Czechoslovakia in 1968. The notification of military activities in advance was seen as the main means of limiting the military activities used for the purpose of political coercion.

However the Stockholm Agreement conceptualized a close link between CSBMs and the renunciation of force in terms of a means-end interaction. During the 1980-81 crisis in Poland, the Soviet "ZAPAD 81" manoeuvres along the border of Poland highlighted the need to constrain opportunities for the use of military activities as a means of political pressure. The offensive-oriented military build-up of the WTO in eastern Europe led to pressure to devise further constraints towards reducing the possibility of large scale-surprise attack. Furthermore the CDE mandate, which combined CBMs and disarmament, needed measures "to undertake in stages, new effective and concrete action designed to make progress in strengthening confidence and security and in achieving disarmament". In fact the adoption of "challenge" verification was a practical measure of helping the implementation of both CBMs and arms reduction.

Thus the concept of CBMs was formulated in the context of hostile military confrontation between East and West in Europe. It is said CBMs were conceptualized as a mechanism of reducing tension and the risks of surprise attack and conducting a bridge-role to the stage of arms reduction.

An ultimate objective of CBMs is to create 'stability' and a 'military status quo' by means of appropriate military control and cooperation measures. This objective is attained by limiting the conditions of military activities without changing the size or quality of military forces. The pattern can be established whereby the states concerned could demonstrate that military forces in peacetime are intended only for defence and not for attack.

The early CBMs were mainly focussed on conceptual or psychological perspectives, not physical constraints. Therefore studies emphasised 'miscalculation', 'mistrust', 'threat perception' and 'intentions'. Richard E. Darilek saw the role of CBMs as reducing miscalculation and mistrust. His argument was that the awareness of what constitutes normal or abnormal military activities can reduce the dangers inherently coming from miscalculation and unintended crisis.[18]

On the other hand Jonathan Alford noted that CBMs are primarily designed to affect perception of potential adversaries, particularly perception of their intentions in confrontation.[19] Like Alford, Hans Gunter Brauch interpreted CBMs as political and psychological measures to prepare for arms control. According to his argument, the role of CBMs is primarily focussed to operate on threat perception, and consists of two elements:

> the subjective perception-the fears and enemy images that have been influenced by historical tradition, own experience and by the interpretation of reality by the media and by the national political actors as well as by service interests;

> the objective threat perception-military capabilities in terms of hardware and troops of the other side, an interpretation of past action and by an assessment of the intention and motivation of the most likely opponents.[20]

The "perceived threat" may be regarded as playing a more important role than the "threat" itself because of the possibilities of a war by misunderstandings and miscalculations. It cannot be denied that much of the emphasis of CBMs on the psychological aspect was to a great extent influenced by the attention given to CBMs relating to nuclear weapons.

However the Soviet offensive military build-up and preparations for a surprise attack in Central Europe helped to shift the focus of debates on

CBMs from modest roles to practical and concrete ones. Thus the question of the surprise attack has been a core subject in the European CBMs negotiations. Lynn M. Hansen argued that military 'openness' or 'transparency' is the essence of CBMs. Her argument was that they must be understood as a means of clarifying political-military intentions, not simply collecting intelligence or data.[21] In practical terms, surprise is achieved when one side has no time to prepare defence. Soviet forces were capable of launching a surprise attack from a standing start. Therefore NATO needed a larger warning period for adequate reaction to the enemy's sudden attack and sought regulations affecting the operations and associated readiness of forces.

Operational measures limiting specified military activities have been devised as a means of realizing the objectives of CBMs: military stability and prevention of a surprise attack. Holst pointed out that CBM objectives can be furthered by increased 'predictability' and 'reassurance'.[22] Many arms control theorists generally have three perspectives in relation to the linkages between CBMs and arms reduction. The first perspective is that CBMs simply contribute to the overcoming of the difficult obstacles to arms reduction by serving as a pacesetter to conventional arms control.[23] It is said that "they constitute a pavement for the traffic of arms control and disarmament".[24] In any case it is difficult to envisage implementing any arms reduction agreement without information and monitoring of deployed forces.

The second perspective disregards prerequisites for arms control, the tracking of the development of European arms control, and the basic attributes of tension arising from imbalances of physical military capabilities. Such a perspective mainly arises from the naive characteristics in early CBMs which were not militarily constraining, thereby emphasising the political aspect of CSCE. However, since the Stockholm Agreement, CBMs have been developed as a militarily important mechanism for reducing the possibility of inter-state war in Europe caused by misunderstanding. The CBMs regimes have in fact been primarily based upon the "cooperation & communication" that Schelling and Halperin defined as a basic objective of arms control and this concept has figured prominently in all the negotiations of conventional arms reduction.

The third perspective seeks further improvements of CBMs with respect to both expanding their scope and sharpening specific regulation through transparency and constraining measures. It is much concerned with providing a mechanism for guarding against circumvention, for verification of compliance and with mandating defence. This perspective stresses the necessity of establishing linkage between the evolution of the CSBMs regime and the suggestion of new directions to arms control negotiations. Such a framework means an institutionalized parallelism between negotiations on conventional forces and effort to further strengthen the CBM regimes.[25]

Figure 3-1 The Functional System of CBMs

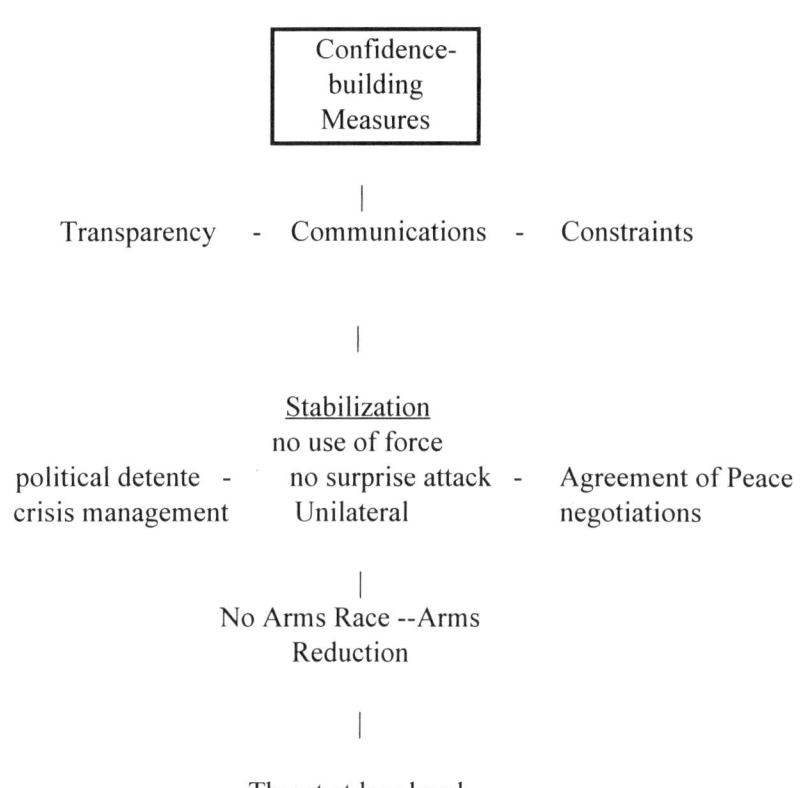

```
                    ┌──────────────┐
                    │ Confidence-  │
                    │  building    │
                    │  Measures    │
                    └──────────────┘
                           │
  Transparency  -   Communications   -   Constraints
                           │
                      Stabilization
                      no use of force
  political detente  -  no surprise attack  -  Agreement of Peace
  crisis management     Unilateral             negotiations
                           │
                    No Arms Race -- Arms
                         Reduction
                           │
                    Threat at low level
```

CBMs were the basis of the Associated Measures incorporated into MBFR: prior notification of out-of-garrison activities and exchange of observers at such activities; ground and aerial inspection; declared troop entry/exit points with observers; exchange of information on manpower and structure and non-interference with national-technical means of verification.[26] The "Associated Measures" and the CBMs are fundamentally concerned with establishing and confirming patterns of routine, non-threatening military activities and verification of troop reduction. The ultimate goal was to help the two alliances to connect with a mutually complementary relationship between the software and hardware of European security. The real impetus to building confidence and reducing mistrust would be the initial reduction agreement itself. MBFR directly tried to address insecurity and mistrust through the reduction of forces.

However, practically and conceptually, it was difficult to envisage the negotiations of conventional arms control being carried on in two different forums. The MBFR reduction area was smaller than the CBM zone of application. The limited reduction area had insufficient militarily significance and could not bring about the desired result. The geographical asymmetry was not favourable to NATO. By the late 1980s dissatisfaction with this situation led to the curtailment of the MBFR negotiations and their replacement by the CFE (Conventional Forces in Europe) talks. The CDE was put forward to integrate the two negotiating bodies. The objective of the conference was to strengthen confidence and security and to achieve disarmament.

The results of the negotiations of the two blocs relating to arms reduction was reported to the 35-states of CSCE. It envisaged a "two circles" regime inside CDE, with the "old" MBFR negotiations constituting the inner circle.[27] By bringing together the identity of CBMs and the arms reduction area, the subject and results of negotiations of the two blocs influenced the security of all Europe. Furthermore, the contents of CBMs developed the hardware part, i.e, the concrete verification, compliance and data exchange which is required in the before and after phases of arms reduction. For these reasons, the regimes of CBMs and arms reduction have a very close linkage in the process of European arms control. As Darilek noted, "CBMs are a necessary concomitant of, not prerequisites for, a reduction and limitation of force levels".[28]

The Application and Implementation of CBMs

CBMs had their first real embodiment in the Helsinki Final Act. However they were only militarily symbols of political detente. Given its political nature, the Final Act provided no ultimate deterrence or sanction against, noncompliance with its CBMs. Therefore the CBMs were faced with many serious problems when implemented in the European area as a part of national security policies. The Soviet military intervention in Afghanistan in 1979 and the Warsaw Pact's military intimidation of Poland in 1981, violated the principles of both the renunciation of the use of force and non-intervention of the CSCE. The Final Act confined CBMs to only an area within 250km of the Soviet Western frontiers. In the case of Afghanistan, the Soviet intervention took place outside the agreed geographic area. Furthermore there were no practical provisions to reveal or deter preparations for attack. Consequently, the CSCE follow-up meetings established CDE in 1986 in order to overcome these limitations.[29] The Conference was the first to produce Confidence and Security Building measures, CSBMs, a second generation of interrelated CBMs; a second phase to deal with limitation and reduction of armed forces in Europe.

The accomplishments of the conference are generally understood in the two dimensions - the political and military. Hence, Richard Darilek observed:

> if the Helsinki CBMs were quasi-military measures intended to build political confidence, the measures to be negotiated at Stockholm were to be more fully military measures whose objective was to promote military as well as political confidence.[30]

Their implementation was politically binding - the document strengthened the commitment by changing the verbs from "may" to "will". There were no escape clauses such as the "if possible" or "are encouraged" or "voluntary" found in the Helsinki Final Act. The Stockholm Document constituted a list of obligations to be respected by the Conference members. The zone of application for military CSBMs was also much wider than that of CBMs: "from the Atlantic to the Urals". The extension of the geographic scope was more realistic and meaningful in that it could be applied to the whole of Europe. All Soviet European territory was included in the CSBMs. Consequently, the Soviet force activities were more regulated. Compared to the CBM regime of Helsinki the Stockholm CDE Agreement amounted to a true "quality leap" with important military significance. The CSBMs thus became theoretically part and parcel of arms control.[31]

The third generation of CBMs was produced on 21 November, 1990 in Paris. The 1986-89 follow-up meetings of Vienna aimed to "build upon and expand the results already achieved at the Stockholm Conference". The aim was to elaborate and adopt a new set of mutually binding CSBMs.[32] The first and second CBMs agreements were concluded and implemented within the context of a divided Europe. With the Paris Accords the former agreements were widened and the CSCE was further institutionalized, taking it beyond what had been a series of negotiations without any formal structure. However the collapse of the Cold War regime and the changing political situation in Europe required new measures appropriate to the future security environment.

CBMs can be divided into three categories: transparency measures, constraint measures and communication measures. Transparency measures may be further categorized into several types; notification, observation, information exchange and verification. Constraint measures include limitation on locations, equipment or operational practices of military forces. Communication measures are means of crisis management for prevention of unintended incidents and escalation in to a full-scale crisis. To a large extent these divisions are artificial and all measures are mutually intertwined.

The Helsinki Final Act was limited to very modest notification and observation measures. In contrast to the Helsinki Final Act, the Stockholm Document included rigorous notification, information and observation measures, as well as new measures dealing with verification, constraints and annual military calendars. The Vienna agreement confirmed the previous agreements and elaborated their regulations and newly devised further communication and crisis management mechanisms.

Transparency Measures

1. Prior Notification of Certain Military Activities

o.	Notification days: Helsinki-21, Stockholm, Vienna-42
o.	Notification thresholds . Helsinki: 25,000 troops or 300 battle tanks, Amphibious landing and Parachute - 3,000, Air forces-200 sorties

Successful implementation of notification measures over a period of years would make patterns of military activities more recognizable. Previously, routine military exercises were used as preparation for launching surprise attack or exerting political intimidation. Examples were well demonstrated by the Egyptian attack upon Israel across the Suez Canal in 1973, the 1968 Soviet invasion of Czechoslovakia and the 1980-81 Soviet intimidation of Poland. In fact central to notification must be the information about the routine or irregular activities. The Vienna agreement required a greater amount of information.[33] The criteria of requirement was also extended from the division level of Stockholm to "brigade/regiment or equal level" in Vienna.

2. Observation of Certain Military Activities

> o. Helsinki:none specified
> o. Stockholm, Vienna: Ground forces - 17,000 troops
>   Amphibious landings and Parachute Assault - 5,000 troops

This plays a useful role in the avoidance of misunderstanding and miscalculation by providing an opportunity for reassurance that "the notified activity is non threatening in character." These measures were voluntarily implemented under the Final Act. Therefore, Warsaw Pact nations often gave a set-piece demonstration rather than showing actual field training.[34] However, the Stockholm agreement elaborated a code of conduct of host states and observer rights. Further the Vienna agreement ensured non-interference with inspections and permitted more aerial surveillance.

3. Exchange of Military Information

> o. Helsinki: none specified
> o. Stockholm: annual calendar and 2-year forecast
> o. Vienna:
>   . troop strength and major weapons systems
>   . down to the level of brigade or regiment
>   . plans for the deployment of major weapons and equipment systems
>   . military budget

The exchange of information is the foundation on which to base a regime of CBMs. One primary result is greater openness and hence, predictability, states know what is supposed to happen in some detail.[35] The Helsinki conference recognized the need for exchange of military information to reduce misunderstanding and miscalculation but failed to specify it. The Stockholm conference defined the conditions of information exchanges but also limited them only to military activities. However, the Vienna Agreement expanded the hardware part of military forces to include the military organization and structure. Moreover, the exchanges of information concerning each country's annual military budget generates greater transparency about their military build-up in the future.[36]

4. Compliance and Verification

> o. Helsinki: none
> o. Stockholm:
> . 3 obligatory on site inspections per year
> . replies to request for inspection within 36 hours
> . termination of inspection within 48 hours
> o. Vienna:
> - a quota of evaluation visits per year
> - established of right to inspect states within the same alliance

One of the most important successes of CBMs was the adoption of compliance and verification provisions. "Without effective means of verifying compliance, even concrete CSBMs become nothing more than mere declarations of intent."[37] The Stockholm Document prescribes a regime of on-site inspection as a means of verification. A state need accept no more than three inspections a year, nor more than one inspection by another state. An inspection must begin within thirty-six hours of the request and must terminate forty-eight hours after the arrival of the team, which is limited to four inspectors. The host country has no right of delay or refusal on demand. This provision may also make it more difficult to prepare to launch a surprise attack under the cover of peacetime military training. The significance of this provision was that it would contribute to the greater credibility of the entire systems of CSBMs. It was also very significant in that this was the first time that the Soviet Union agreed to mandatory inspections on its territory. The Vienna Agreement further increased the credibility of the verification regime by introducing an evaluation mechanism for the given data. In contrast to the Stockholm Agreement, the Vienna CSBMs prominently allow for inspections of each country within the same alliance.[38]

Constraint Measures

> o. Helsinki: none
> o. Stockholm
> . Annual calendar notification-activities with 40,000 troops
> . Notification prior to 1 year-activities over 70,000 troops
> o. Vienna: Notification prior 2 years - activities over 40,000 troops

These measures, which are known as "time constraints", exert a considerable deterrent effect against a state contemplating aggression or staging shows of force for intimidation.[39] Constraints were championed at the CDE by the neutral and non-aligned (NNA) group. Among the NNA, Yugoslavia and Sweden were very enthusiastic for such measures in the CDE conference.[40] The Vienna Agreement imposed on the CSCE members thresholds reduced from 75,000 to 40,000 troops.

Communication Measures

o. Vienna: . The establishment of Conflict Prevent Centre (CPC) . An increment of military contacts and visits to air base

Many analysts proposed the creation of an institution and hot-line as a means of crisis management. The Vienna agreement created a Conflict Prevention Centre. The functions of this mechanism are mainly to consult and cooperate over "unusual military activities" and "hazardous incidents of a military nature".[41] For these a computerized communications network was set up. To improve further mutual relations, the conference agreed to increase military contacts by senior military officers and relevant institutions, including visits to air bases.[42]

The implementation of CBMs on the scale envisaged in the Final Act was not expected to bring about a radical security improvement, but to increase political confidence in East-West relations. The information received from notification had been obtainable before Helsinki and was almost useless. NATO and WTO contrasted very sharply in their implementation of CBMs. As given in the table below, analysis of the CBMs regime reveals that NATO and the Neutrals to some extent implemented their commitments. They notified many military exercises with much lower thresholds and with much longer warning time (between 34 and 53 days) than required.[43] They also often invited observers and provided them with effective means of observation. On the other hand, the Warsaw Pact countries gave very limited advance notice. Furthermore, 13 out of the 32 Eastern exercises did not have any code name or official designation whatsoever.[44]

As a good example the Soviet Union failed to supply the agreed information when notifying its biggest military exercise since the end of World War II. The Soviet Union omitted to specify its code name (Zapad

81), size (100,000 troops) and exact area and there was no invitation of Western observers.[45]

Table 3-1 CBMs Activities under the Helsinki Regimes (1975-1986)

	NATO	WTO	NNA
TOTAL Notifications 130(125)	77(73)	32(33)	21(19)
Invitation of observers 72(66)	50(44)	10(9)	12(13)

Sources: Victor-Yves Ghebali and Fred Tanner, "Confidence- building measures in arms control: the mouse that roared?", *International Defence Review*, 10/1988, p. 1269. (): John Borawski, *From the Atlantic to the Urals* (London: Peragmon-Brassey's, 1988), p.27.

However, the record of implementation of the Stockholm regime was remarkably good. All of the provisions were well exercised and complied with by NATO and WTO as given in the table 3-2. In 1987-90, 147 military activities were recorded in the annual calendar. 56 were by NATO members, 75 by WTO members and 16 by neutral and non-allied nations. Until 1990 NATO had conducted fewer military activities than the WTO. NATO exercises sometimes involved more than 40,000 troops, but the WTO conducted more military activities on a somewhat smaller scale.

From 1990 this trend changed.[46] The total number of notifiable military activities since 1987 has decreased. Political developments in Europe led to the scaling down or even the cancellation of exercises during 1990. The overall decrease in the number of exercises is a reflection of the changes in the political situation in Europe. For the observation requirements, in 1987-90, 44 on-site inspections were also carried out, in nearly equal number, by the East and West. The Vienna conference agreed to hold an annual implementation assessment meeting. The CPC serves as the forum for such meetings. Thus the CSBMs regime has contributed greatly to better mutual understanding and a greater stabilization of Europe. The evidence is very well demonstrated in an official statement of December 1988 on conventional arms control. NATO ministers reported: "we are encouraged thus far by the successful implementation of the Stockholm Document and we consider that the momentum must be maintained".[47]

Table 3-2 Implementation of the Stockholm Regime (1987-90)

Notification   Invitation of Observers   Inspection

	87	88	89	90	91	87	88	89	90	87	88	89	90
NATO	17	13	11	10	5	17	13	11	8	2	7	9	5
WTO	25	22	17	7	4	4	7	7	3	3	6	7	5
NNA	5	3	3	4	1	-	2	2	-	-	-	-	-
TO	47	38	31	21	10	21	22	20	11	5	13	6	10

Sources: This data compiled from *SIPRI Yearbook 1988/89/90 91*-Implementation of the Stockholm Document and Calendar of planned notifiable military activities.

Criticisms and Lessons

There have been some criticisms about the functional effectiveness of CSBMs. One of the main criticisms is that CSBMs have been slow-acting and have not brought any substantial reductions of force levels or defence expenditures. Alexander L. George demonstrated the limited scope and effectiveness of the CSBM Regime:

> the expected contribution by CSBMs to enhance overall security is generally seen as of peripheral rather than central importance since they do not affect the military capabilities as such and thus leave intact the instrument for settling disputes by force.[48]

The other criticism is directed at the premise of CBMs that war is caused by miscalculation and misperception. Such a simplistic approach does not adequately take into account the historical reality that almost all international conflicts are the result of profound clashes of national interests. Nations do not go to war just because of an accident or the odd unfortunate development. Lewis and Lorell contend that "the fundamental drift of nations toward conflict is most critical, not the particular events that serve as benchmarks along the path the drift follows".[49] This may be especially true in the age of weapons of mass destruction, when the results of war cannot differentiate between the winner and the defeated. Unlike nuclear war, a conventional war allows to some extent sufficient time to make rational judgements on enemy military activities and intentions before entering into war. For example, NATO recognized that the "ZAPAD 81" of WTO was implemented as a means of political intimidation relating to the crisis in Poland, and not directed against NATO.

In addition to this point, some critics argue that sensible leaders cannot contemplate a surprise attack under conditions where both sides are deterred from committing any sort of offensive action for fear of the consequences of war. A surprise attack demands a great deal of preparation in order to guarantee success. Such preparations can be detected by means of intelligence activities. For many reasons, Lynn Hansen does not see CBMs as a means of preventing a surprise attack.[50]

On the other hand, many positive lessons can be gathered from the experience of CBMs. The relative success of CBMs to some extent depend on the overall balance of military capabilities between potentially conflicting states.[51] The implementation of CBMs undoubtedly contributed to the stabilization of Europe by reducing the deep-rooted mistrust between the two blocs. CBMs have constituted a new security alternative to arms build-up and arms reduction which make physical changes to current capabilities. Further, the advent of concrete CSBMs reduced the potential for the use of military force as a means of political coercion at the inter-bloc level. It cannot be denied that the CBM regimes have in addition contributed to the political change in Eastern Europe with the attainments of the their basic goals: tension reduction and stabilization. Therefore, the West has given as much credit to the CBM regime as to arms reduction.

Another lesson is that "the history of negotiating CBMs appears to bear out the proposition that the more militarily significant a confidence building measure is, the harder it is to obtain a agreement".[52] The more concrete CBMs are designed seriously to restrain the use of military forces. For example, comparing the negotiation periods of the three CBMs regimes, the Stockholm Agreement needed 10 years, a longer time than the 3 years of the Helsinki CBMs. The Vienna Agreement, supplementary to the former, took only 3 years. Therefore at the first stage of CBMs negotiation it is perhaps very difficult to devise very concrete measures. The gradual approach from modest measures to concrete ones is useful for an easy arrival at an agreement, educating or persuading friendly and hostile states of the value of them as security means.

Applications of the European CBM Model Elsewhere

The CBMs within Europe have been more urgently sought as a security regime than in many other regions. The concept originated in the East-West conflict, but has application to conflict situations outside Europe. Non-European countries have talked about the need for CBMs to eliminate the sources of tension by peaceful means and thereby to contribute to the strengthening of peace and security in the world.

However, there is no clear and common understanding about what constitutes a CBM; about its prerequisites and its area of application. Sometimes the CBM has been employed as a means of demonstrating at home a government's constant effort to achieve disarmament and arms control in the world, while demonstrating abroad that it is keen to make headway on maintaining peace. On the other hand, it has been used for propagandist purposes "the concept of CBM could become an empty shell, and the politics of CBM would then be nothing but diplomatic lacemaking".[53]

There has been a growing awareness in Europe that the concept of CBM was not restricted to European use only, but could and should also be applied elsewhere. The FRG, which played a leading role in including the CBMs in the Final Act and in the MBFR talks, advanced the point of view that the security of Europe and the Third World were inextricably linked, and that therefore CBM techniques should be applied all over the World. Chancellor Helmut Schmidt in the First UN General Assembly Special Session on Disarmament emphatically voiced the view that confidence-building measures could "serve in all parts of the world to improve the political pre-conditions for disarmament and arms control".[54] He noted that suitable confidence-building measures must take regional circumstances into account, while regional agreements could lay the groundwork for an international convention on confidence-building measures.[55]

However, the European CBMs have failed to be extended to the other regions. The non-European countries have voiced criticisms with regard to the European concept. The backers of the European CBMs tried the direct application of their theory without developing a CBM concept required in the specific situations of the other regions. The nature of the potential threat is very different between Europe and the other regions. Europe had long existed in a heavy military confrontation in the bilateral system of the Cold War. From a Western viewpoint there are two obvious instabilities which could be mitigated by CBM mechanisms of a politico-military nature: first, the use of military imbalances, primarily through surprise or preemption;

second, the use of military force for political purposes in time of peace, in particular by threatening military intervention.

On the other hand, most of countries outside Europe respectively have particular military threats mainly arising in the context of various disputes between two or more states. Each region of the world is unique in the threats and threat perceptions which it faces. Therefore, various kinds of types may be described, based upon the specific characteristic of the regions: territorial, border, resource, ethnic, influence and ideological conflicts.[56] For example, in the Asian case there have existed quite a number of disputes, caused by territorial or ideological issues. Such conflicts cannot be stabilized by CBMs without renouncing the use of force or having a non-aggression treaty before the application of CBMs.

In the same mistaken way that European countries have tended to assume the transferability of their security regime without major adaptation to the other regions, the Third World has had a tendency to accept directly the European concept without developing their own principles. Proposals for CBMs regimes exist today for many regions. In the absence of a suitable regional CBMs model outside Europe, there are two successful examples of an application of the sophisticated CBMs. Undoubtedly, the Egypt-Israel peace treaty and the Central American peace process have produced the most comprehensive CBMs outside Europe.

Success of CBMs in the Sinai

One of the most successful CBMs applications was the CBMs-regulations contained in the Peace Treaties between Egypt and Israel. These treaties included many arms control and security arrangements aimed at stabilizing the strategic relationship between the two parties and thereby increasing mutual confidence in the area of security. With the signing of the Sinai Agreement I, Egypt and Israel created a demilitarized buffer-zone in the Sinai and made a thinning out of and specific limitation on military forces along the border as a practical form of security management. The demilitarization of the Sinai was a major stabilizing measure and increased the confidence of the two parties that no surprise attack could take place and that no war or major escalation would develop from a local skirmish. All the wars between Israel and Egypt began with surprise attacks, the Sinai Campaign (1956) and Six Day War (1967) and the October War (1973).[57] The forward development of Egypt in defence of the Suez Canal was always a threat to Israel. Such an exposed forward deployment led to an Israeli preemptive strike. Consequently the Peace Treaty between the two states reduced risks of surprise attack.[58]

The Sinai experience had some particular characteristics dissimilar to European CBMs. In Europe political stability proceeded arms control. But arms control was an integral part of the political settlement between Israel and Egypt. Yair Evron contended that "without arms control measures no enduring political settlement in the Middle East can be achieved".[59] The number of wars and sharply actualized adversary relations between them made military stability or arms control a real and urgent problem. Because of the deep-rooted distrust, in addition to a formal arms control agreement, the establishment of CBMs was required as a means of underpinning any political solution and complying with the Peace Treaty. The institutionalized military disengagement negotiations contributed to a build-up of confidence. Consistent monitoring of events and constant personal interaction have developed habitual cooperation and established a working relationship.

The other prominent point is that a trusted third party can serve a useful purpose for reducing fears of surprise attack and war by miscalculation. The United States assisted verification systems which helped to deter serious violations, bearing much of the financial burden for their implementation.[60] It was very difficult for two countries who had fought each other four times over the previous 30 years to avert conflict without the help of an intermediary which could watch over the execution of an agreement.

Another characteristic of the Sinai model is that the verification function of CBMs is a very important factor in the build-up of confidence even where prior confidence is virtually non-existent. In general, political cooperation and reduction of tension must precede progress in arms control. But the Sinai case strongly suggests that confidence emanating from the successful verification of a military agreement can precede and ultimately advance political accommodation between the parties.[61] Initially, the verification system served an important risk reduction function by giving early warning against surprise attack. The historical precedents of surprise attack helped the two states to concentrate on having sufficient warning time to counter any threat. In fact the signing of the 1979 peace treaty was in large part due to the successful record of the verification system of CBMs between 1976 and 1979.

The Sinai model might be usefully applied and have some prospect of improving the security relationship between non-European regional adversaries. The Sinai experience indicates that the model is most likely to be successful when;

only two parties are involved and other actors can be prevented from interfering with the process of improving risk management, there is a commitment to developing a political and military framework for an agreement,
third parties are prepared;by providing technical expertise and financial support;to facilitate the process of disengagement and assist in verifying the new agreement.[62]

First of all, the Sinai Model has contributed to the development of a military framework for an agreement that would restructure the security relationship between Egypt and Israel. The Joint Israeli-Egyptian Military Commission has played a major role as an arbitration forum for the arms control and verification regime. The military commission meetings have dealt with not only the specific security arrangements to be made in the Sinai but also the military doctrines, military planning and long-term security concerns.[63] Thus the Sinai Model has attained the goals of CBMs and further helped the CBMs to be realized as a paradigm of a military security regime between countries in conflict. The Sinai model provides a typical example where CBMs may be more important for proximate hostile states who perceive their conflict in more immediate terms and have no experience in generating co-operative behaviour.[64]

CBMs of the Contadora Treaty in Central America

The Contadora process of Central American attempted the most comprehensive CBMs outside Europe.[65] They constituted an important framework for regional conflict resolution in Central America. The governments of the Contadora Group have sought the settlement of conflict by confidence-building measures. CBMs similar to the ones practiced in Europe were envisaged as an important component of the peace process in the region. The measures included limitation of military manoeuvres and prohibition of troop concentrations in border areas; exchange of information on military spending, as well as on military manpower and equipment; co-ordination of programmes for arms acquisitions; exchange of military missions and observers; and establishment of joint, third-party or international supervision of the disputed and troubled area.[66] Additionally CBMs also included the establishment of a Verification and Control Commission (VCC) and a region-wide 'hot-line' communication among the governments. Further a staged process of arms and troop reductions were envisaged in the CBMs. "The Contadora CBMs were therefore seen as a prelude to and a complementary part of the partial disarmament process for the states involved."[67]

The CBMs regime of the Contadora treaty closely followed the pattern of the Stockholm CSBMs. States should be notified about military manoeuvres and should supply information about the designation, purpose and area of manoeuvres, as well as about the equipment and weapons involved. Unlike the European model, however notification of manoeuvres was divided into three kinds of manoeuvrers: national manoeuvres, joint manoeuvres with regional states and manoeuvres with states from outside the region. It is noticeable that the Contadora Group have limited each manoeuvre to a maximum 15 days, and prohibited the number of foreign troops from exceeding the number of national troops in the joint manoeuvres with non-Central American Countries.[68] This initiative arises out of the intention to exclude external pressure or influence.

The Contadora treaty has a prominent characteristic in that Central American states use the CBMs as a means for the prohibition of military intervention by powers from outside the area. The CBMs of Europe and Sinai were for superpowers themselves or for assistance or mediation by them. The proposals made by the Contadora Group contain quite a contrasting CBMs-goal to the previous ones:

> To prevent their territories from being used, and to refrain from giving or permitting military logistic support for people, organisations or groups who try to destabilize the Central American countries' government.[69]

Intervention by outside powers has exacerbated the regional conflicts in the past. In particular the United States, which considers Central America to be a region of vital importance to its national security, has carried out a number of military interventions.[70] The Soviet Union and Cuba have assisted revolutionary movements in the region. Thus, Central Americans concluded that the cessation of outsiders' interference would help to achieve a stable and lasting peace.

The Contadora Group seem to be unanimous in demanding the exclusion of foreign military interference. It has, however, been extremely difficult to cast this objective into concrete CBMs which can be applied and verified. It cannot be attained in reality without the consent of outside powers. Given the past experiences with major powers that have intervened in the region in support of their vital interests such an objective may exist in ideal terms, but not practical and real ones.

Table 3-3 The Contadora Treaty's CBMs on Military Manoeuvres

	National	Joint with Central American states	Joint with outside nations
Notification	30 days	45 days	30 days
Troop ceiling	------	4,000 men	3,000 men
Observers	neighbours	<------------all states---------->	
Zones	------	within 50km from adjacent countries	
Duration	------	manoeuvres limited to 30 days/year	

Sources: This is abstracted from Victor-Yves Ghebali and Fred Tanner, "Confidence-building measures in arms control: the mouse that roared?", *International Defence Review* 10/1988, p. 1272.

It should also be pointed out that the Contadora CBM is too comprehensive and ambitious to be applied in an acute crisis. So the Contadora Group will negotiate particular points pending an agreement as regards security, verification and compliance outlined by the Contadora document for peace and co-operation in Central America. In conclusion the Contadora Treaty has a significance in that the European CBM Model was partly attempted in a regional conflict zone outside Europe. It also suggests that the refined model of Contadora CBM can be applied in the countries or regions of competition between major powers.

Conclusion

The experiences of the CSCE offer many lessons for arms control. The CSCE can be first of all be evaluated as a security forum which has contributed to the establishment of the political and military status quo of Europe by solving the post war disputes. The CSCE eliminated political obstacles to arms control. Without the CSCE forum, the advancement of conventional arms control in Europe would perhaps have been slow because of the mixture of political and military issues within one arms control forum. Thus the CSCE played a crucial role in developing European arms control negotiation by building political confidence between NATO and WTO.

To maintain political stability the CSCE produced a new CBMs security regime different from arms race or arms reduction efforts to balance military force. The primary goal was to deter the use of military forces in the situation of high tension between East and West. The CBMs were the most effective alternative for tension reduction and maintenance of the military status quo. The measures aimed first of all to build up confidence and to limit the conditions for the use of force without physically changing military forces themselves.

The CSCE produced concrete CBMs over three generations from the 1976 Helsinki Final Act to the 1990 Vienna Agreement. The main focus of the measures was on the prevention of surprise attack. For this the CSCE member states greatly elaborated the transparency of military troop organization, defence budgets and plans for the development of military forces in the future. The CBMs expansion reached the realm of understanding of military doctrine and defence policy between the CSCE member states.[71]

Thus the CBMs reduced the mutual suspicion and mistrust produced by the possession of huge military forces and minimized the advantages of possession of such forces. The CSCE member states then extended the scope of the CSCE application to the realm of arms reduction. They established the CDE dealing with CBMs and arms reduction covering all Europe from 'the Atlantic to the Urals. The concept of a bridge-role for CBMs towards arms reduction was realized. Thus the two separated realms of CBMs and arms reduction talks were combined in the CDE framework with the products of the third CBMs agreement and the CFE Treaty on 19 November 1990 at the Paris summit meeting.

During of the Cold War, CSCE was a device to overcome the dangers of European division and maintain a political status quo in Europe. CBMs were the most effective formula for constraining the use of military forces and for the management of hostile relations between NATO and WTO. But the end of the Cold War provided the CSCE and CBMs regimes with new challenges. The decay of alliances left a security vacuum in Central and Eastern Europe. There are border disputes and ethnic conflicts among several European countries. There are no clear security regimes to deal with these new political and military changes. Therefore the CSCE and CBMs regimes need a new framework responsive to the new security order.[72] Secretary of State Baker suggested broad security problems posed by the new European realities as following:

> ... our present proposals are oriented primarily toward the danger of Eastern offensive action against the West. We also need to develop measures that would impede an assertion of military might by any European nation against the other.
> ... We consider now proposals to promote greater military transparency between neighbouring states, especially along border areas ... .[73]

CSBMs appear attractive as a means of managing potential crises where the parties wish to avoid war. The United Kingdom proposed the notification of lower thresholds focussing on 6,000-9,000 troops down from 13,000 to compensate for the trend toward smaller, division-level exercises.[74]

Thus the development of a new CSCE and CBMs regime responsible for stability between individual countries may give a good example to regions outside of Europe. Therefore the design of the new security measures based upon the successful precedent in the East-West confrontation certainly presents a typology of a universal security regime applicable to the regions or individual countries outside Europe.

NOTES

1. Wolfgang Klaiber, et al., *Era of Negotiations: European Security and Force Reductions* (London: D.C. Heath and Company, 1973), p. 54.
2. Ibid., P. 8.
3. John J. Maresca, *To Helsinki: The Conference on Security and Cooperation in Europe 1973-1975* (Durham and London: Duke University Press, 1987), p. 212.
4. James H. Wyllie, *European Security in the Nuclear Age* (Oxford: Basil Blackwell Ltd, 1986), p. 127.
5. Maresca, op. cit., p. 225.
6. Maresca, op. cit., p. 81.
7. Ibid., p. 212.
8. Klaiber, op. cit., p. 12.
9. See the Bucharest Declaration of the Warsaw Pact on the European Conference in July 1966. Klaiber, op. cit, p. 104
10. Maresca, op. cit., p.212.
11. Richard E. Darilek, "Reducing the Risks of Miscalculation: the Promise of the Helsinki: CBMs", in F. Stephen Larrabee and Dietrich Stobbe (eds), *Confidence-Building Measures in Europe* (New York: Institute for East-West Security Studies, 1983), p.65.
12. Maresca, op. cit., p. 169.
13. Rolf Berg, "Military Confidence-Building in Europe", Rolf Berg and Adam-Daniel Rotfeld, *Building Security in Europe* (New York: Institute for East-West Security Studies, 1986), pp. 22-23.
14. The NNAs' position on CBMs contained important elements similar to those favoured by NATO: in scope and context, however, it was close to the approach favoured by members of WTO in that the concept of CBM is closely connected to arms limitation and disarmament.
15. Adam-Daniel Rotfeld, "CBMs between Helsinki and Madrid: Theory and Experiences", in *Confidence-Building Measures in Europe*, p. 121
16. Ibid.
17. See the 98th provision of the Final Act of Helsinki.
18. Darilek, "Reducing the Risks of Miscalculation", p. 78.
19. Jonathan Alford, "Confidence-Building Measures in Europe: the Military Aspects, Jonathan Alford (ed), "The Future of Arms Control Part III: Confidence Building Measures" , *AdelphiPaper*, No. 149, pp. 4-13.

20. Hans Gunter Brauch, "Confidence Building Measures and Disarmament Strategy", *Current Research on Peace and Violence* (Tampere Peace Research Institute), 3-4/1979, p. 118.
21. Lynn M. Hansen, "Confidence and Security Building at Madrid and Beyond" in *Confidence-Building Measures in Europe,* pp. 150-151.
22. Johan Jorgen Holst, "Confidence-Building Measures: A Conceptual Framework", *Survival*, Vol. XXV. No. 1,(Jan./Feb. 1983), pp. 2-3.
23. Timothy E. Wirth, "Confidence and Security Building Measures", in Robert D. Blackwill and F. Stephen Larrabee, *Conventional Arms Control and East-West Security* (Duke University Press, Durham and London, 1989), p. 354.
24. Holst, "Confidence-Building Measures", p. 5.
25. Volker Rittberger, Manfred Finger, and, Martin Hendler, "Toward an East-West Security Regime: The Case of Confidence-and Security-Building Measures", *Journal of Peace Research,* Vol. 27. No. 1, (1990), pp. 67-68.
26. Berg, "Military Confidence-Building in Europe", p. 26.
27. Ibid, p. 61.
28. Darilek, "Reducing the Risks of Miscalculations", p. 73.
29. The proposals on CDE were first put forth by French President Giscard D'Estaing at the First Special Session on Disarmament of the UN General Assembly in May 1978. In September 1983 the Madrid Review Conference of the CSCE concluded with an agreement on the Mandate for CDE, to be held in Stockholm beginning in 1984.
30. Richard E. Darilek, "Building Confidence and Security in Europe: The Road to and from Stockholm", *Washington Quarterly*, Vol. 8. No. 1, (1985), p. 132.
31. Victor-Yves Ghebali and Fred Tanner, "Confidence-Building Measures in Arms Control: the Mouse that roared ?", *International Defence Review,* Vol. 21, 10 (1988), p. 1270.
32. *SIPRI Yearbook 1989: World Armaments and Disarmament* (Oxford: Oxford University Press, 1989), p. 419.
33. Carl C. Krehbiel, *Confidence-and Security-Building Measures in Europe: The Stockholm Conference* (New York: Praeger, 1989), pp. 32-39. And see Richard K. Betts, *Surprise Attack: Lessons for Defence Planning* (Washington D.C.: The Brookings Institution, 1982), pp. 68-86.
34. John Borawski, "Accord at Stockholm", *Bulletin of the Atomic Scientists,* Vol.42, No.10, (December 1986), p. 35.
35. Y. Ben-Horin, et. al., *Building Confidence and Security in Europe: The Potential Role of Confidence and Security-Building Measures* (RAND, prepared for the office of the Under Secretary of Defense for policy, December 1986), p. 658.
36. The 1990 Vienna Agreement (From the 10th provision to the 16th provision). Itemising defence expenditures on the basis of the categories set out in the United Nations' Instrument for Standardised International Reporting on Military Expenditures' adopted on 12 December 1980.
37. Krehbiel op. cit., p. 240.
38. *SIPRI Yearbook 1991: World Armaments and Disarmament* (Oxford University Press, 1991), p. 455.
39. Borawski, "Accord at Stockholm", p. 35. For detailed references, see Richard E. Darilek and John K. Setear, "Constraints in Europe" and Manfred Mueller, "Constraints", in *Conventional Arms Control and East-West Security*, pp.379-421.
40. Krehbiel. op, cit., pp. 219-221 and pp. 360-361 (Proposal of NNA on 15 November 1985 in the CDE Conference)

41. For the enhancement of the CSCE`s CPC functions, see James Macintosh "The emerging post-Helsinki security architecture" in Heather Chestnutt and Steven Mataija (eds), *Towards Helsinki:1992: Arms Control in Europe and the Verification Process* (Toronto: Centre for International Strategic Studies, 1991), pp. 229-247.
42. *SIPRI Yearbook 1991*, Articles II, III of the Vienna Agreement (From the 17th provision to the 35th provision)
43. Ghebali and Tanner, op. cit., p. 1270.
44. Ibid.
45. Ibid.
46. Jane Sharp, *SIPRI Yearbook 1990: World Armaments and Disarmament* (Stockholm International Peace Research Institute, Oxford University Press, 1990), p. 516.
47. Statement Issued by the North Atlantic Council Ministerial Session at NATO Headquarters, Brussels (8th-9th December 1988), *NATO Review*, Vol.36, No.6, (December 1988), p. 25.
48. Rittberger, op. cit., p. 63.
49. Kevin N. Lewis and Mark A. Lorell, "Confidence-Building Measures and Crisis resolution: Historical Perspectives", *Orbis*, Vol. 28., No. 2, (Summer 1984), p. 304.
50. Lynn Hansen, "Evaluating the Stockholm Conference: A US Perspective", in *From Stockholm to Vienna: Building Confidence and Security in Europe*, p.28.
51. Brauch, op. cit., p. 132.
52. Berg, Military Confidence-Building in Europe, p. 17.
53. Hugh Hanning (ed), *Peacekeeping and Confidence-Building Measures in the Third World* (New York: the International Peace Academy, Report No.20, 1985), p. 33.
54. Falk Bomsdorf, *'The Third World, Europe and Confidence Building Measures'* quoted in Bulletin of the Federal Government No. 55 of 30 May 1978, p. 534.
55. Falk Bomsdorf, "The Confidence-Building Offensive in the United Nations", *Aussen Politik*, Vol. 33, No. 4, p. 371.
56. Jack Child (ed), *Maintenance of Peace and Security in the Caribbean and Central America* (Report of the International Peace Academy Workshop at Cancum, Mexico, 7-9 October 1983),p. 46.
57. See Betts, *Surprise Attack*, pp. 63-80.
58. Yair Evron, "Arms Control in the Middle East: Some Proposals and their Confidence-Building Roles", in 'The Future of Arms Control Part III', pp. 33-34.
59. Ibid., p. 30.
60. David Barton, "The Sinai Peacekeeping Experience: A Verification Paradigm for Europe", in *SIPRI Yearbook 1985*, pp. 542-550.
61. Brian S. Mandell, T*he Sinai Experience: Lessons in Multi-method Arms Control Verification and Risk Management* (Ottawa: Arms Control Verification Studies, No.3, 1987), p.23.
62. Ibid., p. 32.
63. Barton, op. cit., p. 553.
64. Mandell, op. cit., p. 28.
65. Jozef Goldblat, "Multilateral Arms Control Efforts", in *SIPRI Yearbook 1987*, p. 401. The Contadora Treaty was replaced in August 1987 by the Arias Plan. The Contadora Group consists of Colombia, Mexico, Panama and Venezuela. Argentina, Brazil, Peru and Uruguay formed a support group for the Contadora efforts.
66. Jozef Goldblat and Victor Millan, "The Honduras-Nicaragua Conflict and Prospect for Arms Control in Central America, in *SIPRI Yearbook 1982*, p. 537. For detailed proposals of CBMs to Central America, see Jack Child, "A Confidence-Building Approach to Resolving

Central American Conflict", *Conflict in Central America* (London: The International Peace Academy, 1986), pp. 121-130.
67. Trevor Findlay, "Sinai and Contadora: Non-European Models for Asia/Pacific Confidence-Building" (Australian National University: Peace Research Centre, Working Paper, No.79, 1990), p.7.
68. Ghebali and Tanners, op. cit., p. 1272. The intrusive verification is performed by the Verification and Control Commission (VCC)-an organ entrusted with the talk of compiling all the relevant information resulting from data exchange and notification.
69. Final Document of the Summit Meeting of Five Central American Presidents 7 August 1987, *Survival*, Vol.30, No.1, (Jan./Feb. 1988), p. 84
70. The U.S. objects to the Contadora peace process which excludes its influence-the traditional solution advocated by the U.S. In fact it is hard to envisage a proficient operation without the support of the United States.
71. See "First Successful Step in CSBM Negotiations: the Military Doctrine Seminar", *NATO Review*, Vol.38, No.2, (April, 1990), pp. 10-15. *SIPRI Yearbook 1991*, pp. pp. 501-511. Wendy Silverman, "Talking Sufficiency in the Hofburg Place: The Second Seminar on Military Doctrine", *Arms Control Today*, Vol.21, No. 10. (December 1991), pp. 14-17.
72. Kate Holder and Robert E. Hunter (eds), "Confidence on Security and Cooperation in Europe: The Next Phase", *Significant Issues Series* (Washington D.C. CSIS, 1991), Vol. XIII, No. 7, pp. 1-64.
73. John Borawski, "The Vienna Negotiations on Confidence and Security, Building Measures", *RUSI Journal*, (Autumn 1990), pp. 41-42.
74. Ibid. p. 42.

4. The Arms Reduction Negotiations : MBFR and CFE

The Process of the MBFR Talks

In December of 1967 NATO foreign ministers adopted the 'Hamel Report' on the future tasks of the alliance. The Hamel Report recommended that "the allies would study disarmament and practical arms control measures, including the possibility of balanced force reductions". It also suggested the use of these measures as a vehicle of detente by emphasizing that their active pursuit reflected the will of the allies to work for an effective modus vivendi with the East.[1]

A refinement of the Reykjavik Declaration of principles regarding mutual force reductions was issued in the alliance ministerial meeting in Rome in 1970. The ministers decided upon the principles that guided the exploratory phase of MBFR talks with the Warsaw Pact countries: mutual force reduction based on geographical asymmetry, phased and balanced in its scope and timing, reduction of foreign and indigenous forces and weapons, and adequate verification.[2] These points were employed as nearly unchanged bases of the NATO position through the whole period of the MBFR negotiations.

The WTO at first paid no attention to NATO's arms reduction proposals. However, the East gave an indication that some sort of arms control discussion might be possible based upon the premise of the creation of a body responsible for questions of European security. This was suggested at the meeting of the Warsaw Pact's foreign ministers in Budapest on 22 June 1970. The communique mentioned that "a study of the question of reducing foreign armed forces on the territory of European states would serve the interest of detente and security in Europe".[3] In linkage with the convocation of a security conference, the Soviet Union repeated the suggestion for MBFR participation in the 24th Communist Party Congress in March 1971.

In 1967 the number of Soviet divisions deployed west of Soviet borders was increased from 27 to 31, and a further 100,000 Soviet soldiers were gradually moved into eastern Europe. The Warsaw Pact also added the combat strength of one field army, which included another 1,400 tanks.[4] The balance shifted further to western disadvantage. The NATO alliance was shocked by the Warsaw Pact's invasion of Czechoslovakia in 1968. The shock was triggered by the surprise attack abilities of the Pact forces and the use of military power for political ends in the heart of Europe.

In relation to the threat of the WTO, NATO adopted in 1967 'the flexible response strategy'. The viability of this strategy was dependent upon the creation of sufficient conventional forces to deter and ultimately defeat a conventional attack by the WTO. However, in order to implement the strategy the European members of NATO would be required to increase their military budgets by between five and 15 percent.

The size and distribution of the alliance forces deployed in Central Europe was felt to be inadequate to halt a determined large scale Pact invasion. Jeffrey Record pointed to the vulnerabilities of deployment:

> Most NATO ground force units currently deployed in the Guide-lines Area are not stationed in their assigned wartime positions. In many cases, major combat formations are located on the "wrong side" of the Rhine or otherwise separated from their initial required ammunition supplies.[5]

NATO also depended upon substantial reinforcements from the US but, in the wartime, only three US Army divisions were capable of being moved to Europe by air and most reinforcements would arrive in Europe after M+25 by sea.[6]

Consequently, the MBFR proposals described as "working for an effective detente with the East "might be interpreted as motivated by the inferiority and vulnerabilities of the NATO alliance. In fact the MBFR initiatives by the West were more influenced by political than by military arguments. With the beginning of the SALT negotiations on strategic nuclear weapons in 1969 an "era of negotiations" between East and West was opened. The detente process was based upon pressure for a reduction of US forces in Europe from Congress. Senator Mike Mansfield introduced an amendment calling for a partial and unilateral reduction of US forces in Europe. The amendment asked for a 50 percent reduction of some 300,000 US forces in Europe. According to his argument, such a massive withdrawal would not endanger the security of Western Europe, but rather would lead the Soviets to withdraw their forces from the Eastern countries.

The Mansfield proposal was attacked by the Nixon Administration and by other Senators. Secretary of State William P. Rogers emphasised the need to link the reductions of US forces with the those of Soviet forces:

> We would want to do it in the context of a mutual and balanced force reduction. Why should we in the United States reduce unilaterally and

thereby kiss goodbye to any chance that we might have to negotiate successfully to reduce the Soviet presence.[7]

Senator Robert Dole also made a strong statement that "unilateral US troop reductions in Europe would destroy any hope of mutual and balanced force reduction negotiations at a time when such negotiations appear to be a real possibility".[8] Such arguments were more persuasive than the unilateral reduction proposal. The amendment was rejected. Thus, the MBFR talks were a very important tactic of the Administration in holding off unilateral force cuts.

The Soviet Union which had scarcely shown any concern previously with the MBFR negotiations officially declared in May 1971 in Tbilisi that it favoured MBFR participation. This sudden change of the Soviet attitude, five days prior to the vote on Mansfield's proposal, had a decisive role in defeating it. The reasons for Soviet MBFR participation can be considered at various levels. The Soviet Union saw this as the means for realizing both limited and long-term objectives in Europe. The Soviet Union, as a limited objective, accepted the MBFR talks in return for the convening of the CSCE Conference. "Brezhnev was clearly making progress on MBFR conditional on the successful completion of the CSCE conference."[9] The US policy was also the same. To bring a positive response from Moscow, Kissinger during his visit to Moscow in September of 1972 also linked US acceptance of the opening date of the CSCE to Soviet acceptance of the opening of MBFR.[10]

Other important objectives were drawn from the military aspects. The first was to use theatre nuclear weapons which were regarded as a crucial threat to the East as a means of negotiating down WTO conventional advantages. John G. Keliher made this observation in relation to SALT I: " General Secretary Brezhnev certainly must have had FBS in mind when he issued the call for mutual force reductions in May 1971, once it became apparent that FBS would not be dealt with at SALT I".[11]

Another objective was directed at the regulation of the armed forces of FRG. West German membership of NATO gave the Soviet Union a strong stimulus for entering into the MBFR talks. The German armed forces had become a central pillar in the composition of NATO forces. Against the Soviet forces the FRG had been encouraged to increase further its military strength. The Soviet Union recognized that it was only possible to influence FRG military strength within the bloc negotiations. It feared an increment of West German troops would follow a US force reduction. Moscow therefore desired a regulated withdrawal of American military force.[12]

1973 Preparatory Talks

Preliminary talks on MBFR were initiated in Vienna between NATO and the Warsaw Pact on 31 January, 1973. The geographical area of MBFR covered Central Europe; the two German states, Benelux, Poland and Czechoslovakia. Negotiators consisted of 11 direct participants from the 7 countries whose territory was involved and the 4 countries whose forces were stationed in Central Europe: USSR, the US, the UK and Canada. With special observer status NATO had Denmark, Greece, Italy, Norway and Turkey; WTO observers were Bulgaria, Hungary and Romania.

The West wanted the inclusion of Hungary as a direct participant, while the East insisted on the inclusion of Italy and France. The Soviet Union, particularly, feared that French armed forces and their nuclear weapons would be excluded under the MBFR agreement. As a result of these negotiations French forces of some 50,000 men and 325 tanks in West Germany were included within the Western total. Three countries were excluded in the Guidelines area. With the exclusion of Hungary, which had Soviet combat forces on its soil, MBFR "covered all major US ground forces deployment in Europe while leaving undisturbed a significant Soviet deployment and the USSR's sole military 'window' on a post-Tito Yugoslavia".[13]

The 1973-75 Negotiations

The formal MBFR talks were opened on 30 October 1973 in Vienna. NATO offered the first proposal calling for a two phase reduction. The first phase reduction would be a 15 percent cut each of Soviet and US forces. The United States would pull out some 29,000 troops in return for 68,000 Soviet ones with 1700 tanks. The Second phase would be applied to the indigenous forces of direct participants in the Guidelines area. Each alliance would be limited to the common ceiling figures of 700,000 ground forces. In effect, this would require the respective reduction by the Warsaw Pact of 225,000 men and NATO of 77,000 men.[14]

---

o. NATO proposals
 . Phase I: 15% reductions each of Soviet and US forces
 . Phase II: reductions of participants forces

> o. WTO proposals
> . Phase I: reductions of 20,000 men in 1975
> . Phase II: reduction of 5% in 1976
> . Phase III: reduction 10% in 1977

The NATO proposal was based on asymmetrical reduction of the WTO preponderance in manpower and in tanks for offensive operation. The reduction was otherwise limited to troops, excluding their equipment, air and theatre nuclear forces. The West opposed inclusion of equipment because of the perceived value of these weapons in compensating for the East's advantage in deployed manpower.

The East made a three-stage proposal encompassing nuclear and air force units as well as ground forces. The proposal called for a total reduction by 17 percent of each state's military units, forbidding the leaving behind of stationed forces' equipment. In March of 1975, the East offered the modified position that for stage I the United States and the Soviet Union would each withdraw 10,000 troops in the first six months from the Guidelines area; in the second six months the two Germanys would cut their forces by 5,000 men each, and the remaining Eastern and Western direct participants would divide up another 5,000 in reduction amongst themselves.[15]

A major point of the Eastern proposal was the demand for the establishment of national sub-ceilings of each direct participant. It was intended as a device to block possible future expansion of the Bundeswehr after the application of MBFR. The Soviet Union wished to take the opportunity to further their long-standing goals of reducing the armed forces of West Germany, which comprised roughly 45 percent of NATO's strength. This factor, coupled with the historic fear of the Germans, made reduction of the Bundeswehr an important and logical goal of the Soviet Union.[16]

The profound differences of the MBFR proposals of NATO and the Warsaw Pact can be summarised in the table below. These differences reflected a disagreement over the nature of the military balance in Central Europe, as well as a divergence of objectives sought in MBFR. The different approaches of both sides remained during the whole of the MBFR negotiations.

Table 4-1 The Reduction Approaches of NATO and WTO in the Opening Proposals

	NATO	WTO
reduction method	asymmetry	symmetry
reduction forces	ground	ground, air & nuclear
reduction subject	troops	troops & equipment
reduction phase	two phase	three phase
force ceiling	collective	national sub-ceilings

The 1975-78 Negotiations

o. NATO
   The Option III with the previous phase I,II
   WTO- a reduction of 17,000 tanks and 69,000 men
o. WTO
   Phase I: 1976 proposals; 2-3 % reduction, 1978 proposal; 7%
   Phase II: 1976 proposal; 7%, 1978 proposal; WTO 13% & NATO 11%
o. Convergence: reductions over two stages, common ceilings

In an attempt to break the deadlock of negotiation NATO modified the 1973 proposal on 16 December 1975. NATO offered Option III - withdrawing some tactical nuclear assets in return for the reductions of phase I. The proposal included airmen in addition to 54 Phantom aircraft in order to establish a common manpower ceiling of 900,000 men for each alliance with a sub-ceiling of 700,000 for ground forces.

Option III was a major concession, accepting in effect the Pact's longstanding demand that MBFR should encompass nuclear weapons as well as conventional forces. The removal of nuclear forward-based systems had indeed been a major Soviet arms control objective in Europe. However, NATO's substantial change did not draw any concessions from the Soviets. WTO argued that the nuclear withdrawals under Option III represented ageing and often obsolete ordnance in exchange for new sophisticated weapons. The proposal was in fact made as a means "to relieve Congressional pressures to relocate up to 1000 older tactical nuclear weapons from Europe to the United States and to extract a price for their withdrawal".[17]

On 16 February 1976, WTO made a counter-offer to the NATO proposals. The first stage would reduce 2-3 percent of US and Soviet manpower, freezing the remaining direct participants' forces at their 1976 level. In 1977-78, the direct participants would reduce their forces by 15 per cent and the two superpowers would reduce by an additional 12-13 percent. The proposals also included the reduction of one army corps headquarters, 300 tanks from each side and the trade off of 54 F-4 tactical aircraft for Su-17/20 As & Cs and 36 Pershings for SCUD-Bs. Neither side's proposals addressed the questions of greatest concern to the other side and offered no meaningful concessions for escaping from the negotiation deadlock.

Eventually the two sides made a substantial revision of their original positions. On 19 April 1978 NATO, thanks to a major concession from the FRG, modified the position requiring the phase I withdrawals of 1,500 Soviet tanks from the GDR. Instead, it proposed a reduction of 1,700 tanks and 69,000 men associated with five divisions in the Guidelines area. This provided the Soviets with greater flexibility in selecting the force units of reduction.

The East swiftly made three main counter-offers on 8 June 1978. The first was to accept NATO's position on phase II reduction-a common ceiling of 700,000 ground force personnel and a combined ground and air personnel ceiling of 900,000. Second, in return for Option III, was to withdraw 1000 tanks and 250 armoured personnel carriers. The third was to modify the reduction percentage from the previous 15 percent to 13-11 percent, reducing 7 percent of Soviet and US forces in the first stage.

The proposals of NATO and the Warsaw Pact in 1975-78 failed to bring major compromises. However, this period's offers nevertheless represented significant progress in the MBFR negotiations. For the West, a most important concession was the offer of trading nuclear weapons for conventional ones under Option III. The offer, though it did not produce any fruits and was withdrawn as a one time option, remained a precedent of possibility for the trade-off of incompatible weapons.

Other progress was that the East, for the first time since the beginning of the MBFR talks, submitted data on its forces in the Guidelines area. The data offer, though it did not break the continuing deadlock because of major differences from NATO estimates of Pact forces, was a significant change from the previously inflexible Soviet position. The release of military data was regarded as a turning point in the Soviet Unions reluctant attitude towards the MBFR negotiations.

Another development was the modification of the Pact's rigid position on the national subceiling demand for any one country. The previous demand resulted from the Soviet Union's worry that West Germany would increase its forces in order to offset the reduction of allied forces. The Soviet Union began to show a flexible position on German military issues. Until that time, the Soviet Union had attempted to establish the very kind of national subceiling on German forces that NATO itself had imposed on Germany.[18]

The 1979-86 Negotiations: Associated Measures

> o. NATO: the withdrawal of Option III
> . Phase I - the 7% reduction of US and Soviet Forces
> . Associated Measures
> o. WTO: 20,000 reduction of US and Soviet troops each
> . freezing of manpower levels for three years

On 17 December 1979 NATO tabled an interim proposal on manpower instead of withdrawing Option III in order to proceed to a second-phase agreement. The proposal called for a respective 7 percent reduction by both sides during phase I; 13,000 for the United States and 30,000 for the Soviet Union. It was almost identical to the manpower elements of the 1978 Eastern scheme which proposed to withdraw Soviet 30,000 troops, 1,000 tanks and 250 armoured personnel carriers. The proposal was very significant in that NATO gave up its long-held position that greater asymmetrical reduction by the East must be made. This concession was linked with a NATO decision to upgrade US Pershing Ia missiles and the unilateral withdrawal of 1,000 US nuclear warheads.

NATO officially put forward the Associated Measures for ensuring compliance with any MBFR agreement. The main measures were:

> . Prior notification: out-of-garrison activities, changes over military personnel and all troop movement (division size).
> . Exchange of information and observers: force levels, military movement.
> . Inspection: mutual aerial and ground inspections (18 inspection trips) designation of Exit/Entry.[19]

The Associated Measures, which were issued as an official title in preparatory talks, had been reserved for the final stages of the negotiations. However, the Soviet contravention of the Helsinki Declaration by the invasion of Afghanistan and WTO's growing capability for surprise attack in Central Europe led NATO to insist upon binding verification measures. NATO gave priority to verification measures before the reduction agreement.

At the end of 1980 the East had a counter proposal for the mutual reduction of 20,000 Soviet personnel against 13,000 US ones from ground forces. This offer was consistent with the Eastern Bloc's earlier proposal for an initial reduction of 20,000 men from both sides as a symbolic step of political and practical significance. In addition, the East put forward the freezing of manpower levels on both sides at existing ceilings for three years. The crisis situation in Poland at the time was likely to induce the Soviet Union "to avoid any substantial progress towards an agreement under which Soviet forces would have to be withdrawn from Eastern Europe under mutual control".[20]

In the 1980s the general political environment did not favour MBFR. The declaration of the 1979 Soviet unilateral withdrawal of about 20,000 men and 1,000 tanks from the GDR had the most direct impact on the MBFR talks itself by breaking a fundamental commitment on mutual negotiated reduction.[21] The Soviet invasion of Afghanistan and the West's boycott of the 1980 Olympic games in Moscow signalled a new cold war era. With the beginning of the new Cold War NATO and WTO again recognized arms control talks as an important vehicle for the creation of new detente and made efforts to break the MBFR deadlock. For this, the US proposed a staged implementation of the reductions to a common collective ceiling, comprising a single agreement instead of two separate ones. The Soviet Union also agreed to some form of on-site inspection and to the initial force reductions which embraced a higher proportionate reduction on its side and which it had previously rejected. However, the MBFR negotiations eventually failed due to the lack of compromise over verification procedures, data and the subjects and sizes of reduction.

The Problems and Obstacles of the MBFR Talks

The MBFR negotiations were led by the two superpowers. The analyses of the problems of MBFR must start with the assessment of their intentions for achieving MBFR. Because of the lack of a strong mutuality of interests, neither side went to Vienna with enthusiasm.

The United States proposed an MBFR formula as a device to relieve the Congressional pressures for unilateral reduction of its troops. All other goals were secondary to this consideration. Richard Burt noted that for the

West, MBFR itself was not a means of achieving the real object, viz. a more stable military balance in Central Europe.

> A basic rationale for plunging into the MBFR exercise was to dampen enthusiasm in the Senate for unilateral withdrawal of US troops from Europe. Even though these Senate demands have all but died, MBFR continues with little changes in its focus and negotiation goals.[22]

The real US objective of MBFR is well demonstrated by Kissinger's confession that the proposal to convene the force reduction negotiations was essentially a ploy to forestall unilateral American cuts.[23] The United States was generally active in MBFR when confronted with the pressures of US force reduction. The Reagan Government took a new initiative for escaping from the MBFR deadlock when the calls for US force reduction in Europe re-emerged in 1982 during a Senate vote on economic pressures. After Congressional pressure to repatriate US troops subsided, its enthusiasm cooled. The Soviet Union also attended the MBFR negotiations without having any great desire for their realization. There were no special military incentives for MBFR participation. Moscow's clear aim in Europe was to obtain a general political settlement, not a forces reduction. It insisted that force reductions be considered only within CSCE.

Arms control as an approach towards management of the military confrontation was in fact more a part of the political East-West relationship than of the military one. A reduction of small size was always claimed as a symbol of detente. Apparently the Soviet Union viewed the MBFR talks as a forum for maintaining a degree of detente with Europe after its relations with the US had begun to deteriorate.[24] The Soviet Union used its military powers as a means of political intimidation in crises in Eastern countries. The MBFR agreement, which would result in the loss of the superiority of its conventional forces and weaken its influence over the East, was believed to be very detrimental to the Soviet Union's strategic advantages.

The other line of the failure of MBFR is reflected in the criticism of its emphasis of a reduction of manpower rather than offensive combat units or armaments. Western countries argued that reduced armaments might have to be destroyed, making it impossible to use this equipment for reserve forces. Furthermore, equipment withdrawn by US forces would be returned far more slowly than reintroduction of Soviet equipment in the event of crisis. Therefore they attributed a top priority to achieving equal troop levels because they thought that force levels could be equated in practice more readily than military units of different sizes, organization and equipment. Besides, troop reduction was very attractive due to the financial savings which would be made. The focus on manpower reduction as the first negotiation subject in the MBFR talks seemed to be a sensible choice in that not only was its calculation very simple, but such reduction would in practice result in the reduction of both troops and weapons.

However, the idea proved to be a mistaken judgement. It was in fact more difficult to count servicemen with precision because of their mobility. Furthermore each alliance force structure was too diversified to make the counting exact. The component ratio of men in each unit was dissimilar between alliances or individual nations. The Soviet ground forces in Central Europe, for example, were organized so that 65 percent of all personnel were in a division when compared to 60 percent in the West German Army and 43 percent in the US Army in Germany.[25]

The MBFR approach had an another fault in that it depended on only numerical balance without developing an adequate arms reduction formula bringing stability. Manpower reductions, even if implemented, can be ineffective in reducing the level of confrontation because they bring only common ceilings at somewhat lower levels. In fact the conceptual problem of the MBFR approach arises from the difficulty of evaluating the military balance given the need for taking into account all combat factors-tangible and intangible. According to Generals Lee and Jackson, even in combat, total numbers of troops and armaments are often less important than the skill and determination of individual soldiers, relative mobility of opposing forces, and the respective quality of military leadership.[26] The war between Israel and the Arab countries in June 1967 remains a good example where the numbers of troops did not determine the eventual victory.

The approach problem of the MBFR talks also arises from the assessment of geographic asymmetry. NATO favoured asymmetrical reduction owing to its lack of territorial integrity, its short combat depth, and the proximity of Soviet territory and resources to Central Europe compared to the long distance from the US. However, it is in reality very difficult to reach a refined consensus on how to factor geographic asymmetry into a military balance. The military balance is based on many factors which are subjective or difficult to quantify. Therefore many proposals in MBFR negotiations had continued to rely for their conceptual basis on simple "bean counting".[27] Because of the pivotal concept of MBFR, no agreement could be concluded without setting the conceptual framework about the military balance and the relative military capabilities of two sides. In fact a military balance could not prevent the outbreak of war and provide stability in Europe. Even if both sides were convinced that a balance existed, the question of the relationship between balance and security would come up. [28]

One of the most important reasons why the MBFR talks failed was due to the disagreement over the data between East and West concerning the number of Warsaw Pact troops. The data dispute was mainly about the size of the Eastern ground and air forces in the area of reduction. The Eastern data on its own forces, submitted for the first time in 1976, was in sharp contrast to the Western estimates. As shown in the table below, the Eastern figures were 157,000 below Western estimates for the ground forces while the air forces were almost compatible. The WTO data suggested that a balance already existed and symmetrical reduction should be made in ground forces. WTO, while unwilling to accept NATO's data on WTO forces, rejected the provision of further detailed information needed to resolve the discrepancies on the NATO's estimates. From the WTO point of view it was not in fact necessary for both sides to agree on the current size of their forces before making a force reduction agreement.

Table 4-2 The Difference of Data between NATO and WTO in the Guidelines Area, 1976

unit:000

	NATO Manpower	Pact NATO estimates	Manpower Pact Data	Discrepancy
Ground	791	962	805	157
Air	193	200	182,3	17,7
Total	984	1,162	987	17,4

Source: Jeffrey Record, *Force Reductions: Starting Over* (The Institute for Foreign Policy Analysis, Inc., 1980) p. 53.

Instead the residual force levels could be verified after reducing to the common ceilings of 700,000 and 900,000 men. On the other hand NATO insisted that the size of reductions should be calculated based upon data from an agenda. The data would assist in fixing post-reduction levels and would provide a baseline for testing compliance with manpower ceilings once reduction had taken place.[29]

One important reason for the long dispute arose from lack of agreement over the counting rules. Many arms control analysts held the view that no meaningful progress at MBFR was possible until the development of the counting rules which dealt with specific weapon systems, together with military units of all sizes and various organizational schemes. The precious lesson learned from the MBFR experience is that data and counting rules must be discussed before entering into concrete reduction talks.[30] Otherwise, neither side can be sure of what the other side's data actually represents. By first unilaterally introducing data before counting rules were agreed upon, both sides fell into a dispute over data credibility. WTO might be very reluctant to modify the publicized data because of prestige or reduced credibility. Once the East had provided data it was then committed to defend it.

In conclusion, it was proved by the MBFR experience that the realization of reduction without data agreement is impossible. An agreed data base is a essential element both before and after the reduction phase. An agreement on data is essential in order to verify adherence to the concluded treaty. In the conventional arms reduction negotiations "the best approach to a data solution lies not in data update but in an agreement on counting values".[31]

The other crucial obstacle to MBFR agreement had to do with verification. The basic objective of verification is to confirm the data in the pre-reduction stage. Its implementation also helps to monitor compliance, to prevent violation, to discourage circumvention, to increase mutual confidence and to augment warning time.[32] Therefore, it has always been one of the most complex and sensitive issues of negotiations. The problem of how to verify force levels before concluding an MBFR agreement was a central issue to both sides from the beginning of negotiations.

The West insisted from 1973 onwards on the negotiation of inspection measures as a part of the "Associated Measures". It was not adopted as a formal proposal because of sensitivity to strong West German objections that such measures would impinge on its sovereignty.[33] It was not until 1979 that the West included inspection measures in an associated measures package. The inclusion consisted of three main points: permanent entry-exit point for observation, an annual quota of 18 inspections and noninterference with National Technical Means (NTM) of verification. The West sought to develop specific measures complementary to NTM, namely, on-site inspection. In contrast to Western efforts, the East tried to avoid this subject. Soviet negotiators argued that it was illogical to negotiate the inspection measures without prior agreement on reduction. The East wanted to employ NTM for verification of MBFR. Its intention was to apply the precedent established through the SALT II treaty to MBFR.[34] In February 1986 WTO made some concessions on the principle of permanent checkpoints and on-site inspections. However there remained many differences about how inspection between the East and West should take place. NATO, for example, wanted 30 on-site inspections per year, while

WTO claimed the right to refuse ill-founded requests for inspection. WTO also wanted to avoid formal check-points to monitor the regular rotation of Soviet troops in the area.[35]

Military manpower is the most mobile and concealable of all military resources. It is very difficult to detect when servicemen take off their uniforms and put on civilian clothing. The methods relying on only NTM could prevent the violation of an MBFR agreement. Undoubtedly small-scale reintroduction or increment in armed forces, made gradually over time, would be extremely difficult to detect. On-Site-Inspection, though it is not fool-proof in terms of detection, might well be recognized as an effectual means, complementing to some extent the vulnerability of NTM. It also had the merit of insuring the participation of the countries which did not possess sophisticated NTM.

In MBFR, neither side made progress because of the data issue and divergent views on the conduct of verification. In 1985 president Reagan declared that "strict compliance with all provisions of arms agreements is fundamental, and this Administration will not accept anything else".[36] The United States regarded it as a cooperative measure to ensure undiminished security. In the INF treaty of 1987 the Soviet Union ended the secrecy era by allowing on-site inspection. However, the nuclear weapons systems covered by the INF Treaty were simpler and smaller in numbers than conventional weapons in Europe. Thus, the verification of conventional forces might be harder than any previous nuclear arms control. The verification issue was regarded as a key issue in the post-MBFR era.

The Process and Issues of the CFE talks

The long stalemate of the MBFR talks produced a great deal of cynicism about the talks themselves between East and West. This cynicism generated interest in finding a new forum as a way to escape from the stalemate. The military significance of MBFR was in the mid-1980s scarcely greater for either side than it had been in 1973. The results of the agreed first step-a small US-Soviet troop reduction-would be militarily insignificant. Reducing personnel was also less significant militarily than cutting offensive weapons. A MBFR accord would do little to affect the capacity of the two alliances to wage war. A symbolic reduction of a small number might also encourage subsequent and more sizable reductions. Such an accord would result in lower levels of armament without fundamentally changing the military balance.

The pursuit of a new policy was highlighted in a speech by the new Soviet leader Mikhail Gorbachev in April 1986 in East Berlin. He proposed a complete reformulation of East-West negotiations on conventional forces. His proposal was to aim at substantial reduction of conventional forces over the entire European territory from the Atlantic to the Urals, including land forces, tactical air force and tactical nuclear weapons. The June 1986 Budapest Appeal of the Warsaw Pact confirming Gorbachev's intention offered concrete proposals. The proposals, as a first step, called for a 100,000-150,000 troop reduction of each side within one or two years and as a second stage, some 25 percent reduction of conventional forces of both alliances by the early 1990s. For purposes of verification, on-site inspection (OSI) was for the first time proposed with the establishment of an International Consultative Committee.[37] The extension of the reduction area to the Atlantic-Urals and acceptance of OSI were great concessions to the West and represented a turning point in conventional arms control. Thus, a movement for a new arms control was initiated by the Warsaw Pact. A swift response to Gorbachev's suggestion was made at the NATO ministerial meeting at Halifax on 30 May 1986. NATO set up a High Level Task Force (HLTF) on conventional arms control in Europe to evaluate MBFR and advise on its future, declaring their readiness to open East-West discussions for a new arms control forum. In its report to NATO in December 1986, the HLTF recommended two separate sets of negotiations: expansion of results of the Stockholm Conference and talks about conventional stability at lower levels.[38]

Talks on the new mandate began in Vienna in February 1987. The talks were convened in parallel to the CSCE review conference. The 20 months negotiations produced the mandate for the CFE talks and agreement on objective, rules, organization and procedures. On 15 January 1989, the 35 CSCE countries adopted a mandate for the opening of new negotiations on conventional forces in Europe (CFE) between the 23 NATO and WTO states excluding neutral and non-aligned countries in the reduction area. The opening of the new negotiation was held in Vienna in March 1989. In consequence, the MBFR talks were formally concluded with the starting of CFE.

The geographical area that the CFE talks covered were the territories of the 23 NATO and WTO countries from the Atlantic to the Urals and the Caspian Sea, including the European islands. During the MBFR talks the West worried that, even if Soviet forces were withdrawn from Central Europe, the USSR's heavily mechanized forces West of the Urals would pose a major threat to the West. The extension of the reduction area from

Central Europe to the Urals had been a long-standing Western concern in the East-West conventional talks.

The subject of the negotiations was the participant's conventional ground and air forces based on land. The Soviet Union agreed that only conventional forces were to be included, thereby abandoning its previous insistence that SNF be covered. Naval forces and chemical weapons were also to be excluded. The conventional capability of dual-purpose weapons could be dealt with in the negotiations, but they would not be singled out in a separate category. As a result the mandate limiting the talks to forces in the ATTU region had very different implications for the West and the East. For the Soviet Union, 70 percent of ground and air forces were included in the CFE talks. For the United States, however, only about 30 percent of ground forces and 10 percent of tactical air forces were included. Given its forces on the US territory this asymmetrical reduction was more advantageous for NATO. Over half of the US ground divisions and an even larger share of the US tactical aircraft were formally committed to NATO in the event of war.[39] The bitter experience of MBFR failure helped both sides to have a special concern with verification and accurate information exchange. For an effective and strict verification regime, the participants included the establishment of OSI as a right and exchanges of information.[40] They also agreed upon the exchange of sufficient detailed information which could allow a meaningful comparison of the capabilities of forces and provide a basis for the verification of compliance.

The CFE mandate was indeed devoted to the central security problems in Europe within the framework of the CSCE process. The participants consisted of all countries with essential influence over the security of Europe. The scope of negotiation dealt with the conventional security potential of all Europe, covering the entire region of strategic relevance from the Atlantic to the Urals. It also included other militarily significant measures directly related to the force reductions. The official objectives of the CFE talks were:

> the establishment of a stable and secure balance of conventional armed forces at a lower level;

> the elimination of disparities prejudicial to stability and security;

> the elimination, as a matter of priority, of the capability for launching surprise attack and for initiating large-scale offensive action.[41]

The CFE mandate reflected a long-standing NATO view for elimination of the Eastern superiority in armed forces and a surprise attack or large-scale attack. Unlike the MBFR talks which were directed towards politically symbolic cuts and a status quo at high levels of forces, the mandate suggested deep cuts which could eventually lead to the elimination of risks of war and to stabilization of defence-oriented restructuring of the forces that remained. In order to achieve the objectives, it also included the application of militarily significant measures such as limitations and redeployment provision essentially related to the reductions.

NATO and the Warsaw Pact were quick to table respective draft proposals after the opening of the CFE Talks. Considerable progress was achieved in less than a year. From the start of the talks the general proposals of both sides were considerably convergent though their reasons for putting them forward were different. Such convergences were caused by the WTO's concessions to NATO. The WTO, led by the Gorbachev initiatives, put a higher priority on budgetary savings and improved East-West relations than on traditional military concerns. The Soviet Union narrowed the military gap between NATO and WTO by making unilateral cuts in the size of its conventional forces for pressing economic reasons and was consequently content to accept asymmetric proposals.

In contrast to all the action in the East, NATO adopted a very cautious attitude towards the unilateral reductions and initiatives of the Soviet Union and approached the conventional talks with the traditional perspective. The opening NATO position in March 1989 offered only a 10 percent cut in tanks and a 15 percent cut in combat aircraft below the NATO level. The implementation of the NATO proposal in the ATTU region would result in a US cut of just 95 tanks, out of about 15,600 and about 120 combat aircraft out of about 7,200 respectively in the global inventory.[42]

Despite different attitudes the proposals of both sides revealed a number of convergent approaches. Overall agreement in the first discussions existed; the application of ceilings, a phased asymmetrical reduction, elimination of capability of surprise attack and large-scale offensive action, data exchange, comprehensive verification and a sufficiency rule.[43] Although the proposals were similar there were significant disagreements on detail which were obstacles to rapid progress. The disagreements came from the subjects of reduction. WTO included manpower and 5 categories of offensive weapons; tanks, artillery, ACVs, aircraft and helicopters. As a method of reduction three stages were suggested; to reduce to 10-15 percent below the lower level in each category in stage I (1991-1994), to reduce a further 25 percent in stage II (1994-1997) and to restructure the remaining forces of each side to defence postures in stage III (1997-2000). However, NATO's proposals excluded manpower, helicopters and combat aircraft, and omitted reduction phases.

Soviet Union had plans for withdrawing some troops from Eastern Europe and for restructuring its army at a lower level. It saw CFE as a vehicle for implementing this. Thus the WTO insisted on the inclusion of the manpower limits long before the political collapse of communism in Eastern Europe in late 1989.[44] On the other hand NATO believed that tanks, artillery and ACVs, capable of rapid mobility and high firepower, were crucial to offensive capability. Aircraft and helicopters were excluded in that they were highly mobile and unverifiable. However it was considered that they were weapons systems which could be used in a surprise attack. NATO finally agreed to include combat aircraft and attack helicopters.

As seen in table 4-3, the differences between NATO and the Warsaw Pact were to be too numerous and too varied to achieve easy agreement. On 14 December 1989 the two alliances tabled the texts of comprehensive draft agreements which would be an important basis of the CFE treaty. The most important agreement was that in order to implement reductions from 1992 or 1993 the CFE treaty would be concluded within 6-12 months and submitted to the CSCE Summit Meeting of November 1990 in Paris.

The CFE Treaty, signed on 19 November 1990 after negotiations lasting over 20 months, was an epoch-making agreement in European history. It eliminated what had been the major threat to European security for more than four decades and opened a new security landscape in Europe with the end of the Cold War. The Treaty introduced a number of reduction methods and stabilization measures, directed at the prevention of surprise attack. Five categories of Treaty-Limited Equipments (TLEs) were defined in the agreement; battle tanks, ACVs, artillery pieces, combat aircraft and attack helicopters. Three numerical limits on each category were established: overall ceilings for each alliance, sub-limits for each alliance in each of four 'zones' in Europe and maximum single-country levels.[45] In order to ensure verification of compliance with its provisions, collateral measures were additionally included in the agreement.

The Main Treaty Implications

The five categories of reduction weapons were defined in detail in Article II of the treaty. The definitions of the TLEs (Treaty-Limited Equipments) were a very important criteria for the counting of weapons, reductions and verifications. Without agreed counting rules between the two alliances the exchanged data in 1989 were calculated in different ways and were contradictory. The differences of force structures, weapon systems and weapon possession contributed to a large amount of time spent on the definition of the TLEs in the negotiations. The most serious conflicts concerned the questions of combat aircraft and helicopters. For example, there were differences on the distinction between offensive and defensive weapons. NATO depended on definition by capability, while WTO preferred definition by designation.[46] Under such a definition, the Soviets excluded their own defence interceptors, intermediate bombers, trainers and land-based naval aircraft, while including all of NATO's aircraft because of dual capacity for attack and defence. Difficulties over agreement on technical issues such as the definition of TLEs were the most serious obstacles to the treaty.

Table 4-3   Divergences of Initial Proposals of NATO and WTO in the CFE Talks

---

o. Negotiation subjects
   NATO: tanks, artillery, ACVs
   WTO: NATO + manpower, aircraft, helicopters

o. Sufficiency rules: NATO: 30/60 %, WTO: 35-40/70-80 %

o. Limits in the Sub-zones
   NATO: increasing cumulative totals of permitted TLEs
   WTO: limits on each TLE for each zone

o. Disposition of TLEs
   NATO: a system of interlocking sublimits
   WTO: demobilization and destruction-->monitored storage

o. Verification
   NATO: 900 inspections per year, WTO + doubtful military installation
   WTO: 400 inspections per year, only declared military installations

---

Parity of military strength between East and West has been a central objective in the conventional arms reduction negotiations of Europe. Parity has been seen as essential for stability and security in Europe. The collective ceiling employed in the CFE treaty was based on asymmetrical reduction requiring greater cuts in Eastern European military forces than in NATO forces. Article IV of the treaty set ceilings for each group of states. Each group was obliged to reduce to equal ceilings within 40 months after entry into force of the treaty. Neither could subsequently deploy more than 20,000 tanks, 30,000 ACVs, 20,000 artillery pieces, 6,800 combat aircraft and 2,000 attack helicopters. In particular tanks, ACVs and artillery pieces were calculated in divisions of active units and stored units. Within the overall limits, no more than 16,000 tanks, 27,300 ACVs and 17,000 artillery could be in active units; the remainder could be placed in designated permanent storage sites. The removal of stored weapons from the designated site was under severe constraint. No more than 550 tanks, 1,000 ACVs and 300 artillery pieces can be removed by the members of group at any one time.[47]

The CFE treaty also set the maximum entitlements for each group within each alliance. This is known as the sufficiency rule. No single country possesses more than approximately one-third of five categories of weapons. According to the rule, the levels of maximum possessions of each group are 13,000 battle tanks, 20,000 ACVs, 13,700 artillery pieces, 5,150 combat aircraft and 1,500 attack helicopters. With the rapid disintegration of the Warsaw Pact its non-Soviet members became increasingly concerned about disproportionate Soviet superiority. The Soviet Union argued for a higher sufficiency rule (40 percent) to compensate for its lost allies.[48]

Each country was required to notify all other parties of the portion of the alliance ceiling in each armament category. The announced national ceilings were its maximum entitlement. To increase its maximum entitlement in any category a country must provide 90 days advance notice to all other parties. While individual ceilings for the five categories must not be exceeded, each state has the right to disarm unilaterally. This does not imply an automatic increase in the quotas of the other states belonging to the same group.[49]

The ATTU area of reduction is subdivided into three concentric zones and a flank zone with specific collective sub-ceilings.[50] The divisions of sub-zones have no relation with phase or the time table of reduction. It is only for the purpose of preventing destabilizing force concentrations, or treaty circumvention. The sub-ceilings apply only to ground weapons in active units. The three concentric zones are comprised of successively larger areas, so that each zone aggregated the previous one. NATO did not envisage any ceilings for aircraft or helicopters, for the simple reason that regional ceilings are considered particularly unverifiable. Its basic aim was to constrain the reinforcement potential of the Soviet Union. On the other hand the WTO's proposal was to take stored equipment into account. The Eastern intention seemed to focus upon constraint, by limiting Bundeswehr forces and POMCUS.[51]

Table 4-4 Ceilings of Sub-zones in the TLEs

	Zone 1	Zone II	Zone III	Flank
tanks	75	103	153	47
ACVs	112,5	192,6	241	59
Artillery	50	91	140	60

Source: *SIPRI Yearbook 1991*, pp.465-466 (The CFE Treaty, Article IV)

An effect of these sub-ceilings was that no one single country can exceed the one-third maximum possible under the sufficiency rule. The sub-division of reduction zone and each subceiling was one of the most difficult issues alongside aircraft reduction in the Vienna negotiations.

To enhance verification of treaty compliance the CFE Treaty requires each country to notify all other states with regard to information necessary for its implementation. Verification of compliance with the Treaty is based on a comprehensive exchange of information.

Table 4-5   Passive Quotas for Inspection of Sites

	baseline validation	II reduction phase	III validation phase	V subsequent years
declared sites	20	10	20	15
challenge Inspection	15	15	15	23

challenge inspection: ratio of declared sites quota. Source: SIPRI Yearbook 1991, p. 411, quoted in *The VERTIC Guide to the CFE Treaty* (VERTIC: London 1990), p.14

The information to be provided includes: force structures down to the level of brigade/regiment; overall and sub-zone accounting of the members, locations and types of TLEs in each weapons category; objectives of verifications (OOVs) and declared sites etc. For the purpose of monitoring any declared site each group has the right to conduct a large number of OSI.

The inspection is divided into four phases. Each state has a quota of passive inspections it must accept in each treaty phase. Thus a quota of inspection is assigned to each country of the alliance groups. The CFE treaty provides 'active inspection' that each country may carry out within the same alliance. No party can implement more than five inspections annually on the territory of another party.[52]

The inspection and verification measures of the CFE treaty are similar to the CSBMs of the CSCE process. But CSBMs would be "politically mandatory, while the measures of the CFE treaty would be legally binding under international treaty law".[53] Moreover the CFE measures were narrowly focussed and were applied only to weapons and forces covered by the Vienna reduction mandate.

The Results and Impact of the Treaty

Article VIII outlines the timetable for reductions. Reductions are to be implemented in three phases. Each country is committed to reduce 25 percent of excess holdings of the five categories of weapons within 16 months of the treaty's coming into force. One year later, 60 percent of the reduction must be undertaken. Reductions are to be completed within 40 months. The treaty also detailed various procedures for the reduction of excess equipment. Reductions must be carried out by each state at a maximum of 20 sites simultaneously with advanced notification. Each country can convert the weapons subject to reduction for the use of non-military purposes. Conversion is allowed for 5.7 percent of the main battle tanks and 15 percent of ACVs. Combat-capable aircraft can be converted to unarmed trainer aircraft up to a maximum of 550.

According to data release at its signature, the Treaty requires 44,829 TLE items to be removed from the ATTU zone.[54] The overwhelming majority of reductions are to be made by the Soviet Union/CIS, and its allies. They must cut 10 times as many weapons as NATO. The former Soviet Union and WTO must reduce about 35,000 piece of equipment in total (Soviet Union: 18,700 and Eastern Europe: 16,600).

On the other hand, NATO as a whole had to reduce its TLE inventory by about 13 percent for a total of about 12,000 items of ground equipment. But European NATO members would have to increase to a total of 14,000 piece of weapons for a given ceiling. No combat aircraft or helicopters will be destroyed. Rather, to reach CFE ceilings NATO could add 1231 combat aircraft and 325 helicopters. Thus NATO had no need to alter its force structure to comply with the CFE ceilings.

Table 4-6   Reduction Requirements of the CFE Treaty

Western Europe / US Pre-CFE	Post-CFE	% Cut	ceilings	Pre-CFE	Eastern Europe /Soviet Union Post-CFE	%Cut
16853	15136	10	Tanks	12497	6850	45
5904	4006	32	20000	20694	13150	36
15803	15794	0	Artillery	13125	6825	48
2601	2492	4	20000	13825	13175	4
22450	14450	36	ACVs	13601	10000	26
5747	5372	7	30000	29348	20000	32
4827	5978	+24	Aircraft	1927	1650	14
704	784	+10	6800	644	5150	20
1406	1492	+6	Helicopter	272	272	0
279	518	+ 86	2000	1330	1500	+13
61339	62740	+2	Total	41422	25825	+38
15235	13172	+14		71645	52975	+26

Source: This table is made based on the data offered in *Arms Control Today*, Vol.21, No.1, January/February 1991, P.29.

The basic objective of NATO since the beginning of conventional arms control negotiating has been to establish a secure conventional balance, to eliminate the WTO capacity for disparities in armament, and to eliminate a surprise attack. The three basic objectives were completely realized in the CFE Treaty. The Treaty will be the basis of certainty and confidence between the major European states in an era of change by fixing strict, precise equipment limits on the size of 'Soviet' forces in Europe and also legally-binding limits on the forces of the 22 participant countries.[55]

The Soviet Union by itself had an advantage over NATO of about 2 to 1. Following implementation of the treaty, however, Russia/CIS will at a disadvantage to the order of 0.7 to 1.[56] Further the withdrawal of its forces and the dissolution of the Warsaw Pact will remove the superiority of conventional forces which threatened NATO during the Cold War. The implementation of the CFE treaty does not impose a requirement for substantial reduction on NATO. However, the removal of the forward threat from the Warsaw Pact forces has led to a reformulation of NATO's force structure, doctrine and strategy based on the security situation of pre-CFE treaty. NATO has been led to prepare a new allied military strategy moving from "forward defence". NATO adopted a doctrine and force posture designed for a mobile defence and moved toward creating forces based as far as possible on multinational units integrated at the lowest practicable level.[57]

The CFE treaty allows the reduction obligation to be adjusted through transfers of TLE among members of the same Group. This idea was proposed by NATO. To avoid destruction of their most modern equipment, NATO defence ministers agreed to replace the ageing weaponry of their allies with modern TLE in excess of ceilings. According of NATO some 25 percent its alliance equipment is at least 30 years old; for the 'Soviets', on the other hand, the bulk of their equipment was less than 10 years old.[58] The equipment was transferred to the Northern and Southern flanks. In December 1990, NATO decided to transfer over 3,000 tanks, 1,000 ACVs and 176 artillery pieces from Germany, Netherlands and the US to Denmark, Greece, Norway, Portugal, Spain and Turkey.[59] This 'cascading' was considered cost-effective. The costs and the amount of work involved in the destruction of battle tanks is considerable. For example, the destruction of one T-55 tank was estimated to take 150 man-hours and costs the German tax payer some DM 30,000.[60]

In this respect the Soviet Union also desired to retain some newer equipment. According to some estimates, total costs to destroy all Soviet weapons included by the CFE limits may be upwards of $5 billion; the cost for destroying one tank, $ 36,000.[61] A great deal of Russian equipment has been removed to the Far East and has been used for upgrading old weapons in the region.

The Lessons from the CFE Talks

The success of the CFE talks must first of all be sought in the strong will to achievement by the participants. The CFE talks were far more complex than were the MBFR talks with an increase of participating countries from 11 to 23, the extension of the reduction zone from Central Europe to the ATTU zone, and reduction subjects from a single subject of manpower to five categories of equipment. Consequently the particular threat perceptions of individual participants became more important than ever before and had to reflect even the security interests of small states to reach an agreement.[62]

Under the difficult conditions of negotiation the US and the Soviet Union did not want to repeat the failure of the MBFR talks. In December 1989 they decided to sign the CFE agreement at the Paris Summit

Meetings.[63] The setting-up of a deadline served to concentrate the efforts of delegations over subjects for negotiation and to encourage concessions. The requirement to meet a deadline is one way to reduce the tendency for the negotiating parties to lapse into fossilized and increasingly irrelevant negotiation positions, as in the case of the MBFR talks.[64] In fact many key issues were settled during the final phase of negotiation because of the awareness of the deadline.

The political will for an agreement can be seen in the participation of France in the talks. There is no doubt that French absence from MBFR was a serious problem, especially since France had stationed about 50,000 troops in West Germany. France was highly vocal about arms control, objecting to the talks between the two blocs outside the MBFR forum. In CFE it to some extent contributed to reducing conflicts in the negotiation process and converting the CFE Treaty from the format of the two blocs into that of a Group of States.

The success of the CFE talks was primarily caused by the surprising change of Soviet security policy. Gorbachev adopted a new doctrinal framework based on the concepts of political security, reasonable sufficiency, defensive doctrine and mutual security.[65]

The previous Soviet political leaders viewed military power as the fundamental basis for maintaining security. Political means were merely an adjunct to military technical means. However, Gorbachev argued that "the maintenance of security is a political task and can be settled by political means".[66] Therefore negotiation and diplomacy were more emphasized than the additional allocation of military resources. Of the new security approaches, undoubtedly, the decisive contribution to the success of the CFE talks was the notion of "reasonable sufficiency." The previous leaders believed that military superiority over an opponent could guarantee victory in war. Therefore security policy moved toward the action-reaction arms race. However, the new thinking on security considered that the existing military capability of the Soviet Union was enough to absorb any attack under the worst imaginable conditions and to rebuff the enemy.[67] The Soviet theory of "defence" had prepared for offensive operations to penetrate the depths of enemy positions. To accomplish this, weapons of high-speed mobility had been developed. However, the change of defence doctrine from offensive to defensive by the pursuit of "sufficiency" needed the reconfiguration of the force structure. Consequently the combination of reasonable sufficiency and defensive doctrine presented an opportunity for significant arms reductions.

One of the reasons why the CFE talks were successful derived from the elimination of technical problems. The exclusion of nuclear weapons served to eliminate one of the obstacles to a treaty. The MBFR talks attempted the trade-off of conventional and nuclear weapons which, though they have a mutually complementary relationship, are structurally very different in characteristics. Because of this, the negotiators had difficulties in formulating appropriate counting rules. The separation of conventional from nuclear weapons was a crucial turning point which encouraged the independent development of theories on conventional arms reduction.

The solution of the data and verification problems decisively contributed to the success of the CFE Treaty. One of the most important reasons for the failure of MBFR was the Soviet reluctance to release data and allow effective verification. The Soviet aggressive image among Western countries was attributable largely to its policy of secrecy. But Gorbachev's acceptance of reliable and effective military information and inspection increased confidence in the Soviet Union and helped to forward negotiations in practical terms. The mutual openness of data is a very important basis for the comparison of military forces and the establishment of counting rules. In January 1989 the Warsaw Pact for the first time published data about detailed military equipment and made a comparison between its own forces and those of NATO. Its data implied different counting rules from the methodologies of NATO.[68] On the basis of released data NATO and WTO were able to agree the specification of counting criteria on the TLEs.

Conclusion

During the Cold War the formula of conventional arms reduction in Europe emerged as an alternative to the arms race. The arms race, required an enormous military capability and associated economic burden. It resulted in the escalation of uncertainty and mistrust. But the introduction of an arms reduction formula employed political means such as negotiation or diplomacy. Unlike the arms race based upon "uncertainty" or "secrecy" the formula emphasized the prevention of war by "communication", "transparency" and "deterrence at low level".

During the Cold War the MBFR and CFE negotiations were a symbol of detente and an important channel of communication for the prevention of war between East and West. The negotiators in the MBFR talks preferred the maintenance of political detente and the military status quo through a symbolic reduction of troops, to a change of military environment through substantial reduction of military forces. They neglected the development of methods and techniques for reductions, simply focussing on the numerical military balance. The focus on force levels introduced a channelling effect to improve the combat strength or the efficiency of existing forces so as to minimize impacts on future reductions. Moreover the MBFR talks deterred unilateral reductions due to the expectation of negotiated reduction. From the start the talks were doomed to failure in gaining any reduction because of the lack of desire to achieve agreement. In the negotiation process the problems of data and verification were critical obstacles to progress in negotiations and became more controversial issues than reduction itself. The success of CBMs limited the value of MBFR as a vehicle of detente. After this the work of reduction was handed over to the CFE talks.

The CFE talks started with a strong political will towards substantial reductions, particularly within the Soviet Union. In contrast to past tradition when leaders sought arms control agreements primarily as a way of codifying the status quo or achieving strategic parity with the opponent, Gorbachev used arms control as a vehicle for change and the establishment of a co-operative relationship with the West through mutual security.[69] Gorbachev's positive attitude toward arms control gave NATO a number of concessions.

The superiority of the Soviet Union in conventional forces was given up through unilateral and asymmetric reduction. The veiled military realm was made transparent through the release of data and allowance for inspection on its territory. The adoption of a defensive doctrine and reasonable sufficiency helped pave the way for the CFE Treaty in more immediate terms. No stable and secure balance of armed forces could be expected without the revolutionary change of military doctrine and strategy. These steps towards the fundamental changes taken by its new political thinking helped to increase confidence in the West towards the Soviet Union through the decrease of the perceived threat that existed after World War II.

The application of the concept of "stability" as a model of arms reduction changed the priority of reductions from manpower to offensive weapons. The reduction of offensive weapons rather than manpower was seen as preventing surprise attacks and strengthening stability. Such a change of reduction concepts led to a substantial reduction in the five categories of the TLEs defined as offensive weapons. The effect of the CFE Treaty will be to limit Russian/CIS weapons to levels of about one-third below than NATO totals. NATO will be the dominant military power in the ATTU after the implementation of the CFE Treaty. By eliminating the shadow of Soviet supremacy in conventional forces and retreating its forces in Europe to its territory, "the CFE Treaty chipped away a final foundation-stone of the Cold War."[70]

In conclusion the MBFR and CFE talks between East and West provide a number of lessons for hostile countries in tense confrontation, resulting from large armed forces. The formulas of arms reduction employed in Europe may be used as conceptual models for regions which still exist in the structure of Cold War confrontation.

NOTES

1. The 13th provision of the "Hamel Report on Future Tasks of the Atlantic Alliance", approved at the NATO Ministerial Meeting, Brussels, 14 December, 1967.
2. See the "NATO Ministerial Communique and Mutual and Balanced Force Reduction Declaration", Rome, 26-27 May , 1970.
3. See the "Warsaw Pact Communique and Memorandum on European Security Conference", Budapest, 21-22, June 1970.
4. Lothar Ruehl, "MBFR: Lessons and Problems", *Adelphi Paper* No. 176, (1982), p. 8.
5. Jeffrey Record, *Force Reductions in Europe: Starting over* (Institute for Foreign Policy Analysis, Inc. 1980), p. 9.
6. Ibid.
7. John G. Keliher, *The Negotiations on Mutual and Balanced Forces Reductions: The Search for Arms Control in Europe* (Pergamon Press, New York, 1980), p. 26.
8. Ibid., p. 28.
9. John G. Keliher, *Eastern Arms Control Proposals for Central Europe* (Ph.D Dissertation, Georgetown University, Xerox University Microfilms, 1977), p. 69.
10. John J. Maresca, *To Helsinki: The Conference on Security and Cooperation in Europe, 1973-1975* (Duke University Press, 1987), p. 11.
11. John Borawski, "Mutual Force Reduction in Europe from a Soviet Perspective, *Orbis*, Vol.22, No.4, (1979), p. 860.
12. Keliher, *Eastern Arms Control*, p. 64.
13. Record, op. cit., p. 38.
14. Record, op. cit., p. 44.
15. Ibid. p. 43.
16. Keliher, *The Negotiations*, p. 67.
17. Coit D. Blacker, "Negotiating Security: The MBFR Experience", *Arms Control*, Vol.7, No.3, (December 1986), p. 222.
18. Record, op. cit,. p. 59.
19. Ruehl, op., cit, p.26.
20. Ibid. p. 22.
21. Keliher suggested that the unilateral withdrawal would be related to the MBFR process, especially to the size and comparison of the phase I Soviet withdrawal. According to his reference the Soviet Union saw unilateral withdrawal as a way of circumventing the data stalemate. Keliher, *the Negotiations*, p. 83. But Henry Kissinger in his book, *White House Years*, suggested that Brezhnev's remark had little to do with the scheduled vote on the Four Power negotiations then underway on Berlin.
22. Richard Burt, "A Glass Half Empty", *Foreign Policy* , (Fall 1979), p. 41.

23. Blacker, op. cit., p.220. quoted in Henry Kissinger, *White House Years* (Boston: Little, Brown and Company, 1979), p. 400.
24. April Carter, *Success and Failure in Arms Control Negotiation* (SIPRI: Oxford University Press, 1989), p. 242.
25. Ruehl, op. cit., p. 2.
26. Robert D. Blackwill, "Conceptual Problems of Conventional Arms Control", *International Security*, (Spring 1988), Vol. 12, No. 4, p. 39.
27. Ibid., p. 42.
28. Ernst F. Jung, "Conventional Arms Control in Europe in Light of MBFR Experience", *Aussen Politik*, Vol. 39, 2/88, pp. 160-161.
29. Jonathan Dean, *Watershed in Europe: Dismantling the East-West Military Confrontation* (Massachusetts: Lexington Books, 1987), p.164.
30. Keliher, op. cit., p.124. For further detailed reference, see Eliot A. Cohen "Toward Better Net Assessment: Rethinking the European Conventional Balance" (*International Security*, Vol. 13, No. 1, (1988) pp. 71-76.
31. Ibid., 128.
32. Klaus Wittmann, "Challenges of Conventional Arms Control", *Adelphi Paper 239*, (Summer, 1989), p. 71.
33. Keliher, op. cit., p. 135.
34. Ibid. p. 130. Under Article XII of ABM Treaty and Article V of the Interim Agreement, both the Soviet Union and the United States agreed to the use of "National Technical Means" with no interference with each other's Satellites and not to use deliberate concealment measures which impede verification by NTMs.
35. Carter, op. cit, p.240.
36. Blackwill, op. cit., p.47.
37. "Appeal by Warsaw Pact Treaty member states to the member states of NATO and to all European countries for the Reduction of Armed Forces and Conventional Armaments in Europe 11 June 1986." Lawrence Freedman (ed), *Europe Transformed: Documents on the end of the Cold War* (London: Tri Service Press, 1990), pp. 214-216.
38. *SIPRI Yearbook 1988* (Oxford University Press, 1988), p.331.
39. *Cutting Conventional Forces* (Massachusetts: Institute for Defence and Disarmament Studies, 1989), p. 22.
40. Ibid., *CSCE: Mandate for negotiation on Conventional Armed Forces in Europe,* pp. 139-140. The objectives which appeared in the Mandate accorded with the principles for the CFE talks that NATO set out in Brussels on 3 March 1988.
41. Ibid., pp. 138-139.
42. Ibid., p.72.
43. Rudiger Hartmann, "The CFE negotiations-A Promising Start", *NATO Review,* Vol.37, No.3. (June 1989), pp. 10-11.
44. John Speight, "CFE 1990: Achievements and Prospects", *Faraday Discussion Paper*, No. 15 (London: the Council for Arms Control, 1990), p.4.
45. Lee Feinstein, "The Case of CFE", *Arms Control Today*, Vol. 21, No. 1, (January/February 1991) (Special Supplement, p.4)
46. John Lunn, "The Conventional Forces in Europe Talks" (House of Commons Library, Feb. 1990), *Background Paper* No. 241, p. 15.
47. US 102D Congress, 1st Session, Senate Committee on Foreign Affairs, *The CFE Treaty* (Washington D.C.: GPO, 1991), p. 9.
48. Jane M. Sharp, *Conventional Arms Control in Europe*, p. 413 (in SIPRI Yearbook 1991).
49. Brigitte Sauerwein, "CFE: the Story so Far", *National Defence Review*, 1/1991, p. 35.

50. Zone I:Federal Republic Germany, Benelux, Poland, Czechoslovakia, Hungry. Zone II: U.K., Northern Ireland, Denmark, France, Italy, and the Baltic, Byelorussian, Carpathian and Kiev MDs, Zone III: Moscow, Volga-Ural MDs. Zone IV: Bulgaria, Greece, Iceland, Norway, Romania, Turkey, the Leningrad, Odessa, Transcaucasus and North Caucasus MDs.
51. Victor-Yves Ghebali, "CFE First Years Status Report", *International Defence Review*, Vol.23, 4/1990, p. 369.
52. *SIPRI Yearbook 1991*, p. 420. This rule was established by WTO states, particularly Hungary. Non-Soviet WTO states insisted on inspecting Soviet sites. NATO members were reluctant to inspect other NATO states.
53. Lunn, op. cit., p. 13.
54. *SIPRI Yearbook 1991*, p. 422.
55. Thomas Graham, Jr, "The CFE Story: Tales from the Negotiating Table", *Arms Control Today*, Vol. 21, No.1, (January/February, 1991), p. 9.
56. US Congress, *The CFE Treaty*, p. 35.
57. William Park, "Political Change and NATO Strategy", in Michael C. Pugh (ed), *European Security towards 2000* (Manchester: Manchester University Press, 1992), p. 43.
58. David T. Lightburn, "Enhancing Security-Arms Transfers under CFE Ceilings", *NATO's Sixteen Nations*, (May/June, 1991,) p. 61.
59. *SIPRI Yearbook 1991*, p. 426.
60. Sauerwein, "CFE:the Story so Far", p. 37.
61. Feinstein,"The Case for CFE, (CFE supplement)", p. 4.
62. For references of the matrix explaining the complexity of the CFE talks, see Dai, Dunay, "Conventional Arms Reduction in Europe: What is the Matter?", in Spanger, Hans-Joachim and Hyde-Price, Adrian G.V.(eds) *European Security in the 1990s* (Frankfurt and London: Peace Research Institute and RIIA, PRIF Report No.11-12 1990), p. 75.
63. NATO allies had an initiative to accelerate the schedule. On 13 July, the last day of the second round of the CFE talks, they submitted proposals including the talks timetable for an agreement within 6-12 months and reductions to be carried out from 1992 or 1993.
64. Carter, op. cit., p. 254.
65. Stephen M. Meyer, "The Sources and Prospects of Gorbachev's New Political Thinking on Security", *International Security*, Vol 13, No.2, (Fall, 1988), pp. 124-163.
66. Dunay, op. cit. p. 55.
67. Meyer, op. cit. p. 145.
68. Manfred R. Hamm and Hartmut Pohlman, "Military Strategy and Doctrine: Why they matter to Conventional Arms Control", *The Washington Quarterly*, Vol.13, No.1, (Winter 1990), p.189.
69. Jane M. O. Sharp, "Disarmament and Arms Control: A New Beginning", Ken Booth (ed), *New Thinking About Strategy and International Security* (London: Harper Collins Academic, 1991), p. 122.
70. Congress, *The CFE Treaty*, p. 3.

5. The FRG's Arms Control Policies as a Divided State

Factors Influencing Arms Control Policy Making

West German arms control policy was rooted in its geostrategic environment. The front-line between NATO and WTO was formed along the division line of Germany. The two alliances forces were concentrated on German territory. The exposure on the front-line position meant that in case of war the whole national territory would become the primary theatre of military operations of the two blocs and would be devastated beyond recognition. The country's relatively small geographic area, high population density and extensive industrialization made it particularly vulnerable to war damage.[1] The clearly catastrophic consequences of a conventional war meant that, in the eyes of the West Germans, the vulnerability could not be covered by any perfect defence planning within the NATO alliance. Thus the FRG's special geostrategic situation directly on the border line between the West and the East helped the FRG to move towards arms control.

The FRG's defence obligations under its NATO commitments also influenced its attitude towards arms control. The size of the armed forces assigned to FRG for NATO defence took precedence over a discussion of its national defence policy considerations. The FRG had a substantial share of NATO conventional forces in Central and Northern Europe. In this region its shares were; 50 percent of NATO's ground forces, over 60 percent of its main battle tanks, 50 percent ground-base air defence, 30 percent of combat aircraft, 30 percent of western naval forces and 70 percent of naval units and all NATO's naval-air combat forces in the Baltic Sea. In the initial phase of a WTO attack its active duty force would be expanded to 1,340,000 and have to defend about 65 percent of the entire front between the Baltic Sea and the border between Germany and Austria.[2] Thus the defence of West Europe was inconceivable without the crucial contribution of Germany to NATO.

The FRG was seen as a "NATO Resource Pool"; providing replacements for major Western conventional retrenchment, a *redistribution* of alliance burdens for compensation of allied countries' force reduction, *economical offset* in return for alliance forces, and an *alliance crisis reserve*.[3] It was to be the source of men, money and material needed for the defence of Europe as a precondition for NATO participation. The growth and capability of the West German economy was such that it could afford to provide additional support, first for closing the military gap vis-a-vis a superior WTO and then in sharing the costs for maintenance of allied forces. The FRG's share of the funding for the NATO infrastructure programme was far ahead of that of all the other alliance states. Its cost share for 1985 to 1990 amounted to 26.8 percent and thus followed closely behind that of the United States.[4] These heavy defence burdens led the FRG to have an active attitude towards arms control in the desire for defence burden relief.

The FRG also existed as an anchor of the East-West detente. It made efforts to reduce the tense confrontation resulting from Germany's division and the dense concentration of armed forces along the front-line while maintaining a steady military contribution to Western defence. The East-West detente politics in the late 1960s-early 1970s heightened West Germany's role between the two alliances. The West German normalization with the Soviet Union and the Eastern countries was a momentum for opening the CSCE and MBFR. Throughout the 1970s and the 1980s, the FRG played a major role in the process of conventional arms talks dealing with stability and the reduction of armed forces in Central Europe.

The security policy of the Federal Republic of Germany was based on the combination of deterrence-defence and detente-arms control. The dual security policy was well demonstrated in the 1985 Defence White Paper; "dialogue and cooperation in conjunction with arms control and disarmament on the basis of an assured deterrent and defence capability remain integral parts of our security policy within the alliance".[5] West German governments judged that there was no acceptable alternative to strong defence at the East-West dividing line, because the West had insufficient depth of territory to make any other strategy credible. For this reason the doctrine of forward defence, which rejected a withdrawal and a sacrifice of any German territory for any reason, was seen as a most effective strategy. With the Flexible Response strategy this doctrine needed a credible defence capability as a pillar of Western security and was a high priority in defence policy. Given its exposed position and dense population, any war on German soil would be catastrophic. Conventional deterrence, backed up with nuclear deterrence, was therefore the highest priority.

However, there existed the fear that too much conventional strength might not only weaken the nuclear deterrent, which was seen as the best guarantee for prevention of war, but also exceed a "potential political ceiling" which could reduce the caution of neighbours caused by the German historical legacy.[6] The FRG also feared that the build-up of conventional forces would lead to force reductions by other alliance countries. The maintenance of military forces at viable levels was believed to increase the linkage between nuclear and conventional capabilities. Thus, according to Defence Minister Georg Leber's 1975 response to the US demand that West Germany expand the Bundeswehr to 600,000 men:

> ... if the Germans were to increase their army while the others were to reduce theirs, inner-European problems would arise with certainty, because of the excessive weight that such a German army would then have in the circle of the West European military powers. And I must preserve Europe from that.[7]

There was a broader consensus that war prevention should be built on a much broader set of strategies than mere military deterrence. In fact there was no concrete evidence that the German government closely linked arms control options with force planning or the impact of sophisticated defence technology. But it is certain that arms control has been conducted as an essential option for its security.

West Germany strongly favoured the detente-arms control formula. Arms control was regarded as more important than reducing the East's military edge through increased military spending. The Bonn government wanted to see a military balance achieved through arms control rathe. than by any arms build-up.[8] In a 1983 survey in comparison with the other countries, even the German security elite were much less convinced that military strength was important to national security (the FRG: 61%, US: 89 percent, UK: 74%, France: 90%, Netherlands: 78%).[9] The FRG preferred to overcome the military confrontation of the two blocs in Europe through political means or negotiated arms control.

Conventional arms control talks in Europe were fundamentally concerned with the "German Question". The Western allies frequently linked the unification of Germany with arms control before the beginning of the arms control talks in the 1970s. They argued that, "without German unity any system of European security would be an illusion".[10] From their point of view the reunification of Germany would settle some of Europe's past problems such as the status of Berlin. In this way it could lead to a reduction of tension.

The divided status of the German state imposed a big constraint to the German approaches towards arms control talks. In fact, for much of the post-war period, the Federal Republic's arms control policy was a mere function of various reunificaiton strategies. Arms control agreements presupposed a prior solution of the problem of German reunification.[11] This position was well expressed in the famous peace note of 1966:

All efforts to achieve security, disarmament and arms control will in the end be successful and durable only if the causes of tensions in the world are gradually removed. In Europe, this means above all solving the German question in a must manner by granting the whole German people the right to freely determine their own form of government and their destiny.[12]

Thus arms control talks were a prerequisite for overcoming the division of Germany. The FRG did not have any arms control policy until the late 1960s. However, prior to the unification of Germany, the amelioration of political tensions and the human costs that arose from that division remained a high priority. After Brandt became Chancellor, the Federal Republic redefined the relationship between security and the national question. Arms control was linked to the Ostpolitik policy. His successor Helmut Schmidt denied the formulas of 'peace and reunification', 'reconciliation and reunification', or 'arms control and reunification', announcing an end to the policy of ostracizing the GDR.[13] There was less insistence on linking arms control and disarmament with progress on the German question. The only way to overcome the German problem was to accept the results of World War II; the realities of division and the post-World War II borders. This option was to mean that the German question could not be solved without the coexistence of the two German states. Active coexistence meant trying to improve the relationship between them and finding common responsibilities that provided new and more promising possibilities for reconciling peace and security with the national question.

There was no evidence that either West Germany or other NATO countries linked arms control talks with the unification of Germany after the beginning of the talks in the early 1970s. After the Reykjavik summit in October 1989, a member of the West German parliament pleaded in public for the linking of impending arms reductions with efforts to promote German unification.[14] This interconnection was also suggested in a statement of 1987 by Richard Burt, US ambassador to Bonn; disarmament is the first step on the road that one day should lead to the overcoming of the division of Europe and the division of Germany.[15] This proposition, a reminder of the notions that were prevalent in the 1950s-1960s, was officially disavowed by Chancellor Helmut Kohl.

As a result, German unification was achieved prior to the implementation of the CFE Treaty without a linkage of arms reduction and unification. Hence the European arms talks did not deal with the problem of German unification. Nevertheless, the sequence of events does suggest that a process of rapprochement through the arms talks and the implementation of arms control helped generate German social momentum for a common future and paved the way for the unification.

In the 1950s and 1960s the Federal Republic's reluctance to pursue arms control and dialogue with the GDR was a big obstacle to the establishment of arms control institutions. No arms control institutions in the government organization were established except for the Commissioner of the Federal Government for Arms Control and a small desk with four officials in the Foreign Ministry. Their function was only to respond to external arms control initiatives.[16] The FRG's hostage role for NATO did not make it feel the need of any independent arms control policy at the initial stage of the arms control talks. Moreover the talks of a package by the two blocs did not allow the FRG to have an individual voice.

However, the revival of German national identity and the recognition of special German vulnerability to a WTO surprise attack required the establishment of arms control institutions to support the consistency of the FRG arms control policy and the championship of its interests in the multilateral talks. Thus, Bonn made the institutional adaptations to new arms control requirements. As a result, these helped the German Government to play a more active role in international arms control negotiations and enabled its arms control policy to be institutionally upgraded. There were further organizations of arms control institutions in the 1970s and 1980s. The multilateral negotiations and various measures of arms control needed a further upgrading of decision making structures and arms control policy. These institutional adaptations contributed "to facilitate a closer connection between the arms control negotiations and potential domestic consequences of arms reductions, to improve departmental coordination, and to institutionalize an independent voice of arms control and disarmament within the Federal government".[17]

The primary source of all arms control policies came from the Foreign Ministry. The Foreign Ministry initiated preparatory work on arms control and reserved the right to make final policy decisions. Within the Ministry, the "Commissioner on Arms Control and Disarmament" played a central role, linking the executive political leadership with working level operations. The Commissioners mission was deeply concerned with all issues relating to arms control, covering not only international cooperation but the domestic decision making process and public education.[18]

The Ministry of Defence (MOD) also had an important role in the decision making process. The MOD could have greater influence because the arms control problems had a clear application to defence and military affairs. In fact, in the case of CSCE and MBFR, the most concrete proposals on military security came from the MOD. However, it played only a minor role in the arms control decision-making process. The FRG's positions were determined more on the basis of political considerations than military ones. Therefore, the role of the MOD was less crucial in the final internal decision making process.

The Chancellor's Office had the third executive role in shaping arms control policy. Its major role was to approve the position papers of the Foreign Ministry and the MOD and to adjust them to the government's general policy guidelines. As a consequence of the principle of the autonomy of a respective ministry, its role in the decision-making process generally was quite limited. Its influence was exercised only as a coordinator solving some conflicts between ministries. The lack of an independent bureaucratic infrastructure prevented the Cabinet from acting as a collective decision-making body.[19]

German arms control policy making, as a general attribute of any bureaucratic politics of decision-making, depended to a large degree on the personalities, capabilities, and interests of policy makers. For example, Foreign Minister Hans-Dietrich Genscher played a dominant role, displaying a long term personal and professional commitment in the German arms control policy making process. However, his direct involvement was limited to determining the general orientation of policy. In fact, the multilateral conventional arms control negotiations required complex inter-ministerial mechanisms for close consultation and coordination between the MOD, the Foreign Ministry, and these executive organs. During the negotiation of the CSCE, MBFR and CFE, the Foreign Ministry and the MOD shared responsibilities for the formulation of specific West German position.

In a real sense, the German Arms Control decision-making was more affected by external rather than by domestic factors. Decisions were made through a complex network of consultative decision making processes of the FRG. NATO and the US perspective was injected into the internal decision-making processes of the FRG.[20] NATO's various consultative channels at the working or ministerial level more often functioned "as information clearinghouses than as true collective decision making bodies".[21] Thus, the FRG's independent arms control position was to a great extent constrained by the US input and NATO policy. What is more important was that the Foreign Ministry had initiatives in the process of arms control decisionmaking process. German arms control policy had the character of a political approach rather than a military approach. Further it was seen through the institutionalization of arms control structures that beginning arms control talks requires a number of arms control structures and effective cooperation between arms control and defence policy in the government organization.

Policy-Making for Arms Control as a Pillar of NATO

Up to the 1960s neither arms control and disarmament policy nor scholarly discussions on these issues existed in West Germany. Adenauer and his successors believed that a policy of "strength" was an indispensable precondition for agreements with the Soviet Union. Since the main foreign policy goal of his cabinet was to regain sovereignty and solve the security dilemma of the West German state, disarmament and arms control matters ranked low as a priority.

As earlier mentioned, arms control policy was not formulated by a close linkage of disarmament matters with German reunification. West German policy assumed the prior dissolution of the GDR and the reunification of Germany as a precondition for East-West arms control agreements. Bonn did not accept the existence of East Germany or the overall division of Europe. German arms control participation consequently meant the recognition of the entity of the GDR and the territorial and political status quo in Europe.[22] It believed that, by solidifying Western unity and military power, reunification was more likely.

Adenauer's perspective on German unification was based on two central assumptions that "(1) Washington and Moscow held the key to the German question and (2) with the passage of time the balance of power between the cold war blocs would shift in favour of the West, thus allowing negotiations on the basis of strength which would induce the Soviet Union to settle the German question on Western terms".[23] He thought that regional arms control negotiation with the Soviet Union would create the possibility of German separation from the NATO alliance and also a temptation for Western allies to bargain with the East at the cost of German interests. He was always beset with a deep-rooted mistrust of the Western powers' detente policy due to memories of the four powers' bargaining at Germany's expense during and after World War II: the Yalta and Potsdam complex. His call for multilateralization of the detente policies mainly served the purpose of providing himself with a kind of veto position.[24] Adenauer's brake upon detente was based on a belief that only NATO superiority of strength would defeat the Soviet Union and the Soviet Union would be in the long run not be able to stand an armaments race with West because of the pressure on its resources at home. Then the time would be right to settle, through general disarmament, territorial questions as well.[25]

The United States was at first in agreement with Adenauer's fundamental policy and supported his approach to arms control. But Kennedy adopted a flexible response strategy and put an emphasis on limited cooperation with the Soviet Union. Adenauer's policy-resistance towards accepting the status quo in arms control gradually began to lose support in the West. Washington dropped the close linkage between disarmament efforts and the solution of the German question. After the resignation of Adenauer, his successor moved closer to the defence policy views of the Kennedy and Johnson administrations. Furthermore, with the formation of the grand coalition between CDU/CSU and SPD in 1966, the FRG began to seek for alternative foreign policy conceptions. First of all, the NATO "Hamel Report", advocating the parallel pursuit of military effort and political effort made the FRG adopt an arms control and disarmament policy. Arms control and disarmament, together with deterrence and detente, become an important element in the security policy of West Germany.

The FRG began to have an active arms control policy with the "Ostpolitik" of Chancellor Brandt after 1969. The Ostpolitik policy resulted in the implementation of various bilateral and multilateral treaties. These treaties removed major stumbling blocs for detente by recognizing the territorial status-quo in Europe. Ostpolitik was a turning point of German security policy. The result was not to lessen the FRG's strategic dependence on the United States or its allegiance to NATO, but to remove any rationally conceivable Soviet incentives to apply military pressures to NATO's central area.[26] As a result, Ostpolitik tackled the German security problems at their political roots and became a complementary political part of Germany's security policy. The recognition of political and territorial realities developed a more constructive attitude toward arms control, and fully attuned West German foreign policy to the dynamics of East-West detente.

Brandt was convinced that the German question would be solved only through the comprehensive detente-dialogue with the Soviet Union. Therefore, unlike Adenauer, he no longer considered steps towards the unification of Germany as a precondition for striving towards any settlement on a European scale, but saw a unified Germany rather as something to be achieved as the result of a process of detente between East and West.[27] Consequently, the FRG itself cleared away the preconditions for the CSCE and MBFR negotiations and began to participate actively in the two negotiations and the Committee on Disarmament in Geneva.

West German security policy can be described as comprising three overlapping spheres: military policy, the management of East-West relations and Ostpolitik. Among these, despite slight differences in priorities, there was a consensus on Ostpolitik and conventional arms control after the beginning of the arms control talks.[28] The CDU-CSU government of Helmut Kohl continued the Ostpolitik of the Schmidt government with little change even during the height of the INF controversy. Arms control was also pursued as an important component of West German security policy and as a means of the management of East-West relations.

Threat Perceptions From WTO

In the 1950s and 1960s, West German strategists had very gloomy views with respect to the military capabilities and intentions of the Soviet Union and later the Warsaw Pact. They were apprehensive about what the Korean war might mean for their security. Adenauer was firmly convinced that Stalin was planning the same procedure for West Germany as had been used in Korea, regarding the Korean 38th parallel as the Elbe. At the time West Germany took the assumption of 5 points of danger into consideration: "(1) Full scale Warsaw pact invasion (2) A Soviet attack limited to West German territory (3) An accidental conflict that escalated from border incidents, unrest in East Germany or a crisis over Berlin (4) A 'proxy' attack by East German forces (5) Soviet political pressures against West Germany".[29] Fearing American force reductions, the FRG emphasized the possibility of an all-out Soviet attack in the forefront of NATO planning. Unlike the German threat perception, the United States tended to underestimate the Warsaw Pact conventional capabilities.

However, entering into the 1970s the FRG increasingly scaled down the likelyhood of a massive Warsaw Pact attack. With this trend, it allocated to national defence-only 3.5 percent of gross domestic product from 1970-1974, a far lower level than the 6.5 percent of the US and 5.1 percent of the UK.[30] In fact, few German officials viewed the Soviet military threat in the stark terms used by NATO's military authorities or Washington's policy-makers. While most German leaders acknowledged the need for military plan to consider a "worst case" scenario, the government was not persuaded to adopt national military measures on the basis of NATO's assessment of Soviet capabilities.[31]

Instead of a military threat, a political threat was generally perceived. The FRG's 1970 defence "White Paper" described the real danger as not military aggression, but political pressure or threat. The FRG remained concerned that the Soviet Union might translate military preponderance on the Continent into progressive political pressure. This political pressure might weaken the solidarity of the alliance and lead gradually to hegemony over all Europe. Therefore, the FRG emphasised the threat of Finlandization of its country far more than the danger of a massive Soviet military sweep.[32]

In the 1980s the Federal government perceived a military threat, particularly from the surprise attack capabilities seen in the offensive military build-up of WTO. But political rather than military means were emphasized as a way of overcoming the military threat and gap. Accordingly, responding correctly to the defence requirements of the allied countries, Bonn's security policy focussed upon the neutralization of Soviet political pressure through political means.

Political Remedy of Military Balance

The concept of military balance in the conventional arms control talks in Europe was artificially developed by the West German point of view. NATO authorities and some allied officials argued that Germany must increase its conventional forces to help to reduce the growing NATO-Warsaw Pact military imbalance. However, Bonn held the belief that German defence forces had fully played the role assigned to them by NATO. The German position was made explicit in the 1973 statement of Defence Minister Leber's thesis of sufficiency:

> The defence capability of the alliance rests on the principle of sufficiency of forces. The NATO partners therefore do not need to aspire to a conventional superiority. In as much as NATO is purely a defensive alliance, an equivalence of 'man for man' is not required. So long as NATO ... has command of sufficient forces for deterrence and defence, the situation is not dangerous.[33]

His words meant that, though inferior in each category of forces, NATO had already achieved an overall equilibrium because of its deterrence and defence capabilities. Rather, most Germans thought that too many arms were arrayed on the two sides of the inner-German border. This belief led to a widespread desire to find an East-West balance at lower, not higher, levels of armaments to match the conventional capabilities of WTO.

West German analysts developed the concept of a military equilibrium between the two opposing alliances. The term equilibrium of forces used by them did not mean "equality" at one point of time and in one kind or level of forces and armament. It included a dynamic spectrum of forces and weapons in which particular items would be asymmetrical and unequal.[34] The West Germans believed that the principal threat to them arose from the political consequences of a stark military imbalance on the Continent in favour of the Soviet Union. This perception was very different from that of US strategic analysts. The American view was that Soviet military superiority could credibly be prevented from being translated into aggression or political advantage. The United States called for quantitative and qualitative increases in NATO forces to counter the Soviet threat. However, Germany put more weight on the political and psychological impacts of military imbalance rather than the military option.

The outbreak of a conflict is finally determined by the political objectives, not by the supposed possession of military capabilities for action. Accordingly the West Germans supported the concept that the military imbalance between NATO and the Warsaw Pact could be primarily overcome through political efforts altering the political motivation and interests of the other side, rather than through the equilibrium of armed forces needing much time and resources. In the belief in such an approach, many West German politicians and thinkers on security affairs encouraged a military balance through arms control. Thus the concept of military balance was in harmony with West German and NATO's perceptions of the role of military power and its political cutting edge.[35]

The Positions on the CSCE and CBMs

The basic objective of German security policy was to secure peace by means of nuclear deterrence and conventional defence. Moreover, the security guarantee based on such a strategy was increasingly becoming problematic because it assumed sharp military confrontation and high cost. The East-West confrontation in the territory did not accord with its security interests as a divided state. As an alternative to military security guarantees, West Germany began to pursue a political security policy which lessened the risk of war and the increased military cost after the adoption of the "Hamel Formula". The fact that Germany was divided perhaps created a perception of special security needs. Close relations with the West were seen as indispensable to West German security; at the same time, the FRG had special interests in maintaining political compromise and political stability through good relations with East. The arms control dialogue between the two blocs was seen as the means for East-West detente and improved FRG-GDR relations.

Two basic approaches to arms control may be identified in West German political military thought: as a means of preventing war and stabilizing the mutual deterrence system and an intermediate step towards a strategy of gradual disarmament.[37] In the traditional philosophy of disarmament, "equilibrium" was a precondition for starting negotiations for arms control. However, in the new approach, it became the aim of the arms control process. Arms control was a military effort for restoring the capability for deterrence and defence. The official West German aim was first "to achieve equilibrium by increasing armaments with a view to limiting them afterwards".[38] However the FRG did not undertake extraordinary measures to achieve the 3 percent target for real annual growth in defence expenditures agreed by Ministers in 1978.[39]

The FRG emphasized the political and psychological aspect as having significance equal to strictly military consideration, seeing arms control as an integral element of detente. For example, Paul E. Zinner pointed out that

> In the view of the German government, the confidence-building potential of the arms control process should be better utilized to help build a security partnership between East-West. Arms control should not be regarded as an end itself but as a means to an end, and the process should be institutionalized as much as possible.[40]

The FRG, seeking the solution of the German question through multilateral political negotiation and detente between East and West, assigned great importance to European security conferences, such as the CSCE process and the Stockholm Conference. The Christian Democratic Union during the administrations of Adenauer and his successors had very negative attitudes towards Eastern Europe's proposals for a European security conference. The party regarded such a conference as a threat to the cohesion of the Western alliance and as an attempt to solidify the status-quo in Europe. The deep-seated resistance to the conference project did not change until the Helmut Schmidt government. The CDU/CSU parliamentary faction voted for a resolution asking the Schmidt government not to sign the Helsinki Final Act of 1975 of CSCE.[41] They wanted to achieve progress on the German question and structural changes in the Eastern bloc without giving concessions to the East. In this the party reflected the US reservations towards the CSCE, fearing Soviet political influence in Europe.

The West German progress on security was undoubtedly shaped by the FDP foreign minister Genscher's own perspectives on the requisites of

German foreign policy. From 1974 till 1992 Genscher provided a necessary check on the excess of both the SPD left wing and CDU right wing as a "coalition maker" and "safety valve".[42] Genscher was an especially strong advocate of a multilateral effort at reducing East-West tensions, such as the CSCE and CDE. The multilateral cooperation, in Genscher's scheme was essential because security could no longer be guaranteed unilaterally, but only through cooperation. His view often expressed the relationship with the East as a "survival partnership" or "cooperative security structure". The multilateral security conference was viewed as a means by which the smaller and medium-sized European states might also bring influence to bear, bolstering European interests against the great powers' predominance".[43]

Confidence-building measures in the CSCE became a mainstay of West German security policy. In the West German view, the unique capability of CBMs to enhance stability, specifically in areas of tension were the most suitable security measures in the Central European region. This derived from a view that CBMs can easily result in political detente-namely mediation measures connecting political with military detente. CBMs were also attractive in that they addressed common interests in all European countries without the serious risk resulting from a direct military reduction or radical changes of current military doctrine.

CBMs were proposed by West German analysts prior to the CSCE in parallel with efforts for solving the German question. In 1962 Helmut Schmidt suggested a two phased implementation of CBMs as a means of extensive disengagement for Central Europe: the first phase was the establishment of fixed armed and mobile ground and aerial inspection systems; the second phase was the establishment of two early warning lines along the Rhine River in the west and the Bug River in the East.[44] At the time the CBM proposals were concerned with reduction of tension along the division line of Germany. The other proposal was made in 1966 by the West German Chancellor Ludwig Erhard. His suggestion in a special "Peace Note" was to exchange observers of military manoeuvres with the armed forces of the Soviet Union, Poland, USSR, Hungary, Romania and Bulgaria in order to dispel the distrust relating to alleged German aggressive intentions.[45] It is a significant point that this idea was first focussed to explicitly advertise West Germany's own non-aggressive intentions rather than to find out the enemy's aggressive ones as a means of relaxation of tension.

The 1968 Warsaw Pact surprise invasion of Czechoslovakia resulted in a great shock to the German moderate CBM idea. Up to that time the FRG had kept up with the US concept of political warning-that any Warsaw Pact large-scale aggression would entail political and military changes in Eastern Europe and give sufficient warning time. After the event, West Germany was the first to discount this concept. As well as the warning indicator, the correct interpretation of signals was very important to prevent an accidental war resulting from the dense military concentration in its terrain. CBMs were therefore focussed on the warning of surprise attack.

At the CSCE, the FRG played a leading role in including the CBMs in the Final Act and even at the Vienna MBFR talks likewise stressed their importance.[46] The Federal Government consistently stressed the usefulness of CBMs as agreed upon in the Helsinki Final Act. It attempted to promote its policy as part of a comprehensive East-West dialogue based on a 'realistic' notion of detente. The security policy makers recognized that "the Stockholm CBMs contribute to achieving several of the main goals of West German security policy, viz., to render the behaviour of states in Europe more calculable in general, to reduce the risk of exposure to surprise attack and 'to coercive diplomacy' and to improve the conditions for making progress in arms control".[47] The FRG's policy makers had very positive assessments of the 1986 Stockholm Accord, linking the CSBM with conventional arms control. Foreign Minister Genscher assessed the CSBM as follows:

> The outcome of Stockholm represents an important stage. It is now imperative to make progress in other arms control fora and to exploit every opportunity for achieving substantive results. ... Stockholm proves that the time has become ripe for cooperative solutions to arms control issues.[48]

The FRG also attempted to develop CBMs at the global security level. The FRG submitted a working paper to the First UN General Assembly Special Session on Disarmament in 1978 proposing:

- Information on defence budgets as a precondition to reduction.
- Information on troop strength and a description of composition.
- Prior announcement of any changes in these structures.
- Exchange of military personnel and visits of military delegations.
- Prior announcement of military manoeuvres and of smaller exercises.
- Invitation of observers to manoeuvres.
- Prior announcement of military movements.
- Establishment of observation posts and of electronic monitoring posts in crisis areas and in demilitarized zones.[49]

During the Special Session of the UN, Chancellor Helmut Schmidt gave an address arguing that confidence building measures could "serve in all parts of the world to improve the political preconditions for disarmament and arms control". The FRG emphasized that suitable confidence-building measures must take regional circumstances into account, while regional experiences could make an important base for a global convention on CBMs. However, the government considered it essential that the specificity of CBMs as conceptualized in Central Europe be preserved in order to maintain the unique quality of CBMs as an identical regulator of state behaviour.[50]

The Position on Conventional Arms Reduction Talks

The FRG has been a persistent supporter of negotiated troop reduction in Europe. As early as 1959, Helmut Schmidt outlined a mutual and balanced force reduction project which maintained a residual ceiling of 300,000 troops for the West and 400,000 troops for the East.[51] In 1967, the CDU Defence Minister, Schroeder also elaborated a plan calling for a reduction of 60,000 in the ground forces to 276,000 troops.[52] From 1969 onwards, the SPD Brandt Government hoped to achieve a considerable mutual and balanced reduction in forces on the European Continent as part of a process of detente. The German enthusiasm towards such troop reductions gave the MBFR negotiation a great boost. The German preference for force reduction was caused by three factors; (1) the shortage of manpower, (2) the caution on US forces' withdrawal and (3) the complement of Ostpolitik and detente.

In order to maintain the 495,000 strong FRG army in peace time, 250,000 fit recruits were annually needed. The assumption was made at the beginning of the 1970s that by 1988 there would be a shortfall of 25,000, increasing to 100,000 by 1994.[53] In fact, the West German population has not only been ageing but, since 1974, has declined by nearly 500,000.[54] Therefore, the German eagerness for the force reduction was due to the need of some solution to the continuing manpower problem of the German armed forces.

The other reason resulted from the fear of American force withdrawals from Europe. The US military force level in the whole of Europe had dropped from 434,000 men in 1962 to around 300,000. In 1973, when MBFR began, there were some 193,000 U.S soldiers in the ground forces in Central Europe.[55] The German government thought that more American reductions would be inevitable in the long run and the FRG and the alliance would be obliged to accept a marginally lowered US military presence in

Europe. Therefore it needed a new set of foreign policy initiatives against the US unilateral reduction. The Germans used the negotiated reductions as a bargaining chip vis-a-vis the Soviet Union. The negotiated reduction was to help avoid or slow down American troop reductions in Europe. Consequently this proposal contributed to the creation of a framework which would help the US administration to reject the Mansfield Amendment.

Another reason was used as a means of drawing the Soviet Union into detente. The German military build-up not only might risk a further deepening of the country's division, but also might increase its vulnerability to Soviet counter pressures. The negotiated reduction of Soviet forces was not only to reduce the Soviet threat, but to guarantee the continuation of detente between the superpowers. Further, it was also believed that the negotiations with the Soviet Union would result in the improvement of detente with the GDR and the other Eastern countries.

In the MBFR talks, the FRG, though not enthusiastic as in the CBMs talks, had more active initiatives than the other NATO countries. It often suggested to the Soviet Union a number of concessions for ending the deadlock of the MBFR talks. The deadlock of the MBFR talks was over the exchange of the 68,000 soldiers and 17,000 tank reductions of the Soviet Union for the NATO Option III. The Federal Chancellor Schmidt attempted to resolve the deadlock in the talks by suggesting the Soviet Union withdraw only 1500 tanks. The proposal was to exclude the front-line Group with the most sophisticated Soviet weapons in the GDR.[56]

In 1979 Helmut Schmidt again offered a new proposal to NATO intended to bring an interim result to MBFR from which the negotiations could proceed further to a second-phase agreement. This proposal was almost identical to the manpower elements of the 1978 Eastern Stage I proposal as the modification of its previous phase I proposal. This was to change the long-held NATO position that greater asymmetrical Eastern reductions must be taken.[57]

Such German efforts did not break the deadlock because of the imposition of national ceilings on German forces by the Soviet Union. The Soviet position in the talks reflected a long-standing desire to achieve a contracted ceiling on the peace time size of the Bundeswehr. The Soviet objective was not to allow the FRG to increase above its existing manpower level in the event of additional American withdrawals.[58] The demand for the establishment of national subceilings as a device to block possible future expansion of the Bundeswehr remained a prominent feature of the Soviet Union's bargaining position in Vienna. The Soviet Union's principal intention was demonstrated in its proposals during the early MBFR negotiations. The force reduction ratio of most concern to the Soviet Union was the Soviet Union/FRG ratio rather than the Soviet Union/US ratio. In the Soviet Union's view, the principal counterpart to the Soviet forces stationed in Central Europe was the Bundeswehr, not the United States Army.[59] For example, the Eastern offers of 1973 and 1976 proposed an asymmetrical reduction for the Soviet Union and the United States. However, the force reduction ratio of the Soviet Union and the FRG was nearly symmetrical as shown below.

Table 5-1   Eastern Reduction Proposals of 1973 and 1976

	US	FRG	USSR
1973	44,200	73,700	72,250
1976	35,000	69,000	63,750

Source: John G. Keliher, *The Negotiations on Mutual and Balanced Force Reductions: the search for arms control in Central Europe* (Pergamon Press, 1980), P. 78.

The Germans generally recognized that central Soviet purposes in MBFR were" (1) to constrain West German military capabilities, (2) more specifically to exact from the FRG payment in Bundeswehr capabilities for any Soviet force withdrawals, and (3) more generally to hamstring the NATO defensive options in Central Europe".[60] The Germans were very stubborn about the demands of the Soviet Union. They argued that the principle of a national ceiling should not be compromised by NATO in any reduction scheme put forward in Vienna. Accepting a national ceiling on the Bundeswehr was considered by the Germans to be another impingement on national sovereignty and a surrender to one of the main objectives of the Soviet Union in the MBFR negotiations. Paradoxically Helmut Schmidt proposed that no direct participating state should maintain more than 50 percent of the residual 700,000 troops on each side. His objective was to reduce the Soviet forces comprising 55 percent of the WTO forces in the reduction area, while allowing a 5 percent increase in the Bundeswehr which held some 45 percent of the NATO total.[61] In relation to the national sub-ceilings, they repeatedly assured the Soviet Union that Bonn had no intention of expanding the Bundeswehr after a force reduction agreement, but failed to convince them.

The Germans expected that an MBFR agreement might provide a frame around which political cooperation would grow and further that it might reduce the military asymmetries. However, the main stream of West German military thought was highly sceptical of the ideas about the effects of MBFR. In fact, the original motive of MBFR negotiations followed from a foreign policy design and not a military consideration, focussing on the political effects of nominal troop reductions by both alliances. However, many German military analysts pointed out that an MBFR agreement had many possible dangers and disadvantages. While accepting the effort to establish a military equilibrium on a lower level through the MBFR, they criticised it as endangering NATO doctrine and military posture. Their main arguments were;

- Geostrategic advantage might redeploy the Warsaw Pact force to the reduction area more rapidly than NATO.
- Reductions of conventional forces would endanger the forward strategy and might compel NATO to make earlier use of nuclear weapons.
- Some arms control measures might change the character of the Bundeswehr as a modern armoured and mobile army.
- Arms control might lead to more imbalances of the overall military field.
- The advocacy of arms control would weaken the Bundeswehr's perception of a military threat.[62]

The German military elite's more reluctant attitude derived from the narrowness of the MBFR area as a special disarmament zone. The idea to expand the area of MBFR for the application of CBMs was a basic German arms control concept. This wish was well shown in the West German press:

> The Federal Government want to extend the geographical framework of the confidence-building measures as broadly as possible beyond the MBFR area. Troop reduction in the MBFR alone would not be worth very much if the Soviet Union accumulated just that much more offensive potential behind its border. The Federal Government wants to prevent a marked internationally controlled arms-control zone from emerging in Central Europe.[63]

In conclusion, the FRG originally had a positive attitude towards the MBFR talks, but it became far less active as divisions of opinion grew within its own government on the subject matter of the talks. Its concern moved towards the creation of a new, broader arms control forum.

The FRG perceived arms control as having a political character rather than a military one. However, with the beginning of the CFE talks the traditional German perspective was changed from political to include significant military objectives.[64] The West Germans anticipated the possibility of achieving a substantial reduction in force levels through the CFE talks. Such assertiveness encouraged West Germany to play a more prominent role on serious issues affecting its security.

The German change was crucially influenced by the attitude of the Soviet Union. With the new perspective of the Soviet Union in relation to arms control, the size of the reductions envisaged was much larger, and their geographic area was extended from the Atlantic to the Urals. Furthermore the Soviets agreed in principle to the concept of asymmetrical reductions in order to correct the arms imbalance through the elimination of their military advantage. The Soviet unilateral cuts of troops and weapons in the European theatre was the most influential initial factor. The positive German attitude on the Soviet Union took shape with the emergence of Gorbachev as Soviet leader. Foreign Minister Genscher was very quick to recognize the promise Gorbachev represented for a new era in Europe. He was the first Western leader to recognize Gorbachev's peaceful intentions beneath his arms control policy.[65]

The German ideas of non-offensive defence or sufficiency influenced Soviet civilian thinking. The doctrine of "sufficient defence" that led the Soviet Union to restructure and reduce its armed forces on the principle of adequate defence in fact originated in Germany.[66] The concept of "sufficiency" has been the principle on which the German armed force is based. The Chief of Staff of the Federal German Armed Forces suggested three criteria of defence capability as the establishment of adequate defence:

- The defence capability must be such that attack is not an attractive option to any potential aggressor.
- The defence capability must deny any potential aggressor the ability to seize territory and hold it permanently.
- The defence capability must guarantee the recovery of territory and thus the re-establishment of the status quo ante.[67]

The prominent German role for the CFE Treaty was well shown in the "2 plus 4" talks held as a means of resolving the international issues of German reunification. The four Allies (US, UK, the Soviet Union, France) responsible for Germany after its defeat in World II sought legal constraint on German military power after unification. The Soviet Union certainly linked German reunification with a numerical ceiling on a united Germany's armed forces. The Soviet strong will on limitation of a unified German Army accorded with the views of the US, UK and France. Therefore, the allied countries easily agreed with the Soviet Union's offers relating to the limitation of the German Army in the "2 Plus 4" talks.

The "2 plus 4" talks concluded that a unified Germany would not produce, possess or control atomic, biological or chemical weapons and should reduce its forces to 370,000 within three to four years. It would permit the Soviet forces to remain on the GDR territory for three-to-four years and US, French and British soldiers would be stationed in West Berlin until all Soviet troops were gone from Germany.[68]

The FRG government had rejected any European arms reduction agreement that singled out Germany for limitation of its forces. However, Chancellor Kohl departed from the previous position and actively suggested a future commitment on limitation of unified German forces. The Germans recognized this constraint as not only inevitable given their past history, but also desirable to assuage their neighbours' concerns about German rearmament.[69]

The FRG put a 370,000 ceiling of its forces agreed in the "2 plus 4" talks in the CFE Treaty and confirmed that with a ceiling of its ground and air forces no more than 345,000 would be subject of the CFE Talks. Consequently the Bundeswehr will be confirmed and monitored under the verificaton regime of the CFE Treaty. Through its active commitment the FRG expected to contribute to the follow-on CFE Treaty limiting personnel strengths.[70]

Arms control dialogue between the FRG and the GDR

Until the early 1970s when West Germany recognized the entity of the GDR, the GDR had no independent arms control policy of its own. Against the West German policy, which required the prior dissolution of the GDR and the reunification of Germany as a precondition for East-West arms control agreements, East Germany conversely suggested arms control proposals as a means of gaining its acceptance from West Germany as a sovereign state. After the FRG achieved NATO membership, the GDR become the most loyal member of the Warsaw Pact in order to overcome its own vulnerability to the FRG's military build-up. Therefore, the GDR's arms control suggestions were echoes of the arms control projects of the Warsaw Pact.

However, after 1982, the GDR began to seek its own national security interests, which no longer necessarily coincided in every respect with those of the Soviet Union and the WTO. It was based upon the recognition that its front-line position would be the first theatre of any armed conflict. The GDR's perception of its vulnerability led to efforts for damage limitation and arms control.

The GDR became one of the strongest proponents of the need for arms control in East-West relations, and began to play a more active role itself. It had five major policies of arms control:

. establishment of a zone free of nuclear forces in Central Europe.
. a reduction by 50 percent of strategic nuclear weapons of US & USSR.
. a staunch advocate of a nuclear test treaty.
. an international convention on a ban on chemical weapons.
. the reductions of conventional forces and armaments in Europe.[71]

The various proposals were not new ones but originated from the traditional fears of the West's nuclear weapons superiority against the conventional weapon's of the East.

The collapse of the INF talks in 1983 induced the East Germans to have an independent conventional arms control policy. In the shadow of the threatened deployment of medium-range nuclear weapons in Western Europe, they began increasingly to realize that the Warsaw Pact's superiority of conventional weapons no longer guaranteed the GDR's security. The notion of military balance was again reassessed. In contrast to the earlier concept, which emphasised the pursuit of military parity at an ever-high level, they increasingly focussed their attention on a military balance at low levels. The GDR's aim was to combine parity with disarmament in a process of de-escalation of military confrontation.[72]

The GDR's positive position on conventional arms control was well shown in the statement of Erich Honecker during his visit to France in January 1988. His suggestion was that the "GDR, in particular, because of its geographical position and the high concentration of conventional weapons in Central Europe, has a very special interest in seeing concrete results achieved in this area, and has high expectations of negotiations on conventional disarmament from the Atlantic to the Urals".[73]

However, the East German leaders refused to contemplate a reduction of only conventional capabilities. The reduction of conventional forces was always linked with the nuclear reduction. The military, in particular, sought to apply the brakes upon the enthusiasm of the political leadership for conventional disarmament endeavours. Thus, a mid-1987 article of the NVA's theoretical Journal stressed that "a reduction of conventional weapons can only be contemplated if the primacy of the reduction of nuclear weapons is borne in mind".[74]

Nevertheless, the GDR could not avoid the reduction movements of conventional forces. Dismantling of theatre nuclear weapons and systems by the INF Treaty pushed the GDR towards the reduction of conventional forces. The other Warsaw Pact countries positively supported a far-reaching proposal to reduce conventional forces and armaments in Europe with emphasis on those components particularly suitable for the prevention of surprise attacks. In relation to their domestic economies, the implications of military forces and budget reductions in Hungary and Poland as well as the Soviet Union forced the GDR to follow their policies. The unilateral massive reductions of Soviet forces from the GDR and the other Eastern countries following Gorbachev's UN declaration urged it to follow a similar policy to the Soviet Union. Honecker announced that by the end of 1990, the GDR would cut its armed forces by 10,000 men, disband six tank regiments and an air force squadron and reduce 600 tanks and 50 aircraft while decreasing its military budget by 10 percent.[75] Such a decision was taken to keep the GDR in step with the reduction projects of Gorbachev. The GDR politicians recognized the concept of "conventional stability" with that of common security or security partnership between East and West. The conventional stability was understood as a means of preventing conventional local conflict in an initial phase which could automatically escalate to the phase of nuclear war.

Both German states had a stronger interest than most other European states in acting to prevent war. They shared a common understanding of the likely impact of war on their territories. They were non-nuclear states and neither had chemical weapons of their own. Nevertheless, they would be primary victims of such weapons deployed on their territories.

The arms control negotiation between the two states was founded on the 1972 Basic Principles Treaty. It reads as follows:

> Both states shall support efforts towards arms limitation and disarmament, particularly in the concept of nuclear weapons and other means of mass destruction, for the purpose of achieving general and complete disarmament under effective international control and conducive to international security.[76]

However, no arms control dialogue between them was made during the arms control talks of the two blocs. The two German states played down the arms control discussions to avoid suspicion from their allies. During the MBFR talks inter-German discussions of security issues were formal and restricted mainly to periodic contacts at working level. Their activities focussed on reviews of widely known information on the MBFR talks and did not go beyond a formal exchange of comments.[77]

Nonetheless such contacts widened the mutual understanding and acceptance of German interests in the multilateral negotiations. The

Stockholm Conference clearly helped the GDR to change its traditional negative perspective on CBMs. The GDR, which understood the monitoring and verification measures as a means for collecting military intelligence, began to recognize them as a precondition of arms reductions and stability. The change of the GDR's attitude in this area appeared in the implementation of the regulations in force after 1987. Whereas its allies for the most part showed considerable reluctance and failed to satisfy all but the minimum requirement, the GDR was much more flexible and generous, for example, as regards the observation of manoeuvres on its territory.[78]

During Honecker's visit to West Germany in September of 1987, the joint communique showed that the visit did cover a fairly broad spectrum of arms control issues. The two leaders agreed that "arms control negotiations should produce a stable balance of forces at the lowest possible levels, accompanied by elimination of disparities and effectively verifiable reduction, on the basis of equality and parity".[79] Even for the problem of SNF, both states, to some extent, began to expand the scope of understanding. They also agreed to seek to exercise constructive influence on the bilateral negotiations between the two superpowers and endorsed the pending INF agreement.

Thus, the FRG and the GDR had common views about many arms control issues. The two states' policies overlapped on a number of arms control issues i.e. the Stockholm conference, a comprehensive nuclear test ban and preference for low level's of armed force. In fact, the West German position regarding reduction of the conventional armaments of the two blocs in the CFE region was somewhat closer to that of GDR than it was to that of the United States, France or the United Kingdom.[80]

Dialogues between the SPD and the SED

The party-to-party arms control talks of the two German states gave a priority to German security interests rather than those of the blocs. Therefore, arms control proposals focussed on their territory and reflected security problems and the problem resulting from the division of the state. The talks, though deviated from the European arms control talks, were a possible source of arms control ideas needed for a divided state with tense military confrontation along the division line.

The arms control talks between NATO and WTO were long deadlocked without producing a fruitful result for the two German states. The prolonged arms control talks led the West German SPD and the East German SED parties to create a new independent arms control format. Consequently, the arms control dialogue between the SPD and the SED was seen as "a substitute for a bogged-down East-West arms control process, or as a supplement for a more active process".[81] The SPD spokesman pointed out that its motive was taking action in a European area where the great powers had failed to act. They also argued that "regional agreements were easier to achieve than world wide ones and once achieved would stimulate a worldwide agreement while serving as a model for disengagement zones in Europe".[82]

The strongest motive for arms control discussion between the SPD and the SED was the collapse of the negotiations on intermediate-range nuclear forces in 1983. The two parties tried not only to protect German-German detente from the general deterioration of East West relations, but also to play a more independent role in preserving East West detente. The GDR, along with Hungary, emerged as one of the strongest proponents of East-West detente within the Eastern bloc. For the SED Honecker gave strong backing to "the Hungarian thesis that small and middle European powers can play a role in preserving detente in periods when relations between the superpowers are strained".[83] Even after the West German Bundestag took its final vote to deploy the new INF systems, he declared that the GDR would maintain the inter-German relationship.

The collapse of INF negotiation also gave great impact to the SPD initiative. The SPD put emphasis on "a second phase of Ostpolitik" which could produce party to party agreement between the two parties. As a part of this effort the party began to conduct an intensive arms control dialogue with the GDR. In the 1985 report for the annual Bundestag debate on the "State of the Nation", the Social Democrats emphasized the "contribution of both German states to the consolidation of peace in Europe", calling for new initiatives for peace, arms control, and disarmament which would transcend the military blocs.[84] Wilhelm Bruns of the Friedrich Ebert Foundation, a research institute affiliated to the SPD, listed a number of steps for institutionalizing a security dialogue between Bonn and East Berlin:

. formulation of joint proposals at the Stockholm conference.
. establishment of threatening elements trade-offs between the two blocs such as NATO's adopting no first-use policy on nuclear weapons in exchange for the WTO giving up its superiority in tanks.
. governmental negotiation for establishing a Chemical Free Zone on their territories.
. reduction of military budget, and mutual restrictions on their arms sales and transfers to Third World Countries.

. taking joint steps to speed up progress at the MBFR talks and the US-Soviet negotiation in Geneva.[85]

His proposals aimed to develop a common program to eliminate some continuing 'enemy-image' elements in their views of one another in the official political public media and school books.[86] It meant the need for reduction of "threat perception" as well as physical threat as a precondition of arms control dialogues between the two states. The 1988 party congress platform adopted the new security policies. These policies dealt with problems of arms control: (1) increased arms control (2) defensive structure based upon extensive use of fora such as CSCE, CDE and MBFR (3) nuclear weapon free zones (4) replacement of Flexible Response Strategy (5) common security (6) curtailment of the arms industry.[87] In fact, the platform, which provided the conceptual foundation of the inner-German dialogues, accorded in many respects with the security issues which the SED had proposed.

From 1984 the SPD began to conduct its own bilateral talks with East German officials on a wide range of security issues. After the 1983 election defeat by Chancellor Helmut Kohl, the SPD wanted to exploit strong anti-chemical and anti-nuclear sentiment in the FRG. In March 1984, the SPD began a series of talks with officials of the SED to create a chemical weapons-free zone in Central Europe. In June 1985, the two parties set up an agreement for eliminating chemical weapons from the area covered by the MBFR negotiations.

In September 1985, Willy Brandt and Grich Honecker agreed to create an SPD-SED working group to examine the possibility of creating a nuclear-Weapon-free zone in Europe. The idea, which originated from the Palme concept of a Corridor Free of Nuclear Weapons in Central Europe, was to remove all nuclear weapons in the immediate battle area, instead of maintaining some nuclear weapons for deterrence in West Germany.[88] After six meetings the SPD-SED working group issued a joint document outlining a proposed 150km wide, 300km long nuclear-free zone which would encompass parts of the two German states and Czechoslovakia.[89] Their proposal included all nuclear capable delivery vehicles.

In subsequent discussions, both parties worked out the outlines of an agreement which would link the withdrawal of nuclear weapons with withdrawal of offensive conventional forces. The working groups supported the start of the CFE negotiation before the end of 1987. Their aim was to submit proposals to bring about a mutual non-offensive capability, based on a simultaneous adequate defence capability.[90] Thus, on 15 May 1987 Hans-

Jochen Vogel and Erich Honecker agreed to the institution of a joint working group on conventional stability. Their agreement was similar to the declaration that the SPD and the Polish United Workers Party made in 1984.[91]

In contrast to disarmament measures, their initiatives were to develop independent regional CBM models without the direct participation or interruption of the Soviet Union and the United States. But these proposals could only be implemented with the support of the USA and USSR who possessed the nuclear and chemical weapons in Europe. Among the proposals relating to conventional arms control, a particularly attractive point was the idea for "a zone of confidence and security in Central Europe "with the setting up of a "confidence-building centre". The zone of application was limited to within 50km either side of the border between the alliances. The "centre" and "observation post" were intended for the two German States and Czechoslovakia.[92] Unlike the established measures of the CSCE's or the two bloc's the concept envisaged the CBMs within the two states' bilateral settlements. In this respect, the arms control discussion of the SPD-SED was very meaningful in that they had pursued an independent arms control for military stabilization themselves in the frame of European arms control on the basis of national identity.

Table 5-2 Arms Control Proposals of the SPD-SED

Disarmament measures	
June 1985	. a chemical weapons-free zone: Central Europe
Oct. 1986	. a nuclear weapons-free zone: FRG, GDR, Czecho
May 1987	. an institutionalization of a non-offensive defense: FRG, GDR
Confidence-building measures	
July 1988	. a zone of confidence and security: Central Europe
July 1988	. a confidence Building centre: FRG, GDR. Czecho
	. direct bilateral links:Hotline: FRG GDR Czecho
	. exchange of military attaches: FRG GDR
	. joint European satellite observation: FRG GDR

Sources: Jonathan Dean, "Changing Security Dimensions", in F. Stephen Larrabee (eds), *The two German States and European Security* (Mackmillan Press LTD, 1989), pp. 168-174, and Hans-Joachim Spanger, " The GDR in EastWest Relations, *Adelphipaper* 240 (summer, 1989), pp. 54-74.

FRG's Debates and the Bloc Powers' Response

The CDU/CSU, which had basically resisted an arms control dialogue with East Germany, remained very wary of the SPD-SED arms control discussion. The party always regarded NATO nuclear deterrence and the US security guarantee as a pillar of West German security. Therefore, the party could not accept the SPD-SED arms control dialogue which dealt with the reduction of US nuclear weapons from the Federal soil. Their belief was that SPD-SED arms control dialogue would split Bonn from its Western partners, weaken the alliance, undercut the credibility of America's nuclear guarantee, and hasten the process of 'Finlandization'.[93] Chancellor Kohl criticized the SPD for arrogating to itself negotiating authority which could be exercised only by his government. The collaborative activities of the SPD with the SED were seen as undermining the Western negotiating position.

Unlike the CDU/CSU position, the Foreign Minister, Genscher of the FDP, had some positive attitudes about the inter-German dialogue. He thought that their activities could contribute by giving a new impulse to East-West cooperation, provided neither state was obliged to cast doubt on its own Alliance commitments. His acceptance of the two party discussions was limited to the comprehensive exchange of information. However, he cautioned the SPD against going beyond the limits of party activity and undermining governmental prerogatives or the defence consensus.

The SPD-SED arms control discussions aroused suspicion on the part of leaders of the blocs. In particular the United States feared that the direct FRG-GDR arms control talks might undermine alliance policies. The United States' strong negative position was clearly revealed in the criticism of Genscher's attempt. During the 1984-1986 CDE conference, he raised the idea of advancing the Western position by discussing a possible commitment on non-use of force with East Germany. However, he was advised by the US administration that this agenda was already being dealt with in the multilateral negotiations of CDE and an independent German dialogue could weaken the unity of NATO's negotiation position.[94] Consequently, the SPD-SED dialogue on security issues created new friction and suspicion with the United States.

As well as the United States, the Soviet Union was never an enthusiastic supporter of sub-regional security-building and arms control measures independently initiated by the two German States or the SPD-SED.[95] This came from a fear of a loss of control over its allies. In fact, the 19 Soviet divisions and nearly 400,000 troops in the GDR were the linchpin not only of its military strategy, but also political control and stabilization in Eastern Europe. The Soviet reaction to the Palme Commission's proposal to create a chemical weapons-free zone in Central Europe was very cautious. Rather, as an alternative, it suggested a zone of 250 to 300 km either side of the East-West border.[96] In fact, the SED position on a chemical weapon-free zone in the discussion with the SPD was coordinated with Moscow.

Conclusion

Conventional arms control in Europe was closely concerned with the German question. The creation of the twin bloc' collective defence systems and the two German state's entrance into them escalated the military build-up and its heavy concentration on German territory. The FRG found itself firmly planted on the front line of any future European conflict. Thus, the FRG replaced the security concept of deterrence-defence through high armament level with one of detente-defence and low armament level.

The FRG accepted the political and territorial status quo by recognizing the entity of the GDR and the geographical boundaries left after World War II. It also did not directly link arms control issues with the problems of unification. The FRG's policy and Ostpolitik contributed to the establishment of CSCE and MBFR negotiations in Europe.

MBFR, stimulated originally by a German idea for reducing the intensity of military confrontation was used as a means of preventing some reductions of US troops in Europe. Furthermore, this forum was likely to encourage Moscow to push for limitations of the Bundeswehr. The Federal Republic's geostrategic disadvantages of a front line position and its security dependence upon the US left no room for an individualized security and arms control policy.

However, Bonn modified its earlier ideas regarding the military build-up and adopted a dual security policy combining defence-deterrence and detente-arms control. It saw MBFR neither "as a means of improving mutual constraints nor as a framework within which structural reforms of the Bundeswehr might be carried out".[97] It was regarded as a means of political detente complementing deterrence and defence. As a result, detente and arms control were seen as its functional equivalents.

The application of MBFR was very difficult in a country where the risks of conflict were so high and where preventing war by military strength alone was held to be impossible. Accordingly West Germany gave up the idea of a radical reduction of its conventional forces and the restructuring of residual troops in wholly defensive units. West Germany's approach to arms control was directed towards build-up of the confidence and the establishment of a more cooperative relationship between East and West. The FRG's concern was to develop a more cooperative security system which could prevent surprise attacks or an accidental war. Its efforts were concentrated on the establishment of a CBMs security regime, which could produce military stabilization and lead to political detente.

The Federal arms control policy occurred as a consequence of Genscher's persistent foreign policy perspectives. He argued that long-term security required an institutionalized East West dialogue, such as the CSCE process of multilateral talks, with a more autonomous European voice. This view espoused the importance of political security, resting above all on an active arms control policy. For him, threat and distrust could be eventually replaced with cooperation, interdependence, confidence building and other aspects of cooperative security.

The emphasis on such political security led to arms control discussions between the two German states. Their own interests no longer necessarily accorded with those of their alliance partners. Thus, they began to have their own initiatives with regard to the German question. According to the words of the West German president, Richard Von Weizacker, the FRG had in the early 1980s become "the East of the West and the GDR the West of the East, and both states had moved towards the centre."[98]

The independent arms control discussions between the FRG and the GDR were an outcome of a broad revival of national feeling. Their bilateral arms control attempts gave a new impetus to the long deadlock of the two blocs' conventional arms control. In particular the SPD and SED arms control efforts were a new challenge towards the two blocs' arms control system. Their arms control proposals, which were based upon the situation of a divided state, expressed a national character rather than a European one.

In conclusion, the arms control policy of the Federal Republic has been shaped by a continuing interplay between NATO and the Warsaw Pact. However, the FRG viewed arms control as a means of pursuing detente in the framework of the blocs' military confrontation. Their active role in the conventional arms control field provided many lessons and experiences closely connected with the major powers' interaction. Finally, German arms control policy produced many ideas in relation to conventional arms control. Such ideas can be generalized as a model, applicable to similar regions sharing some of the security situation of Germany for military stabilization and the reduction of conventional forces.

NOTES

1. *German Defence White Paper*, 1976, p. 87. About 25 percent of the industrial production base and 30 percent of the population of the Federal Republic were within 100 km of the Eastern border of West Germany.
2. *German Defence White Paper 1985*, pp. 111-112.
3. Catherine McArdle Kelleher, "Germany and NATO: The Enduring Bargain" in Wolfram F. Hanrieder (ed) *West German Foreign Policy: 1949-1979* (Colorado: Westview Press, 1980), pp.46-48.
4. *German Defence White Paper* 1985, p. 102.
5. Ibid. p. 21.
6. Richard C. Eichenberg, "Strategy and Defence Budgeting in the Federal Republic of Germany", in Stephen F. Szabo, *The Bundeswehr and Western Security* (London: MacMillan Press, 1990), p. 151.
7. Walter F. Hahn, *Between Westpolitik and Ostpolitik: Changing West German Security Views* (Beverly Hills/London: SAGE Publication, 1975), p. 70.
8. Gert Krell, T*he Federal Republic of Germany and Arms Control* (Frankfurt:Peace Research Institute: PRIF Reports No. 10, Feb. 1990), p.11.
9. Peter Schmidt, "Public Opinion and Security Policy in the Federal Republic of Germany", *Orbis*, vol 28, No. 4, (Winter 1985), p. 729.
10. Philip Towle, *Arms Control and East-West Relations* (New York: St. Martins Press, 1983), p. 176.
11. Ibid.
12. Krell, op. cit. p. 4.
13. Ibid.
14. Karl E. Birnbaum, "Peaceful Evolution in Europe and the Role of the CSCE/CDE Process", in Karl E. Birnbaum and Bo Huldt, *From Stockholm to Vienna: Building Confidence and Security in Europe* (Stockholm: the Swedish Institute of International Affairs, 1987), p. 73.
15. Ibid.
16. Hans Guenter Brauch, "Arms Control and Disarmament Decisionmaking in the Federal Republic of Germany: past experience and option for change" in Hans Guenter Brauch and Duncan L. Clarke (eds), *Decision-making for Arms Limitation: assessment and prospects,* (Cambridge: Ballinger Publishing Company, 1983), p.142.
17. Ibid. p. 143.
18. Barry Blechman & Cathleen Fisher, *The Silent Partner: West Germany and Arms Control Policy* (Cambridge: Ballinger Publishing Company, 1990), p. 31.
19. Renate Mayntz and Fritz W. Scharpf, *Policy Making in the German Federal Bureaucracy* (New York: Elsevier, 1975), p. 43.
20. See Stanley R. Sloan, "Arms Control Consultations in NATO", in *Decisionmaking for Arms Limitation*, pp. 219-236.
21. Blechman & Fisher, op., cit, p. 51.
22. John G. Keliher, *The Negotiations on Mutual and Balanced Force Reductions: the Search for Arms Control in Central Europe* (Pergamon Press, 1980), p.7. Before the 1970 FRG-Polish treaty, the FRG continued to regard "the line as provisional because the Potsdam Agreement, which gave Poland the territory up to the Oder-Neisse, declared that the Oder-Neisse Line was provisional pending a peace settlement with Germany."

23. Wolfram F. Hanrieder, "West German Foreign Policy, 1949- 1979: Necessities and Choices" p. 18, in *West German Foreign Policy*.
24. Hans-Peter Schwarz, "Adenauer's Ostpolitik", p.131, in *West German Foreign Policy*.
25. Ibid. pp. 129-130.
26. Hanrieder, *West German Foreign Policy*. p.29.
27. Jan Sizoo & Rudolf Th. Jurrjens, *CSCE Decision-Making :the Madrid experience* (Lancaster: Martinus Nijhoff Publishers, 1984), p. 31.
28. Jeffrey Boutwell, "Party Politics and Security Policies in the FRG", pp. 127-130 in *the Bundeswehr and Western Security*.
29. Robert McGeehan, *The German Rearmament Question: American Diplomacy and European Defence after World II* (University of Illinois Press, 1971), pp. 23-24.
30. Hahn, op. cit., pp.37-38.
31. *NATO Press Service,* "Financial and Economic Data Relating to NATO Defence." (28th Nov. 1989),p. 4.
32. John A. Reed Jr, *Germany and NATO* (Washington D.C.: National Defence University Press, 1987), p. 160.
33. Ibid. p 42. For detailed references of German's perspectives on Soviet military power as means of political instruments, see *German Defence White Paper 1985,* pp. 41-45
34. Ibid. p. 43.
35. Julian Lider, *Origins and Development of West German Military Thought: volume 2, 1966-1988* (Gower Publishing Company, 1988), p. 220.
36. Hahn, op. cit., p. 43.
37. Lider, op. cit., pp. 480.
38. Ibid.
39. Washington expected that the Federal government would be more willing to increase defence spending. But even the Kohl Government of CDU/CSU supporting a strong defence program has done little more than keep pace with inflation in defence spending.
40. Paul E. Zinner, *East-West Relations in Europe: observation and advice from the sidelines, 1971-1982* (Boulder, Colo: Westview Press, 1984), p. 69.
41. Krell, op. cit., pp. 35-36.
42. Boutwell, op. cit. p. 139.
43. Blechman & Fisher, op. cit., p. 172.
44. Keliher, op. cit, p. 141.
45. Hans Guenter Brauch, "Confidence Building Measures and Disarmament Strategy", *Current Research on Peace & Violence* (Tampere Peace Research Institute, 3-4/1979), p. 127.
46. Falk Bomsdorf, " The Confidence-Building Offensive in the United Nations", *Aussenpolitik,* vol.33, No.4, (1982), p. 371.
47. Volker Rittberger, Manfred E. Finger & Martin Mendler, "Toward an EastWest Security Regime: the case of confidence-and security-building Measures", *Journal of Peace Research*, Vol.27. No.1, (1990), p. 66.
48. Ibid. p. 67.
49. Brauch, "Confidence Building Measures", p. 130.
50. Henning Wegener, "CBMs: European and Global Dimensions", in F. Stephen Larrabee and Dietrich Stobbe, *Confidence Building Measures in Europe* (New York: Institute for East-West Security Studies, 1983), p. 168. This article described the Federal Government's effort for development CBMs to the global security measures at the United Nations.

51. Paul E. Zinner, "German and US Perceptions of Arms Control", Wolfram F. Hanrieder(ed), *Arms Control, the FRG and the Future of East-West Relations* (Boulder & London: Westview Press, 1987), p. 12.
52. Lothar Ruehl, "MBFR: Lessons and Problems", *Adelphi Paper,* 176., p. 7.
53. Harald Ruddenklau, "Constraints on German Defence Policies in the 1990s", in Karl Kaiser and John Roper(eds), *British-German Defence Cooperation: partners within the alliance* (London: Royal Institute of International Affairs, 1988), p. 149.
54. Reed Jr. op cit., pp 154-155.
55. Ruehl, op. cit., p. 7. Britain also sought to reduce somewhat her ground forces in Germany which then stood at about 59,000. French ground forces in Germany were roughly 60,000, all French air force units having been withdrawn to France in 1966-7.
56. John Borawski, "Mutual Force Reductions in Europe from a Soviet Perspective", Orbis, Vol.22, No.4, (1979), p. 851.
57. Keliher, op. cit., p. 86.
58. For detailed references, see Borawski "Mutual Force Reduction", pp. 845-873.
59. Keliher, op. cit. p. 78.
60. A Conference Report, *Third German-American Round Table on NATO: The MBFR negotiations* (Institute for Foreign Policy Analysis, 1980), p. 12.
61. Thomas J. Hirschfeld, "MBFR in Eclipse", *Arms Control Today*, Vol.16, No.7, (Oct. 1986), p. 9.
62. Lider, op. cit., p. 533.
63. Keliher, op. cit., p.140.
64. Gale A. Mattox, "The Bundeswehr and Arms Control", p.86 in *the Bundeswehr and Western Security.*
65. Stephen F. Szabo, *The Changing Politics of German Security* (London: Pinter Publishers, 1990), p. 129.
66. Wendy Silverman, "Talking Sufficiency in the Hofburg Palace: The Second Seminar on Military Doctrine", *Arms Control Today,* Vol.21, No.10, (December 1991), p. 16.
67. Admiral Dieter Wellershof (Chief of Staff of the Federal German Armed Forces), "First Successful Step in CBMs Negotiations: The Military Doctrine Seminar", *NATO Review,* Vol.38, No.2, (April 1990), p. 12.
68. "Final Settlement for Germany at '2 plus 4' negotiations", *Financial Times,* 13 September, 1990.
69. Paul B. Stares, *Allied Rights and Legal Constraints on German Military Power* (Washington D.C.: The Brookings Institution, 1990), p. 3.
70. See "Declaration of the Government of the Federal Republic of Germany on the Personnel Strength of German Armed Forces" in the CFE Treaty.
71. Max Schmidt, "The Two German States and European Security", in F. Stephen Larrabee (ed), *The Two German States and European Security* (New York: the Institute for East-West Security Studies, the Macmillan Press, Ltd. 1989), pp. 115-116.
72. Hans-Joachim Spanger, "The GDR in East-West Relations", *Adelphi Paper,* 240 (1989), p. 45.
73. Ibid. p.69. For detailed references on the GDR positions for the CFE talks, see Manfred Muller, "Constraints", pp.405-421, in Robert D. Blackwill and F. Stephen Larrabee (eds) *Conventional Arms Control and EastWest Security* (Duke University Press: Durham & London, 1989).
74. Ibid. A similar view was expressed by the GDR Defence Minister Heinz Kessler at the end of 1987. He emphasised that "there is no more urgent priority than to begin nuclear disarmament."

75. Ian Cuthbertson, "The Political Objective of Conventional Arms Control", in Robert D. Blackwill and F. Stephen Larrabee (ed) *Conventional Arms Control and East-West Security*, p. 106.
76. Schmidt, op. cit., p. 115.
77. Jonathan Dean, "Changing Security Dimensions of Inter-German Relationship", p. 160. in *The Two German States and European Security*
78. Spanger, op. cit., p. 53.
79. Dean, "Changing Security Dimensions", p.175.
80. Ibid., p. 176.
81. Jonathan Dean, "Directions in Inner-German Relations", *Orbis*, , vol.29, No.3, (Fall, 1985) p. 629.
82. Dean, "Changing Security Dimensions", p. 169.
83. Larrabee, "From Reunification to Reassociation: New Dimensions of the German Question", p.5, in *The Two German States and European Security*
84. Dean, "Directions in Inner-German Relations", p. 628.
85. Blechman and Fisher, op. cit., p.139.
86. Dean, "Changing Security Dimensions", p. 164.
87. Matthew A. Weiller, "SPD Security Policy", *Survival*, Vol.30, No.6 (Nov./Dec., 1988), p. 516.
88. "Breaking with Convention: the start of new European Force Talks", *Arms Control Today*, April 1989, p. 9.
89. Weiller, "SPD Security Policy", p. 521.
90. "SED-SPD Working Group in Favour of Continuing Process of Disarmament", *Foreign Affairs Bulletin* (Ministry of Foreign Affair of GDR), Feb. 1987, Vol. 28.
91. Dean, "Changing Security Dimensions", pp. 171-172. The SPD/PUWP decl ration advocated eliminating offensive components of NATO and Warsaw Pact forces including the disparities and asymmetries, so that neither alliance was able to launch a surprise attack.
92. Spanger, op. cit., p. 54.
93. Blechman and Fisher, op. cit., p. 71.
94. Dean, Direction in Inner, p. 630. The US also discouraged the Kohl-Honecker discussion of inner-German commitment on no use of forces, arguing that the independent German dialogue outside the CDE talks would weaken the Western position.
95. Spanger, op. cit., p. 56.
96. Ibid. p. 61.
97. Uwe Nerlich, "A New Look at MBFR Talks", *The German Tribune* (Political Affairs Review), No.29, (10 July, 1977), p. 3.
98. Spanger, op. cit., p. 76.

Part III
Arms Control in Northeast Asia

6. The Application of the European Arms Control Model to Northeast Asia

The Arms Control Links between Northeast Asia and Europe

When the Korean War occurred, the NATO countries regarded the war as a preliminary theatre for the Soviet Union's attack upon Western Europe and took steps to create strengthen the alliance. The Korean War deepened the divisions between East and West because it reinforced the aggressive image of the Soviets. North-East Asia and Europe seemed linked as theatres of the superpowers' strategies.

In the early 1980s US Defence Secretary Weinberger promoted the strategy of 'horizontal escalation' - an attack by the Soviet Union in Europe would be countered by United States' strikes against Soviet weak points. The rationale for attacking the Soviet military assets in Asia in the context of a European war was explained by Richard Solomon, director of the policy-planning staff of the US State Department. His comment was that against the Soviet strategy for minimizing its two-front problem the US would open a second front line in Asia which could divide the Soviet forces.[1] The Soviet Union also viewed Northeast Asia in the context of the security of Europe. After the 1969 Soviet-Chinese clash, Brezhnev asked his allies in Eastern Europe to contribute forces to Central Asia in defence of the Soviet Union.[2] The Soviet's great willingness to participate in the MBFR talks also coincided with the development of the new strategic front-line in Northeast Asia through the 1971 Sino-American rapprochement. Moreover, an intensive US-Japanese military cooperation was, in the Soviet view, part of a US effort to establish a link between the two theatres through increasing contacts between Japan and NATO on security matters. In regard to the Japanese foreign minister's visit to NATO headquarters TASS stated in 1986 that "Japan is being increasingly drawn into NATO military-political consultation" and that it is "turning into a 'NATO far-Eastern member".[3]

A further arms control linkage between Europe and Northeast Asia was developed in the course of the INF talks between the United States and the Soviet Union. The INF agreement based on the 'zero option' was made possible by the demand of the North Asian countries for the principle of equal security for Europe and Asia. At first, the two superpowers considered the agreement limited to only the European region. In 1983, Soviet Foreign Minister Gromyko announced that his country would "shift the missiles withdrawn from Europe, according to the treaty, to Siberia whence they could no longer reach Europe".[4] Japan, China and South Korea saw the deployment of SS-20s in Asia as a critical new element in the Asian security equation and viewed the US-Soviet arms limitation talks on INF as having a direct impact on their national security. Indeed, the USSR made its initial deployment of SS-20s against China, Japan and major US bases in Northeast Asia, not in Europe.[5] In the process of the INF talks the USSR also employed a negotiating strategy of trading off Pershing IAs, which the FRG sought to retain, for its SS-20s in Asia.[6] Therefore, Asian countries regarded 'the zero option' as raising important principles regarding the US commitment to them. They encouraged the United States to negotiate an agreement in a global, not merely a Europe-centred context. The outcome of the INF talks operated as an important factor linking security between Europe and North East Asia. The arms control link between the two regions through the INF talks contained valuable lessons. If the elimination of INF was limited to only the European area, it might have been very difficult to have mutual monitoring and control given the geographical mobility of the nuclear missiles. A ban on all INF contributed to the simplication of the verification tasks, taking away a role for the Asian SS-20s as a strategic reserve for the European theatre. The progress of the negotiations for the INF treaty showed that, at least on certain, issues the security of Europe and Northeast Asia had become closely interdependent. The treaty itself, although principally initiated for European security, had not only direct implications for the military balance of the Asian theatre, but more importantly, changed the regional countries' perspective on arms control. Furthermore, the security situation in Northeast Asia was also substantially improved by the CFE treaty of Europe. The elimination of Soviet conventional-force preponderance in Europe and the concrete steps taken to reduce the Soviet offensive threat to Europe would mitigate the need for the US 'horizontal escalation' strategy in East Asia in response to a Soviet attack on NATO forces.

Notwithstanding these benefits, the CFE Treaty has not benefitted Northeast Asian countries security significantly. Rather it resulted in increasing potential threat in the region. The Soviet Union redeployed much sophisticated equipment withdrawn from Europe to Asia prior to the signing of the CFE Treaty.[7] As a result the armed forces of Russia in Northeast Asia were significantly modernized in qualitative terms compared to the pre-CFE Treaty situation. The CFE Treaty necessitated a close arms control link between Europe and Northeast Asia. Thus the build-up of the potential threat demonstrated the need for an arms control mechanism similar to Europe in the region.

The Dynamics of Regional Strategic Environment

Northeast Asia is one of the most heavily armed areas in the world. The interests of four of the world's most powerful nations - the US, Russia, Japan and China converge in the region. Because of its strategic complexity this region is very unstable and the danger of an intensive war may be higher than in other regions.

During the Cold War North-East Asia reflected the geostrategic classification of the US and the Soviet Union as a seapower and landpower respectively. Geographically the US relied on long range power projection and command of critical ocean areas in order to maintain its strategic influence in a region such as the North Pacific. The Soviet Union on the other hand was in a position to dominate neighbouring states with its formidable land-based military power. Both sides took steps to moderate this asymmetry: "the US through bases closer to the Eurasian land mass and the Soviet Union through a belated but determined effort to acquire a blue-ocean navy".[8] As a Pacific power US maritime strategy aimed to contain the Soviet Union through early offensive operations and forward deployment of forces in the North Pacific region such as in Japan and South Korea. The Soviet Union challenged the US dominance in the region through an enormous military build-up. It has encouraged the US and its allies to enforce the security relationship and this has led to arms competitions.

From the postwar period onward to the early 1960s, the bipolarity of international politics between the superpowers affected Northeast Asia. The confrontation between them resulted in the development of respective alliance networks. The US, for example, concluded bilateral security treaties with Japan in 1952 and South Korea in 1954. The Soviet Union had bilateral alliance agreements with China in 1950, North Korea in 1966 and Mongolia in 1966. China also signed a similar treaty with North Korea in 1961. As a result, the Cold War produced two opposite triangle systems; the northern triangle - the Soviet Union, China and North Korea and the southern triangle - the United States, Japan and South Korea. The establishment of these triangle systems represented the most stern cold war confrontation during the 1950s and 1960s.

However, from the mid-1960s the "iron bipolar system" was turned into a strategic triangle of the Soviet Union-China-US by the deepening of Sino-

Soviet conflicts and the Sino-American rapprochement. Since then the security of Northeast Asia has depended not upon the bilateral superpower game, but rather the multilateral interactions of the three-power strategic alignment triangle in response to the changing nature of Sino-Soviet, Sino-American, and Soviet-American relations.

The Sino-Soviet conflict arising from different perspectives on ideology and world politics was widened by the Soviet Union's invasion of Czechoslovakia in 1968 and the Sino-Soviet border clashes in 1969. Faced with a serious threat from the Soviet Union, China used the United States' power as a means of countering the "polar bear" in the ancient tradition of "controlling barbarians with other barbarians".[9] Taking the avoidance of a two-front war into consideration, the Soviet Union also sought detente with the United States by opening the 'era of negotiations' leading to treaties such as the SALT Agreement, the Sea-Bed Treaty, the beginning of CSCE and the MBFR talks in the early 1970s. The Soviet Union and China were eager to make better relations with the United States to counter the other side. Thus, the strategic triangular system was established by the active "swing diplomacy" of the United States.

Regarding the China factor, the interaction between the two superpowers was highly complicated, and volatile, with a great impact upon the geopolitical configuration of the region. China became a key factor in the respective strategic calculus of the two superpowers. As a result the two superpowers' influence in Northeast Asia was to some extent limited by the flexible manoeuvres of China as 'balancer' in the central strategic equilibrium between them.[10] The Chinese strategy was to maintain a little distance from the United States, while preserving a strategic cooperation against the Soviet Union.

However, the rise of Japan to become the world's second largest economic power transformed the triangle structure into a loose economic "rectarchy" in the region.[11] Further, the rapid economic growth of the newly industrializing countries (NICs) of East Asia began to shift the structure to a multipolar structure, severely limiting the strategic options of the regional powers. A spreading and deepening network of economic ties has been steadily transcending ideological-political lines. As a result, this trend is increasing the interdependence among the states of the region and is underwriting a "soft regionalism".[12] With the decline of the superpower's hegemony and economic multipolarization, the two revolutionary events in Northeast Asia were the normalization of Sino-Soviet relations with the summit meeting in 1989 and the establishment of formal diplomatic relations between South Korea and the Soviet Union (1990) and China

(1992). Strategically, this means that a new diffusion and realignment of power has already taken place. They may also mean a reformation of strategic structure to open up new possibilities for functional multilateral cooperation in the region. The Sino-Soviet arms reduction agreement created a new security landscape in the region, effecting a gradual reduction of military tension. Neither China nor the USSR/Russia now regards the other as an immediate security threat.[13] The normalization of relations between South Korea and the Northern Powers may mean the collapse of the Cold War system in Northeast Asia.

Regional Military Balance

During the Cold War, the military balance between the major powers in Northeast Asia was traditionally assessed by comparisons of military forces of the Soviet-US and the Soviet Union-China or Soviet Union-anti Soviet alignment; the US China and Japan. The main possible arenas for military conflict between the major powers in the region were the Sino-Soviet border, Northern territories, and the West Pacific.

The Soviet ground, naval and tactical air forces in the region were steadily increased during the 1970s and 1980s to ensure the independent viability of the Far East theatre of military operations (TVD) in any circumstance.[14] This Military District contained the single most important concentration of Soviet forces east of the Urals, with 43 percent of all the motorized rifle, tanks and artillery divisions and 54 percent of all tactical aircraft.[15]

The Soviet Defence Minister revealed the total number of Soviet forces east of the Urals as breaking down into two parts: one to defend against US and Japanese forces in the Pacific area; and the other to oppose the Asian countries facing the Soviet Union on the Eurasian Continent.[16]

The Soviet Union undoubtedly possessed overwhelming military power with which to face either China or Japan alone in Northeast Asia. As a consequence, these countries relied heavily on friendship or alliance with the United States to balance Soviet power. However, strategically the Soviet Union was fundamentally vulnerable in the region, notwithstanding its superiority of military forces. Geographically the Soviet Far East was separated from the European theatre of the Soviet Union by 5,000 km of largely empty land-mass, and the two parts were connected only by two rail routes. These factors motivated the Soviet Union's heavy military build-up in the region.

128 *Ending the Last Cold War*

Table 6-1   **The Comparison of Armed Forces between the Major Powers in East Asia**

	Soviet Union A	B	TO.	China	Japan Asia/	US Pacific
Aircraft	820	870	1690	4970	422	619
Tanks (00)	81	45	126	75-80	12	2.04
Vehicle (00)	102	41	143	28	5.74	5.19
Artillery (00)	94	70	164	145	5.53	?
Troop (00)	2714	3262	5976	30300	2460	1350
Surface Ship	-	55	-	56	66	55
Submarine	-	46	-	94	17	17

The Soviet Union; A: against China, B: Against US & China, Sources: Research Institute for Peace and Security, Tokyo, *Asian Security 1989-90* (Brassey's 1989), pp. 73-4; The forces of China and Japan: *The Military Balance 1991-92*, US forces: Korean Defence White Paper 1991-1992 (Seoul: Korean MOD, 1991), p.49.

The other important aspect of military competition was the build-up of naval forces between the Soviet Union and the US in the North Pacific. From the early 1970s the Soviet Union greatly reinforced the Pacific Fleet, which now constitutes the largest of the four Russian fleets. It comprised 30 percent of the total Soviet navy. Two of the three Soviet Kiev-class aircraft carriers were included in this fleet. This expansion of the Pacific Fleet was meant to challenge the United States for control of the SLOC (Sea Lanes of Communications) in the Asia-Pacific region. Against the force build-up of the Soviet Pacific Fleet, the United States adopted an offensive maritime strategy. John Lehman, Secretary of the Navy, sought power projection through the deployment of 600 ships to counter the Soviet forces. In wartime the 3rd Fleet, which had responsibility for operations off Alaska, the Bering Sea and Eastern Pacific had orders to support the 7th Fleet. American naval exercises in the northern Pacific operated in close proximity to Soviet naval bases. Its aircraft and submarines also intruded into air and sea spaces.[17]

However, the collapse of the Soviet Union resulted in a change to the Cold War formula of military balance. The USSR and the US no longer regarded the other as an enemy. The USSR and China also ended 30 years of hostility with the conclusion of the Sino-Soviet border treaty. There is now no definite military balance in the region because of the change of strategic relationship between the regional powers. Now it is important to understand the regional military balance in the assessment of military capability or potentiality between the regional rival countries. There have been no arms reductions responding to the end of the Cold War. The deep-rooted bilateral rivalries have helped to preserve the enormous military assets which were built up in the Cold War and which are a big obstacle to regional stability.

The USSR and China reached agreements on the reduction of their armed forces deployed along the Sino-Russian border. However, the border still remains an area of potential instability in the region. The huge concentrations of armaments along the border are far in excess of the level of force deployment in normal relations. The military asymmetries between them are an other potential factor of instability. One Chinese author warned that "despite the border treaty the Soviet army presently remains an offensive force; even if the change to a defensive structure is realized in the future, the Soviet Army will still carry tremendous potential of launching an in-depth attack".[18]

The "Northern Territories" have been a focal point of military confrontation between the USSR and Japan. The forces of the USSR have been built up in the islands north of Hokkaido quite dramatically since the signing of the Sino-Japanese Friendship treaty in 1978. Two army divisions are in Sakhalin. On Etorofu there is now stationed a 10,000-16,000 men composite division of the regular army with 40 MIG-23s. The USSR also substantially increased the amphibious capability in the area, which would presumably be directed against Hokkaido.[19] Against these Soviet forces Japan locates four of the twelve Ground Self Defence Force divisions (GSDF) in Hokkaido. These divisions consist of a total of 31,000 troops and include Japan's only armoured division.[20]

The Japanese argue that the reduction of Russian forces along the Chinese border does not change the nature of the military threat to Japan. Furthermore they have complained that Russian forces withdrawn from Afghanistan and Central Europe have been transferred to Japan's northern front.[21] This anxiety is extended to the argument that China continues to build up and modernize its naval capability, expanding its naval operations from coastal patrols to blue water missions. The Chinese naval force projection centres on the development of sea combat forces, including warships, submarines and aircraft.[22]

China is also very cautious about Japan's naval build-up. The level of attention paid to Japanese military developments is significantly more pronounced than that paid to those of any other countries, upon the assumption that Japan aims to become a regional military power. In fact the Japanese Maritime Self-Defence Force (JMSDF) has deployed 66 destroyers and frigates, more than China. Of most concern to Chinese military planners is the Japanese orientation to a more forward-based defence posture. The primary Chinese motive for the build-up of naval forces stems from the extension of the JMSDF's security responsibilities in the 1980s to 1,000 nautical miles from the Japanese coast.[23]

Yet in Northeast Asia, even after the end of the cold war, Moscow has not substantially reduced its enormous naval and air forces which were built up in the arms race with the US After the collapse of the Soviet Union Russia declined in prestige as a European or global power. However, its formidable forces in the region are still regarded as a potential threat to regional countries, although the degree of its threat has declined.[24]

The Territorial Disputes and Arms Control

Border disputes serve as an adversarial symbol and a big obstacle to stability and arms control between nations. In the Northeast Asian region, unlike Europe, many territorial disputes remain unsolved. These problems have been one of the major reasons underlying the military confrontation of the Major Powers in the region.

The most serious obstacle today to a major improvement of the security of Northeast Asia is the long-standing and bitter dispute over the Northern Territories between Russia and Japan. The territories in question, the islands of Etorofu, Kunashiri, Shikotan and Habomai have prevented the two countries from erasing officially the legacy of World War II. The solution of these island problems is a basic precondition for arms control and stability in Northeast Asia.

The USSR recognized the strategic significance of the islands as the key to access between the North Pacific and the Soviet Far East. Stalin said in September of 1945 that:

> South Sakhalin and the Kuriles "will henceforth serve not as a means for isolating our country from the ocean or as a base for Japanese aggression in our Far Eastern area but as a means for linking the Soviet Union with the ocean and as a base for our defence against Japanese aggression.[25]

In fact, the strategic value of these small islands has increased because of the military confrontation with the US. The islands, which guard the southern entrance to the sea of Okhotsk, can guarantee the activities of

SLBM's in targeting strategic objectives in the US and deny access to US hunter-killer submarines.[26]

The attitude of Moscow has moved to a conciliatory stance since the Sino-Japanese Treaty of 1978. The Treaty showed Moscow that the border disputes with China and Japan were politically and strategically detrimental to the Soviet Union. After Gorbachev took office, Moscow recognized that some form of rapprochement with Japan was essential in order to benefit from East Asian economic dynamism. Russia has suggested several possibilities, such as the return of two islands or even all four, the development of joint enterprises and the creation of joint sovereignty or joint administration over them. The possibility of returning the two islands was apparently mentioned by Gorbachev during the visit of Japanese Prime Minister Nakasone to the USSR in 1988. Boris Yeltsin also proposed a long term solution of five stages: (1) official recognition of the problems existence and reshaping of public opinion for a settlement over 23 years (2) demilitarization of the islands for 5-7 years (3) establishment of a free enterprise zone over 3-5 years (4) signing of a peace treaty (assuming some 15-20 years to reach this fourth stage) and (5) finally the settlement of all remaining issues by a new generation.[27]

However, there are a number of constraints to the return of the islands. The residents of the disputed region are strongly opposed to any territorial concessions. Nikolai Danilyuk, Chairman of the Far Eastern Association (FEA), said that his group would establish a Far Eastern Republic if the Russian Government decided to transfer the Kuril Islands to Japan.[28] The military pressure may also make it hard for the government to concede a potentially strategic piece of territory. The strategic significance of the islands has greatly increased since 1956 when the Soviets were prepared to make concessions to Japan over the islands. Moscow still has a strong security interest in keeping the islands out of the hands of its strategic rivals.

The settlement of the territorial issue has been near the top of Japan's foreign policy agenda toward the Soviet Union since 1945. Japan has made the return of the islands a precondition for a peace treaty and the development of good relations with Moscow. In the 1956 joint declaration Japan gained the Soviet concession that the islands of Habomai and Shikotan would be returned to Japan after the signing of a peace treaty. However, the Japanese government demanded the immediate return of all four islands. There has also been some political interest at stake in the Japanese government's unyielding stance on the territories issue. The continued Soviet military build up on the islands served to increase the security concerns of Japan and permitted an increase of the defence budget.

For ten years, the government has held annual "Northern Territories Day" rallies and collected signatures requiring the return of the islands.[29]

Japanese politicians and scholars have made various proposals, in response to the Soviet flexibility on border issues. Japan dropped its previous insistence that all four should be handed over together. In line with the pledge of the Soviet Union in 1956, it proposed the return of two first and the others later. During Gorbachev's visit to Japan in April 1991, a proposal of $26 billion in aid was made in return for the islands: $4 billion as an emergency loan for consumer goods, $4 billion for withdrawal of troops and residents, $8 billion for oil and gas projects in Sakhalin and $10 billion for a long-term economic plan.[30] Subsequently Japan offered a new proposal of four principles: (1) Russian acknowledgment of an illegal occupation (2) simultaneous conclusion of a peace treaty and the return to Japan of the Habomai group and Shikotan islands (3) an acknowledgment of Japanese sovereignty over the two remaining islands (4) Japanese acceptance of continued administration of the islands for a certain period of time and in return trillions of yen of full-scale aid.[31] However, no real progress towards the settlement of the dispute was made.

There are a number of possible solutions to the border dispute in the medium or long term. Russia's desire to play a greater role in the Pacific and its need for Japanese investment and technology in the Russian Far East are inducements for making concessions. Japan also has a long term economic interest in gaining access to the huge natural gas, oil and pulpwood resources in Eastern Siberia and Sakhalin. The possibility of a solution of the border dispute was suggested by former Soviet foreign minister Shevardnadze, "who pointed to the long but successful negotiations between Peking and Moscow over their disputed border as a model for a settlement".[32]

There is an other important potential territorial dispute over islands between China (with Taiwan) and Japan. The island group, Diaoyutai in Chinese and Senkaku in Japanese, some 120 miles northeast of Taiwan and some 250 miles southwest of Okinawa have been contested periodically by Beijing and Tokyo since the 1970s. There are claims and counterclaims in this dispute much like those in the Northern Territories.[33] Japan's claim to the "Senkaku" - a group of eight small islands is said to be based on records showing that the islands were "occupied and administered" by Japan in the late 19th century. These islands were placed under US administration after the defeat of Japan in World War II. By the "Okinawa Reversion Treaty" of 1971, the United States returned administrative rights to Japan. But this action was challenged by China. Twice there were risks of military clashes over the sovereignty of the islands, between China and Japan in 1978 and between Taiwan and Japan in 1990.[34] Recently China legislated its right over the islands. The Chinese law affirmed territorial sovereignty and explicitly reserved the right to use military force in the area.[35]

As seen from their attitudes on the border disputes with the Soviet Union-China and the Soviet Union-Japan, China and Japan have been sensitive about the border problems. They did not make any concessions to the Soviet Union. But because they had shared a common task of seeking the solution to border problems with the Soviet Union, China and Japan were unwilling to quarrel. Recently the Senkaku dispute has again surfaced. The potential oil deposits of the maritime area around the islands may result in an escalation of the dispute.[36] Rivalry between them as regional greater powers may make more difficult the solution of the island problem.

The Application of Arms Control Along the Sino-Russia Border

The border dispute between China and Russia along the Amur-Ussuri basin was resolved in 1990. As a result the two countries normalized their relations and introduced CBMs and arms reduction in the border region. An agreement on basic principles of mutual arms reductions and CBMs was signed between the Soviet Union and China in Moscow in April 1990. A joint commission at the level of vice-foreign minister was established to discuss these problems and several talks followed leading in 1990-91 to the "Agreement on Mutual Reduction of Military Forces on Sino-Soviet Borders and the Guiding Principles of Trust in the Military Field".[37] This agreement was a turning point for them to put aside the hostile relations of over three decades and coexist as good neighbours. The border dispute between them directly concerned the security of Northeast Asia. The solution of this problem provided a basis for regional security and arms control.

The point of the dispute, which had lasted over three centuries, was the use of the Amur-Ussuri waterway. The territorial dispute, which originated from the competition for a slight commercial advantage, had escalated to a concern of strategic importance through the over-deployment of armed forces along the border.

Along the Amur-Ussuri basin, the Chinese faced a direct Soviet threat to their vital strategic and industrial interests in Manchuria. China's heavy industrial zone, extending northwards from Mukden to Harbin was especially vulnerable to a Soviet blitzkrieg. From the Soviet point of view the holding of certain islands, known by the Chinese as "Bear Island" and by the Russians as the "Ussuriysk island" provided very important strategic advantages. The large pair of islands at the convergence of the rivers was vital to the security of Khabarovsk, through which runs the Trans-Siberian Railway.[38]

The Soviet Union has threatened China through a heavy arms array along the Sino-Soviet border. The Soviet threat had also increased through the countries which share common frontiers with China; Afghanistan, Mongolia and Vietnam. The 115,000 Soviet troops in Afghanistan and 75,000 in Mongolia maintained the highest category of readiness.[39] The continuation of military confrontation with China was a very heavy burden. The forces arrayed against China accounted for about 15-20 percent of Soviet defence spending.[40] Therefore the Soviet Union had a strong motive to begin arms control talks with China along the frontiers.

Table 6-2   Comparison of Army Divisions in the Sino-Soviet Border (1970-1980)

	Soviet Union		China	
	Total	border (percent To)	Total	border (percent To)
1971	160	33 (20.6)	140	33 (23.6)
1975	157	43 (27.4)	162	96 (59.3)
1980	173	46 (26.6)	136	75 (61)

Source: White, Yalando Simmons, *The New Arms Control-Mindedness of the Chinese* (University Microfilms International, 1982), p. 83.

China demanded from the Soviet Union concessions in five areas as a prerequisite to border talks: (1) withdrawal of its troops from the Sino-Soviet border, withdrawal of its forces from (2) Mongolia (3) Afghanistan, (4) the recognition of existence of "disputed areas" and (5) the end of its aid to Vietnam.[41] These demands were dismissed by the Kremlin. The border talks were stalemated on this preliminary question until 1987.

The long stalemate of the border problem was broken by "the new thinking" policy of Gorbachev. The Soviet Union acknowledged for the first time that its frontier with China ran through the centre of the Ussuri and

Amur rivers, rather than along the Chinese bank. This meant that the disputed Damanski Island belonged to Chinese territory. Thus Gorbachev's unilateral arms retreat from the Sino-Soviet border and Mongolia and Afghanistan was a turning point that ended the antagonism between China and the USSR. Gorbachev's plan to cut 500,000 men announced at the UN in December 1988 included 200,000 men in Asia. 120,000 men of the proposed reduction came from Far Eastern Asia, including 12 divisions of ground forces, 11 air force regiments and 16 warships.[42] The withdrawal of two tank and three motor rifle divisions in Mongolia, which could serve as a blitzkrieg force for any attack on China, contributed to the change in China's security policy.

From the early 1980s, Chinese leaders began to judge that the Soviet threat was not as powerful as it had been. China and Mongolia signed an important border demarcation agreement in 1984. Along the Sino-Soviet border there existed some indications of a reduction of tension after the mid-1970s. In 1976-77 two-thirds of the Soviet troops were in categories 1 and 2 of high readiness. However, this fell to 50 percent in 1977-1983, and from 1984 only 35 percent were said to be at this state of readiness.[43] China also withdrew the requirement for the Soviet Union's acknowledgement of 'unjust treaties' imposed on China by the Tsars, which was invariably demanded in Mao's time. In response to this the Soviet Union began major reductions in its armed forces after 1987. The initiation of these unilateral reductions proceeded the border arms control talks between the Soviet Union and China.

The 1991 Sino-Soviet Border Treaty was made on the basis of the CBMs conceptual framework. The Soviet Union was particularly keen to apply European CBMs to the Sino-Soviet border. It placed greater emphasis on the introduction of the Helsinki CBMs than on troop reduction. It proposed that the agreement include prior notification of military exercises and an exchange of observers at large-scale manoeuvrers.[44] In the Gorbachev period, the CBMs policy on the border was elaborated by the 1986 Stockholm agreement in Europe. During his visit to China in 1988, Shevardnadze proposed a package of CBMs which would produce 'almost total transparency' along the border. He also proposed mutual notification of military exercises, the exchange of observers at exercises, and no military movements without agreement.[45] Following Gorbachev's visit to China in May 1989 a joint working group was established to negotiate CBMs proposals. This paved the way for security cooperation on the basis of arms control between the two powers. Reciprocal visits of military officials at a high level began in April 1990.[46] This was the first formal official visit for three decades following the withdrawal of all Soviet military advisers from China in 1960. These moves led to reciprocal visits by defence ministers. These frequent contacts contributed to mutual understanding and cooperation on a variety of subjects. Similar to the experience of Europe, the build-up of CBMs between them successfully resulted in an agreement upon arms reduction.

With the application of CBMs, the Border Treaty is now moving towards troop reductions and the restructuring of military potential along the border within the framework of non-provocative defence.[47] The new Commonwealth of Independent States (CIS) suggested a plan to demobilize 60,000 troops in the border region in 1992 - in addition to the withdrawal of 120,000 men from the region in the past few years.[48] Though the border treaty applied to the 7,000 km-long border, the demarcation of around 10 percent of it still presents some problems. There is in fact an obvious asymmetry in the application of the Border Treaty. This asymmetry was demonstrated by Soviet researcher Andrei Kouzmenco of IMEMO (Institute of World Economy and International Relations):

> In view of such asymmetry the process of arms reductions along the Sino-Soviet border requires definition of the term "border zone". For instance, if the territory 600 kms or less along the border (300 kms on each side) is defined as "border infrastructure and power supply", Chinese troops will mostly not be restationed. On the other hand, disbandment of Soviet divisions is difficult because of problems of redeployment, retraining and social security of the retired personnel.[49]

Despite this asymmetric width of border zone for the two nations, the follow-up discussion of the Border Treaty has concentrated on the production of a concrete agreement within its framework.

In conclusion, the Border Treaty between China and the Soviet Union served to solve a major problem of regional security. Furthermore the arms reduction and CBMs introduced in the Treaty was a first application of European conventional arms control in the Asia-Pacific region. This offers a successful precedent for the application of European conventional arms control in the region. As seen from the experiences of Europe and China-Russia, as long as the disputes remain, no arms control can be expected. On the other hand, the potential of arms control for tension reduction is even more evident in the region where territorial claims persist.

The Regional Powers' Policies towards Arms Control

Conventional arms control has been energetically discussed and successfully put into practical use in Europe since the early 1970s. But, except for the recent bilateral arms control between China and the Soviet Union, no regional arms control process has been made in Northeast Asia. Neither the United States nor the Soviet Union paid any attention to regional arms control despite the energetic arms control efforts that occurred in Europe. Furthermore, regional powers such as, China and Japan kept a distant watch on the activities of arms control in Europe. They were wary of regional arms control. However, after the advent of Gorbachev to power in 1985, the Soviet Union became the primary initiator of arms control proposals for Asia. With the end of the Cold War, Asians have also given much concern to the arms control models of Europe.

The Asian Security Conference

The Soviet Union sought the application of European models to the Asian region. The agendas of arms control currently applicable to Asia are almost entirely based upon the European experiences. After Gorbachev proposed a "joint, comprehensive approach" to security during Prime Minister Rajiv Gandhi's visit to Moscow in May 1985,[50] the Soviet Union repeatedly reaffirmed its commitment to hold an Asian security conference. The Soviet intention was demonstrated in Gorbachev's speech in Krasnoyarsk on 16 September 1988:

> We suggest discussing at any level and in any composition the question of creating a negotiating mechanism for considering our and any other proposals relating to security in the Asian Pacific region. This discussion could be started between the USSR, the PRC and the USA as permanent members of the UN security council.[51]

At the Sino-Soviet summit meeting on 16 May 1989, Gorbachev emphasised the creation of a mechanism of regular multilateral consultation that would allow the participation of all interested countries. Three specific suggestions were also made in his speech of April 1991 in the Japanese parliament: "a five-nation conference about security problems to be attended by China, India, the US, Japan and the USSR; a border meeting of the Asian Pacific nations in 1993 and three-way consultations between the Soviet Union and America and Japan".[52] Thus the Soviet Union searched for a comprehensive security conference similar to the Helsinki Model to solve many of the outstanding Asian issues.

Gorbachev's conception of an Asian security conference was similar to the Brezhnev proposals for an Asian collective security system whose principles were almost identical to those incorporated into the Helsinki model. However the Brezhnev proposals excluded the invitation of the major regional powers, especially the US and China. It was viewed as a means to isolate the US and to establish a coalition of states hostile to China. On the other hand, Gorbachev emphasized the need for Chinese and American participation.[53]

The Brezhnev era's misplaced emphasis on military power as a means of security led to a strengthened American military presence and created an alignment of forces that heightened Soviet insecurity.[54] Therefore, the Gorbachev era's policy makers changed Soviet security policy from military means to political ones. Gorbachev believed that the European-CSCE model, though its application would not be mechanical, could be copied in the Asia Pacific region by the same policies, method and tactics that were used in Europe. But, most regional countries were suspicious of Soviet intentions because her previous policies had provoked regional fears of Soviet expansion. Therefore, the Soviet Union needed to cultivate a pacific image in regional countries and create an atmosphere that would be conducive to discussing security matters.

The Soviet Union approached the creation of a new security regime in Asia from three directions. These were: 1) improved bilateral and multilateral relations among regional states; 2) settlement of conflicts in the region; 3) easing of military confrontation through arms control.[55] Soviet scholars and officials believed that the Asia-Pacific region could convene a Helsinki-style conference by the year 2,000.

Gorbachev's attempt to apply the European style CSCE to Asia met with coolness from most regional countries. Scepticism towards Gorbachev's initiatives was most obvious in the United States. The negative US position revealed itself in a speech by US Assistant Secretary of State for East Asian and Pacific affairs, Richard Solomon:

> For our part we remain doubtful about the utility of an all-Pacific security grouping. The sources of tension that remain in the region-indeed, the nature of the security challenges we anticipate in the years ahead do not easily lend themselves to region-wide solution. ... In our view, it is preferable to adapt existing, proven mechanisms to meet challenges of changing circumstances before creating new ones. To the extent that a

border collective framework can help resolve regional security problems the United Nations is proving to have new capacity to play such a role.[56]

US officials maintained that any US negotiations with the Soviet Union on security matters would strengthen Moscow's political position and erode the United State's superiority of influence in the region. In fact, most of the region was in the US sphere of influence. The Soviet Union had greater disadvantages in alliance and diplomatic relations with regional countries than the United States. The United States' allies in the region did not see the need to hold the security conference as a means of enhancing regional security because regional governments shared many US threat perceptions and security objectives.[57]

Japan paid scant attention to the Soviet proposals for collective security in Asia. For Toyko, the Brezhnev scheme calling for "respect for inviolability of national borders" was seen as an attempt to undermine Toyko's claim to the Northern territories. In fact, the Soviet Union was not prepared to tie the territorial questions to the Asian collective security conference even after the Gorbachev proposal. It had no overriding interest in obtaining international recognition of borders in East Asia as it did in Europe. The Japanese Government called for the return of the northern territories as a precondition for the security conference. Its argument was that the Helsinki process was made possible only by West German recognition of the territorial status quo in Central Europe.[58] The position of the Japanese government was that Asian problems had to be solved on the basis of individual talks, not in a larger forum, and the Soviet idea was dismissed as premature. Japan has made efforts to increase its role in regional issues, politicizing the status of economic superpower. In the event of the establishment of collective security systems officially involving the regional powers, it is natural that Japan feared that its influence would be eroded.[59]

China was also disinclined towards the Soviet proposal of an Asian security conference. This is because the idea stemmed from the Brezhnev plan which was intended to create an anti-Chinese military alliance. China justified its resistance to the security conference by referring to its long-standing position that the United States and the Soviet Union were largely responsible for regional conflicts. China's reasons for opposing a multilateral forum were on the grounds that a Helsinki-type conference violated the principles of superpower arms control responsibility.[60] Moreover,

In an Asia-Pacific forum, China's behaviour and capabilities would come under more intense scrutiny. China would be viewed by a number of smaller actors as a dominant player - as part of the 'problems' of security in the region, not just part of the solution - and it would be pressed to accept responsibility for arms competitions and insecurity in the region, particularly in South-East Asia. It would be lumped in with the superpowers.[61]

The Chinese government kept a watchful attitude on Gorbachev's proposals for the Conference, reserving official pronouncements. Unlike the Brezhnev proposal, Gorbachev invited China to the conference, recognizing that it is impossible to achieve peace and security in Asia without the support of China.[62] However, China, like Japan, did not wish the USSR to play a leading role through the conference, as she had in Europe with the establishment of CSCE.

Confidence Building Measures

The Soviet Union was the most enthusiastic proponent of CBMs in East Asia. Brezhnev considered East Asia as the most promising other region for European-style CBMs, and initially put forward the establishment of CBMs between the Major Powers at the 26th Party Congress in 1981:

> That region is the Far East, where such powers as the Soviet Union, China and Japan border on each other. There are also US military bases there. The Soviet Union would be prepared to hold concrete negotiations on confidence-building measures in the Far East with all interested countries.[63]

The proposed CBM ideas were analogous to the measures included in the Helsinki Final Act, viz. prior notification of military exercises and an exchange of observers at these manoeuvres. The Soviet Union advanced these as a means of improving relations between USSR-China and the USSR-Japan. However, because of its heavy military build-up in the region, regional countries doubted Soviet seriousness.

Under Mikhail Gorbachev, new attempts were made to increase confidence among the regional countries. Gorbachev wished to "get rid of the burden of the past and seek new approaches", acknowledging the mistaken policies of predecessors.[64] In contrast to Brezhnev, he emphasised the non-military aspect of security and the application of the Helsinki process of dialogue, talks and agreements in operation. Glaser and Findlay summarise a number of CBMs ideas that were proposed by the Soviet Union.

CBMs conferences
 . 3-way naval talks between USSR, US & Japan.
 . CBMs between the USSR, China, Japan & the two Koreas.
 . the non-use of force.
 . notification of movements & manoeuvres of ground, air and naval forces.

Naval CBMs
 . limitations of the number and scale of naval exercises.
 . ban on naval exercises in international straits and adjacent region.
 . prohibition of the use of combat weapons during exercises.
 . prevention of incidents on the sea.
 . an "open seas" agreement.

ASW
 . the creation of ASW-free zone.
 . ban ASW activities (including air activities) in specified zones.

Air space
 . air communication security and anti-air terrorism.
 . no participation of regional states in the militarization of space.[65]

Unlike the Brezhnev era's mechanical application of European CBMs, most later Soviet CBMs proposals were put forward in a separate context from the Asian security conference and upon a bilateral basis vis-a-vis such individual regional countries as China and Japan. On the other hand they were intended to limit the naval activities of the United States and its allies, while attempting to improve the bilateral relationship with China and Japan. Moreover, many of them were offered by previous Soviet leaders and were parts of applications of Soviet global naval arms control initiatives. The naval CBMs for the Asia/Pacific region were consistent with the initial WTO proposals for the CFE Treaty tabled in Vienna in March 1989.[66] In the absence of "negotiated CBMs" Russia unilaterally applied CBMs to its naval exercises in the region. Foreign military observers and correspondents were invited to watch its Pacific Fleet navy exercises. Military units in the Far East were opened to foreign pressmen in order to make clear whether there was military threat or not.[67]

The United States rejected a number of Soviet CBMs proposals in the Asia/Pacific region, despite its enthusiasm for the application of CBMs in Europe. Secretary of State George Schultz criticized CBMs in Asia on the grounds that they would "weaken strategic deterrence" and "won't close off opportunities for military aggression or reduce the temptations for political intimidation".[68] In fact many of the CBMs proposed by Moscow were designed to constrain US naval operations. Commander-in-chief of the Pacific Fleet, Admiral Lason warned that if implemented they could weaken the West's deterrent postures and consequently increase the risks of aggression.[69]

The American reluctance was not the result of a weakness of its deterrence. In March 1988, Pentagon Director of Naval Intelligence, Rear-Admiral William O. Studeman told Congress that the Soviet navy's out-of-area operations world wide had dropped sharply over the previous three years.[70] An Australian report, quoting highly placed Australian defence officials, stated that the amount of time the Soviet Pacific Fleet had spent out-of-area had halved in the previous three years.[71] One of the main reasons that Washington retained a cautious attitude came from a perceived desirability of not eroding its superiority at sea. As a maritime power, the US saw a need for naval superiority through the forward deployment of its naval forces and consequent guarantee for free and unhindered activity, with access to all international waters.

However, under President Bush, the US attitude on CBMs slightly changed. Some of his advisers were reportedly prepared to "accept discussion of CBMs such as joint notification and observation of larger naval exercises, seeing CBMs as the lesser evil of naval arms control".[72] As shown in the case of the 1972 Incidents at Sea Agreement and the 1989 Prevention of Dangerous Military Activities Agreement, the US Naval opposition was not to CBMs as such, but to CBMs which constrain US advantages.[73] The Bush administration no longer considered Russia as the primary threat. Accordingly, the possibility of the change of US attitude towards the applications of CBMs cannot be ruled out in the region.

The Japanese responses to the Soviet proposals have been very cynical. The Soviet Union approached Japan with regard to CBMs, specifically directing the 1981 proposal to "all interested countries". During his visit to Japan in 1988, Schevardnadze proposed several CBMs between the two countries for the prevention of naval and air incidents in the crowded seas and skies around Japan. His proposals, during his second visit in 1990, were extended to all military activities, including the exchange of observers at military manoeuvres, exchanges on military doctrine, and direct contact between military officials. However, Japan rejected the Soviet proposals on the grounds that the Far East's situation was very different from the European one. Japan demanded the Soviet return of the Northern Territories as a precondition. A prominent official at the Japanese Ministry of Foreign Affairs argued that "even if the USSR gives prior notification of its military manoeuvres in Siberia, it will not be of much use to Japan".[74] However, Japanese advocates of CBMs have criticized the Japanese government for attaching preconditions clearly unacceptable to the Kremlin. Hiroshi Kimura strongly criticized Japan's intention which was to "confuse intentionally or unintentionally, two closely related yet distinct concepts-CBMs and arms control", arguing that the return of the territories belongs to the latter category.[75] Trevor Findlay mentions that Japan intentionally used the CBMs talks for the opposite purpose "as a bargaining chip to secure a political goal rather than to lower tension as a prelude to political accommodation".[76] In fact, as Reinhard Drifte stated, the Japanese Government may fear that the growing consensus over greater defence efforts would be weakened by any official advancement of proposals for CBMs in East Asia.[77]

China accepted the Soviet CBMs proposals along the Sino-Soviet border. Though the application of the CBMs is limited to the border area, it is the first example of European CBMs being applied to East Asia. As in Europe, the CBMs resulted in the reduction of forces along the border and the development of military "transparency". It cannot be denied that the CBMs were facilitated by a number of Soviet unilateral concessions to Chinese demands such as troop withdrawals from the border. China is more in favour of the idea of CBMs than the United States and Japan. The Chinese publicized detailed information on a large-scale military manoeuvre carried out in Northern China in 1981, although it was only after the manoeuvre.[78] Moreover, China had an agreement with Mongolia for building confidence along the frontier through the withdrawal of Soviet troops from Mongolia.

Conventional Arms Reduction

Arms reductions in Northeast Asia have taken place unilaterally without formal agreements. Such unilateral reductions have been made in tacit response to the situation of regional countries and in accord with domestic requirements for adaptation to new security environments. Russia and China have carried out informal, non-negotiated reductions from areas close to their frontiers.[79]

Most of the Soviet Union's arms control approaches towards the region have followed European models such as the "security conference" and "CBMs". However, the reduction approaches are clearly different from European ones. The adopted method of reduction, though at first favouring "specific steps aimed at a balanced reduction", was eventually unilateral or bilateral, not balanced and negotiated multilaterally.[80] The Soviet Union's arms reduction approach can be divided into two stages; ground force reduction on the Sino-Soviet border in the first stage and naval arms reductions in the Northeast and Southeast Pacific in the second stage. The 597,600 forces east of the Urals were reduced by 200,000 men, which included 120,000 men in the Far East.[81] In addition to such reductions a number of changes in force structure were made. The Central Asian Military districts and the Urals Military District were abolished. The national border forces, the internal ministry forces and the railroad construction forces were separated from the Soviet military organisation.

The Soviet Union sought to implement the principle of "reasonable self-sufficiency" in relation to China. IMEMO's 1987 Yearbook emphasised the return of Soviet military forces to pre-1965 levels along the border.[82] The Soviet desire was to reduce border troops to the minimum level required for defence, so that there was "absolute trust". It was well demonstrated in Gorbachev's speech in China: "we are prepared to work for the withdrawal. ... of all military units and armaments from border areas leaving only personnel required for performing routine border guard duties".[83] Such approaches were enough to draw China to the negotiation table of arms reduction.

The adoption of radical reduction in Far East Asia resulted from a variety of reasons. The Soviet military pressure against China led to political rapprochement between China and the US, and between China and Japan. From a Soviet perspective there seemed to have developed a de facto, quasi - or semi-alliance among the three countries for the encirclement of the USSR along its Far Eastern flank. The arms reductions along the border were conceived to loosen the Chinese security relationship with the US and to make the Chinese equidistant in the Sino-Soviet-American triangle.

Another concern which prompted the USSR to introduce unilateral and radical reductions in Asia was its concern over the recruiting of troops. The average manning level of Soviet units deployed in the east was on the whole lower than the average manning level of forces in the west. Consequently mobilization of units to full strength in crisis produced a greater shortfall in Asia than in Europe, so that almost inevitably, sizable manpower reserves west of the Urals were required to complete mobilization in Asia.[84] A further reason came from a labour shortage for the development of Siberia. Around 75 percent of the Soviet population is concentrated in the western part. After World War II the deployment of large-scale forced labour in the eastern part ended and many workers left Siberia.[85] A high turnover of labour had been a constant problem for the construction of the BMA (Baikal-Amur Railway) launched in 1974. Because of the labour shortage, a large proportion of the troops in Siberia had played an economic role in the region. Only 15 percent of the troops were in Category I combat readiness and the remaining 85 percent were engaged in some form of economic activity.[86] Thus the Soviet enthusiasm to develop the resources of the Soviet Far East automatically led to the reduction of the Far East Military District forces.

The Soviet union's arms reduction approach toward China was very successful. Its approach subsequently evolved into the next stage, which focussed on naval arms reduction, especially with the US and Japan. Reports indicate that a number of ships have been cut over the past five years from the Pacific Fleet.[87] From January 1990 it began withdrawing naval and air forces at Cam Ranhn Bay in Vietnam. Even Vladivostok, the most important naval base in the Pacific, begun to be opened to the regional economic special zone.

The Soviet experiences of ground force reduction talks in Europe may have helped the reduction agreement on the Sino-Soviet border. But, its efforts towards naval arms reduction were not successful. Post-Soviet Russian diplomacy has been no more successful on this score. As in Europe, naval arms reduction agreements may not be expected in Northeast Asia in the near future.

Until the 1970s China had maintained a very negative attitude toward conventional arms reduction which was based on its traditional military doctrine of "People's War". The Chinese criticized the MBFR talks, fearing that the reduction of arms on the European front would help Russia increase its threat to the Chinese "Front".[88] Therefore, China was very reluctant to bind itself to any substantial commitment to regional arms control. There were few indications as to the Chinese position on the regional conventional arms control issues, except occasional hints in Chinese government statements and in strategic analyses about China's response to regional arms control.[89] The consistent Chinese argument was that the US and the Soviet Union were largely responsible for the arms build-up in East Asia, and as a first step must take the lead in reducing arms levels with the withdrawal of their foreign troops from the region. Such Chinese proposals were used as political tools for enhancing China's peaceful image, especially in the Third

World, rather than for the practical purpose of solving specific bilateral or multilateral security problems.

But since the early 1980s China has begun to realize the need for arms control as an important means of promoting its own security. The main approach to arms control was unilateral reduction. Thus a unilateral arms reduction of one million troops was slowly carried out between 1982 and 1986. A number of troops in the PLA (People's Liberation Army) such as construction engineers, railway troops, and domestic security and border guard units were transferred to the civilian sector as a result of these structural changes.[90] As well as troop cuts, a number of defence industries were converted to the civilian sector or systems of combined military and civilian production. According to a Chinese newspaper, 42 percent of military factories were already producing civilian goods, while another 29 percent were developing civilian business. The value of civilian goods made by the military in 1990 had increased 6.1 times compared with 1980.

One of the main reasons for the radical and unilateral Chinese reductions was the result of a change of Chinese threat perception of the Soviet Union.[91] China's security outlook in the 1980s had forecast that for 50 years there could be little risk of a major conflict embroiling China. Chinese military analysts had quite sanguine views about a Soviet attack. Bao Shixiu, a researcher at the Academy of Military Sciences noted:

> During a long period after the founding of the People's Republic in 1949, we made a major error in over-estimating the danger of war. The whole national defence and military construction was centred on a full preparation for 'an early war', a major war and a nuclear war.[92]

The Peking Institute for International Strategic Studies analysed that the Soviet Union would have needed four million to five million solders to invade China and would still have been defeated by China's enormous mobilized manpower.[93] It is in fact doubtful whether the Soviet army could have sustained a conventional war against China. Senior Chinese military leaders seemed to believe that the change of Soviet military doctrine from an offensive to a defensive stance based upon "sufficiency" of military forces would strengthen the increased orientation towards peace, as long as Gorbachev remained in power.[94]

The second reason for the Chinese arms reduction was caused by a revision of the traditional People's War strategy which envisaged defeating the enemy through protracted warfare after drawing its armed forces deep into the Chinese territories. The strategy was for a full-scale war to fight off powerful Soviet invasion thrusts, heavily depending upon manpower without taking into account the importance of weapons. However, after the 1979 Vietnam War, Chinese security policy-makers began to devote increasing attention to localized and unexpected conflicts. The war vividly demonstrated the PLA's inability to conduct a limited war on the border opposite to the Sino-Soviet frontier. One of the major reasons why China felt it necessary to keep the war limited was the deterrent function of the Soviet force position upon the Sino-Soviet border.[95] The change of defence strategy led to a more forward defensive posture and consequently helped a shift from quantitative to qualitative-from relying on sheer weight of numbers to emphasizing the need for a more technological, mobile, three-dimensional and machine-oriented posture.[96]

The principle emphasis in China's military cutbacks was centred upon the concept of 'economic disarmament' - reduction of the military's burden on the economy. In fact China stood in a war readiness posture for Sino-Soviet war. Maintenance of the conventional sector was the most expensive item of the Chinese military budget. From the onset of the 1 million reduction, the defence proportion of the national budget has fallen below 10 percent: in 1984;11.9. 1986;8.8, 1987;8.6 and 1988;8.2.[97] In the late 1970s military modernization was listed as the fourth of the Four Modernizations and in the late 1980s as the tenth in the list of ten important tasks facing the nation.[98]

Despite the implementation of the unilateral reduction and the reduction agreement with the USSR along the border, China has still shown no positive response to the proposals for multilateral regional arms control. This may have come from a fear that China would have very little bargaining leverage in multilateral arms talks with the superpowers, because of the inferiority of her military forces. China's participation in such a forum would help China to play a brokering role rather than as a central actor and would thereby undermine her preferred image as a weaker, militarily disadvantaged and purely defensive player.[99]

The United States has maintained a very reluctant attitude towards arms reductions in East Asia. This is in sharp contrast to its positive attitude towards negotiated reduction in Europe. The most important basis for US opposition originates in the belief that regional security should be maintained by preserving its military superiority rather than by negotiating arms reduction agreements which threaten to undermine that superiority. Unlike in Europe the US perceives no urgent requirement to engage in regional multilateral arms reduction talks. In fact there may be no need to address the conventional military balance in the region because of the favourable military situation to the US. The application of the parity-oriented European arms reduction model to Asia would mean the loss of its regional strategic superiority.[100] With the end of the Cold War and collapse of the Soviet Union, there is no longer an obvious enemy for the United States. There is no actual threat to the US in the region. Therefore the US has no need for arms reduction talks to improve regional stability as was the case in Europe. Furthermore the institutional arms control mechanism in the region would help weaken its dominant role as a security guarantor and its influence on the alliance countries. Despite the above, the United States, though strongly opposing a negotiated arms reduction, is however conducting a unilateral reduction in the Pacific. In April 1990, the United States completed a master plan to reduce and reorganize its military presence in the Pacific in three phases over a ten year period.[101] According to the plan, during the first phase (1-3 years) 14,000-15,000 troops are to be reduced from the 135,000 stationed in the region (50,000 in Japan, 44,000 in Korea, 14,800 in the Philippines, 25,000 naval personnel and 800 others). During the second phase (3-5 years), proportionately greater reductions in combat forces will be made. The third phase (5-10 years) will meet with further cuts if situations permit.

The United States still perceives a number of rationales for maintaining a forward deployment of forces in the region, with only small initial reductions despite the change of regional security environment. The US presence in the region is presently justified to maintain regional stability rather than to counter Soviet power. Paul Wolfwitz, Undersecretary of the Department of Defence (DOD), argued that US forces in Asia, which constitute a "relatively small investment" of only 6 percent of the nation's total military establishment, were playing the role of "a regional balancer, honest broker and ultimate security guarantor".[102] During his visit to Japan on 24 February 1990, Defence Secretary Cheney also said US forces had a role in Asia beyond fighting communism.

> If we were to withdrew our forward-deployed forces from the Asia Pacific region, a vacuum would quickly develop. ... There almost surely would be a series of destabilizing regional arms races, an increase in regional tension and possibly conflict.[103]

The principle argument made by US administration officials is that a US withdrawal would eventually result in Japan's reemergence as a giant regional military power which could dominate Asian countries militarily as well as economically. Maj. Gen. Stackpole, commander of Marine Corps Bases in Japan said in an interview with the Washington Post, March 1990, that the American force presence is "a cap in the bottle" to prevent a resurgence of Japanese military power.[104] He argued that US troops should remain in Japan at least for the next decade.

By and large Asia-Pacific countries accept the US logic for its military presence in the region. Most of them see a strong US military presence as the linchpin that prevents a dangerous arms race between Japan and other countries. Bob Hawke, the Australian Prime Minister said that in the changed strategic circumstance of the collapse of the Soviet threat, the main objective of a US military presence should be to encourage regional powers "to refrain from acquiring military force capabilities of a size that would prove destabilizing and set off a regional arms race".[105] In practice, Asian countries have been cautious about the continuing expansion of Japanese industry and capital into Asia. The regional countries' reliance on US military protection is a way of offsetting Japan's economic dominance.

The present "regional balancer role" of the US is based upon the assumption of existing regional forces being maintained at a high level. This may have increased the military burden for the US in the region. The role of the US cannot be maximized without the reduction of the regional forces to a low level. Thus a "negotiated reduction" with the regional powers, rather than a unilateral adjustment of its forces to the new security environment will increase the US role in regional stability, effectively limiting the military forces of China and Russia inside an arms control framework.

Japan has to some extent observed unilateral arms control either voluntarily or through coercion since 1945. Japan's military power is quite incommensurate with its economic status, particularly since she is faced with large and militarily powerful neighbouring countries, China and Russia. The constraints on her military power derive from both internal and external factors.

The origin of arms control in Japan may first of all be found in Article 9 of the Japanese constitution. Article 9 states the renunciation of both war and the threat or use of forces as a means of settling disputes. This has made the neighbouring countries less likely to need to build up forces to counter possible Japanese aggression.[106] The legal constraint on Japan's defence program has contributed to the creation of a relatively modest military power-lacking in long-range strike aircraft, aircraft-carriers, and amphibious or marine forces which could be used for offensive purposes. Consequently the constitution helped produce a variety of arms control measures constraining possible militarism. The major measures are 1) the three non-nuclear principles, 2) the limit on defence expenditure and 3) a ban on sending military personnel for combat abroad.

The three non-nuclear principles which prohibit production, possession and entry into its territory were first enunciated by Prime Minister Sato in December 1967. The nuclear umbrella of the US has helped Japan to keep this policy despite being faced with a nuclear threat from China and the USSR. The limit on defence expenditure had also made an important contribution to arms control because of Japan's huge economic capability for military build-up. Between 1976 and 1987 Japanese governments maintained a ceiling on the defence budget of 1 percent of GNP. This self-imposed limit was symbolic of both the Japanese people's determination not to resurrect Japan's militarist past and the commitment to maintain only those forces needed for self-defence. Forces designed for other purposes could not be acquired without a significant increase in spending. The other major policy covered by the concept of "self defence" is the ban on troops' dispatch abroad for military purpose. [107]

The reason why Japan has continually maintained a limitation upon its military build-up stems from the United States's influence rather than from domestic considerations to limit Japanese military power.[108] Japan has depended upon the security commitment of the US. However, the abolition of the US-Japan security treaty would compel Japan to seek its own military strategy-including perhaps, on option of nuclearization or the pursuit of a position capable of challenging the US and Russia.

It is undoubtedly true that Japan's national arms control measures have to some extent contributed to regional stability. However, they have not translated into a more active regional arms control. There is a clear discrepancy between a high profile arms control policy on the national level and a low profile on the regional and global level.[109] This can be seen in its attitudes towards nuclear and conventional arms control. With China, Japan had a crucial role in extending the INF zero option from Europe to Asia. The Japanese propounded their views during the INF talks to the extent that one US official suggested that the US had "taught the Japanese to speak German".[110] Their enthusiasm for the limitation of nuclear weapons also played an important role in bringing a reluctant China to join the IAEA in January 1984.[111] On the other hand the concept of regional conventional arms control is still not on the agenda of Japanese policy-makers. They have argued that all such negotiations should be delayed until regional political issues, viz. Cambodia, the Korean Peninsula and the disputed territories, have been resolved. They have cited the European example that the problems of Berlin and the borders were agreed before NATO opened conventional force discussion. Gerald Segal says that "Japanese have so far usually raised the territorial dispute as a reason for avoiding regional arms control".[112]

The Japan-USSR border dispute remains the core variable in regional security between the Major Powers since the Sino-Soviet border treaty was concluded. Japan has become a prisoner of the territorial issue. In the long run, the continuation of the territorial precondition for regional arms control runs counter to Japan's interest in seeking stability in the Asia-Pacific region. Japan should realize that the European CSCE and conventional forces talks were held after the FRG completed the multilateral border treaties with West German concessions. Japan also might note the warning of its arms control expert, Tsuyoshi Hasegawa that "unless we think seriously about our approach to Asian arms control both intellectually and at the policy level, we will face a serious strategic crisis".[113]

The Applicability of the European Arms Control Model

It is generally said that arms control measures institutionalized in Europe are not applicable to the Asia-Pacific region. The reasons are mainly based upon the dissimilarities of the strategic environments between Asia and Europe. There exist a number of obstacles to arms control agreement because of the geographic asymmetries and different force structures between the two military superpowers, asymmetric threat perception and the regional diversity and historical rivalries.

Given the unique circumstance of the arms control process in Europe, the Asian region constitutes a very different strategic environment from Europe. Thus, the strategic environment of the Asia-Pacific region is more complex and undefined, and the regional security problems are less amenable to arms control solutions than in Europe.[114] Most Asian countries, which are committed to the security umbrella of the US, also oppose regional arms control that would result in a limitation of US military power in the region. Such states have negative attitudes towards applicability of European models to the region.

However, given that these models enhanced stability in Europe, even in the situation of the sharp confrontation between two heavily armed blocs, there are many potential areas where the European models could be applied to unstable or conflict-ridden areas of the Asia Pacific. The potential areas are as follows: the Korean Peninsula, the Northern Territories, China/Taiwan, China/Vietnam, India/Pakistan, Indochina-Vietnam/Cambodia, Thailand/Cambodia, Spratly Islands. Among these areas, the most critical region is Northeast Asia which has high potentiality of conflict between powerful regional nations because of dense force concentration and interest convergence. The region is a relatively compact region, so that the naval and air forces of disputing countries come into frequent and close contact with the attendant risk of misadventures. Events during the 1980s demonstrated the possibilities of the risk of direct confrontation. In September 1983, a South Korean airliner was shot down by the Soviet air forces over Sakhalin Island because of the misunderstanding of its intelligence collecting activity. In March 1984, a Soviet submarine collided with an American aircraft carrier and a month later the Soviet aircraft carrier 'Minsk' hit an American Frigate.[115] Even though Russia has greatly reduced its forces, its potential threat to the regional countries still remains. Furthermore, small regional countries perceive threats from China and Japan as potential military powers in the near future.

Faced with a common Soviet threat, regional countries coalesced and some conflicts between them were neutralized. The traditional antagonisms were not readily apparent on the surface because of the requirement for strategic alignment in the days of the Cold War. But, as relations between the superpowers eased, regional rivalries have become less constrained by past strategic alignments. The historical antagonisms and rivalries are increasingly resurfacing in the region. The rival nationalisms have long been apparent. Under such circumstances, the risk of major conflict is growing. However there are potentially a number of traditional basic arms control objectives which can be met thereby minimizing the risk of an accidental war by miscalculation and reducing the arms competition of the military equations in North-East Asia. The strategic situation provides the most obvious reason to manage the instability and reduce the risks of war.

Arms control in Europe was a product of the Cold War. The Asian countries might appear misguided if they seek to apply the European model to the region in a situation characterized by the end of Cold War. In fact such a model cannot be applied without modifications because of the divergent nature of threat and conflicts in the region. The Asian-Pacific region calls for particular measures that are responsive to the special needs of the regional situation.

Table 6-3   Comparison of Strategic Environments between the Asia-Pacific Region and Europe

	Asia	Europe
Geography	vast ocean	continent
Politics		
culture	not shared	share
territory	disputes	solved
mediators	none exist	neutral nations
Defence		
common threat	no	existed
alliance	no blocs	bipolar blocs
Superpower		
main strategy	maritime	land
power balance	US dominance	parity
Arms Control		
experience	no	yes
CBMs	naval	ground
verification	difficult	easy

Sources: Trevor Findlay, "North Pacific Confidence Building: the Helsinki/Stockholm model", *Working Paper,* No. 44 (Canberra: Peace Research Centre, June 1988), Andrew Mack, "Arms Control in the North Pacific: problems and process, *Working Paper*, No. 88 (Canberra: Peace Research Centre, August, 1990), pp. 1-10.

The Application of a Security Conference

It is important to observe that European arms control has been primarily approached in the context of political security. The political security conference has played a major role as a vehicle for arms control. Due to the differences of security environment between Europe and Asia, many observers dismissed the applicability of a security conference similar to CSCE for the region. However, recently the application of a European style security conference has increasingly been suggested as an useful model for solving the security problems in the region.

The idea that the Asia Pacific region should have its own security forum has been slowly promoted between countries outside Northeast Asia. On 27 July, 1990, Australian Foreign Minister, Gareth Evans proposed a Europe-Style CSCA-the Conference on Security and Cooperation in Asia.[116] His argument was that a new system was needed to give a new impact to the gradual change in Asia and respond to the global shift from US-USSR bipolarity to multipolarity in power including Japan, the European community, China and India as powers of actual or potential global influence. Canada has also made a similar proposal. During his visit to Japan in 29 July, 1990 Canadian Foreign Minister, Joe Clark proposed a European style security regime. His version was very much a North Pacific-oriented body, involving Canada, the Soviet Union, the United States, Japan, China and if possible, the two Koreas and Taiwan.[117]

Apart from the proposals of officials, some analysts suggest the establishment of a security commitment or arms control regime in the region. Desmond Ball proposes "the establishment of 'building blocks' - a multiplicity of sub-regional arrangements dealing with various security issues and involving various memberships" prior to a CSCA for the creation of political conditions conducive to formal arms control agreement.[118] Advancing a similar view, Patrick M. Cronin proposes to "try to seize the half-full side of the basin and start with a building-bloc approach that revolves around specific issues such as nuclear proliferation and economic prosperity" on the basis of the present bilateral security arrangement.[119] Given most Asian countries' security commitment to the US, different geostrategic circumstances, too many outstanding issues of territorial claims and a collection of identifiable sub-regions, the security-related sub-regional building block approach might be a more realistic idea at the present time than the notion of a broad CSCA.

There are a number of reasons why an institutionalized arms control mechanism is required to improve the stability of the Northeast Asian region. Even though the Soviet/Russian threat is fading, there are still potentially many possibilities for conflict between the regional countries. The military confrontation of North and South Korea is the most immediately dangerous to regional security. The continuation of Moscow-Tokyo military tension is still beyond the thaw of the cold war because of the border dispute. China and Japan also continue to develop as regional military powers. The regional countries share a long turbulent record of military rivalry. In this century the four major powers experienced many wars against each other; Russia-Japan in 1904, China-Japan in 1936, Japan-USSR & US during World War II, the Sino-Soviet War in 1967 and 1969 and Soviet-US Cold War. The divergence of their interests, potential enmities and possession of high levels of military force might surface to produce another military confrontation in the future.

The other reason for arms control derives from the possibility of potential conflict between the US and regional countries. Some conflict can be caused by a big trade imbalance between the US and regional countries. Out of a $109 billion US trade deficit in 1989, Tokyo ($49 billion), Taipei ($13 billion), and Seoul ($6. 3 billion) accounted for $ 68.3 billion, nearly two-thirds of the total. Many Asian officials fear that military links with the US will be strained by a possibility that Washington tries to use its power to exact trade concessions from Japan and other economically dynamic Asian countries.[120] Some scholars warn of a possibility of a trade war between the US and Japan. Friedman and Lebard argued that America should regard Japan as a greater threat than the Soviet Union. They argue that within 20 years the US and Japan will probably again be at a war in the Pacific because of the trade deficit.[121]

Thus, if conflicts occur between the US and regional countries or between its allied countries, who will play the role as balancer or protector of regional security? US Congressman Solarz suggests the ambiguity of the commitment of American military power to one side or the other in any potential future regional conflict.[122] The present security situation which relied heavily on the US against the Soviet threat may not solve these problems. Until now the Soviet threat has helped East Asian countries to ally with the US or between themselves. However, in the absence of a single threat, a number of simmering potential conflicts may boil over in the region. Therefore the regional countries ought to assume some urgency to establish institutionalized security regimes such as an arms control mechanism for managing military power at low levels and discouraging the use of force.

The Application of CBMs

The military confrontation between the regional powers has recently been reduced in the region. But the deep seated mistrust arising out of the rivalry between such states still remains. Therefore, even a slight military accident or conflict of interests can escalate to crisis situation or a military clash because of the historical legacy. Following the experience of the application of land CBMs along the Sino-Soviet border, naval CBMs could be primarily considered in the context of prevention of crisis.

The already established naval CBMs between the Soviet Union and the US can be extended to the other states in the North-Pacific region. The most relevant CBMs are the "Incidents at Sea Agreement" and the "Prevention of Dangerous Military Activities". The Soviet Union had bilateral arrangements with several western countries; UK, US, the FRG, France,

Canada, Italy and Norway. However, China and Japan are not currently signatories of such an agreement.[123]

The other potential area for CBMs is the maritime boundaries of Northeast Asia: the Yellow Sea, East China and the Donghae Sea (Japan Sea). The claims of the territorial seas overlap because of national ownership of marine resources. China and North Korea declared so-called military warning zones in excess of the limits permitted by the international law of the sea.[124] Thus the maritime boundaries of the region create the potentiality of conflict.

The potential CBMs in the air is the revision of the "Air Safety Agreement" concluded in 1985 between the US, the Soviet Union and Japan. In the aftermath of the shooting-down of the Korean airliner, KAL 007 off Sakhalin Island in September 1983 the three countries concerned had a regional agreement increasing the safety of civilian air traffic in the North Pacific. The key factor of the agreement was to exchange information between aviation control centres in Tokyo, Anchorage and Khabarosvsk when civilian airliners encounter problems and airliners enter the Russian flight information region.[125] However, the agreement omitted efforts to solve some conflicts in the context of regional stabilization. It applies only to civil flights and does not include military activity. The signatories to the agreement also consist of only the countries directly concerned in the 1983 incident without the participation of China. The inclusion of China and extension from the civil flights to military ones could prevent crisis in the air space of the region.

For crisis management, hot lines can be listed in the application of CBMs between the regional powers. The regional nuclear powers in Europe, UK and France, have individually maintained such hot lines with the Soviet Union/Russia. However, China (and Non-nuclear Japan) have no means of direct communication with Russia in a crisis. The establishment of hot lines between the nuclear countries is the most urgent agenda for the prevention of a nuclear crisis in the region.[126]

The most potentially relevant CBMs to the region will be "transparency measures" which were successfully applied in Europe. Through transparency, suspicion and prejudice can be reduced between regional countries. In the absence of reliable information about potential enemies, intelligence assessments tend to be based toward worst-case scenarios because of the dense concentration of forces in the region. Andrew Mack suggests the application of a wide range of specific transparency or information measures:

- to exchange data on military budgets, force levels, weapons platforms building program, retirement program and so forth.
- for the advance notification of agreed categories of exercises.
- for the exchange of observers on agreed categories of exercises and
- for the institutionalization of high-level dialogue on military doctrine and the particular concerns each side has about the other's strategy and force structure, etc.[127]

In fact the absence of actual threats might to some extent reduce the importance of information measures such as advance notification of military exercises or verification of military activities. On the other hand, because of rivalry, each regional power has very deep concerns about the military condition of other regional powers. Therefore the exchange of data such as force levels, structures and military programs could provide states with the certainty of each participating powers benign intentions. Further such measures can contribute to not only a build-up of confidence against any potential threats, but also an early warning of a particular state's change of intention.

The Application of Multilateral Arms Reduction

The enormous military forces of the regional powers have not been reduced despite the advent of a new security environment whereby the Soviet threat has faded in the region. Though partly reducing those ground forces built against the Soviet threat, China has simultaneously increased its defence budget since 1989. Instead of ground forces, emphasis is also being placed on the development of naval and air forces. Its development plan to the end of the century calls for a three-stage expansion of the navy: a bigger and better navy comprising nuclear and conventional submarines and more naval aircraft-probably including aircraft carriers.[128] With the increment of its marine resources, the navy is being transformed from coast-hugging status to a blue-water force able to operate in the Pacific, a development of growing concern to other states in the region.

Japan also gives many indications of development into a military power, gradually relaxing its establishment arms control measures. The limitation of defence expenditure within the 1 percent ceiling of GNP was abandoned in 1987 by Nakasone's cabinet. Nakasone pointed out that the standard must be what is needed for Japan's defence without dependence on budget figures. According to the amendment, the Cabinet adopted a multi-year objective; that is 1.04 percent of the projected GNP for five years.[129] The surprising change of national arms control measures is an attempt to expand the role of its Self-Defence Forces.

Japan failed to send its troops to the Gulf war for the peace-keeping missions of the UN As a result, Japan was left standing on the side-lines at the end of war, whilst contributing $11 billion to the US-led multinational forces.[130] Thus the Kaifu Cabinet decided to send minesweepers to the Gulf. The four wooden-hulled anti-mine boats and two support ships hardly constituted a major display of military power. However, it had a particular meaning in that it was the first time Japanese forces had served overseas since the end of World War II. What is more important is that opinion polls and editorials were generally supportive whereas four years earlier, when the Western allies asked Japan to send minesweepers to the Gulf to find Iranian mines, the idea sparked such bitter controversy that it was quickly dropped.[131] An exercise involving some 300 troops with their tanks, 203 mm self-propelled guns, 155 mm howitzers and anti-tank helicopters was conducted on a firing range in Hawaii in late 1992. Japan's Defence Agency says that the military drill overseas was planned because of the limited space for the exercise within Japan.[132] This was the first overseas combat drill by the Japanese military since World War II. Japan has also been very enthusiastic to protect the 1000 nautical miles SLOC. Fulfilling that mission will require the build-up of maritime forces.

These regional military escalations are paradoxical on the ebb of arms reduction in Europe. The cause of the reverse tide first of all derives from the absence of regional multilateral arms reduction talks. Many observers dismiss the possibility of multilateral arms reduction and instead support bilateral arms reduction talks. It is true that because of the lack of symmetry in military requirements a balanced force reduction of European style is very difficult. However, conversely, such divergences of potential threat manifest an increased possibility for multilateral arms reduction talks. In the light of regional rivalries, the result of bilateral arms reduction between two opposing countries would be very problematical. For example, naval forces reduced on the basis of the Japan-Russia bilateral talks will be vulnerable to the Chinese naval forces not involved in the reduction. As seen from the experience of the Sino-Soviet border treaty, the reduction of ground forces between China and the Soviet Union did not affect Japanese military considerations.

The other rationale for negotiated multilateral talks is based upon the prevention of strategic alignment between regional states. Off and on in modern history, the change of strategic alignment has changed the "balance of power" in the region. Unlike the long continuation of bipolarity between

NATO and WTO, the bipolar structure of US-Japan vs USSR-China was broken by the "China Card". China's role has made it difficult to maintain the balance of strength in the bilateral structure between the superpowers. As a result it resulted in the Soviet military build-up. Thus multilateral talks limiting the role of the balancer, playing off bilateral relations against each other, will contribute to bring a stable balance in the region.

There is also an obvious parallel between European concerns about a resurgent Germany and Asian concerns about Japan. Andrew Mack and Desmond Ball make a similar point:

> NATO's key tasks were to 'keep the Russian out of Western Europe, the Americans in and the Germans down'. For many Asian states (and Russia), the US-Japan security Treaty is valued more as an institution for restraining potential Japanese military resurgence by 'enmeshing' Japan in a tight alliance relationship, than as an alliance for defending Japan from aggression.[133]

The Soviet Union attempted to enmesh German forces by binding the ceiling of the united German Forces through MBFR and the CFE treaty. Thus German potential military resurgence was restrained. The absence of actual threat in the region may cause the US-Japan security treaty, which has ruled out any possibility of renewed Japanese militarism, to be weakened. As in the German case of the CFE Treaty, Japanese militarism can be restrained through a regional multilateral arms control mechanism in the same way that Germany is constrained in the CFE Treaty.

The sceptics argue that because of the lack of common ideological, political or economic interests common security thinking akin to Europe could not be applied to the region. This explanation had some persuasiveness in the period of the Cold War. Now, however, ideological competition between the regional powers no longer exists. Even the Chinese attachment to communist ideology is not a serious obstacle to the development of political and economic relations. They have sufficient interest in promoting closer economic cooperation. Trade volumes between regional countries are increasing. The cooperation on capital, labour and information including technology is rapidly growing in the region. Regional states, particularly China and Russia, have suffered a domestic economic burden from the maintenance of enormous military forces which itself was a big obstacle to economic cooperation with the other regional developed states.

Russia and China will be likely to informally cut their forces by the "economic disarmament" standard and domestic defence planning.

However, there remains the possibility that the reduced forces will be again mobilized unilaterally as long as the reductions are not binding in any negotiated rules of arms control. The level of their informal reduction could be reciprocated with the other regional states in the framework of institutionalized regional arms talks.

Conclusion

There is no enthusiasm for regional arms control in Northeast Asia except for the 1990 Sino-Soviet arms control agreement. The regional powers have expressed little interest in multilateral negotiated arms control mechanisms similar to CSCE, CBMs and CFE in Europe. They each have a different perspective on regional arms control. The Soviet Union took initiatives in the past and China to some extent still has a positive attitude, while the US and Japan are very reluctant to enter into regional arms control talks. Unlike Europe, as seen from the case of the Sino-Soviet border treaty, arms control has been made at the bilateral level rather than at the multilateral negotiated-arms control level. The other regional powers were completely negative to the Soviet Union's introduction of European models to Asia.

It is true that unlike Europe the security situation in the region has not the same urgency to engage the reluctant countries in arms control talks. Even in the absence of negotiated regional arms control agreements, relative stability has been maintained. East Asia has traditionally been a region of US dominance in alliances and in military power-though this was challenged by the Soviet Union's rapid military expansion in the late 1970s. Because of the certainty of the US security commitment, the regional countries' threat perception has been abstract and intellectualized rather than pressing and personal.[134] It may also be said that in the current climate of relaxed tension there is no imperative to a speedily negotiated arms control agreement, since there is no real threat. However, in the long run the alliance security framework of Northeast Asia that was formed in the context of Soviet threat is no longer appropriate to the new regional order. It would be wise for the Major Powers to start thinking about developing a new framework to fit the new realities.

Europe is committed to produce a new security framework for maintaining regional stability and to continue arms control even in the absence of the Soviet threat. Unlike Europe, in Northeast Asia arms control takes place tacitly without formal mechanisms. But it is doubtful that this conduct will contribute to regional stability in the long run. It cannot be excluded that, with the decline of US and Russian influence in the region, some conflicts will emerge between regional countries and between the superpowers and regional countries. Moreover, the regional countries' uneasiness is growing over Japan's expanding military potential. As in Europe, Northeast Asia is obligated to establish an institutionalized arms control mechanism to manage the potential regional conflicts between rival countries. In the context of prevention of regional conflict, the European multilateral arms control mechanisms could be applied to this region.

NOTES

1. Richard H. Solomon, "The Pacific Basin: Dilemmas and Choices for American Security", *Naval War College Review*, Vol. XXXX, No.1, (Winter 1987), p. 38.
2. John Borawski, "Mutual Force Reductions in Europe from A Soviet Perspective", *Orbis*, Vol.22, No.4, (1979), p. 864.
3. Rajan Menon, "New Thinking and Northeast Asian Security", *Problems of Communism*, (March-June 1989), p. 20.
4. *International Herald Tribune*, 18 January, 1983.
5. Herbert Y. Schandler, "Arms control in Northeast Asia", The *Washington Quarterly*, (Winter 1987), p. 70.
6. Stephen Kirby, "Linking European and Pacific Strategies.", *The Pacific Review*, Vol. l,. No. 3, (1988) p. 241.
7. Gerald Segal, "A New Order in Northeast Asia", *Arms Control Today*, Vol. 21, No. 7, (September 1991), p. 15. He argued that Soviet Union moved some 57,300 ground weapons from Europe to Asia after the conclusion of the CFE Treaty.
8.. Bill Hayden, "Security and Arms Control in the North Pacific" in A. Mack & P. Keal (ed), *Security and Arms Control in the North Pacific* (Sydney: Allen & Unwin Australia pty Ltd, 1988), p. 2.
9. Byang-Jun Ahn, "The Strategic Trends in East Asia and their Implications", presented at the 3rd KIDA/CSIS International Defence Conference (Seoul, 5-6 November, 1990), p. 4.
10. Samuel S. Kim, "Superpower cooperation in Northeast Asia", in Roger E. Kanet & Edward A. Kolodziej, *The Cold War as cooperation: Superpower cooperation in regional conflict Management.* (London: Macmillian Academy and Professional LTD, 1991), P. 386.
11. Ahn, op. cit., p. 8.
12. Robert A. Scalapino, *Major Power Relations in Northeast Asia* (University Press of America: New York, 1987), p. 4 and 20.
13. China sought advanced Soviet SU-27 fighters from the Soviet Union, *The Korean Herald*, 31 October, 1990. In return for providing the USSR with food, tea, cigarettes and other consumer goods worth $ 730 million, China wanted to buy combat aircraft, missiles and tanks. *Time,* 1 April 1991, p. 19.
14. Richard H. Solomon & Mastaka Kosaka (eds), *The Soviet Far East military build-up: nuclear dilemmas and Asian security* (Auburn House Publishing Company: Dover & Massachusetts, 1986), p. 49.
15. Menon, op. cit., p. 14.
16. Research Institute for Peace and Security, Tokyo, *Asian Security 1989-90* (Brassey's, 1989), p. 73. The US estimates put Soviet Far East assets at 57 divisions (averaging more than 10,000 personnel in each division, 14,9000 tactical aircraft and a Pacific Fleet of some

77 major surface warsphips and 98 submarines. "Asia: a shift in balance", *Jane's Defence Weekly,* 3 March, 1990. p. 390.
17. Admiral F. Lehman, Jr. "The Maritime Strategy", *Proceedings,* February, 1986, (Supplement), pp. 30-40.
18. Georges Tan Eng Bok, "How Does the PLA cope with Regional Conflict and Local War", in Richard H. Yang (ed), *China's Military: The PLA in 1990/1991* (Boulder, CO.: Westview Press, 1991), p. 152.
19. Sarah M. Taylor, "Military balances in Northeast Asia", in Stephen P. Gibert (ed), *Security in Northeast Asia: Approaching Pacific Century* (Colorado: Westview Press, 1988), p. 146. For reference on Soviet military deployment in areas close to Japan, See *Defence of Japan 1991* (Japan's Defence Agency, 1991), p. 31.
20. Ibid.
21. Masahi Nishihara, "Soviet Threat" in Eric Grove (ed), *Global Security: North American, European and Japanese Interdependence in the 1990s* (London: Brassey's, 1991), p. 55. Japan argues that Russia has deployed the latest T-80 tanks in the Far East which were previously seen only in Europe. *Defence of Japan 1991* (Tokyo: Defence Agency, 1991), p. 30.
22. Tai Ming Chung, *Growth of Chinese Naval Power: Priorities, Goal, Missions and Regional Implications* (Singapore: Institute of Southeast Asian Studies, 1990), pp. 19-36.
23. Ibid.
24. Defence of Japan 1991 reported that Russia deployed in the Far East one-fourth to one-third of the total Russian strategic missile forces-38 of 175 army divisions, 75 of 240 major surface combatants, 105 of 290 submarines and 2060 of 8,380 combat aircraft.
25. David Rees, *Soviet border problems: China and Japan* (London: Institute for the Study of Conflict, 1982), p. 22.
26. Andrew Mack & Martin O'Hare, "Moscow-Tokyo and the Northern Territories Dispute", *Asian Survey,* Vol. xxx, No. 4. (April, 1990), p. 389.
27. SUPAR Report, No. 9. (July 1990), p. 50. *New Times,* No. 6, (February 1990), 6-12.
28. FBIS, SOV. December 31, 1991, 91/251, p. 55. The Far Eastern Association, composed of leaders of the Yakut Autonomous Soviet Republic, the Khabarosk and Primorskii (Maritime) Krai, the Jewish Autonomous, Amur, Kamchatka, Margadan and Sakhalin regions, was formed in mid-August 1990 at a meeting in Khabarovsk to promote social and economic cooperation. *Pacific Research,* Vol. 5, No. 2, (May 1992). The disputed islands are inhabited by 25,000 Russian citizens. Seventy-four percent of those living in the Province of Sakhalin and the Kuriles are opposed to giving up a 'single island'.
29. *The Korea Herald,* March 22, 1991.
30. "Japan, Gorbachev and price of peace", *The Economist,* 30 March 1991, p. 55.
31. "Plan to Settle Russo-Japan Dispute Offered", *Los Angeles Times,* 19 April , 1992.
32. *Financial Times,* 9 September 1990.
33. James F. Giblin, "National strategies and Japan's Northern Territories", *Naval War College Review,* (Winter, 1987), p. 62.
34. For references about the 1978 China-Japan conflict, see Daniel Tretiak, "The Sino-Japanese treaty of 1978: the Senkaku Incident prelude", *Asian Survey,* vol. xviv no. 2. (Dec. 1978) p. 1235. and about the 1990 Taiwan-Japan conflict, see The Free China Journal, Oct 25, 1990, and *The Independent,* 22 October, 1990.
35. "Testing the Waters", *Far Eastern Economic Review,* 12 March 1992, p.8. China also included the sovereignty over the "Spratly" and "Paracel" islands in the law. It renewed the disputes with neighbouring countries.

36. "Seismic" surveys indicate that the islands are sitting on top of potential rich oil deposits, though there has been little exploitation so far. *Far Eastern Economic Review*, 1 November, 1990 p. 19.
37. "Sino-Soviet Joint Communique (Moscow, 19 May, 1991)", *Beijing Review*, 27 May - 2 June, 1991.
38. Rees, op. cit. pp. 14-15.
39. *The Military Balance 1985-1986* (London: IISS, 1985), p. 31.
40. Menon. op. cit., p. 13.
41. Dan L. Strode, "Arms Control and Sino-Soviet Relations", *Orbis,* Vol. 28, No. 1, (Spring 1984), pp. 184-185.
42. *Far Eastern Economic Review,* 25 May, 1989.
43. Gerald Segal, "Arms control and Sino-Soviet relations", in Gerald Segal (ed), *Arms Control in Asia* (London: The Macmillian Press Ltd, 1987), p. 45.
44. Strode, op. cit., p. 187.
45. *Pacific Research*, Vol.2, No.3. August 1989.
46. *Far Eastern Economic Review*, 26 April, 1990, p. 13.
47. Alexei V. Zagorsky, "Confidence-Building Measures: An Alternative for Asian-Pacific Security ?", *The Pacific Review*, Vol.4, No.4, (1991), p. 355.
48. *Far Eastern Economic Review*, 19 March, 1992, p. 13.
49. "Sino/Soviet Border Talks", *Pacific Research,* , Vol.4, No.1, (February 1991) p. 14.
50. *The New York Times,* 22 May, 1985.
51. "Excerpts from Mikhail Gorbachev's speech in Krannoyarsk on 16 September, 1988. *Far Eastern Affairs*, no. 1. 1989
52. *The Independent*, 18 April, 1991
53. Elizabeth Wishmick, "Soviet Asian Collective Security Policy from Brezhnev", *Journal of Northeast Asian Studies,* Vol 7 (1988), pp. 3-28.
54. Menon, op. cit., p. 27.
55. Bonnie S. Glaser, "Soviet, Chinese and American Perspectives on Arms Control in Northeast Asia", *Working Paper*, no. 28 (Australian National University, Peace Research Centre, 1988), p. 13.
56. *Pacific Research*, vol. 4. no. 1, (February 1991), p. 20. Sources: Richard H. Solomon, 'Asian Security in the 1990s: Integration in Economics; Diversity in Defence', address to the University of California, at San Diego, Graduate School of International Relations and Pacific Studies, (30 October, 1990), pp. 5-6.
57. Andrew Mack, "Problems and prospects for arms control in the North Pacific", in Andrew Mack and Keal P.(eds), *Security & arms control in the North Pacific,* (Sydney: Allen & Unwin, 1988), pp. 252-270.
58 Reinhard Drifte, *Japan's rise to international responsibilities: the case of arms control* (London: The Athlone Press, 1990), p. 69.
59. For Japan's role in Northeast Asia, See Edward J. Lincoln, "Japan's role in Asia-Pacific cooperation: Dimensions, prospects and problems", *Journal of Northeast Asian Studies,* vol. viii, (1989), pp. 5-23.
60. Alastair Iain Johnston, "China and arms control in the Asia-Pacific region", in Frank C. Langdon and Douglas A. Ross (ed), *Superpower maritime strategy in the Pacific* (London: Routledge, 1990), p. 193.
61. Ibid. p. 185.
62. "Neoglobalism-a source of tension in Asia and the World at Large", *Far Eastern Affairs,* Vol.135, No.1 (1987), p. 26.

63. Report of the Central Committee of the CSPU to the 26th Congress of the Communist Party of the Soviet Union (Moscow: Novosti Press Agency publishing House, 1981), pp. 38-39. Quoted in Asada, "Masahiko, Confidence Building Measures in East Asia: A Japanese Perspective", *Asian Survey*, Vol.XXVIII, No.5, (May 1988), pp. 491-492.
64. Text of speech by Mikail Gorbachev in Vladivostok, 28 July. 1986 in Ramesh Thakur & Carlyle A. Thayer (eds), *The Soviet Union as an Asian power* (London: Westview Press, 1987). p. 226.
65. Glaser, op. cit, pp.11-2 and Trevor Findlay, "Asia/Pacific CSBMs: Prospectus", *Working Paper*, No. 90 (Canberra: Peace Research Centre, 1990), p. 17.
66. US Congress, *Arms Control in Asia and US Interests in the Region*, Hearings before Subcommittee on Asian and Pacific Affairs, One Hundred First Congress (Washington D.C.: GPO, 1991), p. 39.
67. *The Korea Herald*, 7 November, 1991.
68. Banning N. Garret and Bonnie S. Glaser, "Arms control in the management of US security interests in the Asia-Pacific region", in *Superpower maritime strategy in the Pacific* p. 155.
69. *Pacific Research*, vol.2, no.4, (November 1989), p.11. The objections of US officials on the application of naval CBMs were well demonstrated in the US Congress Hearings, *Arms Control in Asia and US Interests in the Region*
70. Andrew Mack and Andrew McClean, "The growing interest in Asia-Pacific arms control issues, *Working Papers*, No. 75 (Australian National University, Peace Research Centre, 1989), p. 3
71. Ibid.
72. Findlay, "Asia/Pacific CBMs", p. 19.
73. Ibid., p. 18.
74. Hiroshi Kimura, "The Soviet Proposal on Confidence-Building measures and the Japanese Response", in Joshua D. Katz and Tilly C. Frieman Lichtschein (eds), *Japan's New World Role* (London: Westview Press, 1983), p. 25.
75. Ibid. p. 90.
76. Findlay, "Asia/Pacific CSBMs", p. 12.
77. Drifte, *Japan's rise to international responsibilities*, p. 68.
78. Asada, "Confidence-Building Measures in East Asia: A Japanese Perspective", p. 496.
79. For detailed references, see Gerald Segal, "Informal Arms control: The Asian Road to Conventional Reductions," *Arms Control Today*, (May 1989), p. 16.
80. 115. In his speech in Vladivostok, 28 July 1986, Gorbachev declared that "the USSR is prepared to discuss with the PRC specific steps aimed at a balanced reduction in the level of land forces". Thakur & Thayer, op. cit., p. 224.
81. Gen. Viktor I. Novozhilov, commander of the Russian Far Eastern Military District revealed in 1990 that equipment reductions since 1988 were; tanks by 66 percent, armoured personnel carriers by 80 percent, artillery systems by 60 percent and combat planes by 50 percent see "Soviet Views on the Problems of Security in the Asia-Pacific Region" at the 3rd International Conference (Seoul: 4-5 November , 1991).
82. *Disarmament and Security* (IMEMO, 1987), p. 429-430.
83. *Far Eastern Economic Review*, 25 May, 1989, p. 13.
84. Harry Gelman, *The Soviet Military Leadership and the Question of Soviet Deployment Retreats* (RAND cooperation, R-3664-AF, 1988), p. 32.
85. "Glasnost's Asian Frontier", *Far Eastern Economic Review* 4 August, 1988. p. 4
86. Tsuyoshi Hasegawa, "Soviet Arms Control Policy in Asia and the Japan US Alliance", *Japan Review of International Affairs*, Fall/Winter, 1988, p. 228.

87. See the reference "81". Gen. Novzhilov argued that in 1984-1990 the Pacific fleet of the USSR navy was cut by 73 battle ships and the nuclear submarine patrolling was limited only by the waters close to the USSR.
88. John Borawski, "Mutual Force Reduction in Europe from a Soviet Perspective", *Orbis*, vol.22, no.4 (1979), p.865. For a detailed reference to Chinese views on MBFR, see Alastair I. Johnston, "China and Arms Control: Emerging Issues and Interests in the 1980s" (The Canadian Centre for Arms Control and Disarmament, *Aurora Paper* 3, 1986.), pp. 50-52.
89. Alastair Iain Johnston, "China and arms control in the Asia-Pacific region", p. 173, in *Superpower maritime strategy in the Pacific.*
90. See *Asian Security 1985 and 1986* (Research Institute for Peace and Security, Tokyo), p.78 and p.81. *Far Eastern Economic Review*, 27 February 1992, p. 15. Tai Ming Cheung argued that Peking would further cut some 260,000 out of the PLA` 3.2 million troops in the 1991-95 five year defence plan in a bid to modernize the military.
91. The changes of Chinese perception of the Soviet threat were well demonstrated by Yolanda Simmons White, *The New Arms Control-Mindedness of the Chinese* (Ann Arbor, University Microfilms, 1982.), pp. 49-101.
92. "Modern PLA Advance Along the Road to Peace", *China Daily*, 30 July 1987.
93. White, op. cit., p. 95.
94. "China's Changing Doctrine", *Jane's Defence Weekly*, 10 March, 1990.
95. Gelman, "Soviet Military Leadership,", p. 28.
96. Tai Ming Cheung, "Disarmament and Development in China", *Asian Survey*, Vol.xxviii, no.7, (July, 1988), p. 773.
97. *Asian Security 1988-89* (Research Institute for Peace and Security; Toyko, 1988), p. 66.
98. *Asian Security 1989-90* (Research Institute for Peace and Security; Tokyo, 1989), p. 92.
99. Johnston, "China and Arms Control in the Asia-Pacific Region", p. 185.
100. Andrew Mack, "Arms Control in the Pacific: the Naval Dimension", *Working Paper*, no.88, (Canberra, 1990), p. 7.
101. US Department of Defence, A Report submitted to the Congress, *Strategic Framework for the Pacific Rim* (19 April, 1990)
102. "US Report on future Asian Defence unveiled Flurry of Signals", *Far Eastern Economic Review*, 3 May 1990, p. 10.
103. "Cheney's message: US troops to stay in Asia", *The Korea Herald*, 27 February, 1990.
104. " US troops must remain in Japan.", *The Korea Herald*, 28 May, 1990.
105. "US pre-eminence welcomed by Asian", *International Herald Tribune*, 13 June, 1991, p. 1.
106. Paul Keal, "Japan's security policy and arms control" in *Security & Arms Control in the North Pacific.*, pp. 123-144.
107. The Japanese Self-Defence Forces are authorized only for the defence of the physical area around Japan. The dispatch of armed forces to foreign land, sea and air space for purpose of using force is not permitted by the constitution, because it goes beyond the minimum necessary for self-defence.
108. James E. Auer, *The Postwar Rearmament of Japanese Maritime Forces, 1945-71* (Praeger publishers: New York, 1973), pp. 39-52.
109. Drifte, *Japan's rise to*, p.5. He also said that its unilateral arms control and disarmament measures were primarily designed by the government to bridge the gap between the political streams of the Peace Constitution of 1947 and the Japanese-American security alliance.
110. David T. Janes, "Post-INF Treaty attitude in East Asia", *Asian Survey*, vol. xxx no.5, (May 1990), p. 483.
111. Drifte, *Japan's Rise to*, pp .37-38.

112. Gerald Segal, *Normalizing Soviet-Japanese Relations* (Royal Institute of International Affairs, London, 1991), p. 20.
113. Hasegawa, "Soviet arms control policy in Asia", p. 206.
114. Garret and Glaser, op. cit., pp. 157-159.
115. Xu Kui, "Peace, Security and Arms control in the Asia/Pacific Region" in *Pacific Regional Security* (Washington D.C, National Defence University Press, The 1985 Pacific Symposium, 1988), p. 105.
116. "Why Asia needs a European-style CSCA", *International Herald Tribune*, 27 July, 1990.
117. "Creation of North Pacific security body", *Choongang-Ilbo* (Korean newspaper), July 29, 1990
118. Desmond Ball, *Building Blocks for Regional Security* (Canberra: Strategic and Defence Studies Centre, 1991), Paper No.3, p. 27.
119. Patrick M. Cronin, "Pacific Rim Security: Beyond Bilateralism", *The Pacific Review*, Vol.5, No.3, (1992), p. 220.
120. "US pre-eminence welcomed by Asian", p. 2.
121. George Friedman and Meredith Lebard, *The Coming War with Japan* (New York: St. Martin's Press, 1991), pp. 378-403. The authors dismiss the argument that the US and Japan are too interdependent to go to war.
122. US Congress, *Arms Control in Asia and US Interests in the Region*, p. 54.
123. Trevor Findlay, "Asia-Pacific CSBM: a prospectus", *Working Papers,* no.90, (Australian National University, Peace Research Centre, 1990), p. 20. He lists a number of CBMs currently applicable to the Asia/Pacific region. The most relevant CBMs to the Asia/Pacific are; "Incident At Sea Agreement", "Law of the Sea", "Regional Air Safety Agreement", "Agreement on Notification of Ballistic Missile Tests" and "Agreement on Advance Notification of Strategic Exercises".
124. Charles E. Morrison, *Asia-Pacific Report: Trends, Issues and Challenges* (the East-West Centre: Honolulu, 1987), p. 46.
125. *Far Eastern Economic Review,* 25 May, 1989, p. 13.
126. Retired Admiral James A. Winnefeld suggests the establishment of hot line between the headquarters of major commanders in the region, e.g., the US Commander in Chief in the Pacific (USCINCPAC) and the Russia Commander in Vladivostok. US Congress, *Arms Control in Asia,* p. 66.
127. Andrew Mack, "Reassurance vs. Deterrence Strategies for Asia-Pacific Region", Gerrit W. Gong and Richard L. Grant (eds), *Security and Economics in the Asian Pacific Region* (Washington D.C.: CSIS, Significant Issues Series, vol. xiii, no. 9, 1991) pp. 71-72.
128. "Noodles and Nukes", *Far Eastern Economic Review*, 7 January 1988, p. 19.
129. John K. Emmerson& Harrison M. Holland, *The Eagle and the Rising Sun* (Addison-Wesley Publishing Company, 1988), p. 133.
130 "Japanese Poll: Support for Pacifism Ebbing", *The Korea Herald*, 3 May, 1991.
131. "Japan's Warships Leave for Gulf amid Dispute", *The Korean Herald*, 28 April, 1991.
132. "Asian Nations Wary of Signs of Japanese Expansionism, *The Korea Herald, 10 May, 1991.*
133. Andrew Mack and Desmond Ball, "The Military Build-up in Asia-Pacific", *The Pacific Review*, Vol.5, No.3, (1992), p. 204.
134. Jones, "Post-INF Treaty", p. 492.

7. Regional Stability and Korean Arms Control

US Forces Stationed in Korea and Korean Arms Control

The US forces in Korea (USFK) have long been a central issue in regional politics between the Northeast Asian powers. During the Cold War the Soviet Union and China demanded the withdrawal of all US troops and the liquidation of US its military bases and facilities. For Soviet leaders makers, the USFK were seen as intended to enhance the regional and global projection of US power in an effort to undermine Soviet security. Because South Korean troops were fully integrated with the US forces, under the operational control of the US 8th Army, the continuous American presence was seen as a means of making South Korea "a strategic colony under Washington control".[1]

The Chinese objection to the USFK is very different to that of the former Soviet Union's. During the period of the Sino-Soviet conflict China's demands for the withdrawal of the USFK were far less categorical than its rival. A rationale for this attitude can be perceived from China's strategic alignment with the US against the Soviet Union. The tacit Chinese support for the USFK was as a strategic counterweight to the threat of Soviet encirclement of China.[2] A decline in US military strength in the region would enhance Soviet influence there and increase China's military burden. The lukewarm Chinese attitude to the military problem of the USFK was also related to concern for the revival of Japanese militarism. Here evidence can be sought from a statement by Chou En-lai in an interview with the New York Times:

> The Korean question is also linked up with the problem of Japanese militarism. If things do not go well, Japan might use the treaty it has concluded with South Korea, i.e., the Japan-ROK treaty, to get into South Korea immediately upon withdrawal of US forces.[3]

Thus China saw the USFK to some extent in a positive light because it deterred Soviet expansion and the recurrence of Japanese militarism. For China, the timing and method of withdrawal could be a subject of negotiation between the countries concerned.

Faced with the Soviet threat, successive Japanese governments linked South Korea's security with Japan's. They emphasized that "peace in Korea is essential to the peace and stability of East Asia, including Japan". Therefore Japan opposed a reduction of the US forces within Korea. For example, when President Carter made a plan for troop withdrawal, seven Japanese cabinet ministers and 235 legislators jointly stated that the withdrawal would present "an invitation to instability in the Korean Peninsula ... and Northeast Asia as a whole".[4] Japanese opinion formers placed advertisements in major American newspapers opposing the withdrawal plan. Because the USFK was a forward deployment against Soviet southward military expansion, Japan interpreted any withdrawal as a weakening of the US defence commitment to it.

The end of the Cold War reduces the strategic value of US forces as a deterrent against any threat from Moscow and suggests a reduction in the USFK. Russia and China propose the withdrawal of foreign troops as a question of principle. It would suit the general security interests of the two countries not to have US troops in an area so close to their frontiers, even though the small size of the USFK poses no significant threat to them. Japan's demands for a US presence no longer have any real persuasiveness, in the context of a threat from Russia.

The United States seeks a rationale for the continuous stationing of the USFK in terms of regional power politics. The commander of the USFK, General Ricassi said in testimony to Congress that:

> Every nation in the region has a central interest in the geostrategic position of Korea. None would be content to see it fall under the domination of any one of the others. Almost every nation in Asia feels comfortable with the American security presence in Korea.[5]

Historically the Korean Peninsula was often used as a route for the imperial policy of the continental and sea powers. Over one century three major international wars were waged over the control of the Peninsula; the Sino-Japanese war (1894-1895), Russia-Japanese war (1904-1905) and the Korean War (1950-1953) which involved the US and China in the military conflict between capitalists and communists. During the Sino-Soviet conflict the two powers competed to have a dominant influence in North Korea.

Given the strategic importance and many wars on the Korean Peninsula, it is very advantageous to South Korean security that the role of the USFK is defined as a "buffer" or "honest broker" in regional politics. But for the US it leads to higher costs that will be challenged in its domestic politics in the long run. Consequently the US is unilaterally reducing the level of the USFK in the new strategic environment, as part of the global reductions pursued by the Clinton administration. Unlike the past, the US is in the best position now to play a "catalytic role" for stability in Korea by converting the troop reduction into a negotiated arms control mechanism. Its balancing role can also be maximized in the regional power struggle.

The US forces in Korea have been the central problem in arms control talks between the DPRK (The Democratic People's Republic of Korea) and the ROK (The Republic of Korea). The DPRK has consistently demanded the withdrawal of the USFK as the first step for arms control, while the ROK position is that the USFK cannot be the first issue of arms control.

The ROK believes that the USFK have deterred a DPRK invasion since the end of the Korean War in 1953. The USFK presently consist of the 2nd infantry division, the Seventh Air Force, several support units of the US Eighth Army and the fighting liaison unit of the Seventh Fleet. At the end of 1994 its troops numbered roughly 36,000, including 26,500 army, 9,750 Air Force, 400 Navy, 950 Marine. Its main equipment were 84 fighters (5 squadrons), and 100 tanks.[6] The 2nd Infantry Division is the only Army combat unit West of Hawaii. The Division is stationed South of the DMZ, on the main battle line of the DPRK's attack in the Korean War. Its location might be considered as a reserve location capable of moving into either of the two major corridors that approach Seoul. The stationing of ground combat troops at the nexus of the major invasion corridor means that a North Korean attack would almost certainly involve US forces. In the event of such an attack, the 2nd division would be automatically involved in fighting as a so called 'trip wire'. Any US government faced with such an attack on US forces would have little choice but to commit additional US forces to Korea. The USFK are equipped with large numbers of the most sophisticated, top-of-the line weaponry in terms of mechanization and fire power. The 7th Air Force plays an essential role in intelligence gathering and analysis and early warning with a highly sophisticated strategic warning system that the ROK does not have.

The other important reason why the ROK objects to the withdrawal of the USFK derives from considerations concerning the defence burden. Without the US military presence, the ROK would have had to spend a far greater amount of its resources on defence in order to cope with the threat from the DPRK. The Ministry of National Defence has estimated that the ROK would have to increase the present 5 percent of GNP to 8 percent in order to replace the strength of the USFK within five years. Moreover, the obligatory term of military service would require extension from the current 30 months to 50 months.[7]

North Korea considers the withdrawal of the USFK as the precondition for Korean Unification. Citizens in the DPRK are routinely told that the US has turned South Korea into a colony and the South Koreans into slaves of American monopoly capital. Kim Il-sung's perspective on the USFK was that

> the US imperialists want to keep South Korea under their thumb partly because they want to make South Korea their permanent raw material base. It is a fact that they lust for the material in South Korea ... [8]

Such a belief has been deeply inculcated into the DPRK people. To liberate the ROK from the rule of the US is the first and most important goal of the DPRK.

The US forces are the primary threat to the DPRK's security. During the Korean War, after recovering the ROK's territory, the US forces crossed over the 38 parallel line in a counter-attack upon the Northern forces and arrived at the North-Chinese border line, occupying almost all the DPRK's territory. The bitter experience in the Korean War and the American intervention in the Vietnam War helped deepen North Korean perceptions of the threat from the US Kim Yong Nam, Foreign Minister of the DPRK, declared in an article:

> The United States considers South Korea a "forward line of American strategy" and is working hard to set up a system of military aggression in the area. Building up forces and nuclear armaments in South Korea, it is spearheading its offensive against our Republic.[9]

Thus, for the DPRK, the US forces are the first threat to its national security and the biggest obstacle for unification on its terms. From the DPRK's point of view, arms control between the two Koreas is meaningless as long as the problem of the USFK withdrawal remains unresolved.

The Regional Powers' Security Assistance to Korea

During the Cold War the security assistance of the Soviet Union, China and the US to North and South Korea contributed to the maintenance of stability on the Korean Peninsula. But it also resulted in an arms race and heightened military confrontation between the two Korean states. At the present time the significant level of military strength created for stability during the Cold

War should be the subject of arms control concerned with parity based upon low a level of military strengths on the Korean Peninsula

The Soviet Union, China and North Korea

After its establishment on 9 September, 1948 North Korea depended on the Soviet Union and China for help in achieving its objectives: security, economic development, and ultimately the reunification of the Korean Peninsula. In 1961 North Korea concluded treaties of friendship and alliance with both China and the Soviet Union respectively. The contents of these treaties established that, should North Korea be attacked by a third party, China and the Soviet Union would provide security support.

Based on these treaties, North Korea has received massive weapons assistance from the Soviet Union and China. Such arms transfers to the North have played an important role in the militarization of North Korea. During the Sino-Soviet dispute the two countries were competing for influence in Pyongyang. North Korea was perceived as an important strategic asset of the Soviet Union and the PRC. China saw North Korea as "the lips to her teeth". If the Soviet Union used her as a base for an attack on China, and Manchuria, the core Chinese industrial complex, was made more vulnerable to the Soviet threat. From Moscow's viewpoint, enemy use of North Korean airfields and ports and basing of medium range missiles on North Korean territory would pose a serious threat to Vladivostok, the principal Russian naval base in the Pacific.[10] When the Sino-Soviet dispute intensified, the North faced a dilemma over which side to align. These two powers could not but recognize the advantage of the strategic barrier provided by North Korea. Kim Il-Sung used this strategic location as a leverage for diplomatic manoeuvering. His 'pendulum swing diplomacy' - periodically leaning one way and then toward the other - was utilized to maximize the acquisitions of weapons from China and the USSR.[11]

During the Sino-Soviet conflict the level of Chinese and Soviet arms transfers to North Korea was determined by the conditions of their diplomatic relations. When the North was close to the Soviet Union, its arms supplies to the North were increased and Chinese supplies were stopped or reduced. On the other hand, when its relations with China were good, the two Powers' arms supplies were reversed. Since the Armistice Agreement in 1953 the general trends of their arms transfers have been identified as follows:

Period 1 (1953-56): unilateral Soviet aid
Period 2 (1957-60): massive Chinese aid
Period 3 (1960-64): low-level aid from both sides
Period 4 (1965-72): massive Soviet aid
Period 5 (1973-84): Increasing Chinese aid and decreasing Soviet aid
Period 6 (1984-88): Increasing Soviet aid and decreasing Chinese aid.[12]

On the other hand, during any period of low intensity dispute, North Korea could attempt to get a balanced amount of weapons from both sides.

The most impressive period of arms supply was between 1965 and 1972 when the Soviet Union provided massive assistance. Seven years of massive Soviet aid decisively contributed to the North's military superiority over the South. As a result, North Korea adopted a more offensive military posture against South Korean and American forces.

Table 7-1   Chinese and Soviet Arms Transfers to North Korea (1950- 1990)

	armoured vehicle				aircraft	vessel
	SU	PRC	SU	PRC	SU	PRC
period 1	100	-	260	-	24	-
period 2	250	-	100	468	2	24
period 3	450	-	-	-	11	-
period 4	1020	20	171	-	38	4
period 5	-	70	114	-	12	6
period 6	-	64	-	-	-	-

This data is correlated from four books. *Arms Trade Registers: The Arms Trade with the Third World* (SIPRI, 1975), pp.10-12. Michael Brzoska and Thomas Ohlson, *Arms Transfers to the Third World, 1971-85* (SIPRI, 1978), pp.203-204. *SIPRI Yearbook 1988, pp.255-256, SIPRI Yearbook 1989*, pp.253-254.

During this period North Korea launched a series of military provocations such as the seizure of the US Pueblo vessel in 1968, the shooting of the US EC-121 flight in 1969, an attempted commando raid attack by 31 agents against Chong Wa Dae, the official residence of the ROK President and the infiltration of 120 armed agents into the 'Ulchin-Samchok' area in the South.

Despite the Soviet Union establishing full diplomatic relations with the South in 1990, the Soviet Union continued to emphasise its defence ties with Pyongyang. In 1988 North Korea received 30 MIG-29 and 18 SU-25 fighters from the Soviet Union.[13] In January 1991, North Korean and Soviet military chiefs signed an accord pledging to strengthen military cooperation. As a result, an agreement was signed to produce MIG-29s under licence from the Soviets.[14] According to the SIPRI Yearbook 1991, North Korea received conventional weapons worth 4406 million dollars from the Soviet Union and 494 million dollars from China between 1986 and 1990.[15]

The United States and South Korea

The United State's security assistance to South Korea consists of the Mutual Defence Treaty, combined defence posture and arms supply. The institutional mechanism of its security assistance comes from the 1954 US-ROK Mutual Defense Treaty. The Treaty stipulates that the two countries "would act to meet the common danger" in the event of an attack in the Pacific area involving aggression against either of the parties.

On the basis of the Defence Treaty, the two governments have maintained the combined defence posture. A signficant development of defence cooperation was the establishment of the ROK-US Combined Forces Command (CFC) in 1978. This establishment was primarily to fill the security vacuum created by the partial pullout of US forces from Korea. The CFC is the only US/Allied command outside of NATO. The purpose of the CFC is to integrate ROK and US forces into command systems and to develop combined operations plans, including wartime logistics supply plans. Before the establishment of CFC, the USFK was in fact not organized for war readiness insofar as strategic directives and missions and force assignments in wartime were concerned. It was limited to conducting the tasks relevant to the Armistice Agreement under the UN.[16]

US military assistance to South Korea has been crucial to the security of the ROK. Until the 1960s most military assistance was served by grants without any cost to ROK. The massive assistance of the mid-1960s was made in return for the dispatch of 50,000 Korean troops in the Vietnam War. In 1965 and 1966 two agreements between the US and the ROK were made for improving the ROK's defence capability.[17] To fill the power vacuum following its deep involvement in the Vietnam War, the US supplied large amounts of weapons to Korea. The modernization of all front-line ROK units was expedited by the help of the US The ageing F86s were replaced by F-5 Freedom fighters.[18] After the declaration of the Nixon Doctrine, the US commitment in Asia was changed from the involvement of troops to material assistance. The withdrawal of the 7th division's 20,000 troops in 1971 was followed by a substantial amount of aid and extensive technical assistance in security. The United States promised to largely underwrite the South's "Force Modernization Plan" (1971 to 1975). During this five year period the United States provided nearly $1.3 billion in military assistance, including $890.4 million in grant aid and FMS Credits and $140.1 million in excess defense equipment transferred against the $250 million goal.[19] In 1971 South Korea received 18 F-4D phantom fighters, 50 M-48 tanks, APCS, heavy artillery, and 12 Honest John SSMs at a cost of $ 95 million, all financed under MAP. Most of the 7th Division's equipment was left to the South including approximately 50 M-60 main battle tanks.[20] At the time of the withdrawal plan of the 2nd Division in 1977, in return for the removal of the Division, equipment of the withdrawing forces was to be transferred to Korean forces.[21] During the period of the South's Five year Force Improvement (FIP, 1977-81), of $3.5 billion foreign acquisition costs, the US assisted with a loan of about $105 million.[22] The increment of arms supply to Korea has been closely related to the reduction of US forces. Thus subsequent US governments have advocated more arms transfers to confirm its security commitment.

US security assistance policy which provided grants to the ROK has undergone a tremendous change from the mid-1970s. MAP aid, the core of earlier US security assistance, decreased from 1975. Grant aided support of Operations and Maintenance (O&M) costs ended by 1974, and grant aid funding was terminated in 1976.

By 1987, only a small-scale International Military Education and Training Program remained in place. Beginning in FY 1974 the US provided increasing amounts of FMS credit. During the period of the Second FIP (1982-1986) South Korea's arms purchases were heavily dependent upon FMS credits. But, the accumulation of the principal and high interest of the FMS credit since the 1980s has placed a tremendous burden on the South's defence budgets. Therefore, in recent years, South Korea's arms imports depended more on cash purchases and direct commercial purchases than FMS credit. In 1983, 991,3 billion Won (Korean Current) was spent on Foreign purchases: 289.5 billion Won (28.5 percent) on FMS purchases and 701.8 billion Won (71.5 percent) on commercial purchases.[23] With its previous grant programs the United States arms supplies provided the crucial impetus for the South's forces as they exist today. The South's weapons have come almost exclusively from the United States.

Table 7-2 US Military Assistance to South Korea (1948-1986)

$ US Million

	1948-53	1953-61	1962-65	1966	1967	1968	1969	1970
Grants	11.9	1471	908	210	272	389	479	330

	1971-2	1973-4	1975-6	1977-80	81	84	85	86
Grants	1056	440	142	806	-	-	-	-
Loans	32	81	185	562	550	275	230	230
Total	1020	520	327	1368	550	275	230	230

Sources: US Overseas Loans & Grants preliminary FY 1974 Data Obligation & Loans Authentication, July 1, 1973-June 30 1974, 1975 AID Possessed, p.73. Senator Hubert H. Humphrey & John Glenn, US troop withdrawal from the Republic of Korea, A report to the Committee on Foreign Relations, United States Senate, 95th Congress 2nd Session (Washington D.C.: GPO, 1976), p.44. US Department of Defence, *Defence Security Assistance Facts as of September 30, 1986* (Washington D.C., 1986).

Even after the end of US aid the South's weapon imports from the US have not changed despite a worldwide trend toward diversification of arms suppliers. During 1986-1990, the South imported armaments worth $3,125 million from abroad. Of these it imported $2,887 million from the US[24]

Table 7-3 The Arms Imports of South Korea (1951-1990)

	1951-5	1956-60	1961-5	1966-70	1971-5	1976-80	1981-85	1986-90
I.T.	496	675	603	1091	1185	3020	3140	3125
US	99	100	100	100	98	95	97	92

IT Import Total (M$ 1985 prices), US: US Supply(percent), Source: Nfichael Brzoska & Thomas Ohlson, *Arms Transfers to the Third World, 1971-85* (SIPRI, 1987), p.344. The data of 1986-90 comes from *SIPRI Yearbook* 1991, p.208.

As long as the US ROK security cooperation and the North-South Korean arms race continue, South Korea's arms dependence on the United States will remain at a high level. As seen from the past pattern of US-ROK security cooperation, a reduction of the USFK will lead to an ROK arms build-up through a transfer of equipment of withdrawn forces.

The Military Confrontation of North and South Korea
Comparison of the Military Strengths

The Korean Peninsula is now one of the world's most militarized regions. There are over one and a half million troops along the 155 mile demilitarized zone separating North and South Korea. When compared to other theatres in the world, these forces are the most heavily concentrated in a small area. Despite the advent of the new detente prevailing in Korea with the end of East-West confrontation, both sides retain the inheritance of the Cold War with a high level of tension. During the last four decades, South and North Korea have steadily increased their military strength. According to the Military Balance 1991-92, the North and the South have the world's fifth and seventh largest armed forces respectively and their combined forces are fourth after the CIS, US and China.[25]

The military strengths of the two Koreas can be measured in terms of a number of tangible and intangible elements.

Table 7-4 The Military Balance: North and South Korea

	North	South
troops (000)	1030	655
tanks	3800	1950
APC	2500	2100
artillery	10,800	4600
combat vessels	434	190
submarines	26	2
combat aircraft	850	520

Source: *Korean Defence White Paper 1994-1995* (The Ministry of National Defence, ROK, 1995), p. 80.

The overall situation can be summarized as three different points of views; North Korean superiority, South Korean superiority, and mutual balance. The view of North Korean superiority gives more weight to the qualitative analysis of military power. On the other hand, the view of South Korean superiority has more emphasis on the qualitative analysis. The view of mutual balance simultaneously analyses the qualitative and quantitative aspects of military forces. The ROK government has argued that the North has quantitative advantages over the South in troops and equipment. Such a military imbalance has arisen from the gap in military investment between both sides. The South has been limited to 5 percent of GNP, while the North has consistently allocated 20-24 percent of GNP. Moreover, the North implemented its defence build-up in 1962, 12 years earlier than the South.[26] As a result, the South is the underdog in terms of regular active forces readily available for the initial phase of war.

The North's numerical superiority is marked in ground troops. The superiority in tanks and artillery is prominent. It means that DPRK ground forces are highly mechanized with enormous fire power. The former ROK Defense Minister, Sang Hoon Lee, explained the superiority of North Korea in terms of a sophisticated static analysis that the joint military strength of South Korea and USFK amounted to 68.1 percent of North Korea's strength; respectively South Korea, 62.1 percent and US, 5.4 percent. He went on to predict that in order to cope with North Korea, the South-US military capability would achieve defensive capability, 70 percent of that of North Korea in 1991, deterrent capability, 80 percent in 1996 and offensive capability, 90 percent in 2006.[27] To assess the military balance, the Korean Institute for Defense Analysis (KIDA) developed a standard unit as a method of comparison.[28]

Table 7-5 The Military Balance and Prospect of 1990-2005 in Korea

	1989			1995			2000			2005
	NK	SK	FR	NK	SK	FR	NK	SK	FR	NK
Inf. div 1.6	55	46	1.2	55	42	1.3	55	38	1.4	55
Mec div 1.6	22	4.5	4.8	25	9	2.8	27	13	2.1	30
Art. 1.5	160	40	40	180	60	3	190	90	2.1	200
Surface 1.2	74	57	1.3	80	67	1.2	90	77	1.2	100
Sub 1.6	24	-	-	25	6	4.2	26	12	2.2	28
F-16 1.2	345	219	1.6	400	273	1.5	420	327	1.3	450

NK: North Korea, SK: South Korea, FR: Force Ratio, Inf div: infantry division, Mec div: mechanized division, Artillery, Surface; destroyer, Sub: submarine. Source: Oh Kwan-chi, "The Military Balance on the Korean Peninsula" in William J. Taylor, Jr.& Cha Young-Koo (eds), *The Korean Peninsula: Prospects for Arms Reduction under Global Detente* (Westview Press, 1990). p. 103.

North Korean officials and revisionist scholars claim that the military forces of the South are superior to those of the North. In an interview with a Korean daily newspaper, Vice-Chairman of the Committee of Peace Unification of Korea, Bae Gem Chul said "We have neither strength enough to attack the South nor intention to do so ... For Southward invasion, we need a strength three times that of the South's".[29] North Korean officials argued that the claims of unreasonable superiority of the North are made in the context of a pretext for perpetuating the stationing of USFK and war preparation of the South and the US forces. North Korean officials have not publicly advanced any military data. Their position on military balance has directed itself towards the comparisons of war potential; i.e., military capabilities, the size of population rather than those of present military force levels.

Recently theories of a military balance between North and South Korea have been begun to prevail among many scholars of the US and the South. Most of them admit a slight advantage to the North in terms of qualitative strength. However, they emphasize a more comprehensive concept, namely a total war potentiality rather than a superficial comparison of figures. For example, Stephen D. Goose argues that the quantitative edge of the North is offset by the South's superiority of non-quantifiable elements i.e. weapon quality, training, war experience, geography, terrain and defensive posture.[30] Most analysts have pointed to the military strength of the combined South and US forces. Even US and Korean officials have indirectly acknowledged the military balance by stressing that the combined forces provide a strong deterrent to North Korean aggression. The former commander of USFK, General Livsey, stated in 1985 that Korean and US forces were currently able to defeat any renewed aggression from North Korea and the South would achieve a military edge during the 1990s.[31] Some Korean analysts agree that the two Koreas have achieved a strategic balance. Tae-Hwan Kwak argues that under the strategic parity conditions North Korea is unlikely to strike first at South Korea when faced with the risk of being defeated, suggesting that, because military strategic equivalence is being maintained without the presence of US ground forces, the South Korean government should accept the North's arms reduction proposal.[32] Ha Young-Sun also claims that because of the rough military and strategic balance there is in the minds of decision makers of both sides a "psychological balance" with both fearing the potential results of war.[33]

More recently many analysts have been persuaded that the military balance is moving towards the superiority of the South through the growth of economic capabilities and defence expenditure of South Korea.

Table 7-6 The Defense Expenditure of North and South Korea

	1970	1975	1980	1983	1986	1989	1990
DE.	753	1286	3309	5535	6593	7865	7827
SK GDP (percent)	3.7	3.4	4.3	5.3	4.7	4.4	-
DE.	936	878	1337	1583	1783	1821	2003
NK GDP (percent)	11	11	10	12.3	-	8.8	-
DE.Dif. (SK-NK)	-183	408	1972	3952	4810	6044	5824

DE.: Defense Expenditure, DE Dif.: Defense expenditure difference. SK: South Korea, NK: North Korea. Sources: 1975-1980; *The Military Balance 1987-1988*, p.220 (US Million at 1980 price), 1983-1990: *SIPRI Yearbook 1991* p. 171 & 176. (US Million at 1988 price).

According to the data of the Military Balance 1994-5, South Korea spent $11.4 billions on defence, compared to $5.3 billions for North Korea in 1994.

It is very difficult to decide which side is currently dominant because of differences of mutual assessment methods and the military build up. The problem of the military balance caused great controversy in the arms control talks between the NATO and the Warsaw Pact. But the MBFR and CFE talks depended more on 'bean counts' and operational considerations more than potential military capabilities. Moreover, the assessment of a military balance based upon military potentialities may be out of date because modern wars are often very short. Therefore it is important to assess the Korean military balance using European assessment methods applied during previous arms control talks. As in Europe, the most important factors for the military balance in the region will not only be the types of military forces and weapons, but also the quality of operational planning and readiness such as offensive strategy, force locations and geographical considerations.

The Surprise Attack Capability

The danger of a second Korean War stems not so much from the huge military capability itself, but from the adoption of offensive strategies and force structures by North and South Korea. These offensive force structures and strategies have increased fear and suspicion, providing incentives for arms races, for pre-emption in crises, and for escalation once the war occurs.

There is no doubt that North Korea is primarily responsible for the destabilising of the Korean Peninsula. The North's strategy is clearly offensive in its nature. The North has focussed on securing the ability to launch a surprise invasion. It has adopted 'blitzkrieg' or 'daring thrust' tactics based upon the use of mobile corps which the Soviets had earlier planned in the European theatre. The strategy is to seize the operational initiative with the occupation of major strategic centres and Seoul, capital city of the South, in the early phases of war. The Minister of National Defence of the ROK, Lee Ki Back noted that "North Korea had worked out a so-called '5-7 day strategy'" and was intensifying the training of military units in offensive operations in accordance with it.[34] Upon the completion of operations in the frontline, successive offensive operations are expanded into the remaining portions of the rear area within 16 days, to be then followed by the final occupational operations within one month.[35]

To implement this strategy, beginning in the 1980s the North Korean armed forces have undergone a sweeping reorganization. As a result, their overall offensive capabilities to execute the blitzkrieg have vastly improved. The main offensive forces comprise 23 mechanized infantry brigades, 14 armoured brigades, and 1 armoured division supported by self-propelled artillery. These forces, together with motorized infantry units, constitute four mechanized and one armoured corps. The artillery forces are highly mobile. Of 9,000 artillery pieces, more than 2,800 are self-propelled and 2,500 are multiple rocket launchers.[36]

A more offensive aspect is the forward deployments of forces within 50 miles of the DMZ. The forward deployments are concentrated just north of the western part of the DMZ, the shortest distance from Seoul. New airfields have been constructed in the region of the DMZ in order to reduce the flight time to Seoul to 8 minutes. About 60 percent of naval forces are also deployed forward towards the south.[37] The most offensive posture arises out of the digging of tunnels under the DMZ, capable of allowing the passage of thousands of light infantry troops into the South, The tunnels can be used for infiltrating guerrilla troops in peacetime or for neutralizing the defence of command posts and front combat zones of the South in the early stages of hostilities.

Table 7-7 The Construction of DMZ Tunnels by North Korea for Troop Infiltration

	No.1	No.2	No.3	No.4
discovery	1974	1975	1978	1990
size (High wide)	1.2m	0.9m	2m high	2m wide
length	3.5km	3.5km	1.6km	unknown
capability	infiltration 39,000 men passing per hour			

Sources: *The Korea Herald*, 4 March, 1990. *Korean Defence White Paper 1990*, p.77.

The North's forward deployment closer to the DMZ has significantly shortened the South's warning time of the North's attack from 24 hours to 6 hours.[38] It has increased the chances of a successful surprise. Admiral Crowe declared in a interview, "I think we probably have put more attention and emphasis on our communications and warning systems in Korea than we have any other single piece of real estate in the world ... it (warning time) has certainly made us work a little harder to compensate in other ways".[39] The first priority for improving Korean peninsula security lies the issue of forward deployments of forces and the offensive strategy of the North and the short warning time, rather than the North's military force levels themselves.

In contrast to the North's offensive posture, that of the South can be characterized as clearly defensive. This is apparent from the strategy, force level and structure, and the deployment of troops. Up to the mid-1970s, the South adopted a very passive defence strategy, because its military forces were manifestly insufficient to defend its territory. So it built a phased withdrawal plan from the front line to three delaying lines to allow the US reinforcements to reach the combat zone. However, the South was faced with a major strategic problem in that Seoul lies within 40 km of the DMZ. Because of Seoul's proximity to the DMZ, South Korea was very concerned about its vulnerability to a surprise attack. One forecast, for example, was that "within the first 90 seconds of another war, 20 percent of the South's defending forces would be destroyed. Within the following 48 hours North Korea's T62 tanks would assault Seoul".[40]

These circumstances encouraged the South to establish the forward defiance strategy, the so called "Hollingsworth Line". The "Hollingsworth line" strategy was to sustain the front line by destroying assailant forces through the concentration of massive firepower and the establishment of strong points. Emphasis is also placed on aggressive counteroffensives for limited objectives and continued firepower and concentration tactics well into the North's second echelon, which might be as deep as 120 km from the North's FEBA.[41] Simultaneously the North's echelon forces would be neutralized by the mobilization of all the US air power in Northeast Asia. The adoption of this strategy meant a change from passive defence doctrine to that of offensive defence doctrine.

The more offensive strategy of South Korea can be seen in 'the Airland Battle' concept employed from 1983. The strategy is primarily to destroy the first and second echelons of the DPRK forces with manoeuvre, the concentration of firepower, and the full use of new technologies. It means that with the beginning of war the whole area of the North is struck by bombardment by the South and the US air force. The strategy is expanded to involve the South and US ground forces in a counter-attack or a counter offensive for limited objectives.[42]

The most decisive threat to North Korea was the combined annual "Team Spirit" (T.S.) exercise of the ROK and US forces. Excluding the "Reforger" exercise in Europe the 'T.S.' was the largest exercise in which US forces participated each year. It involved offer 200,000 US and Korean military personnel, including 60,000 US troops deployed from the US homeland, other US military bases in the Pacific and the US Seventh Fleet. Generally the exercise consisted not only of conventional warfare training, but also training for chemical and nuclear warfare.[43] Undoubtedly the exercise was perceived as deeply threatening by North Korea. North Koreans saw the exercises as "a preliminary war and a test of nuclear war aimed at surprise pre-emptive strike at the North". Therefore, since 1983 the North has put its armed forces and militia on full combat alert during the T.S. exercises.[44]

The South and US forces' counter-attack or counter-offensive strategy is a response to the North's offensive strategy and readiness for a war. Considering Seoul's proximity to the DMZ and the very short warning time, the South directs its strategy to a more offensive defence, in order to reduce the vulnerability to the North's surprise attack and thereby reinforce its deterrent posture. Furthermore, the possibility cannot be excluded that the South would launch a preemptive strike to defend the capital area if deterrence fails and the indication of an attack by the North clearly appears.

Missile Attack Capability

The North and South Korean possessions of tactical ballistic missiles may become very significant because of their potential to penetrate air defence or to conduct non-conventional operations. Without the redeployment of troops or weapons, such missiles can make simultaneous attacks on multiple major targets. Further, such attacks can be conducted without any warning time. Because both Seoul and Pyongyang fall within the ranges of existing missiles, there remains the possibility of a preemptive attack on population centres or strategic objectives. The special status of ballistic missiles which reach their targets at long range, and high speed and deliver their payloads with accuracy, has made the military planners of the two Koreas more concerned about their possession of them.

The North's missile programmes have been developed with the help of the former USSR, the PRC, Egypt and Iran. During 1969-70 North Korea obtained its first surface-to-surface missile with the Soviet delivery of the FROG-5 and FROG-7A and during the mid-1970s initiated a programme to indigenously produce a reverse engineered version of the FROG-7A.[45] A small number of Soviet Scud Bs were transferred to the North during the early 1980s. With the technical assistance of the PRC and the financial support of Iran, North Korea manufactured the Scud B with a range of 320-340 km, which is slightly greater than that of the Scud-Bs (280-300km range) which the Soviet Union provided the Third World and that have a range of 280-300 km.[46] Furthermore, North Korea is revitalizing the Scud-PIP of 600 km. The new and longer range version is able to threaten not only Southwest Japan, but also Beijing, Vladlvostok and Khabarovsk.[47] The North presently has one Scud B regiment, which is organized with a HQ element, 3 missile battalions and some service units. It is capable of producing more than 50 Scud B missiles a year and has at least 12 mobile launchers about 40 to 50 km north of the DMZ.[48]

Faced with the threat of missile attack, South Korea has developed a long-range surface-to-surface missile which is able to counter the Frog-7 and Scud. In 1978 the South had a first test flight of the ballistic missile based on a conversion of the US Nike-Hercules surface to air missile to a surface-to-surface configuration. The NH-K was designed as two versions of a surface-to-surface missile; one version with a range of 180 km and the other 220 to 260 km.[49] However, its attempt to upgrade Nike-Hercules failed due to pressure from the United States. In return for the abandonment of its missile project, the United States granted Korea access to a wide range of advanced technologies. This contributed to the development of its missile program. A modified Nike Hercules surface-to-air missile, the US 'Honest John' unguided tactical missile, the Hawk SAM System, and an anti-ship missile have been produced. According to the Korean Defense White Paper of 1989, the South has since 1982 had a plan for producing sophisticated equipment such as surface to surface missiles.[50]

Table 7-8 Missile Capability of North and South Korea

	Missile	Range(km)	Launchers	Numbers
North	Frog-5	50	9	50
	Frog-7	70	18	54
	Scud-B	280	12	hundreds
South	Honest-J	37	7	36
	Nike-H	240	?	100

Source: *SIPRI Yearbook 1991*, pp. 341-342.

North Korea has a significant advantage in short-range missile systems against the South's NH-K missile and old US Honest John. The range of the North's missiles is presently longer than that of the South. In particular, a number of Frog Missiles with a range of 50-70 km could attack Seoul in eight minutes. The Scud B missile is able to strike the South's rear, the "Sangju and Kimcheon" region.[51] Of the 109 active airfields/bases within the South, 91 are within operational range of the Scud-B and 48 are within the range of the Frog.[52] On the other hand the South's missiles are very limited in their ability to strike the strategic targets of the North because of their short range and the US control. The possession of ballistic missiles by North and South Korea has increased the possibility of a surprise attack or a preemptive war on the Korean Peninsula. Moreover, the Scud-PIP program of Pyongyang is encouraging Seoul's aspiration to develop a missile which can deter or retaliate against Pyongyang. The North's possession of the PIP missile, which is able to carry chemical and nuclear warheads to Japan further undermines regional stability.

Nuclear Crisis on the Korean Peninsula

The nuclear issue on the Korean Peninsula has been a source of major international concern. The main focus of concern is about the North Korean nuclear bomb programme. There is some evidence that North Korea has attempted to acquire nuclear weapons.

In May 1989, the United States informed the South Korean government that its CIA had obtained "crucial evidence proving North Korea's capability of developing nuclear weapons on its own".[53] Japanese satellite photographs also confirmed US intelligence reports that North Korea was building a facility at Yongbyon as a part of nuclear weapons program. The first signal of the North's nuclear programme came from North Korea itself. During Shevardnaze's visit to Pyongyang in September of 1990, the DPRK's Foreign Minister, Kim Youngnam, suggested it would develop nuclear weapons if Moscow further developed relations with South Korea. He declared that:

> Pyongyang would have no choice but to take means to provide for ourselves some weapons for which we have so far relied on the alliance. ... This move would lead the arms race to an acute phase on the Korean Peninsula and carry the situation there to an acute pitch of strain, worse still it will aggravate the situation of the Asian-Pacific region in general.[54]

It is known that the North is presently capable of producing 7 kilograms of plutonium a year enough for one bomb. The larger reactor, which is expected to be completed in 1994, has the ability to produce 18 to 50 kilograms of plutonium a year - two to five atomic bombs with a yield twice as high as the one dropped on Nagasaki.[55]

The North can easily obtain the fuel source for a nuclear reactor without any dependence on foreign supply. Natural Uranium is currently mined in Pyongsan, 54 km Southwest of Yongbyon. There are a large number of graphite mines within 70 km. Since its nuclear cooperation agreements with the USSR and China in the 1950s, the North has also accumulated technology enough to build nuclear weapons, receiving much material and technology for the construction of atomic power facilities.[56]

The crisis triggered by North Koreas announcement that it was withdrawing from the NPT (12 March 1993), was resolved on 21 October 1994 when the Clinton Administration concluded an agreement with North Korea. This agreement not only established mechanisms by which the international community would be able to monitor North Korea's progress towards establishing a reliable and purely non-military nuclear energy programme, but also pledged the two states to 'move toward full normalisation of political and economic relations'.[57] The agreement also included a commitment by North Korea to 'engage in North-South dialogue'.[58]

The North may be dominated by the perception of a growing strategic need for nuclear weapons. The superiority of armed forces is moving inexorably in the South's favour. The deterrent value of Pyongyang's nuclear weapons may be increased by "a no-win dilemma and failure to keep up with the South militarily".[59] Moreover, as seen in the past countries isolated from neighbouring countries, South Africa, Israel and China became quickly determined to possess nuclear weapons. North Korea, isolated from world society may have followed such a precedent as a means of escaping such isolation.

Should it become clear that the North was determined to build nuclear weapons, the South would also have a strong temptation to possess nuclear weapons against the North. The first years of mutual possession would be an extremely dangerous period. There would be the temptation to conduct a preemptive strike to reduce vulnerability in a crisis, as seen in the precedent of the Israeli strike at Iraq's Osirak nuclear reactor in 1981. Seoul hinted at the possibility of a preemptive strike against the Yongbyon reactor.[60] Washington officials also fear that Seoul would be compelled to match any North Korean program or to destroy it through pre-emptive action.[61]

Possession of nuclear weapons by North Korea would pose the most serious threat to the peace of Northeast Asia with the development plan of Scud-B ballistic missiles capable of delivering nuclear warheads. Andrew Mack sees the impact on the regional stability as the following:

> Strategic stability on a nuclearised Korean Peninsula would be further undermined by the absence of sophisticated and reliable command, control, communication capabilities or any arms control measures ... The prospect of a nuclearized Korean Peninsula could have profoundly destablizing impact on Japan strengthening the hand of the so-called 'Japanese Gaullists 'who believe that Japan should have a nuclear weapons capability.[62]

As seen in the European experience, conventional arms control talks were long deadlocked due to the nuclear problem. The nuclear problem in the Korean Peninsula may help further to complicate the Korean conventional arms control talks.

The Regional Powers' Policies towards Korean Arms Control

Status quo and war deterrence for the Korean Peninsula has been one of the most important policies of the Major Powers. The inherent objective is to avoid a war, which would be likely to trigger the deep involvement of the regional powers. The Powers have already implemented "informal arms control measures" in Korea in an effort to avoid risk of war.[63] The Korean War led the major states to recognize the limits of their powers. The lesson of the Korean War was that the regional powers would not allow one side to achieve a unified Korea through military cooperation with any regional power. It also demonstrated that none of the powers could gain a dominant advantage without unacceptable or costly consequences. Samuel S. Kim argues that since the Armistice, the Soviet Union and the United States have carried out 'tacit cooperation' in the preservation of the postwar status quo, as each superpower refrained from military attack on the ally of the other superpower, both superpowers followed tacit rules of cooperation not to tresspass into the other side of the DMZ.[64]

The desire of the major powers for stability in Korea is also apparent from the patterns of their behaviour in the crises of the Korean Peninsula. Despite North Korea's numerous provocations against the United States such as the capture of the surveillance ship Pueblo, the shooting down of the EC-121 aircraft, and the "Poplar Tree incident", the responses of the US have been limited to demonstrations of force or military warnings. Until now the US has not employed any military retaliation despite the North's repeated provocations.

The Soviet Union and China have also maintained very cautious attitudes towards North Korean adventurism. The two countries' responses to the crises by the North have always been passive and unwilling to risk confrontation with the United States over the North's interests.[65] In response to the attack threats of the United States on North Korea, Moscow and Peking did not offer Pyongyang any counter-military actions as security guarantors. In the Pueblo crisis it was only after the threat of war had passed that Moscow brought its naval deployment up to task force size. In the EC-121 crisis the USSR also discouraged the North's adventurism. Soviet President Podgorny, mentioned the Soviet-North Korean Mutual Defence Treaty only as the basis of friendship between the two countries, not in the context of countering the US 'imperialist' threat.[66] As well as the Soviet Union, China always limited itself to verbal support of the North Korean Position. In the Poplar crisis, China played a major role in bringing about Kim Il-sung's apology message to the United States.[67]

The major Powers had a 'tacit agreement' on the peaceful solution of the Korean question. None of the Powers supported the idea of solving the Korean question by military means. They have preferred to live with a divided Korea rather than face the dangerous uncertainties that would accompany an attempt to reunify it by military force. The Powers have given rhetorical support to the peaceful unification of Korea. However, their priorities have been the preservation of the status quo based upon a divided Korea.[68] A reunified Korea could be a source of serious misgivings to all interested countries with a combined population of near 70 million and with the military power of over one and half million well armed and trained soldiers. Moreover because of the significance of its geostrategic position, a united Korea would in all likelihood maintain strong ties with one of the regional powers, imposing burdens on the regional power balance. In such a case none of the powers would wish Korea reunified. Instead, each would rather maintain the more comfortable and manageable status quo.[69]

A desire for limitation of the Major Powers' arms transfers has been one of the traditional ways of thinking about arms control on the Korean Peninsula. The limitation of weapons was recognized as a way of achieving stability from the establishment of the two Korean governments in 1948. Soviet General Zakharov and the politburo refused an appeal by North Korea for an air force. According to the General:

> It is necessary to be careful with these Koreas. ... We are going to form a modern army, ... but we are going to act like the sorcerer's apprentice, creating a force which could make mischief in the Far East.[70]

At the same time the weapons transfers by the US to South Korea were also very limited for fear of President Syngman Rhee's offensive rhetoric about 'northward toward Pyongyang'. The first US ambassador John J. Muccie recalled:

> President Rhee had a very unrealistic attitude towards that whole issue. He thought that people in the North were waiting for him to arrive on a white charger. ... That tied our hands, for there was a danger that the aggression would occur from the South.[71]

As a result, whilst withdrawing US forces from South Korea in 1948-49, the US decided to leave limited weapon quantities in Korea. However, after the Korean War, the Major Powers changed their arms transfer policies from limitation of the quantitative to the qualitative. Their logic was that the achievement of stability would be made through an increase in the amount of weapons, instead of the mutual control of sophisticated weapons. An analyst described their policies for stability of the Peninsula as

> the Major Powers have instituted regional arms control in the Korean Peninsula, not a written agreement, but rather a tacit understanding in which certain types of weapons and levels of sophistication are not introduced.[72]

Such policies were retained till the 1970s. The Soviet Union refused to provide Pyongyang with high technology weapons systems such as long range surface-to-surface missiles, a sophisticated air defence system or Mig-23s supplied to some Middle East countries e.g. Egypt, Libya and Syria. The United States responded with similar restraint towards South Korea as shown by the US rejection of the South's request for the transfer of M60 tanks and two Lance battalions. The US also pressed the South to abandon its missile project in 1978.[73] Thus the level of weapons and their quality has been decided by the threat perceptions of the major powers rather than by the recipient clients.

Notwithstanding the above, the tacit arms control was broken with the growth of the recipient nations' economies. The US commenced selling F-4 and F-5 fighters to the South in the early 1980s; 36 F-16 sales followed in the mid-1980s.[74] In response to the US delivery of F-16, the Soviet Union provided North Korea with 46 MIG-23 and 24 MIG-29 fighters, 10 Su-25 light tactical bombers and sophisticated ground-to-air missiles and surface-to-surface tactical ballistic missiles.[75] Moreover, despite the end of the Cold War, there is no indication that the major powers have begun to downgrade the transfer of arms to the Korean Peninsula.

It cannot be denied that the arms supplies of the Major powers to Korea temporarily contributed to stability and status quo by announcing respective security commitments. However, the large influx of arms has surely heightened the recipients' threat perception and has maintained the stability through a high level of arms.

The amount and quality of arms are now decided by threat perceptions and purchase capabilities of North and South Korea, not by a criteria of stability. The 'tacit agreement' between the Major Powers no longer exists in the Korean Peninsula. Consequently it must be a useful subject for arms control negotiations between them.

The Implications of the European Arms Control Model

The Major Powers have attempted to solve the Korean question through agreement between themselves. The 1945 Yalta Agreement decided upon the division of the Korean Peninsula and considered a trusteeship by the US, the USSR, and China. Since that time a multilateral conference of concerned countries on the Korean problem has been recognized as an ideal formula for solving the Korean question. Proposals for a multilateral conference were put forward by Western policy makers. A former American ambassador to Seoul stated, "the potential for progress toward stabilization of the two Koreas may lie more in developing arrangements among the outside powers than through a process of North-South talks".[76]

The concept of maintaining of the status quo by the cooperation of the powers was based on a 'two-Korea policy' patterned after 'a two-German policy'. In fact the proposals for the multilateral talks were to follow European experiences which established the status quo in Europe and international acceptance of the two German states through the CSCE conference. On the basis of the CSCE model, a former US official called for a 'Conference on North-East Asian Security' (CNEAS) including the four powers, North and South Korea, and other countries. His proposals were that:

> continuing the German analogy, such a proposal for (CNEAS) should be thought of as much like the proposed European Security: ... The important result of a conference, perhaps even the purpose of merely calling for one, would be to tie up the parties in a negotiating process and all the preceding diplomatic byplay.[77]

Secretaries of State Henry Kissinger (1975), Cyrus Vance (1977) and Howard Baker (1991) called for six-party talks consisting of the four powers and the two Koreas. Kissinger's main concern was that through the conference, the concerned countries would discuss the issue of replacing the Armistice with a permanent peace treaty, including the cross-recognition of the two Koreas and the simultaneous admission of them into the United Nations.[78] The Reagan administration also indicated a four-party conference. Although it has objected to the application of the CSCE model to Northeast Asia or Asia, the US has however recognized the need for major powers' talks for settlement of the Korean question. The Soviet Union kept in mind the application of the German model of peaceful coexistence for Korea, criticizing the North's tripartite talks between the US and the two Koreas as an unrealistic approach.[79] Moscow's multilateral talks position following the pattern of settlement of the German question can be understood more clearly through the Soviet initiative for the CSCE which confirmed internationally the existence of the two German states. The Soviet Union indicated its desire to participate in any negotiations dealing with the Korean problems.[80] Because of that, it was natural that Moscow did not respond favourably to the North's tripartite conference proposal excluding its participation. The exclusion from such a conference would have reduced its influence on future developments in the Korean problem. As a result it supported Kissinger's proposal for 'a four-power conference' to discuss the problem.

However, the Soviet position was fundamentally different from that of the US The US proposed a conference of six-countries to solve the Korean question, while the Soviet Union suggested a conference dealing with all the security problems of Northeast Asian coastline countries - the four powers and the two Koreas without being limited to the Korean problem. The conference was to work for arms reduction and restrictions on the powers' naval forces activities.[81] Its logic was that the Korean question could be automatically solved through the creation of an institutionalized multilateral security organization dealing with regional problems.

Since the post-war period Japan has not been directly involved in the Korean question as one of the regional powers. Such a diplomatic attitude was based upon the fact that a substantial element of the Korean problem was a legacy of Japanese rule. However, successive Japanese governments have recognized that peace and stability on the Peninsula are essential to Japan's own security. Therefore, Japan has maintained the position that it cannot be excluded from any conferences dealing with the Korean problem. The Kissinger conference including Japan and the cross-recognition of the two Koreas has been the most popular model to Japan.[82] In fact though it only established diplomatic relations with the South, Japan has kept a balanced equidistant policy towards both North and South Korea.

Unlike the other powers, China has objected to any conference of four powers and six countries. Instead, it strongly supported the North's tripartite conference proposal. China's negative position could be the result of the fear that its direct involvement in the conference would draw the other major powers to the conference and weaken its traditional influence on the Korean Peninsula. China's prime interest in Korea has historically been to keep the Korean Peninsula within the Chinese sphere of influence.

Clearly, the Major Powers have proposed different forums for solving the Korean question. However, they are close to an accord with the view that a North-South dialogue or agreement is required as a first step for the conference. The Kissinger proposal for a six-nation conference was grounded on the basis of the success of a North-South dialogue. North and South Korea should have a preliminary conference first, and the participation of the United States and China would depend on the satisfactory results of this preliminary conference. If this process of North-South dialogue were successful, a more comprehensive conference including Japan and the Soviet Union would follow.[83] A similar proposal to the Kissinger idea was suggested by a Soviet-American special group. A Joint proposal of the group stressed that:

> the Koreans themselves must be responsible for creating their spirit and the mechanisms that can lead to the peaceful reunification of the Korean nation. The United States and the USSR should work to gain the support of other interested nations for such a course of action, especially the People's Republic of China and Japan.[84]

Thus the Major Powers themselves recognize that with regard to the Korean problem, they have not a leading role but a supporting role such as the guarantee on the North-South agreement or the participation in the stage of verification of arms control. Because it was a product of the Cold War, it would be only rational logic that the Korean problem must be solved by a compromise between the regional Cold War powers. But, with the end of the Cold War the Korean Peninsula is no longer the arena of struggle between East and West or the subject of bargaining between the regional powers. Their influence on the two Koreas is now very limited. Thus the Korean question is in hands of the Korean people.

The regional powers have long recognized the necessity of CBMs to the Korean Peninsula. A number of CBMs have been proposed for reducing military tension and bringing stability. Most of their proposals, though expressed as different measures, have principally followed the experience acquired in Europe.

The US believes that because of the very asymmetric conditions between Asia and Europe, no comparable arms control measures can be applicable to the Asian region. However, it considers that the Korean Peninsula is a region which urgently requires the application of CBMS. Richard H. Solomon, Assistant Secretary of State for the East Asia and Pacific region, said that the "Korean Peninsula is one place in Asia where European style CBMs can reduce tensions and ultimately lead to stabilizing arms control agreemen".[85] According to a report of the President to Congress, the US adopted an institutionalization of CBMs to reduce political and military tensions. The first step would be to negotiate 'transparency-style' measures such as data exchanges and exchanges of observers at military exercises.[86]

In fact, the application of CBMs to Korea was proposed before the Stockholm CBMs Agreement. In April 1984, Secretary of State George Shultz suggested four forms of CBMs to the Chinese foreign Minister:

> restoration of the non-military character of the DMZ by pulling forces back and removing heavy weapons from the area; regular inspection by teams composed of neutral nations to ensure the non-military character of the DMZ; prior notification by the North as well as the South of military exercises; mutual assignment of observers to such exercises.[87]

The United States has already carried out parts of their proposed CBMs on a unilateral basis. Annually, since 1982, North Korea and China have been notified of the T.S. exercises and invited to send military observers.

Russia also shares with the US the desire for CBMs application to reduce tensions. The CBMs adopted from the Stockholm agreement would be suitable to the circumstance of Korea as a basis for discussion of arms control. Soviet analysts had previously developed ideas about CBMs applicable either by the superpowers or the two Korean states. The Soviet suggestions included troops withdrawal from the MDL (Military Demarcation Line), advance notification of measures, regular meetings of military officials, reductions of offensive weapons and establishment of communication measures such as a hot-line.[88] The Soviet Union included South Koreans in an invitation to foreign observers for an inspection of the Pacific Fleet navy exercises. Its joint naval and air exercises with North Korea, which had been held since 1986, ceased from 1990.[89]

The Soviet Union fully supported North Korean arms control positions on issues such as the adoption of a non-aggression declaration, phased arms reduction, the establishment of a nuclear-free zone and withdrawal of American troops. The Soviet Union under Gorbachev attempted to play a mediatory role in Korea. As the only country of the major powers with diplomatic relations with the two Koreas, Russia is in a good position to play a role as mediator and promote arms control negotiations.[90]

Unlike the other powers, China did not give any detailed explanation for CBMs and opposed formal, bilateral CBMs in that bilateral CBMs would set a precedent for other types of arms control with the former USSR. However, since the border agreement with Moscow in April 1990, China has applied numerous European CBMs models to its territory, such as mutual notification of military exercises, the presence of observers at exercises, a ban on exercises in particular border regions, and no military movement along the border without prior agreement.

The Chinese have not been the initiator of CBMs proposals for the Peninsula except for advice upon the tripartite talks. However, China supports a number of CBMs in Korea, e.g. widening the demilitarized zone, notification of military exercises, limits on military manoeuvres and limits on arms transfers to the two sides.[91] China already fully supports the North's idea of a nuclear free zone on the Korean Peninsula for its security.

Chinese policy is still largely reactive and sensitive to North Korean interests. Therefore, the Chinese are unlikely to be the initiator of CBMs proposals injuring the advantages of the North in the near future. Japan, which fears getting involved in a Korean conflict, has always had a great concern for the stability of the Korean Peninsula. It would therefore seem natural for Japan to propose CBMs for the area. However, Japan has not suggested any constructive, concrete ideas of CBMs and arms control for the Peninsula even though it feels a need for CBMs application. It is understandable that Japan has not proposed some CBMs and arms control proposals for the region, because it rejected the Soviet CBMs and arms control proposals. The other reason why Japan has not proposed an active role for CBMs is due to its traditional equidistant policy toward North and South Korea. Therefore, for Japan, it may be difficult to propose the CBMs that North Korea has rejected. Japan understands that Korean people would be reluctant to accept any Japanese initiative because of their anti-Japanism. Above all the crucial reason comes from the American monopoly on Korean military affairs. In fact, Americans lack any interest in Japanese support because of their conviction that Korean affairs are an American concern, particularly when they concern military affairs like CBMs.[92]

Despite their different perspectives on the application of CBMs in Korea, the major powers have an agreed view about a ban on the nuclear possessions of North and South Korea. In the period between 1971-72 which saw the withdrawal of the 7th US Infantry Division and the fall of Saigon, South Korea initiated a series of efforts to obtain its own nuclear weapons capability with the establishment of an ad hoc "Weapons Exploitation Committee". After pressure from the US, the South gave up and signed the NPT.[93] In 1976, The South again attempted to purchase a small pilot processing plant from France or Canada and Israeli missiles but was unsuccessful.[94]

The major Powers' pressures on the North's nuclear program have been persistent. In 1985 North Korea signed the NPT under Soviet pressure. As a sanction the Soviet Union temporarily suspended all nuclear assistance to

Pyongyang until its acceptance of the IAEA inspections. China, like the Soviet Union, urged Pyongyang to allow these inspections. Pressure from Tokyo may be stronger because of its own security interests. Tokyo stopped the negotiations for full diplomatic relations with Pyongyang, requiring in advance the acceptance of inspections by the IAEA.[95]

Thus, the proposals of CBMs to achieve stability on the Korean Peninsula have come from the Major Powers. However, ideas for arms reductions have seldom been found in their official statements and documents. They assumed that the flash points of the Cold War involving the Superpowers would be the front line of Germany in Europe and the division line of Korea in Asia. The superpowers have simultaneously sought in Europe two ways of CBMs and arms reduction such as the MBFR and CFE, while they have not followed suit in Korea. It means that they have pursued a stability at the low level of armed forces in Europe and on the other hand, a stability at the high level in Korea. Arms reduction proposals have focussed on withdrawal of US forces from Korea, rather than a reduction of Korean forces. With the beginning of North-South arms control talks the Major Powers now show concern about the reductions of Korean forces. However, their proposals still only stress a need for arms reductions following the European experience without offering any concrete ideas.

The United States' position is "a withdrawal of combat force from the DMZ, equalization of troop levels and mutual balanced reduction of offensive weapons".[96] This means that the DPRK forces are unilaterally or asymmetrically reduced to the level of the South. Richard H. Solomon, Assistant Secretary of State argued that Pyongyang should follow the Soviet example of reducing forces into a posture of 'reasonable sufficiency'.[97] Such a position is in line with the ROK one, giving more priority to political and military CBMs than to arms reduction. These measures would be proceeded by verification for a common assessment of military forces of the two sides.

Some analysts have suggested that the four phased-arms control process can be applied to the Korean Peninsula. The phases are: first, the normalization of North-South relations; second, the Major Power's guarantee on a nonuse of force treaty between the two Koreas; third, the implementation of military CBMs and the creation of buffer demilitarized zones; and finally, a balanced reduction of North and South forces with the withdrawal of US forces.[98]

The enormous Korean military build-up is a remnant of the Cold War. The sizes of forces far exceed the requirements of defence. A low level of forces would be more conducive to Korean and regional stability. As in

Europe, the simultaneous implementation of CBMs and arms reduction talks must be considered for the Korean Peninsula. Now it is time for the regional powers to spur the application of European arms control mechanisms such as CBMs and arms reduction talks in Korea.

Conclusion

Historically the Korean Peninsula is a consequence of power political practice between Major Powers in Northeast Asia. Japan gained an opportunity to rule Korea for 36 years from 1910 as a victor in regional wars with China in 1894 and Russia in 1904. With the end of World War II the US shared the Korean problem with the regional powers. The Korean War was a limited war between the major communist and capitalist powers in support of the international bipolar state system beyond the military conflict between North and South Korea. Since then the Korean Peninsula has been an arena of the Cold War. During the period of the Sino-Soviet conflict in particular, North Korea was an area of competition for influence between the Soviet Union and China. Thus the Korean Peninsula has been in the shadow of regional power or global ideological politics over this century.

The Major Powers, which failed to establish exclusive influence in Korea through the Korean War, have guaranteed the security of their allies through arms supply. The rationale for the arms supply has been stability through military balance. However, the phenomena of their arms transfers has escalated military tension and helped to create a high level of threat perception. Furthermore, during the Sino-Soviet conflict, the competitive arms supplies of the two countries to North Korea helped the military balance tilt towards the North. Thus the competitive arms supplies of the major powers for military balance has led to the Korean arms race. In recent years there has no longer been the rule of "tacit arms control" between the powers which has limited the supply of sophisticated offensive weapons. Major Powers' sales of such weapons have increased upon the basis of commercial interests. Moreover the Korean arms race has developed from a qualitative to a qualitative dynamic in the absence of formal or informal arms control mechanism between the suppliers or receivers.

North Korea has consistently allocated a high portion of national resources to its defence build-up in order to achieve the unification of the Korean Peninsula on its terms. As a result, the military balance on the Korean Peninsula has been maintained to the advantage of the North. On the basis of such military superiority, North Korea has threatened the South and has through numerous military provocations escalated various crises. Faced with the North's threat, the US has conducted deterrent postures for the South. Of such postures, the stationing of US forces as a "trip-wire" has been the most significant.

The North's dream of communization of the entire peninsula has been obstructed by USFK. Consequently North Korea has maintained the belief that the withdrawal of the USFK would provide the shortest road to unification. They suggest its withdrawal as a precondition for tension reduction and for North-South arms control talks. On the other hand, the ROK and the US have staunchly opposed this and have rejected the link of US withdrawal with arms control talks. In particular South Korea has argued that the withdrawal of USFK would invite the DPRK's invasion southward. This belief is very concrete because of the past experience that the DPRK waged the Korean War as soon as the US forces were completely withdrawn from Korea in 1949. The US and some regional powers add the role of balancing for regional stability beyond the function of deterrence to the North's adventurism. The regional stability role of USFK beyond the Korean problem makes any agreement more difficult between the two Koreas on the problem of US forces. Thus although the presence of the USFK has decisively contributed to stability of the Korean Peninsula, it has on the other hand been a big obstacle to Korean arms control.

The urgent need of Korean arms control derives from the necessity for the prevention of surprise attack and crisis escalation rather than the rectification of the military balance. The heavy forward deployment of armed forces of both sides could lead to a small clash or an accident along the MDL and cause an escalation to a total war between them. The brevity of warning time and combat zone depth, together with the short distances of both capital cities from the MDL, are conditions that could suggest a surprise attack for strategic advantages to either side. Moreover, the growing shift of military superiority from the North to the South, together with the North's attempt to possess nuclear weapons would heighten the possibility of a preemptive war by either side.

This high state of tension and potential for war between the two heavily militarized Korean states has been a focus of international concern for four decades. The major powers concerned with the Korean problem have implemented a status quo and war deterrent policy in the region. They have suggested conferences and some measures associated with the European experience as solutions to the Korean problem.

The close connection of the two Koreas in the regional Cold War structure has limited the possibility of arms control by the Major Powers and in particular within the two Koreas. However, with the collapse of the Cold War system, regional environments are now changing from geopolitical to geoeconomic configuration or from balance of power to balance of interests. Such a regional security environment certainly provides a new, practical opportunity for the reduction of tension and a greater degree of arms control on the Korean Peninsula.

NOTES

1. Joseph M. Ha, "The Soviet Policy toward East Asia: Its Perception on the Korean Unification", *Asian Perspectives, Vol.* 10, No. 1, (Spring-Summer, 1986) p .1 16.
2. Senator Hubert H. Humphrey and John Glenn, *US Troop Withdrawal from the Republic of Korea,* A report to the Committee on Foreign Relations of United States Senate (US, GPO, 1978), p. 12.
3. Ralph N. Clough, A Doak Barnett *et al, The United States, China and Arms Control* (Washington D.C.: The Brookings Institution, 1975), p. 118. Quoted in *The New York Times,* 10 August, 1971.
4. William J. Taylor, Jr. Michael J. Mazarr and Jennifer A. Smith, "US Troop Reduction from Korea, 1970-1990", *The Journal of East Asian Affairs,* Vol. IV, No.2, (Summer/Fall, 1990), p. 270.
5. *Far Eastern Economic Review,* 2 May , 1991.
6. *Military Balance* (IISS, London, 1994), p. 181.
7. The Ministry of National Defence of the ROK, *The Korean Defence White Paper 1989,* p. 132.
8. Byung Chul Koh, *The Foreign Policy Systems of North and South Korea* (Berkeley: University of California Press, 1984), p. 91.
9. Yong Nain Kim, "A View from Pyongyang", *International Affairs* (Moscow), January 1990, p. 142.
10. Western analysts have said that the strategic location provided the Soviet Union/Russia with the use of ice-free ports in the Far East, a role of a buffer state against seapowers and the route for the air line between the Russian Far East and its base in Indo-china.
11. Helen-Louise Hunter, "North Korea and the Myth of Equidistance", *Korea and World Affairs,* Vol. 34, No. 2, (Summer 1980). pp. 268-279.
12. Young Koo Cha, "Northeast Asian Security: A Korean Perspective", *Significant Issues Series* (Washington D.C.: The CSIS, 1988), Vol. X, No. 1. p. 24.
13. *SIPRI Yearbook 1989,* p. 255.
14. "Economic Weapons", *Far Eastern Economic Review,* 23 May, 1991.
15. *SIPRI Yearbook 1991,* p. 209
16. For references of the establishment, organization, functioning and mission of USFK, see Ronald D. McLauin and Chung-In Moon, *The United States and the Defence of the Pacific* (Colorado: Westview Press, 1989). MyungKi Kim, "Some Legal Problems Concerning Withdrawal of the United Nations Forces", *The Journal of East Asian Affairs,* Vol.IV, No.2, (Summer/Fall, 1990), pp. 287-310.
17. For detailed references, see Richard P. Cassidy, *Arms Transfer and Security Assistance to the Korean Peninsula 1945-1980: Impact and Implications* (Monterey, Calif.: Naval Postgraduate School, 1980), pp. 91-93. and; Hearing before the Subcommittee on the United

States Security Agreements and Commitments abroad of the Committee on Foreign Relations, 91 st Congress, 1971, p. 1 569, 1618.
18. SIPRI, *The Arms Trade Registers: The Arms Trade with the Third World* (MIT Press, 1975), p. 12. The US transferred 76 Northrop F-5A, B Freedom Fighters to Korea between 1965 and 1971.
19. Cassidy. op. cit., pp. 119-120.
20. Cassidy, op. cit., pp. 101-102. To improve firepower and mobility, the US promised South Korea $275 million in FMS credits in FY 1979. The equipment of the 2nd Division such as upgraded M48 tanks, Tows, Honest SSMs and Howitzers was to be transferred to Korean forces.
21. Ibid. pp. 217-218. Actually 37 F-4E Phantom Fighters and air defence missiles such as Honest John 1-Hawk SAMS and MIM-23B Hawk were supplied between 1977 and 1978.
22. Humphrey and Glenn, op. cit., pp. 43-45.
23. Korean Defence White Paper 1989, p. 189. FMS Credit for South Korea was terminated at the beginning of 1987 on the basis that the Korean economy was healthy enough to permit the procurement of US military articles without US-finance credit.
24. *SIPRI Yearbook* 1991, pp. 208, 260.
25. *The Military Balance 1991-1992,* pp. 212-214. The number of troops in 1000's were: The CIS; 3400, China; 3030, the US; 2029, India; 1265, DPRK; 1 1 1 1, Vietnam; 1041, ROK; 750.
26. The Ministry of National Defence of the ROK, *Korean Defense White Paper 1989,* pp. 99-100.
27. *Wolgan Chosun* (a Korean monthly Journal), Vol.9, No.8, (August), pp. 2515.
28. Oh, Kwan-Chi, "The Military Balance on the Korean Peninsula", in William J. Taylor, Jr and Cha, Yoong Koo (eds), *The Korean Peninsula: Prospects for Arms Reduction under Global Detente* (Westview Press, 1990), p 102-103. Author assumed that GNP growth rates of South Korea would be in the range of 6 to 7 percent per year for the 1990/2005, and those of the North, 3 percent per year. The South was estimated to be spending 4.5 percent ; the North was estimated as spending 21.5 percent of GNP on defence.
29. *The Chung Ang Ilbo* (Korean Daily Newspaper), 25 August, 1990
30. Goose, Stephen D. "The Military Situation on the Korean Peninsula", in John Sullivan & Roberta Foss (eds), *Two Koreas-one Future* (University Press of America, 1987). p. 57.
31. *The Korea Herald,* 7 July, 1985.
32. Kwak, Tae Hwan, "Peace Process and Military Capabilities on the Korean Peninsula", Presented at the Joint Annual Convention of the British International Studies Association and the International Studies Association (London, 28 March-1 April, 1989), p. 16.
33. Ha, Young Sun "The Korean Military Balance: Myth and Reality", Presented at CSIS /KIDA (the Centre for Strategic and International Studies & the Korean Institute for Defence Analyses), International Conference(Seoul, 12-13 September, 1988), pp. 20-22.
34. Lee, Ki-Baek, Minister of National Defense of ROK, "Present and Future Security Problems of Korea", A speech delivered at the Centre for Strategic and International Studies, Georgetown University, 8 May, 1987)
35. Chung, Tae-Dong, Assistant of DIA of Ministry of National Defense of ROK, "The Security Situation on the Korean Peninsula", a speech delivered at the Korean Ilhae Institute (Seoul, 18 March, 1987)
36. Oh, Kwan-Chi, "The Military Balance", p. 98.
37. *Korean Defence White Paper 1990,* p. 70.
38. Gertz, Bill, "N. Korea Troops near Border Alarm US," *The Washington Times, 2* May, 1985, p. 5.

39. *Armed Forces Journal International,* August 1984, pp. 39-44
40. Atta, Dale Van and Nation, Richard, "Kim's Build-Up to Blitzkrieg", *Far Eastern Economic Review,* 5 March, 1982, p. 26.
41. Chung Min Lee, "Holding the Hollingsworth Line : Conventional Deterrence in the Korean Peninsula", Harold C. Hinton, Donald Zagoria and Jung Ha Lee, *The US-Korean Security Relationship: Prospects and Challenges for the 1990s* (Washington D.C.: Pergamon.Brassey's, 1988), p. 72.
42. Ibid. pp.76-79. Cushman, John H. "South Korea: the ROK / US Partnership for Peace", *Pacific Defence Monitor,* (May 1984), pp. 39-44.
43. Goose, "The Military Situation", p. 79.
44. "N. K Puts Military on Full Alert against Team Spirit", *The Korea Herald,* 27 February, 1991.
45. Bermudez, Joseph S. Jr and Carus, W. Seth, "The North Korean Scud B Programme", *Jane's Soviet Intelligence Review,* (April, 1989), p. 177.
46. Bermudez, Joseph S. Jr., "New Developments in North Korean Missile Programme", p. 344. This source said in June of 1987 North Korea and Iran concluded a $500 million arms agreement which included the purchase of 90-100 North Korea produced Scud-Bs and apparently assistance in establishing a missile production facility in Iran.
47. Ibid, p. 345.
48. "N. K. deploys Scuds close to DMZ; 12 launchers detected", *The Korea Herald,* 3 February, 1991.
49. Nolan, Janne E. *Trappings of Power: Ballistic Missile in the Third World* (The Brooking Institution, 1991), p. 50
50. *Korean Defence White Paper 1989,* p. 165.
51. *Korea Defense White Paper 1989,* p.27. Chung-in Moon, "US Third Country Arms Sale Regulation and the South Korean Defence Industry" in Manwoo Lee, Ronald D. McLaurin and Chung-in Moon, *Alliance under Tension: The Evolution of South Korean-US Relations* (Seoul: Westview Press, 1988), p. 85.
52. Bermudez Jr & Carus, "The North Korean Scud B Programme," p. 180.
53. Mack, Andrew, Nuclear Issues and Arms Control on the Korean Peninsula (Pacific Research : Australian National University, *Working Paper* 96), February 1991, p. 2
54. "Signs of a Thaw ?", *Pacific Research,* Vol.3, No. 4, (November 1990), p. 17. and N. Korea will build Nuclear Weapons, *Jane's Defence Weekly,* 12 January, 1991.
55. "Nuclear Jitters", *Newsweek,* 29 April, 1991
56. Bermuda Jr, Joseph S. "N Korea-Set to Join the Nuclear Club ?", *Jane's Defence Weekly,* 23 September, 1991.
57. Davis, S. *et al,* 'Korea: Procedural and Jurisdictional Questions Regarding Possible Normalisation of Relations with North Korea', *CRS Report for Congress* (Washington, DC, USGPO, 1994), Summary.
58. Ibid, p. 9.
59 Mack, "Nuclear Issues", p. 14.
60. On 12 April, 1991, South Korean Defence Minister Lee Jong Koo suggested the probability of a commando raid. "Nuclear Jitter", p. 22.
61. *International Herald Tribune,* 4 June, 1991.
62. Mack, "Nuclear Issues", p. 17.
63. Gary Klintworth, "Arms Control and Great-Power Interests in the Korean Peninsula", *The Korean Journal of Defence Analysis,* Vol 111, No. 1, (Summer 1991), p. 166.
64. Roger E. Kanet & Edward A. Kolodziej, *The Cold War as Cooperation: Superpower Cooperation in Regional Conflict Management* (London: MacMillan, 1991), p. 387.

65. The behaviours of the Soviet Union and China in the crises on the Korean Peninsula by North Korea are described in Donald S. Zagoria and Janct D. Zagoria, "Crises on the Korean Peninsula", in Stephen S. Kaplan and others,, *Diplomacy of Power.. Soviet Armed Forces as a Political Instrument Part* 11 (Washington D.C.:Brookings Institution, 1981), pp. 357-411.
66. Ibid. pp. 394.
67. Ibid. pp. 405-409.
68. Clough et al. 111- 114.
69. Tae-Hwan Kwak and Chonghin Kim (eds), *Korean Reunification: New Perspectives and Approaches (Seoul:* the Institution for Far Eastern Studies, 1984), p. 230.
70. This statement was revealed by Colonel C. D. Kalinow, who had been a member of the Soviet military mission to North Korea at the end of 1948, and attached to the Soviet General Staff under General Zakharov in 1949. Cassidy, op. cit., p. 46.
71. Ibid., p.42. President Syngman Rhee's rhetoric about "moving North" was misinterpreted by many Americans to be more than the moral boosting rhetoric it actually was.
72. Ibid. p. 209.
73. Franklin B Weinstein, "Korea and Arms Control 11", in John H. Barton and Ryukichi Imai (eds), *Arms Control ll: A New Approach to International Security* (Cambridge: OGII, 1981), p. 165.
74. *The Korea Herald,* 31 August, 1991.
75. Alexei G. Arbatov, "Sheathing the Korean Dagger: Problems and Opportunities for the Northeast Asia Arms Control and Security Process", in *Arms Control on the Korean Peninsula: what lessons can we learn European experiences?* (Seoul: Institute of Foreign Affairs & National Security, 1990), pp. 93-94.
76. Richard Sneider, "Prospects for Korean Security", in Richard H. Solomon (ed), *American Security in the 1980s: Problems and Policies for a Time of Transition* (Cambridge, MA: Oegeshhlager, Gunn & Hain, 1979), p. 139.
77. Morton Abramowitz, "Moving the Glacier: the Two Koreas, and the Powers" *Adelphi Paper* 80 (IISS, 1971), p. 24.
78. Hak-Joon Kim, "The Tripartite Conference Proposal for Korean Settlement: its origin, evolution and prospects", in Tae Hwan Kwak and Chonghan Kim (eds), *Korean Unification,* p. 105.
79. Ralph N. Clough, *Embattled Korea: the Rivalry for International Support* (Westview Press, 1987), p. 243.
80. Young C. Kim & Abraham M. Halperin, *The Future of the Korean Peninsula* (New York: Fredrick A Praeger, 1977), pp. 120-12 1.
81. "From Mikail Gorbachev's Speech in Krasnoyarsk on September 16, 1988", *Far Eastern Affairs,* No. 1, 1988, p. 2.
82. *The Korea Herald,* 13 January, 1984. Rejecting the tripartite talks proposals of China and North Korea in 1984, Japan responded that it would favour the six-party conference. "Kaifu to Propose six-nation parley on Korean Peninsula", *The Korea Herald,* April 15, 1990.
83. Hak-Joon Kim, "the tripartite conference proposal", p. 108
84. The International Strategic Institute at Stanford and the Institute of Far Eastern Studies, Academy of Sciences of the USSR, "On Strengthening Security and Developing Cooperation on the Korean Peninsula" (September, 1988).
85. *Overview of Recent Events in the East Asian and Pacific Region,* Hearing before Subcommittee on Asian and Pacific Affairs of the Committee on Foreign Affairs House of Representatives (one hundred and first Congress, Second Session, GPO., 22 February, 1990). p. 48.

86. *The President's Report on the US military Presence in East Asia,* Hearings before the Committee on Armed Services of the United States Senate (one hundred first Congress, second session, G.P.O., 19 April, 1990), p. 21.
87. Reinhard Drifte, "Arms Control and the Superpower Balance in East Asia", in Generald Segal, *Arms Control in Asia* (MacMillan Press, 1987), P. 35.
88. Stephen Blank, "Soviet Perspectives on Arms Control in the Korean Peninsula", *The Korean Journal of Defence Analysis, Vol* 111, No. I (Summer, 1991) p. 120.
89. *Asian Security 1991-1992* (Tokyo: Research Institute for Peace and Security, 1991), p. 161.
90. "Shevardnaze Sees Soviet mediation role in Korea", *The Korea Herald,* 7 April, 1990.
91. Alastair Iain Johnston, "China and Arms Control in the Asia-Pacific Region" in Frank C. Langdon C. & Douglas A. Ross, *Superpower Maritime Strategy in the Pacific* (London: Routledge, 1990), p. 194.
92. Reinhard Drifte, "The Missing Link of Neo-Detente: Arms Control in East Asia" in *Toward one World beyond all Barriers* (Seoul: Poong-nam Printing, 1989), p.282.
93. Cassidy, op. cit. p. 246.
94. Ibid. p. 247.
95. Leonard S. Spector and Jacqueline R. Smith, "North Korea: the next nuclear nightmare?", *Arms Control Today,* March 1991 pp. 10-11.
96. *The President's report of the US military presence in East Asia, p. 54.*
97. *Overview of Recent Event in the East Asia and Pacific Region, p. 48.*
98. Alexei Bagaturov and Mikail Nosov, "The Korean Aspect", *New Times* (6-12 June , 1989), p. 26.

Part IV
Korean Arms Control and the Application of the European Model

8. The North-South Arms Control Negotiations

The History of Arms Control Talks

North and South Korea have long believed that security can only be achieved through strengthened military power. Using arms control to enhance security has not been prominent in their thinking. North Korea has continuously developed its military strength in the hope that unification might be achieved by use of force. In addition, with the experience of the UN counter-offensive of 1950, it has identified a genuine military threat from the ROK and USFK forces to the South. Faced with the threat from the North, South Korea has responded with the same option of increasing military strength to maintain parity. Therefore, arms control issues have seldom been subjected to serious bilateral negotiations. Instead, both states have announced a number of unilateral, declaratory arms control statements as tactics in domestic politics and foreign policy without promoting them in serious negotiation. According to South Korea's National Unification Board, the North and the South made a total of 294 arms control proposals between 1948 and 1988. The North made 235 proposals on 29 subjects, while the South made 59 proposals on 18 subjects.[1] This seems to show that in arms control the North was considerably more active, However this does not necessarily mean that the North really wanted arms control. Rather, the North used such initiatives to attempt to project a non-threatening image overseas.

The first arms control dialogue between North and South Korea dates back to the multilateral Geneva Conference in 1954. At that conference North Korea demanded the withdrawal of all foreign military forces from Korea within six months and a mutual limit on the size of Korean forces at a level of 100,000 men. South Korea countered with a call for the withdrawal of all Chinese troops one month in advance of the election's designed to bring about the unification of Korea and the continued stationing of the UN forces until the completion of unification.[2] In reality, neither side was ready to compromise after the bitter experience of the Korean War.

In the 1960s the hardline policies of both sides excluded any possibility of arms control negotiation between them. In 1961 the South established a very strong anti-communist government. In response to this in 1962 the North began the modernization and expansion of its armed forces with the adoption of the 'Four-point Military Guidelines'.[3] With the beginning of the Vietnam War such harsh policies were enforced even more. The South demonstrated a rigid anti-communist stand through the dispatch of its troops to South Vietnam. The North increased intensive military provocations against the South. Thus, the internal and external situations did not provide any room for arms control dialogue.

However, in the early 1970s improvements in the international environment, such as the Soviet-American detente and the rapprochement between the US, Japan and China, permitted a change from military confrontation to negotiation in Korea as well as in Europe. Further the removal of 20,000 US troops from the South as a result of the implementation of the Nixon Doctrine encouraged South Korea to adapt to the changing situation on the Korean Peninsula. South Korea felt a strong need for negotiation with the North to establish a stable equilibrium after the unilateral reduction of American forces. North Korea also hoped that its moderate policy toward South Korea would encourage America to pull out all its remaining troops from the South.[4]

For the first time North-South direct contacts were made in 1971, after more than two decades of frozen hostility. On 4 July, 1972, North and South Korea agreed a joint communique on measures for reducing military tension and developing peaceful steps toward unification. The communique elaborated three principles of unification and confidence building. The principles of unification were:

- achievement of unification through independent efforts without external imposition or interference.
- achievement of unification through peaceful means, without the use of force
- achievement of national unity as a homogeneous community, transcending differences of ideologies and system.

Major confidence building measures proposed were:

- to ease tensions and increase the atmosphere of mutual trust.
- not to conduct armed provocations.
- to prevent military accidents.
- to carry out exchanges in various areas.
- to seek an early success of the Red Cross talks.
- to install a direct telephone line to prevent military accidents.
- to establish a South-North Coordinating Committee to settle problems.[5]

The Red Cross talks, which aimed at the reuniting of families separated through the Korean War, opened in August 1972. The mutual slander and defamation through loud speakers was stopped along the Armistice line. The key developments were the establishment of the "North-South Coordinating Committee" and a direct telephone line between the representatives of the committee. The committee's purpose was to use diplomacy to manage crises including tension reduction and prevention of accidental conflicts.

However, the two sides had very different views regarding the implemention of the agreement. North Korea made a five-point proposal: 1) a halt to the North-South arms race 2) mutual reduction of troops to 100,000 or less 3) a halt to the introduction of military equipment from foreign countries 4) withdrawal of all foreign forces 5) signing of a peace agreement to guarantee these measures.[6] On the other hand South Korea insisted upon the discussion of non-military issues such as trade and cultural exchanges, opposing the priority given to military issues. The sudden dialogue, which started as a means of adapting to the uncertainties of the external environment, failed to narrow the divergent views. Furthermore both sides held the talks essentially for political reasons rather than due to any military needs. This was evident from the fact that no military representatives were included among the delegations and a direct telephone line was installed only between the political authority and not the military.

Beyond that point North and South Korea subsequently exchanged only declaratory statements of 'tit-for tat', proposals for propaganda or counter-proposals. For example, in January 1974, the South proposed a non-aggression pact between Seoul and Pyongyang. In March 1974 the North countered with a proposed peace treaty between Washington and Pyongyang. In 1979 the US and the South proposed tripartite talks between Seoul, Washington and Pyongyang. In subsequent years North Korea called for a tripartite conference similar to the previous South-US proposal.

This pattern lasted up to the second half of the 1980s. The expectation was that neither side's proposals would be automatically accepted by the other side. In fact, after the North-South dialogues of 1972-73, there was little room for negotiation between them. Pyongyang's provocations against the South were clearly evident: the shooting of President Park and the killing of his wife in 1974, the 'Axe-Murder Incident' of two US officers in 1976 and 'Rangoon Bomb Terror' aimed at killing President Chun and his ministers during their visit to Burma in 1983. North Korea's subsequent provocations destroyed any confidence established through the 1972-73 dialogue and deepened mistrust. Moreover, the North replaced the South with the US as a security negotiation partner. No negotiations on the military issues took place between them up to the mid-1980s.

However, from the mid-1980s, the domestic and international environments pushed the two Koreas towards arms control negotiation. On 16 June, 1986 North Korean Defence Minister Ochin-u proposed tripartite military talks between Defence Ministers of both sides and the commander of the USFK for dealing with tension reduction.[7] North Korea's subsequent proposals were: high level talks on political and military affairs in 1987, 'a comprehensive plan for peace' in 1988 and a disarmament proposal for peace in 1990. The contents of the proposals of 1988 and 1990 were similar to earlier ones. However, a desire for negotiation was more evident. First of all, it showed some flexibility. Unlike the previous proposals, the period of reduction of armed forces was not concretely fixed. A phased withdrawal of American forces was also considered in keeping with the arms reduction of the North and the South. What was a more significant event however was that the language of CBMs was used for the first time. The most surprising change was a proposal for 'high level talks' between the Prime Ministers of both Koreas, replacing the US with the South as the primary negotiation partner.

South Korea has made great efforts towards institutionalizing peaceful coexistence between the two Koreas since President Roh's accession in 1988. The taboo against discussion on arms control and disarmament in the North-South dialogue disappeared within the South. At the 3rd Special Disarmament Meeting of the United Nations in June 1988, Foreign Minister Choi Kwang-Soo put forward a three-stage approach towards disarmament on the Korean Peninsula; first, to build up mutual trust and confidence, secondly, to conclude a non-aggression pact and thirdly, to achieve the goals of disarmament.[8] In his speech at the UN Assembly in the same year President Roh declared unilaterally the South's first no-first-use of force against the North and proposed a summit meeting between the two Koreas for resolving all the problems, including disarmament, arms control and other military matters raised by both sides.[9] It was a turning point in South Korea's arms control position, changing from the negative to the positive. South Korea put pressure on the North to come to the negotiation table through its 'Northern Policy' towards the Soviet Union and China, pillars of the North's security. With the success of this policy, it began to have the initiative for the first time in the history of the North-South arms control dialogue. The hitherto dominant pattern has been that Pyongyang acted and Seoul responded. Since 1988 South Korea has taken the initiative.[10]

From 4 September 1990, both sides have discussed the implications of arms control through the high level talks between Prime Ministers. On 13 December 1991, An "Agreement on Reconciliation, Non-aggression and Exchanges and Cooperation" was made in the fifth round talks. The long game of arms control has already started in the Korean Peninsula.

Arms Control Approaches

The arms control approach of North Korea has been based on its strategic objective of unification. Korean national unification has been the linchpin of its domestic and foreign policies. It can be said that the Korean War itself was caused by the North's drive towards unification. After meeting with Kim Il-Sung US Congressman, Stephen J. Solarz stated that "the unification of Korea is not only the major objective of North Korea, but the primary touchstone against which different policies and proposals for resolving the Korean problems are evaluated".[11] No North Korean proposals for arms control have been separated from the objective of the unification. On 7 November 1988, the Central People's Committee of the North emphasized that "peace on the Korean Peninsula should serve the idea of national unification and become a prerequisite for national unification, rather than for the establishment of 'two Koreas' masked by a preservation of peace".[12] Thus, for North Korea, unification is a necessary condition of peace and no peace is guaranteed without unification. In fact, arms control proposals based on the status quo or tension reduction have been recognized as disregarding unification. The report of Solarz emphasised the relation between arms control and unification:

> They (North Koreans) fear that agreement on tension-reducing political and military measures, ranging from dual membership in the United Nations to the genuine demilitarization of demilitarized zones, would be more likely to result in the perpetuation of the status quo than in any real progress toward the establishment of a unified nation.[13]

In theory, the North's pursuit of unification leads it to oppose the status quo and tension reduction. Any measures for stability or status quo are understood as maintaining the division of the Korean Peninsula. As a result, the North's arms control approach in the context of unification means that it uses arms control proposals as a means of unification, not as an end in itself.

North Korean arms control proposals are based upon an unrealistic premise in terms of the process of negotiation or implementation. The reduction of North and South Korean troops and the withdrawal of US forces from Korea are called for in a very short time-frame without taking into account the phases of arms control. For example, the 1988 proposal, the so-called "Comprehensive Peace Plan", argued that the nearly one million strong Northern forces and the 650,000 strong Southern forces should be reduced to 100,000 men respectively in four years and the withdrawal of all US forces should be made in two years. The time-table North Korea suggested is so rapid that it cannot be physically arranged. Thus the North has generated credibility in terms of the process and steps needed to reach the successful final stage of arms reduction.

North Korea also argues that disarmament measures are a necessary precondition for building confidence. The introduction to the 1990 proposals declared that: "without disarmament it is impossible to build confidence between both sides, bring the dialogues for reunification to a success, realize cooperation and exchange or achieve the peaceful reunification of the country".[14] The North's proposals have not been primarily aimed at arms control but rather are political propaganda. Its proposals have been tactical ploys directed at the South's domestic political situation and US force reductions in Korea.[15] As seen in table 8-1 the frequency of its proposals have been highest the times of US force reductions and political unrest in the South.

Table 8-1 The Pattern of the North Korean Arms Control Proposals

	1960-61	1972-73	1977-78	1986-87
situation	P.U	7th W.	2nd W.	P.U
frequency	12	33	16	30

P.U: Political unrest. 7th. W.: US 7th division withdrawal. 2nd. W: US 2nd division withdrawal plan. Sources: This is compiled through a paper of Young Koo Cha, "Arms Control on the Korean Peninsula" presented for the International Conference of the Korean Institute of International Studies (4-6 July,1989).

Thus arms control proposals have been used as a means of political tactics rather than military stabilisation. It is not clear that the many proposals of the early 1970s and the mid-1980s were influenced by the development of the conventional arms control negotiations of Europe. Unlike Europe, North Korean proposals were almost always in abstract terms, unilateral declaratory statements which did not suggest concrete and detailed plans to reach any meaningful conclusion. Further the proposed subjects were far removed from those of European arms control. This suggests that North Korea had the intention of improving its image, rather than solving pending military issues.

The arms control approaches of South Korea are fundamentally different from those of North Korea. Its perspective on national unification, unlike the North's "unification first, peace later", is that peace is a necessary condition for unification. For the South, national unification is a long term goal to be achieved through the creation of a status quo that admits the reality of the division. Therefore, South Korea has argued a formula of 'Peace first, unification later'. It has advocated, for this purpose, an incremental, functional and step by step approach. It is believed that the incremental implementation of cooperation in non-military fields helps military issues, difficult to negotiate, to be settled more easily. On the basis of this perspective, the establishment of political and non-military CBMs such as mutual recognition between Seoul and Pyongyang, exchange of liaison offices in both capitals, cessation of verbal attack and the promotion of cultural and economic cooperation has been emphasised prior to arms control.[16] The South Korean insistence that improvements of such exchanges and cooperation must precede the resolution of military confrontation is intended to eliminate political and psychological suspicions which have accumulated over the past four decades.[17]

The priority goal of arms control is to ease tensions and to build trust. Therefore, South Korean arms control proposals have consistently aimed at creating an atmosphere conducive to substantive arms control. To South Korea, confidence building measures are the best option for this purpose. In contrast to the North's position that without disarmament CBMs are impossible, the South's belief is that the implementation of CBMs is a necessary precondition for disarmament. South Korea upholds a procedural formula of "building-up of mutual trust, secondly arms control and then arms reduction". South Korean officials have dismissed most Northern proposals not based on the build-up of trust and confidence-building measures as unrealistic and propagandist. Consequently, the South is in favour of operational CBMs such as exchanges of information, advance notification and exchange of observers at troop movements, deployments, exercises, and inspections.

The South's arms control ideas have been much more cautious than those of the North. Its arms control approach are designed to enhance deterrence. Deterrence is partly achieved through the alliance with the US The operation of the ROK/US combined forces command system is a central feature of security maintenance. Such an approach is clearly suggested in the basic guidelines for arms control:

- arms control should be based upon the ROK/US security cooperation regime and pursued in line with military modernization in order to meet the North's threat.

- arms control should be comprehensively approached in pace with the regional environment and development of North-South relations in a linkage with unification and security policy.

- arms control should be approached by gradual and step by step methods, minimizing security risk on the basis of military stability.[18]

Because of its military inferiority to the North, the South has been preoccupied with how to catch up with the North in each sector of military preparation. Some analysts argue that "since the military balance is moving inexorably in the South's favour, there is no real need for arms control and certainly not until the North is ready to accept Seoul's terms".[19] The evidence was well demonstrated in a recent speech that "strengthened military power in the South would lead the North to give up the arms race and to come to the table of mutual arms reduction, a precondition for peaceful unification".[20] Thus, in fact the South is very reluctant to deal with arms reductions with the North until military parity is achieved. For the South, any hasty and drastic arms reduction could disturb the military stability on the Peninsula.

Negotiation Forum

North and South Korea have long exchanged arms control ideas. Unfortunately all the ideas were seen as political propaganda. One of the most important reasons why such ideas were not developed was due to the lack of an institutionalized negotiation forum where proposed views could be discussed in depth. Both Koreas argued their claims through unilateral statements without establishing any appropriate forums for devising procedures and methods for arms control. Even though the proposed ideas were propagandist, common interests could have been identified through the process of filtration in the negotiation forums.

In fact, the negotiation forum itself became a controversial issue and a major obstacle to the beginning of negotiation towards arms control. The focal point of the argument concerned the question of negotiation partners. The North demanded direct negotiations with the US, while the South insisted on direct bilateral negotiations with the North. The North's basic strategy was to talk with the United States first, then with the South. An example of this was the 'tripartite conference' proposed by Pyongyang in 1984. The main subjects of the conference were to replace the Armistice Agreement with a Peace Agreement between the US and the North and to adopt a declaration of nonaggression between the North and the South.[21] Though the North's tripartite conference invited the South as 'an equal partner', the South could not take part after the opening of the North-US meetings, and would be seated as an observer.[22] The North's intention was to bring about the withdrawal of the USFK in direct talks with the US with the exclusion of the South.

In fact, the idea of the tripartite conference was originally proposed in July 1979 by the South's President Park and the US President Carter. They called for the convening of a meeting of senior official representatives of South and North Korea and the United States in order to seek means to promote dialogue for unification and to reduce tension.[23] But, the North rejected the proposal on the grounds that the unification issue was an internal affair and that the South was not a party to the 1953 cease-fire agreement. Thus, Pyongyang has insisted on a format of talks that seeks to diminish Seoul as a negotiation partner.

The South's basic position was to solve all the Korean problems including military matters through bilateral negotiation between the North and the South. South Korea consistently proposed 'settlement measures' confined to the bilateral context. Its first proposal was a North-South non-aggression Pact of 1974. Its preference for bilateral negotiation was an attempt to resume the meeting of the "South-North Coordinating Committee" which had been stopped by the North's unilateral declaration. In fact, the South was never enthusiastic about the tripartite format declared by the communique of the 1979 summit meeting of the South and the US President. South Korean President Park agreed reluctantly to the tripartite proposal of President Carter in order to ensure the suspension of the US troop withdrawals and in the expectation that the North would turn it down.[24] Since the main task of the North's tripartite talks focussed on dealing with the withdrawal of American forces, it was natural that the South strongly rejected the idea of the talks.

The South's alternative was a North-South summit meeting. In 1981, President Chun suggested face to face talks between the two leaders in either exchange visits, in Panmunjom, or in a third country.[25] His successor, President Roh, also emphasised the meeting as a basic framework for ending the military confrontation and resolving all the problems related to disarmament and arms control and other military matters.[26] As an alternative to the South's summit talks, the North suggested "high level political and military talks".[27] On 28 December 1988, as a response to the North's proposal, the South suggested high level talks between the Premiers. Eventually Pyongyang accepted bilateral talks on arms control issues with Seoul. Pyongyang declared on 31 May 1990, that:

> The United States yet being unwilling to accede to tripartite talks, we cannot delay the discussion of arms reduction for an indefinite period till the US respond. The tripartite talks must be held at an early date, but a way must be found to discuss the disarmament before the talks.[28]

The North did not basically give up the goal of direct negotiation with the US and regarded negotiations as preliminary talks prior to the tripartite talks. However, its acceptance of the South as a negotiation partner eliminated the biggest obstacle to the progress of arms control negotiation. Since the high-level talks of 1990 a number of constructive proposals have been bilaterally exchanged between North and South Korea. The North-South high level talks have broadly been used as a forum of arms control negotiation. The December 1991 "Agreement on Reconciliation, Nonaggression and Exchanges and Cooperation" established three South-North joint committees within the framework of the "high level talks"; the Political Joint Committee, the Military Joint Committee and the Joint Exchanges and Cooperation Committee. The Military Joint Committee now operates as an apparatus for easing tension and devising arms control measures. It will be required to develop as an institutionalized, elaborated forum dealing with arms control subjects and promising the continuation of negotiation without following the abortive precedent of the 1972 North-South Coordinating Committee.

Confidence Building Measures

The Korean Peninsula has long appeared to be the most obvious region for the application of classic European-style CBMs. However, until now, no military CBMs have been initiated in the region. The South has been eager to introduce broad-ranging CBMs to the North as a means of functional incrementalism, while the North has only emphasised the idea of force reduction. But, recently both sides have introduced a number of military CBMs in their proposals.

From the May 1990 disarmament proposals the North Koreans began to use the term 'confidence-building measures' and elaborated some measures. South Korea also placed military CBMs on the table of the first high-level talk. They began to recognize that CBMs are important for tension reduction and stability. In the December 1990 Agreement both sides provided a base for the application of CBMs by concluding an agreement on nonaggression. The nonaggression agreement declared (1) no use of force (2) peaceful resolution of dispute through dialogue and negotiation and respect of the Armistice MDL and the jurisdiction of each side. The CBMs are intended to help to implement the nonaggression agreement. The listed measures are:

- the mutual notification and control of major movements of military units and exercises.
- the peaceful utilization of the Demilitarized Zone.
- exchanges of military personnel and information.
- prevention of surprise attack.
- verification.
- establishment of a hot line between the military authorities.[29]

Thus, both sides have a common view that a legal framework on nonaggression is a first step for arms control. However, they have opposite positions with regard to its implementation.

South Korea first emphasises reconciliation between the North and the South conducive to non-aggression. It believes that a non-aggression agreement not based on the improvement of relations would not guarantee its faithful compliance. For example, the 1972 South-North Joint Communique which contained the provisions of a nonaggression pact failed to ensure the compliance of the North.[30] The South's belief is that a promise of nonaggression can be consolidated by the implementation of exchanges and cooperation, including inter Korean travel, communications and economic exchanges and cooperation.

Figure 8-1 Basic Formulas of North and South Korea for Arms control

South:	confidence build-up --> tension reduction --> non aggression
North:	nonaggression --> withdrawal of USFK --> tension reduction --> confidence build-up

At the outset the adoption of a nonaggression declaration was given top priority in the dialogue of the two Koreas. The North's position was very different to the South's. The North argued that unless peace by a non-aggression declaration was guaranteed, the military confrontation and the deep-rooted distrust would never be removed. For the North, confidence building is not a problem to be solved before the adoption of a nonaggression declaration but its adoption is a most solid and reliable measure for confidence-building.[31] The North's basic objective in the non aggression declaration is to lead the US forces to withdraw. The North stated that:

> If the North and the South are committed to refraining from fighting each other, US troops who are in South Korea allegedly to prevent the outbreak of war, must get withdrawn from there (the South)[32]

Though the agreement simultaneously accepted the concepts of both "confidence build-up" and "nonaggression", there remains a very controversial question over the priority and the method of its implementation.

There are numerous similarities in their military CBM proposals. Both sides share a desire to improve communications. The top-level army commanders of both sides are included as delegates at the high level talks and military problems discussed between them. Further, the installation of a direct telephone line which connects the senior military authorities has already been agreed in order to minimize unintended incidents and to prevent the escalation of a full scale crisis. Similarities are also found in their information proposals. The South proposes to notify the movement of military units and military manoeuvering of brigade size or larger 45 days in advance. The North also suggests a notification of military movements in advance, but has not proposed specific measures.

The South is very keen to reduce the military secrecy of the North through exchanges of data such as defence expenditure and military structure and observer teams. However, North Korea has not emphasised such 'transparency measures' which are very important components of confidence building measures. Both sides accord completely on the goal of the real demilitarization of the DMZ and its conversion into a peace zone. On the other hand they differ significantly with regard to the measures of constraint on military exercises. The North puts much weight on a number of constraint measures on operational steps, while the South is comparatively silent over such measures. The reason for the opposite positions relates to the combined T.S. exercises of the South and the US North Korea's proposal has been extended from a ban on the T.S. exercises to a ban on joint military exercises with foreign countries even outside the

Korean Peninsula. It is actually intended to ban the South's participation in a joint naval exercise, so-called, 'Rimpac' manoeuvres by the US, Japan and other countries in the Pacific.[33]

South Korea rejected a ban on the T.S. exercise, regarding it as a symbol of the US security commitment. However, it has unilaterally applied confidence building measures to the T.S. exercise. From 1982 the South notified the exercise plan in advance through the Military Armistice Commission (MAC) and invited observers from the North, China and the four members of the Neutral Nations Supervisory stationed in Korea.[34] Further, from 1989 the size of the T.S. exercise was gradually scaled down and finally ceased in 1991.

Both sides now accept on-site inspection (OSI) in principle. South Korea has stressed the necessity to devise firm verification measures during the entire period of CBMs and arms reduction implementation before entering the phase of reduction. From its point of view verification is a means for the mutual disclosure of military information and further a solid guarantee for compliance with the nonaggression agreement. It also expects the participation of regional powers or an international safeguards apparatus in order to ensure compliance with the nonaggression agreement and increase the credibility of CBMs implementation.[35] On the other hand, North Korea has failed to propose adequate verification measures. The North "see verification of confidence building measures as two times intelligence - intelligence on intelligence".[36]

Table 8-2 CBMs Proposals of North (N) and South (S) Korea

Legal Measures
. Nonaggression Agreement between the North and South (S)
. Replacement of Armistice with S-N Peace Agreement (S)
. Adoption of a nonaggression declaration between S and N (N)
. Peace Agreement between N and US (N)
. International guarantees of nonaggression (S)

Communication Measures
. A direct telephone line between military authorities (S,N)
  - Defence Ministers and Chairman of JCS (S)

Information Measures
. Exchange of military information and military personnel(S,N)
. Notification of military manoeuvres or movements (S,N)
. Invitation of observer teams (S)

Table 8-2 continued

Constraint Measures

. *Military manoeuvres and exercises*
   - Ban on joint military manoeuvres and exercises with foreign troops (N)
   - Ban on military exercises in excess of one division (N)
   - Ban on military manoeuvres along the MDL (N)
   - No allowance of foreign troops' manoeuvres on the Korean Peninsula (N)
   - Ban on military provocation along the MDL (S,N)

. *The DMZ*
   - Conversion of the DMZ into a peace zone (S,N)
   - Withdrawal of all military personnel & equipment (S,N)
   - Dismantling of all the military set-up (S,N)
   - allowance to access of civilians (S,N)

Verification Measures

. on-site inspection
   - Phase of implementation of CBMs and arms reduction (S)
   - Phase of arms reduction (N)
   - A joint verification group (S)
. Peace guarantee
   - The Major Powers or international systems (S)
   - The deployment of a neutral nation inspection force in the DMZ and along the MDL (N)

Source: These measures are compiled from the proposals of North and South Korea up to the 7th round of the high-level talks (September 1990-May 1992).

North Korea has resisted suggestions that agreements be verified by a third party negotiation teams - Americans or some sort of international system.[37]

Arms Reduction

Unlike the case of CBMs, North and South Korea are strongly contrasted in their perspectives on arms reductions. With regard to arms reduction proposals the North has been very positive, the South, has been negative. The North's core idea is to reduce forces of both sides to a level of 100,000 men in the short term. On the other hand, the South's idea is that before the achievement of an overall military balance, no reduction can be considered.

  The North's proposal to reduce to 100,000 men has been a longstanding theme since its announcement in the Geneva Conference of 1954. According to the statistics of 'the National Unification Board' of Seoul, of its 235 proposals on arms control from 1948 to 1988, the North has proposed 'the 100,000 men idea' 22 times. It ranked third, coming after the withdrawal of US forces, (80 times) and the conclusion of the peace treaty, (28 times).[38] From North Korea's perspective, only the reduction of troops would contribute to the reduction of tension and build-up of mutual confidence and further would be a prerequisite for the realization of reunification of Korea.

South Korean has ignored the North's proposal. To Seoul, the North's proposal for reducing troop strength to 100,000 men is nothing but a propaganda ploy as a projection of a peace image and not worthy of serious consideration.[39] Moreover, the North's reduction proposal included the condition of the withdrawal of US forces which have been pillars of the South ability to deter the North's attack. Furthermore, except up to the 1970s for troop strength, the South's military power has historically been far inferior to the North's. As seen in the diagram 8-1 its superiority of manpower to some extent had contributed to offset the imbalance before the North achieved superiority of manpower in 1979. Thus, it is natural that the South has continually rejected proposals mainly focussed on troop reductions. The differences between both sides on arms reduction have been clearly demonstrated in the proposals at the high-level talks. To begin with, a very sharp contrast is seen between arms reduction proposed by the North vs structural arms control called for by the South.

The North proposes troop reduction over three stages: first stage; 300,000, second stage; 200,000 and third stage; 100,000. The three stages are to be completed in three to four years after an arms reduction agreement is signed. Given the North's one million soldiers compared to the South's 650,000, the North is required to reduce far more troops than the South. There is no denying that the North's asymmetrical reduction idea, based on the principle of 'equal outcome' without emphasising its present advantage or considering its major inferiority in terms of longer-term potential manpower to the South is to some extent persuasive.[40] However, the proposal is still propagandist. Pyongyang has put forward this proposal of 100,000 men periodically, regardless of the prevailing situation. Furthermore, the proposed reductions of over 500,000 men in the South and 900,000 men in the North within three to four year without building mutual confidence are probably unrealistic.

With regard to the reduction of troops, South Korea's position accords with the North in that forces of equal number after reduction should be maintained. However, the South argues that the side with larger armed forces should first reduce them to the level of the weaker to achieve an equilibrium and then the forces of both sides can be reduced step by step to equal numbers. From Seoul's point of view, as long as both sides continuously keep their military forces organized and deployed for offensive purposes, it is hard to verify the commitment to peace or to prevent another war.[41]

The South's efforts, prior to any arms reductions, are concentrated on transforming the offensive military structures into defensive ones. This implies that through arms control negotiations the capability for launching a surprise attack and large scale offensive action, as may be prejudicial to stability and security, should be firstly removed. Currently, North Korea, which has deployed forward over 65 percent of its forces, could make a strategic surprise attack without reinforcements with virtually no preparation time. As a consequence, the South has paid more attention to the withdrawal of the North's forward deployed offensive arms from the frontline. For the South, the redeployment of forward deployed armed forces capable of a surprise attack with little warning may well be more important than overall reduction of aggregate levels of forces.

Table 8-3 Arms Reduction Approaches of North and South Korea

	South (S)	North (N)
basic concept	structural arms control	troop reduction
reduction priority	weapons & equipment	personnel
reduction method	asymmetry	
reduction stage	step by step	
final strength	balance	
troop ceiling		
reserve forces	reduction	
forces level after the unification	500,000-700,000	
US forces withdrawal	after peace settlement	with the N-S non aggression accord

Source: These are compiled from the proposals of North and South Korea in the high level talks, (September 1990-May 1992).

For the prevention of a DPRK surprise attack, the ROK puts more weight on the reductions of weapons and equipment for launching a surprise attack and for initiating large-scale offensive action prior to troop reduction.[42] Many officials and analysts from the South agree with this idea since it is easily verifiable and believe that, since they are central to the seizing and holding of territory, overall levels of offensive weapons such as tanks, mobile artillery and armoured vehicles should be put in the first stage of reductions. As in the case of troop reductions, ROK also emphasises that Pyongyang with higher weapons totals should first reduce them to levels of the inferior Seoul to maintain a parity. On the other hand Pyongyang has not given priority to reduction of weapons and has remained silent on the need to disengage dense offensive forward forces near the DMZ.

However, Seoul and Pyongyang are agreed upon the principle of simultaneous reductions of troops and weapons. Since the proposal of the 'Comprehensive Peace Plan', the DPRK has talked about weapons and equipment. Seoul has also moderated its objection to arms reduction. Both sides agree to "realize arms reduction" in the Nonaggression Agreement, particularly focussing on "phased reduction in armaments including the elimination of weapons of mass destruction and surprise attack capabilities"(Article 12).[43] However, the positions on implementation are fundamentally different in that the South maintains its position on the reductions of troops followed by reduction of weapons, whilst the North calls for weapon's reductions or dismantling in proportion to the phased troop reduction.

Another sharp difference is found in the problem of reserve and paramilitary forces. Seoul calls for their reduction. Pyongyang counters that at the first stages of regular force reductions they should be dissolved. According to the Korean Defence White Paper 1991-1992 Seoul's military reserves are estimated at 4.2 millions whereas Pyongyang can mobilize 6 millions.[44] Though the number of reserve forces are similar, Seoul has a big advantage of about 2 times in the number of the population in the potential combat age of 18-32 (Seoul:6.73 millions vs Pyongyang 3.12 millions) and in the size of populations (Seoul: 44.3 millions vs Pyongyang: 23.3 millions).[45] Seoul's absolute superiority led Pyongyang to demand the dissolution of reserve forces. However, from the South Korean perspective, this proposal would certainly work to their disadvantage. Given the kind and quality of reserve system Pyongyang has, as well as the nature of its politico-social system, it would be possible for North Korea to convert the dissolved reserve forces into a wartime mobilization with greater ease and rapidity, though North Koreas steady economic decline is reducing this danger.

Finally, a contrast between the North and the South is seen on the issue of a troops ceiling. The North has called for a 100,000 man ceiling on both sides as a way towards unification. However, the rationales on the ceiling have not been explained since the time of the first proposal of 1954. Further, the North has not suggested if such ceilings are appropriate force levels needed for self defence. The South does not propose a force ceiling after the final reductions. Instead, a plan is being drawn up to reduce to 500,000 from the current 700,000 by 1996 in preparation for unification. The South seems to assume 500,000 men as a finally reduced size on the premise that the unified Korea would maintain 600,000-700,000 men or equal to one percent of the population.[46] The South is presently reluctant to reduce below 500,000 men. Officials and analysts whose concerns extend beyond Seoul's traditional strategy against the threat from the North, assume a potential threat from outside powers. They particularly keep in mind the Japanese military build-up, and insist that ROK military power should not be restricted to the role of a mere deterrent to an actual North Korean threat. Given the geostrategic location of the Korean Peninsula and the historical experiences of frequent invasion by foreign powers, such concern may be considered prudent. However, the simultaneous consideration of potential threats alongside the North's actual threat creates a greater defence burden and further obstructs arms reduction.

Under these very different perspectives, arms reductions are not likely to occur on the Korean Peninsula in the near future without compromises derived from 'new thinking'. The South assumes that the North-South military confrontation will continue until 1995 and that peaceful co-existence and arms reduction will be possible after 1996 when a military balance is achieved.[47]

Denuclearization

The denuclearization of the Korean Peninsula has been one of the core issues in the regional security. During the period of the Cold War a number of proposals for the denuclearization of the Korean Peninsula were advanced by international security analysts. Allen S. Whiting proposed the establishment of a nuclear free zone in Northeast Asia in order to prevent a nuclear arms race between regional countries. His intention was to limit the attraction of Japan's entry into the nuclear club which was a possible consequence of China's nuclear development. Likewise he wished to negate the North's pursuit of nuclear power status through the withdrawal of the US tactical nuclear weapons from the South.[48] Thus the issue of the denuclearization of the Korean Peninsula was essentially an outcome of the desire for nuclear stability between regional major powers rather than the security of the Korean Peninsula itself.

The denuclearization problem gained in salience with the South's attempt to possess nuclear weapons in the mid-1970s. As an alternative to withdrawals of US forces and tactical nuclear weapons, President Park suggested a nuclear option in an interview with the Washington Post in June 1975: "If the US nuclear umbrella were to be removed we would have to start developing our nuclear capability to save ourselves".[49] The Foreign Minister also stated in June 1977 that the nuclear option could not be ruled out for the maintenance of national security. Many analysts feared that Seoul's acquisition of a nuclear capability would stimulate Pyongyang to follow suit and in consequence quickly lead Japan to seek nuclear weapons.[50] Though the ROK nuclear option disappeared after President Carter cancelled his plan for the withdrawal of US forces in 1979, it provided the North with a strong motive to promote the establishment of nuclear free-zone in Korea. The October 1980 the Sixth Party Congress of the DPRK called for a transformation of the Korean Peninsula into a nuclear free zone. On 16 March, 1981, the North Korean Workers Party and the Japan Socialist Party made a joint declaration calling for the creation of a nuclear free peace zone in Northeast Asia.[51] The North's attempts were intensified as a result of the anti-nuclear movement in Western Europe and particularly the anti-Americanism of the urban youth and students in South Korea in the early 1980s. Pyongyang's objective was to impede any attempts Seoul might make to develop nuclear weapons under the circumstances of a US withdrawal. The ultimate objective was directed towards the withdrawal and elimination of the nuclear threat posed by the US tactical nuclear weapons in South Korea. North Korea has long been faced with nuclear threats since the Korean War. In fact, US governments have maintained a long standing position suggesting first use of nuclear weapons as a means of deterring a North Korean attack.[52] Therefore, South Korea has opposed North Korea's proposal on a nuclear-free zone. For the ROK, American nuclear weapons have not only neutralized the superior conventional force of North Korea but also served as an important deterrent to its aggression. South Korea also argues that the nuclear umbrella of the US would blockade the North's blitzkrieg strategy for occupation of Seoul.

However, with the narrowing of the military gap between Seoul and Pyongyang, the reliance on nuclear threats as a means of deterring Pyongyang's attack has lost credibility. Furthermore the military balance has increasingly leaned to the South's favour. The utility of deployment of tactical nuclear weapons for deterrence has produced doubts in both the scholarly and decision-making communities of Seoul and Washington. Lt. Gen. John Cushman, former commander of USFK, argued in September 1988 that they were no longer necessary for the defence of the South, implicitly indicating the presence of nuclear weapons in the South when they had not been clearly declared by the NCND policy of the US.[53] Former Chairman of the US Joint Chiefs of Staff, Admiral William J. Crowe also suggested that:

> ... the actual presence of any nuclear weapons in South Korea is not necessary to maintain a nuclear umbrella over the ROK; in fact, such a presence would likely become a political football in US-ROK relations over time.[54]

The South has also to some extent begun to be flexible on the nuclear free zone issue. To halt the North's nuclear program was seen as a very urgent and essential South Korean objective. There were some hints by the South for non-nuclearization of the Korean Peninsula. The creation of a nuclear free zone for the Korean Peninsula was on the agenda of the high level secret meeting between Washington and Seoul held in Honolulu in August, 1991 prior to the declaration of the withdrawal of US tactical weapons abroad by President Bush.[55] However, since its establishment would place big limitations on US military activities in Northeast Asia, it might be very difficult for the US to accept the idea. As a result Seoul made plans for non-nuclearization of the Korean Peninsula similar to the three non-nuclear principles.[56]

The inclusion of the South in the declaration of the Bush government on 27 September, 1991 was a crucial turning point in the nuclear debates on the Korean Peninsula. Seoul's declaration of the absence of the US nuclear weapons signalled to Pyongyang a change in Seoul's attitude on the nuclear issue. The fact that the South's approach to 'non-nuclearization' was similar to the North's nuclear free zone pushed the North to follow the South's proposal. Both sides included the "denuclearization" of the Korean Peninsula in the agreement on "reconciliation and nonaggression". The agreements were:

. not to test, manufacture, produce, receive, possess store, deploy, or use nuclear weapons.
. to use nuclear energy solely for peaceful purposes.
. not to possess nuclear reprocessing and uranium enrichment facilities.
. to conduct inspections in order to verify denuclearization.
. to establish a N-S joint nuclear control commission.[57]

However, despite the agreement of the denuclearization the ultimate objectives of both sides are fundamentally unchanged. Their approaches to the issue of denuclearization are very different.

Pyongyang has not given up the objective of the establishment of the nuclear free zone. It attempts to realize it through the adoption of a guideline protocol for the implementation of the agreement. It believes that the nuclear threat from the US can be automatically eliminated through the legal guarantee of no use of nuclear weapons by the regional nuclear powers. On the other hand, Seoul aims at the abandonment of Pyongyang's nuclear development through denuclearization. The South's dependence on the nuclear umbrella of the US is also unchanged, even after the declaration of the absence of nuclear weapons. Seoul opposes any proposals to remove the nuclear umbrella. It believes that despite the declaration of the non-nuclearization the nuclear umbrella of the US would be tacitly valid as in the case of Japan. The problem of verification is the most controversial issue on the implementation of the agreement. Seoul and Pyongyang have an accord on the mutual inspections and the exclusion of third countries. However, Seoul wants the inclusion of all military bases in the lists of inspections in addition to the inspection of the North's nuclear facility and one military base and stresses a special inspection system, which would allow either side to unilaterally see certain sites of the other side upon a regular basis. Such demands are due to the belief that Pyongyang is engaged in an elaborate deception similar to Iraq's effort to hide its nuclear weapon project.[58] On the other hand, Pyongyang suggests all the US military bases in the South should be inspected but only nuclear facilities in the North.

The nuclear issue is a basic premise of development of North-South relations and a big obstacle to the progress of the talks upon conventional arms control. Without solving the North's nuclear problem no arms control measures are likely to be agreed in the 'North-South high level talks.'

The agreement signed on 21 October 1994 between the United States and the DPRK is therefore crucial. Under the agreement North Korea agreed to close down and dismantle its nuclear facilities. In return the Clinton Administration agreed to arrange for an international consortium, the Korean Energy Development Organisation, to build two light water nuclear reactors by the year 2003. In addition the US agreed to supply North Korea with heavy oil from January 1995 onwards. It agreed also to provide security assurances against the threat or use of nuclear weapons against North Korea. North Korea agreed to take steps to implement the North-South Joint Declaration on the Denuclearisation of the Korean Peninsula. While the administration of South Korea's President Kim Young Sam was not convinced that its interests were fully accommodated by the US-DPRK talks, it welcomed the agreement. While the agreement still has to stand the test of effective implementation, it can be seen as a crucial confidence-building measure.

Table 8-4 The North (N) and South (S) Approaches for Denuclearization of Korea

Goal
. nuclear free-zone (N)
. denuclearization(S)

Objective
. removal of the US nuclear arms and umbrella (N)
. halt of the North's military nuclear program (S)

Proposals
. ban on manufacture, possession, store, deployment of nuclear weapons (N.S)
. ban on use of nuclear weapons (N,S)
. no passage of nuclear weapons through airspace and territorial seas (N)
. no test of nuclear arms (N)
. no nuclear exercises (N)
. no possession of nuclear reprocessing and uranium enrichment facilities(S)
. peaceful use of nuclear energy (S)

Controversial Issues in the implementation of the agreement
. priority
    - adoption of a guide-line protocol for denuclearization(N)
    - inspection guide line (S)
. verification
    - inspection by the IAEA Safeguard Agreement (N,S)
    - direct mutual inspection by the North and the South (N,S)
    - all US military bases in the S and nuclear facility in the N (N)
    - military and civilian bases (S)
      nuclear weapons and nuclear bases
    - regular inspections (N)
    - regular inspections and irregular special inspection (S)
. guarantee
    - no nuclear umbrella (N)
    - respect of denuclearization by the regional nuclear powers (N)
    - protection by nuclear umbrella (S)

Conclusion

The Korean attempt at dialogue towards tension reduction and reconciliation coincided with the beginning of European arms control talks. Europeans stabilized the theatre through continued talks and have now proceeded to arms reductions to low levels with the subsequent developments of CBMs. However, in the Korean case the attempt at tension reduction through dialogue failed. Military tension has continued because of the close array of formidable armed forces. After the end of the Cold War, the two Korean states resumed arms control talks in the light of international and regional detente. They have now begun at an inaugural level the non-aggression agreement which Europe established 20 years ago.

The lessons of the failure of the early Korean attempt were complex, but the most important factor was the lack of an arms control talks mechanism. The 1991 North-South agreement adopted elaborate non-aggression provisions and established a Joint North-South military committee which guaranteed the implementation of the agreement. Notwithstanding the agreement the two states retain a very different approach towards arms control. The North seeks arms control "as an end", whilst the South regards it "as a process".[59] For the North, arms control remains a means to the achievement of its core objectives: national unification and withdrawal of US forces in Korea through a peace treaty with the US Its strategy is to connect the non-aggression agreement and arms reduction between Seoul and Pyongyang to the withdrawal of the USFK. The withdrawal of the USFK would be a best option for Korean unification on its terms. By contrast the South regards arms control as a process of building confidence and a national partnership with the North. The South believes that arms control and unification can be achieved through a step-by-step process on the basis of mutual confidence.

The crucial divergence of the North-South arms control approach is over the actual application of CBMs and implementation of arms reduction. From the North's point of view, the source of tension is the possession of a great number of heavily armed forces. Therefore, the guarantee of a non-aggression agreement and confidence build-up can be achieved only after arms reduction, particularly troops. Consequently, despite its advantage over the South in standing forces, the North's demand is for the achievement of the withdrawal of US troops. On the other hand the South views political confrontation as a substantial source of tension. It proposes a three-stage process for arms control: political CBMs, military CBMs and arms reduction. Arms reduction itself focuses primarily upon equipment rather than troops.

Despite the difference in the priorities of arms control application, unlike the past, the two Korean states strongly feel the need for arms control. A number of similarities can be seen in their proposals. In principle both introduce European CBMs such as communication, notification and verification measures. In particular they both advocate the conversion of the DMZ into a peace zone or a real buffer zone. There is less agreement on the objective of arms reduction. Both agree that military balance should be maintained at a reduced level. Therefore an asymmetrical reduction could be applied without considering current asymmetrical military conditions which were such an obstacle to the progress of arms reduction talks in the European context.

Another area of convergence between the two states is on the question of the denuclearization of the Korean Peninsula. Both Korean states seek to eliminate the danger of nuclear war through denuclearization. Production, possession and testing of nuclear weapons are banned in Korea. Despite the agreement the nuclear problem of the North is currently the most critical issue in the North-South arms control talks. Without the solution of the nuclear problem, no conventional arms control in the North-South arms control talks will permit the achievement of true denuclearization for Korean security.

NOTES

1. Young Koo Cha, "Arms Control on the Korean Peninsula: A Korean Perspective", A paper presented for the 18th International Conference of the Korean Institute of International Studies (Seoul: 4-6 July, 1989). These data were compiled from the South Korean National Unification Board, *A Comparison of the Unification Policies and Major Contents of South and North Korea*, June 1984, pp 112-168 and *A White Paper on South-North Dialogue in Korea*, 1988, pp. 491-571.
2. In-Young Chun, "Potential for Arms Control on the Korean Peninsula: A South Korea Perspective", A paper presented at the 3rd KIDA/CSIS, International Defence Conference (Seoul, 5-6 November, 1990), p. 2.
3. The Four-point Guidelines are (1) arming the entire population, (2) transforming the whole country into an impregnable fortress (3) converting the whole army into an army of cadres and (4) modernizing the military establishment.
4. Ralph N. Clough, *Embattled Korea: the Rivalry for International Support* (Boulder, Colorado: Westview Press, 1987), p. 114.
5. The National Unification Board of ROK, *A White Paper on South-North Dialogue in Korea* (Seoul, December 1988). pp. 54-56.
6. Byung-Joon Ahn, "Arms Control Proposals of North and South Korea, and their Implications for Korean Security", A paper prepared for the conference on arms race and

arms control in Northeast Asia by the Korean Association of International Relations (Seoul, 28-29 August, 1886), p. 9.
7. *A White Paper on South-North Dialogue in Korea*, p. 570.
8. A speech of Kwang Soo Choi, Minister of Foreign Affairs of the ROK at the 3rd Special Disarmament Session of the General Assembly of the United Nations 10 June, 1988.
9. Tae-Whan Kwak, "Peace Progress and Military Capabilities on the Korean Peninsula", A paper prepared for at the Joint Annual Convention of the British International Studies Association (London, 28 March -1 April, 1989), p. 2.
10. Tong Whan Park, "Security Dilemma and the Politics of Arms Control between the Two Koreas", A paper prepared for the International Conference of Korean Association of Political Science (Seoul, 25-27 July, 1991), p. 5.
11. US Congressman, Stephen J. Solarz, *The Korean Conundrum: A conversation with Kim Il Sung*, Report of a study mission to South Korea, Japan, the People's Republic of China and North Korea, 12-21 July, 1980 (Washington D.C.: GPO, 1981), p.6. He also emphasized that "The Commitment on the part of both Kim (Kim Il Sung and his Minister of Foreign Affairs, Kim Young Nam) to reunification was not just verbal but visceral".
12. Yuri I. Ognev, "Principle Background and New Developments in the DPRK approach to Peace Settlement on the Korean Peninsula", pp. 127-128, in *Working Group Meetings on Issues of Peace and Cooperation in the Asia-Pacific Region* (Stanford University: the Center for International Security and Arms Control, 1990), pp. 127-128. Author quoted this sentence in 'On the complex of measures to provide peace for independent and peaceful unification of the country', Joint Session of the Central People's Committee, 7 November, 1988.
13. Solarz, op. cit, p. 6.
14. "Disarmament Proposed to Ease Tension on Korean Peninsula and Create a Peaceful Climate for Reunification", *The Pyongyang Times*, 9 June, 1990.
15. Chung In-Moon, "Potential for Arms Control", p. 8. He says that North Korea initiates and acts against the South on the basis of its perceptions and calculations; North Korea seems to initiate or respond if its perception of political change in the South is directly reflected in its behaviour. For a detailed explanation of the North's arms proposals as a means of a propaganda, see Cha, "Arms Talks on the Korean Peninsula", pp. 11-15.
16. On 1 February, 1982, the ROK's national unification minister suggested to North Korea a set of 20 pilot projects promoting contact and exchange and increasing mutual confidence.
17. For the South's arms control approaches, see Yong-Ok Park, "Bilateral and Multilateral Approaches to Peace on the Korean Peninsula". A paper prepared for the fourth KIDA/CSIS International Defence Conference (Seoul, 4-5 November, 1991), pp. 1-3.
18. *The ROK Defence White Paper 1991-1992* (in Korean), p. 155.
19. "Asia/Pacific Security Background", *Pacific Research*, p. 3.
20. "Min. Lee rebuffs proposal for defence budget cut", *The Korea Herald*, 30 August, 1991.
21. "Letters to the US Government and Congress adopted at the Joint Meeting of the Central People's Committee and the Supreme People's Assembly Standing Committee of North Korea, 10 July, 1984. *Korean Unification: Sources Materials with Introduction* (Seoul: Research Center for Peace and Unification of Korea, 1986), pp. 324-325. This letter was reprinted from the Pyongyang Times, 14 January, 1984, p. 1.
22. "Speech Delivered by North Korean Premier Lie Jong Ok at the Sixth Summit Conference of Non-Aligned Countries", in *Korean Unification: Source Materials*, p. 131.
23. "Joint Communique of President Park Chung Hee of the Republic of Korea and President Jimmy Carter of the United States, Proposing the Convening of a "Meeting of Official Representatives of South and North of Korea and the United States", Seoul, 1 July, 1979, in *Korean Unification: Source Materials*, p. 115

24. Clough, *Embattled Korea*, p. 191.
25. "Speech of President Chun Doo Hwan at the Inaugural Ceremony of the Advisory Council on Peaceful Unification Policy, in *Korean Unification: Source Materials*, p. 192.
26. Address by President Roh Tae Woo of the ROK at the 43rd Session of the General Assembly of the United Nations (19 October, 1988), *Korea and World Affairs*, Vol.xii, No.4, (Winter 1988), p. 842.
27. In a letter from North Korean Premier Li Gun-Mo to South Korean Prime Minister Lee Hyune-Jae, proposing a high-level South-North political and military conference (16 November, 1988). *Joong-Ahang Ilbo* (Korean Daily Newspaper), 9 July, 1990. A North Korean Scholar who participated in the conference of the North, the South and the US held in July 1990 by Stanford University confirmed that the North position changed from tripartite to bilateral talks.
28. "DPRK Central People's Committee, SPA Standing Committee and Administration Council meets", *The Pyongyang Times*, 9 June, 1990.
29. *The Korea Herald*, 14 December, 1991
30. In fact, no nonaggression agreement by itself can guarantee that there will no war. Good examples can be seen from the German-Soviet and Japanese-Soviet non aggression pacts in the past.
31. Keynote address by the South's Prime Minister, Kang Young-hoon in the 3rd round high level talks in December 1990 in *South-North dialogue in Korea* (Seoul, International Cultural Society of Korea, No. 051, February 1991), p. 51.
32. Ognev, op. cit., p. 130.
33. The Rim of the Pacific (RIMPAC) Exercise is a large-scale combined maritime manoeuvering exercise that has been held biannually since 1971 under the US 3rd Command. South Korea has participated from 1988 in the exercise which has been conducted by the US, Australia, Canada and Japan.
34. In fact, the T.S. exercises have been watched by 27 foreign military attaches stationed in Seoul and in 1990 overseen by Polish Army officers, one of the four member-nation Supervisory Commission (NNSC) of the Armistice.
35. See "keynote address by the Korean Prime Minister at the Third High-Level talks" in *South-North Dialogue in Korea* (Seoul: International Cultural Society of Korea, No. 052, May, 1991), p. 32.
36. *Arms Control on the Korean Peninsula: what lessons can we learn from European experience?*, (Seoul: Institute of Foreign Affairs & National Security, 1990), p. 157.
37. Ibid. John W. Lewis, the Co-Director of Center for International Security and Arms Control, Stanford University, organized the first Conference on Peace and Security on the Korean Peninsula: A Meeting of Scholars from the North and South of Korea and the United States in July 1990 at Stanford. He had many opportunities to hear the North Korean scholars' views with regard to arms control issues.
38. National Unification Board of the ROK , *A White Paper on South-North Dialogue in Korea* (Seoul, 1987), pp. 491-571.
39. In the proposals of its, so-called, "Comprehensive Peace Plan", the North proposed an ambitious timetable for completion of reduction; the North and the South would be cut to the level of 400,000 strong by the end of 1989 and to the level of 250,000 strong by the end of 1990 to be less than 100,000 strong from 1992.
40. Andrew Mack, "Nuclear Issues and Arms Control on the Korean Peninsula", *Working Paper*, No. 96 (Canberra: Peace Research Centre, 1991), p. 23. He criticizes the South's refusal. He said that "to outsiders, the North's proposals sounds perfectly reasonable, but from the South's point of view it is highly problematic".

41. Keynote address by the South's Prime Minister at the first high level talks, in *South-North Dialogue in Korea*, No. 051, p. 50.
42. "Preparation of Arms Control Plan: more emphases on weapons than troops", *The Joong Ahang Ilbo*, 27 December, 1989.
43. *The Korea Herald*, 14 December, 1991.
44. *The Korean Defence White Paper 1991-1992* (in Korean), p. 139.
45. The Military Balance 1994-1995 estimates reserve forces in the South, 4,500,000 and the North, 540,000, pp.178-180. Kwak, "Peace Process and Military Capabilities, p.5. According to his analysis, South Korea has para-military forces of 7,400,000 (Civilian Defense Corps 3,500,000; Reserve Forces 3,300,000; and Student Homeland Defense Corps 600,000), whereas North Korea has 5,222,000 (Security Forces 1,012,000; Workers-Farmers Red Guards 3,084; Youth Red Guards 1,070,000; and Border Guards 56,000).
46. "Armed forces could be cut to 500,000 by 1996", *The Korea Herald*, 25 September, 1991.
47. "Minister Lee rebuffs proposal for defence budget cut", *The Korea Herald*, 30 August, 1991.
48. Allen S. Whiting, "New Perspectives in Asia: Arms Control in Northeast Asia", *Pacific Community*, Vol.3, No.2 (January, 1972), pp. 272-274. For detailed references for these proposals, see Lee Ho Jae, "Debates on the Nuclear Armed and Nuclear Free Zone on the Korean Peninsula", in Lee Ho Jae (ed), *Arms Control on the Korean Peninsula* (Seoul: Bapmoonsa, 1989, in Korean), pp. 292-312.
49. William H. Overholt, "Nuclear Proliferation in Eastern Asia", *Pacific Community*, Vol.8. No.1 (October, 1976), p.54. This was quoted in *Washington Post*, 12 June, 1975.
50. John H. Barton and Ryukichi Imai, *Arms Control II: A New Approach to International Security* (Cambridge: OG&H, 1981)., p. 173.
51. Young C. Kim, "The Politics of Arms Control in Korea", *Korean Journal of Defence Analysis*, 1989, No.1, Summer, p. 122. The main points of the declaration were that: 1) all the nuclear weapons deployed in the Northeast Asian region should be withdrawn and destroyed and the development, test production, possession, carriage, storage, shipment and use of nuclear and biochemical weapons in this region be totally prohibited. 2) The Northeast Asian nuclear-free, peace zone would cover Korea, Japan and their surrounding waters.
52. Peter Hayes, "American Nuclear Hegemony in Korea", *Journal of Peace Research*, Vol. 25, No.4,(December, 1988) pp. 354-359.
53. Andrew Mack and Andrew McClean, "The Growing Interest in Asia-Pacific Arms Control Issue", *Working Paper* (Canberra: Peace Research Centre, 1989), No. 75, p.4.
54. William J. Crowe, Jr. and D. Rombert, "Rethinking Security in the Pacific", *Foreign Affairs*, Vol. 70, No.2 (1991), pp. 123-140, *Pacific Research*, August 1991, p. 12.
55. *Pacific Research*, 3 August. 1991, p. 14.
56. *The Korean Defence Daily News* (in Korean), 19 November, 1991. On 19 November, 1991, President Roh declared the denuclearization of the Korean Peninsula: firstly, no possession, manufacturing, deployment, storage, use of nuclear weapons, secondly, IAEA Safeguard inspection on nuclear materials & facilities and thirdly, no possession of nuclear reprocessing and uranium enrichment facilities.
57. *The Korea Herald*, 14 February, 1992.
58. *The Korea Herald*, 7 May, 1992. Stephen Solarz said after visiting Pyongyang that it most likely intends to permit inspections while continuing to develop atomic weapons in underground complexes as Iraq did during the Gulf War. in *The Korea Herald*, 7 February, 1992.

59. Byung-Joon Ahn, "Arms Control on the Korean Peninsula: Its Prospects and International Context", in Gerrit W. Gong and Richard L. Grant (eds) "Security and Economics in the Asia-Pacific Region", *Significant Issues Series* (Washington D.C.: CSIS), Vol XIII, No. 9, (1991), pp. 100-104.

9. The Application of the European Arms Control Model to Korea

Relevance of European Arms Control to Korea

The strategic environment of the Korean Peninsula differs in significant ways from that of Europe in the Cold War era. European arms control was based on multilateral negotiations between the two blocs lead by the US and the Soviet Union and included the whole European continent. In contrast the arms control of the Korean Peninsula is on the basis of bilateral negotiation between North and South Korea, covering a very much narrower region. The most fundamental difference is that European arms control was a product of the Cold War, while Korean arms control, though it has obvious Cold War overtones, must be discussed beyond the end of the Cold War. Adam D. Rotfeld says; "European arms control forms are not applicable in ways which they were in Europe because they were not the product of intellectual thinking but rather the reaction to a concrete, specific situation".[1] However, despite the limits to similarities with Europe, the Korean Peninsula in certain respects parallels the European example.

The first similarity is the confrontation of massive ground forces across a land frontier. As in Europe, the dense forces are concentrated along the division line in the forward area. As NATO was very vulnerable to a surprise attack by WTO along the central front of Europe, the South is likewise vulnerable to a surprise attack from the North. Through the forward deployment of North Korea's forces a surprise attack against the South could be implemented without reinforcements and with no warning or a short-warning attack. The Korean Peninsula has short combat depth as well as a short warning time. Therefore it is necessary to introduce CBMs in order to increase stability and prevent surprise attack or a preemptive war. Furthermore, because of the density of offensive forces in forward areas, the Peninsula seems to require a parallel agreement analogous to the CFE-thinning out and demobilizing of offensive military formations, resulting in a regime of limited forward deployment.[2] In such respects, the European CBMs and CFE models may be relevant to Korea.

Secondly, South Korea faces some of the same defence problems that existed in NATO. The South is far inferior to the North in terms of the military balance. The numbers of personnel and offensive weapons such as tanks, armoured personnel carriers and artillery clearly favour the North. The North's numerical superiority has been offset by the technological edge of the South and until recently, by the US nuclear umbrella. Like the W.T.O. the North seeks to eliminate the deterrent role of US nuclear capabilities. Thus the Korean Peninsula has exhibited a close link between conventional and nuclear forces in defence and arms control issues, in much the same way as was the case in Europe.

Thirdly, the division of Germany has some analogies with Korea. The existences of the two ideologically and politically opposed regimes were the result of the rivalry and antagonism between the two global powers. Germany and Korea had been central to the military confrontation of the two powers up to the end of the Cold War. The superpowers had recognized that a war in the two regions would automatically involve them. Because of that, during the Cold War, they made efforts to stabilize the two regions; through arms control in Germany and through military assistance in Korea. Furthermore, Germany and Korea were very similar in respect of bloc structure. FRG and GDR were central poles of NATO and WTO in Europe. Similarly North and South Korea were also central poles of a loose military triangle of China-the North-USSR vs US-the South and the US-Japan alliance in Northeast Asia. The Northern triangle system has been loosened by the collapse of the USSR, but still remains extant in terms of legal treaty and military assistance.

The present situation of Korean arms control is similar to that at the beginning of arms control in Europe. Federal Germany initiated the 'Ostpolitik' policy and improved its relations with the Eastern countries, the Soviet Union and particularly East Germany. FRG and GDR each obtained separate membership in the UN and declared a status quo by admitting the other side as an entity through the FRG-GDR treaty of December 1972. FRG was stronger, GDR was very suspicious Therefore GDR felt that dialogue with FRG would weaken and undermine its security. Dialogue between both sides began with the FRG's acceptance of the East Germans as equal negotiating partners.[3] At present South Korea has improved its relations with Russia and China and begun a dialogue with North Korea through a 'Nordpolitik' policy. The two Koreas separately joined the UN and declared the mutual administration of two regimes and agreed to respect the present border through a nonaggression agreement. While South Korea is stronger, North Korea remains very suspicious about the improvement of North-South relations.

Both European and Korean arms control have been closely linked with the problem of the US forces. European arms control talks were initiated by the need to address such problems. FRG was very reluctant to see the withdrawal of US forces. Similarly the North has dealt with it as the first item on the agenda in its arms control proposals. The onset of Korean arms control coincided with the US force reductions in 1990. Like the FRG the South strongly opposes the withdrawal of US forces.

Moreover, the Korean Peninsula parallels Europe in that arms control negotiations take place between capitalist and communist states. Therefore arms control approaches and the negotiation strategy of the two Koreas are very similar to those of the blocs in Europe. Furthermore, North and South Korea accept the European model as a useful paradigm for Korea. They recognize the need for prevention of surprise attack and war and the withdrawal of forward deployed offensive arms. As in Europe, on the basis of geographical characteristics, their proposals are also related to ground forces without suggesting naval and air forces.

Korean Perspectives on European Arms control

North and South Korea have different perspectives about the applicability of the European multilateral arms control model to Korea. These different perspectives derive firstly from differences of perception of the historical legacy. The perception and behaviour of the Korean peoples has been coloured by historical experiences in which their country was often squeezed, invaded or sometimes protected by the regional powers surrounding it and became an arena of the powers' competition. From such experiences, the Koreans have developed two contradictory attitudes towards outside powers; distrust and dependence.[4] They have recognized that a major cause of the competition between surrounding powers is due to Korea's geopolitical importance. However, the two Korean states have very different perspectives concerning the solution of the Korean problem.

Generally, South Korea has recognized a deep involvement of the major powers in the problems of the Peninsula, while still believing that the key to their solution lies with the two Koreas themselves. Therefore the South believes that the Korean problem cannot be solved by the exclusive dominance of some major power or conversely, total isolation from its relations with surrounding nations. On the other hand, the North has felt some threats from its borders with the continental powers, though it capitalized upon the advantage of its strategic location as a means of gaining competitive military assistance from China and the USSR during the Sino-Soviet split.[5]

In the light of the South's perspective, it is natural for Seoul both to propose and support a multilateral conference with major powers participating. South Korea's preference for a multilateral conference was evidenced by its support for Kissinger's "six-nation conference". In the face of the failure of the inter-Korean detente in 1972-73, the South's efforts have concentrated upon an arrangement based on detente among the major powers to guarantee peace in the Korean Peninsula. The 1988 UN speech of the ROK President arrayed its preference by proposing "a consultative conference for peace". The South's conference proposal differs from the Soviet proposal of setting up a collective security system through a multilateral conference in the region. The South argued that the Soviet proposal should be discussed after resolving the Korean question. Hyun Hong-Choo, South Korean ambassador to the US said:

> the idea (of an Asian CSCE) was met with both hope and scepticism but there is now a semblance of a consensus that the idea and the model could be applicable to the Korean Peninsula, though its regional application would still be premature.[6]

Thus, South Korean recognizes "a six-nation conference" as a forum for Korean arms control. Furthermore, it hopes to extend this conference to a forum for Korea unification similar to the "two plus four conference" which produced German unification. However, unlike Europe, there is no legal basis for the four powers to commit themselves to any resolution for the Korean question.

North Korea has rejected any multilateral conference for the settlement of the Korean problem with the exception of the tripartite conference. Its argument is that the Major Powers' conference for a peace settlement would perpetuate the division of Korea. In this context, it is no surprise that the North dismissed the Kissinger proposal based on cross-recognition of the two Koreas by the powers. However, North Korea supported the Soviet collective security system in Asia on the ground that it required the withdrawal of US forces and proposed a nuclear free-zone on the Korean Peninsula. However, it had a very negative attitude towards the Soviet idea regarding the application of the European CSCE model to Asia or the Korean Peninsula. The argument is that the question of peace, security and cooperation in Asia must be resolved "in an Asian manner with the Asian people being responsible for it". A spokesman for the North's Foreign Ministry declared that:

we consider that mechanically applying an organization like the CSCE to Asia does not suit the reality of Asia. The security affairs in Asia are different from those of Europe. In Asia there remain many pending issues over which the interests of countries in the region conflict with each other.[7]

The North objects to the adoption of a similar "two plus four conference" in Korea as used to facilitate German unification. The North argues that the "manner of German Unification is only the maintenance of capitalism's management".[8] In any event North Korea may not be any more amenable to CBMs or arms reduction in a multilateral forum than they have been in a bilateral or trilateral context.

North and South Korea recognize the significance of European-style arms control negotiations for the Korean Peninsula. Their proposals express the use of the concepts of arms control that have been developed in Europe. The timings for arms control talks are also in accord with those of Europe. The North-South Coordinating Committee Meetings, were established in the early 1970s during the climate of the beginning of the CSCE and MBFR negotiations in Europe. The present North-South arms control dialogue was also begun in 1990 around the time of the conclusion of CFE-I.

The frequency of the North's arms control proposals has been considerably influenced by the process of European arms control talks. The North's proposals were very frequent during the successful implementation of arms control in Europe. Of a total of 236 proposals by the North between 1956 and 1988, 55 were made in the 1972-1974 period of the beginning of CSCE and MBFR negotiations and 20 were in the 1986-1987 period of the Stockholm Agreement and INF treaty.[9] However, the contents of these proposals were not related to European talks. For example, no CBMs were included in the North's proposals of 1986.

With the success of CFE-I Koreans began to have very positive perspectives towards the European arms control model. Accordingly their proposals have been based upon European ideas. Generally the two Korean states tend to follow the ideas put forward by the two blocs in the initial negotiations stage of the CSCE and MBFR. South Korean approaches are very close to previous ones from the West. On the other hand, North Korean ideas are very similar to those of the East and the Soviet Union. The North's approaches to arms control lag behind the Soviet proposals by 5-10 years. Recent trends show the North Korean propositions as reducing this time lag.[10]

The parallels between the West-South and the East-North can be seen in their perspectives on the Helsinki Final Act. At the Helsinki process for the application of CBMs the West required the inclusion of human rights and free movement for citizens, while the East attempted to limit restraints to military CBMs. The South, like the West, is insisting upon the inclusion of humanitarian concessions such as meetings of separated families between the North and the South in line with the military CBMs. The South's position is that "without first resolving this urgent humanitarian problem any tasks for improving inter-Korean relations or mutual confidence building are meaningless".[11] However, the North is opposed to the inclusion of any items relating to the opening of its closed society because of the high risk that such talks could destroy its leadership cult. This fear was well evidenced by the forced withdrawal of all North Korean students from eastern Europe in 1989-1990 after the collapse of Eastern Communist regimes.

During the MBFR negotiations, the East and Soviet Union pursued the objective of breaking the security links between the US and the West. The West kept in mind a geographic asymmetry in which reinforcement by the US forces across the Atlantic would be slow, in comparison with the conditions of the Soviet force's capacity for rapid redeployment to Eastern Europe. Similarly the North still appears to consider arms control as a primary tool to break the security links between the US and the South. South Koreans fear that the redeployment of US forces would require a considerable amount of time because of the long distance - approximately 9,000 miles - involved, should North Korea launch a war after the withdrawal of US forces from Korea.

A more obvious similarity in practical terms is revealed through the perspectives on transparency and verification measures. Like the West, South Korea seeks to introduce these as a first stage of arms control. North Korea sees such measures as a means to attain unilateral advantage relating to intelligence. Consequently they do not propose transparency and verification measures and resist those of the South. This is similar to the Eastern position during the initial phase of CSCE and MBFR.

Thus the similarities of the perspectives of West-South and the East-North are caused by their respective defence cultures. The North and the East premised their defence upon superiority of conventional forces and an offensive strategy, while the South and the West have been faced with military insecurity because of an inferiority of conventional forces and consequent dependence upon the strategy of nuclear deterrence and the security umbrella of the US As a result, the common perspectives of the

South-West and the North-East on defence have helped the two Koreas each to learn different lessons from the West and the East. However, despite their different perspectives, the North and the South have achieved some convergence in the application of parts of the Helsinki and Stockholm Agreements and the CFE Treaty through the December 1990 preliminary arms control agreement.

Table 9-1 The Convergence of Arms Control Proposal between Europe and Korea

	West-South	East-North
negotiation approach	military-technical	political
human rights	inclusion	exclusion
arms control priority	CBMs	arms reduction
arms control phase	CBMs->reduction	reduction->CBMs
priority of CBMs	non-military & military	military
exchange of data	before reduction	after reduction
verification	first phase	negative, final
reduction method	asymmetry	ceiling
reduction priority	offensive weapons	manpower
nuclear free-zone	negative	active
US forces	station	withdrawal

The Potential Conditions for Application

The Korean Peninsula has already matured in the light of three basic arms control objectives; reduction of risks of war, diminished potentiality of destruction in war and reduced economic burden from defence build-up. North and South Korea pursue arms control objectives out of consideration for these objectives. South Korea emphasised these arms control objectives in the Defence White Paper of 1991-1992:

> Our arms control objectives are to reduce the risk of war by improving common security, and reduce the political, military, economic, and social burden by deterring the arms race and the destruction if war occurs through disarmament oriented armament management.[12]

The 1990 Nonaggression Agreement between the North and the South confirms these objectives.

Both sides recognize the possibility of unintended war which may be touched off by any slight accident because of the array of heavily armed forces along the MDL. Therefore their common concern is first of all focussed on the application of arms control measures which could "prevent accidental armed clashes and their escalation" to a total war. The instalment of a telephone hot-line and the conversion of the heavily militarized DMZ into a real buffer zone are included as the first priority of arms control in their proposals.

Both sides have already recognized the degree of catastrophic physical destruction that would be imposed on both victor and vanquished if war should occur. In June 1986, the Defence Minister of the DPRK viewed the prospect of a war as a rationale for 'three-way military talks' in his letter to ROK Defence Minister,

> I think you will not deny the fact that if a war breaks out in our country it will devastate the land and plunge the whole nation into a nuclear holocaust and this will bring nothing good to both the North and the South.[13]

The South's conclusion on the potential results of war is similar to that of the North; "should another war break out, it would bring about untold destruction and massacre, damage the nation's history to an irrevocable extent ... ".[14] The 1989 Korean Defence White Paper drew a picture that another war would destroy half the population and most of the industrial infrastructure on both sides.[15]

Both states had the bitter experience of formidable devastation of the whole country through the Korean War. A Second Korean War would result in irrevocable damage through the presence of heavily armed forces with sophisticated weapons. Furthermore, given the lesson of each failure on the verge of national unification and the heavy burden from military confrontation through the division of the country, both sides would attempt to achieve unification at any cost if the war should occur.

Another important factor is the economic burden from high defence expenditure. North and South Korea have been spending respectively around 20 percent and 5 percent of their GNP for defence. As a result military spending has placed a tremendous strain on their economies. Many analysts argue that particularly in the case of the North, the culminated burden is about to reach a point of financial suicide.[16] In fact after the implementation of the military build-up under the "Four Military Guide

Lines" the North's rate of annual growth of industrialization dropped from 36.6 percent in 1957-60 to 12.8 percent in 1967-70 and averaged 14.2 percent in 1971-84.[17] On the other hand the South has allocated about 5 percent of its GNP and nearly 30 percent of the annual budget to defence. Though this figure is smaller than the North the high allocation for defence has been a serious obstacle to improvement of welfare and social services.[18]

The most favourable condition for Korean arms control can be sought from the ethos of a single political entity which provides a rationale beyond the three classical arms control objectives. The Korean people maintained a single national community from the ninth century up to 1945 and during that period lived in a single ethnic society based on the same language, culture, tradition and homeland. The division of the Peninsula and the Korean war were the outcome of the confrontation between capitalism and communism and are therefore viewed as an unnatural arrangement in the light of the single, homogeneous Korean history. The North and the South have commonly recognized tension reduction and disarmament as the first condition for national unification. Therefore the present North-South dialogue is expected to produce useful results towards arms control given the strong desire for unification.

Lessons Learnt from the European Experiences

An important lesson which Koreans should have gained from European experience concerns the institutionalization of the negotiations on arms control. European arms reductions were made after a nearly 20 year negotiation process. The institutionalization of negotiation mechanisms gave a legitimacy to the process even under conditions where NATO and the Warsaw Pact held very different positions. Though arms control mechanisms were used for propaganda purposes at the outset, later on they became a practical instrument for dealing with European security. In the 1980s it proved to be impossible for either the West or the East to stop and revoke this enterprise.[19]

In the light of the European experience the first task for the North and the South should be to create a mechanism for institutionalizing and legitimatizing the dialogue on security and arms control. Koreans have spent much time in proposing concrete measures that could not be easily accepted by one side without designing a practical forum within which to discuss them. Despite the simultaneous beginning of arms control in Europe and Korea in the early 1970s, the former produced successful results through the continuation of dialogue within the framework of the institutionalized arms control forums. On the other hand, the latter made a direct attempt to discuss arms control measures without developing the 'North-South Coordinating Committee' into a firm arms control mechanism. Currently Koreans has made efforts to set-up arms control forums through 'the Premier High Level Talks'. As a result the North-South Military Committee was established within the framework of the Premier Talks. The North-South Joint Military Commission was established for the discussions about CBMs and arms reduction. A subcommittee was also set up for cooperation between working levels.[20]

The configuration of arms control talks mechanisms within the High Level Talks for the improvement of dialogue and relations is similar to the organization of the CSCE and the Helsinki Final Act which was largely organized into 'three baskets' dealing with security, economics and human rights. The North and the South also attempt to deal with the problems of arms control as part of the overall improvement of their relations. This package negotiation approach has some merits in that bargaining chips between the measures are increased. In practice, bargaining between measures of different character may be very difficult.

The European arms control problems have been managed through the separation of conventional and nuclear arms control. The separate establishments of conventional and nuclear commissions is very sound given that they are very different subjects. However, the negotiations for the application of CBMs and arms reduction in a military commission may produce many problems in the process of the talks. The problems of CBMs and arms reduction, though mutually complementary, have very different subjects. As seen in Europe, the CBMs can easily be applied without causing any damage to existing capabilities. On the other hand, arms reduction may need much time and effort to get an agreement. In future the separation of these 2 areas may be discussed as the arms control talks progress.

However, from the initial phase of the talks, the establishment of subcommittees dealing separately with them is essential for prevention of any deadlock through linkage. This is obvious since in terms of arms control priorities, the South calls for the prior implementation of CBMs, while the North demands implementation of arms reduction first.

What is more important than the effectiveness of arms control talks is the continuation of the talks mechanism. In the light of past experience of the termination of the North-South Coordinating Committee by the North, both sides must first of all reach an agreement upon mechanisms which can guarantee the continuation of arms control talks. This may help either side to prevent an escape from the negotiation table by unilateral declaration.

European CBMs present an essential model for hostile countries with heavily armed forces. Despite the high level of military forces NATO and the Warsaw Pact did not experience any serious crises after the application of CBMs. The CBMs helped the creation of mutual security cooperation and stability. The situation of the Korean Peninsula is very similar to that of the European environment. The antagonism of the two Koreas has lasted over forty years. Both sides have maintained high combat readiness. Therefore European CBMs constitute an ideal model for confidence build-up and stability between two hostile Korean states.

CBMs are understood as two kinds of concept; comprehensive and narrow. Those who advocate the comprehensive concept of confidence seek to apply it to economic, scientific and technological, cultural and other sectors. CBMs for them are incremental measures of every type which are conducive to the promotion of mutual understanding and political confidence between countries.[21] Europeans have focussed upon the narrow concept of Europe's security and attempted to create stability in the operational theatre through reduction of the threat from the adversary. Unlike Europeans South Koreans connote the application of 'comprehensive CBMs' with security CBMs. Their intention is to conduct exchanges and cooperation in the non-security field in line with military CBMs. This means that they follow the model of the Helsinki agreement which failed to adopt militarily elaborate and binding CBMs and concentrated on 'comprehensive CBMs'. This is understandable in that they concentrate on the creation of political confidence as the basis for military CBMs. However, Koreans must keep in mind that the Stockholm Agreement, which created more elaborate military CBMs than the Helsinki Agreement, provided a crucial turning point to bring stability in the European theatre. The Stockholm and Vienna CBMs should be applied to the Korean Peninsula in order to stabilize the tense theatre and to reduce the utility of deployment of huge military forces.

The European CBMs can largely be categorized into three groups: transparency, constraint, and verification measures. These are the most practical measures which can be applied to the Korean Peninsula.[22] Among these, transparency measures may be the first agenda for application. Koreans have shrouded all military activities in secrecy. Greater military openness is necessary in order to assess the military situation without prejudice and to reduce threats caused by misunderstanding. Such measures can more easily be agreed upon because they have no influence upon the two side's military capabilities. Such measures might include:

. Exchange of military information
- information on military forces; military strength, organization, deployment
- plans for major weapons deployment
- defence budget

. Prior notification of major military activities
- exchange of annual calendar
- movement and deployment of military units
- military exercises and manoeuvres

. Observation of major military activities
- invitation of observers at the major exercises and manoeuvres

. Exchanges of military personnel

North Korea has kept military data secret by not releasing information officially or unofficially. Data on North Korean is mainly based upon the estimates of some Western military institutions. Such data has not been found even in statements and dialogue from the North's officials or scholars in conference. The principal arguments are that the North has neither the military capabilities or will to attack the South, because it is inferior to 1 to 2 to the South in population and its military strength is far behind the principle of 3 to 1 ratio usually regarded as necessary for successful offence. Because it is a very closed society, the collecting of information is very difficult. Thus, secrecy may help the negotiating partner to overestimate its counterpart's military power. To avoid this North Korea should not be reluctant to reveal its military capabilities. Prior to the argument for disarmament, the North must release reliable official data which could constitute basic sources in the arms control talks.

The application of 'constraint measures' is essential to the Korean security situation, which is very vulnerable to surprise attack. The capital cities are a short distance from the forward defence line. Warning time in Korea is much shorter than it was in Europe. Therefore the prevention of surprise attack in Korea would be achieved by regulating certain military activities and forms of deployment. Such measures would increase the duration of attack preparation and expose the intention to attack. In the light of existing practice and proposals in Europe, it seems possible to categorize constraints applicable to the peninsula in terms of the following:

- Limitation on size, duration and number of military activities.
- Invitation of observers at military activities above a certain level.
- Ban on military activities above a certain size without annual forecast.
- Limit to set-up size and interval of manoeuvre and movement in forward area.
- Ban on forward deployment of major offensive weapons.
- Limitation on logistic deployment in forward area.[23]

The DMZ and the forward defence area are heavily militarized with huge troop concentration and extensive offensive equipment deployments. Because of that, the application of constraint measures in the area should be considered in line with arms reductions

Taking into account European experiences, verification is a key issue in successful arms control implementation. Verification is a means to an end, not an end itself.[24] The adopted CBMs would always be doubtful if there were no measures for confirming that the treaty partner was abiding by the rules. This is a first step towards confidence and a final guarantor of it.

During the Cold War in Europe the demand for verification symbolized the depth of ideological confrontation and distrust between the East and West. The West insisted on verification measures, but the East was reluctant to accept them.[25] The 1975 Helsinki military CBMs were not conducive to compliance because of the absence of verification measures. The 1986 Stockholm CBMs were a turning point of conventional arms control through the inclusion of inspection measures, particularly on-site-inspection measures. After the Stockholm agreement, for the East, verification was no longer viewed as spying for unilateral advantage, but rather as a mechanism for mutual reassurance.

The Korean attitude towards verification is now similar to the European one. The two Koreas both propose on-site-inspection. However their approaches are fundamentally different. South Korea calls for the inspection of military CBMs to prevent surprise attack. On the other hand North Korea applies verification to the implementation of arms reduction, ruling it out in the CBMs stage. The mutual distrust of the two Koreas is so deep-rooted that agreements without verification will result in increased suspicion about the other side's cheating. Given the Helsinki experience and Korean circumstances, measures for inspection are essential elements in Korean CBMS. The measures should include:

- Inspection on compliance with CBMs implementation
- Inspection on exchanged data
- On site-inspection
- Challenge inspection: annual quota and special inspection
- Aerial inspection

In recent years the nuclear weapons issue has produced agreements such as the 1994 US-DPRK agreement. The successful implementation of these agreements could become a turning point for building confidence between the two Koreas and establish a very important precedent for devising verification measures for CBMs and arms reduction in Korea.

South Korean officials assume a phased arms control formula. The formula is first, political CBMs; second, military CBMs; third; arms reduction.[26] For the South, negotiations for arms reduction would be possible only after a certain level of political and military confidence had been fostered.

The important lesson in relation to this problem is that in the European case negotiation for CBMs and arms reduction began simultaneously in 1973. The process of CBMs was initially separate from that of arms reduction. CBMs were achieved prior to arms reduction. Even the Stockholm Agreement did not produce any arms reduction. As seen in the 1990 CBMs and arms reduction agreements these have been separately negotiated in Europe. The concepts and objective of arms control and disarmament are substantially different. Furthermore, in reality one does not necessarily lead to the other.

The European arms reduction talks were bilateral between the two blocs. Like Europe, Korean arms control is essentially bilateral. Furthermore, the maintenance of the present massive armed forces is a heavy burden for both Koreas. Therefore the three stage order of arms control is not essential in the Korean security situation. Even though the negotiation of arms reduction will be prolonged, the negotiation should be begun in line with the CBMs negotiation. As a US analyst pointed out, the security situation of the two Koreas is more favourable towards arms reduction than was the case in Europe and can be engaged in an Asian version of MBFR.[27]

The data issue was very problematic in the European arms reduction negotiations. The important thing in any negotiation is to count exactly the number of forces and weapons. At the beginning of MBFR, NATO and the Warsaw Pact did not have an agreement on counting rules. The data put on the negotiation table was produced by each side's own counting standards. The data could not be corrected easily due to the constraint of diplomatic credibility. Furthermore, the data issue was sometimes used as a means of slowing down negotiations or diverting them from central issues. Thus, the debates on data significantly blocked progress in the MBFR negotiation.

The way to bypass the mistaken European experience is first of all to prepare a counting rule and standard measures before discussing the amount of reduction. North and South Korean weapon systems have almost without exception depended upon those of the Soviet Union and the US respectively. Therefore the definition of TLEs developed within the CFE Treaty can be easily applied to Korean weapon systems. For this it is very important to establish a consultative mechanism for exchanging military information and setting the rules.[28]

The European experience demonstrated that success in arms reduction is best achieved by dealing simultaneously with forces and equipment. MBFR sought to limit only manpower. The CFE treaty deals with forces reduction only after the agreement an equipment reduction. However, in relation to the process of reduction, priority was given to equipment. The US and the Soviet Union began the MBFR negotiation as a means of preventing the unilateral withdrawal of their forces from Europe. Except for the difficulty of dealing with the withdrawal of foreign troops, manpower reductions carry many problems such as the difficulty of verification because of troop mobility. Further the problem is greater in that the demarcation between active-duty and reserve units is difficult to establish and demobilization, unlike the scrapping of equipment, can be swiftly reversed in a short time. The basic European arms control principle - to prevent surprise attack and reduce the scope of destruction if the war occurs - may have given priority to equipment reduction, rather than manpower reduction, because of considerations of equipment attributes of mobility and destructive capability.

North and South Korea explicitly agree with the reduction of forces and equipment. However, the methods of approach differ markedly. The South proposes to reduce troops in accordance with equipment reduction. The North suggests a limit upon the equipment reduction commensurate with the stages of troop reduction. The numbers game was one of the main reasons for the failure of the MBFR negotiation. If force reduction is prioritised in Korea, similar problems will appear to those of Europe. The two Koreas have developed mobilization systems to convert a great number of regular military reserve and para-military forces into regular forces in a very short time in wartime.[29] The ease of mobilization will limit the effect of regular force reduction.

The present serious destabilization factors in Korea result from significant disparities in holdings of offensive combat units. Equal limits on the equipment for offensive operations should be the urgent subject of negotiation. These are tanks, artillery, armoured vehicles, helicopters and aircraft which are defined by the CFE Treaty as major combat equipment. The levels of reductions are a complex matter, which would need to be studied quite carefully. There is little doubt that the European method of a common ceiling can applied to Korea.[30]

Given the existing procedure of reduction and the prevention of surprise attack, the weapons reduction might be the first agenda of negotiation. However, in the light of the particular Korean security situation which involves maintaining too many forces for such a small nation, forces reduction should be simultaneous with the equipment reduction. As seen in table 9-2, the maintenance of forces which do not exceed over 1 percent of total population is seen as a reasonable force level for a nation according to the criteria of developed countries. The two Koreas have suffered economically from the maintenance of disproportionately forces. North and South Korea's forces represent about 4.7 percent and 1.7 percent of total population respectively. These figures are the highest ratio of the major military powers. In particular over one-third of the North's youth are committed to military service. Because of a shortage of labour a large number of troops work in civil construction.[31] South Korea also allocates nearly half of the defence budget to the maintenance of salaries, food and clothes.[32]

Table 9-1 Military Percentage of Major Military Powers

	DPRK	ROK	USSR	US	Japan	PRC	UK	France	FRG
F/P	4.7	1.7	1.2	0.8	0.2	0.3	0.5	0.8	0.6
F/Y	36	11	10	6.8	1.9	11	4.6	7.0	5.2

	India	Vietnam	Iraq
F/P	0.1	1.5	1.9
F/Y	1.1	11	16

F/P: forces/population, F/Y: forces/youth population (18-32 age) Source: These figures are arranged from *Military Balance 1991-1992*.

Until now the maintenance of a great number of forces has been the security pillar of the two Koreas. A massive force reduction without a concomitant building of confidence would generate alarm and stimulate fear about security. Thus a step-by-step force reduction over the long term would reduce the problems of the psychological impact.

Lessons from German Arms Control Policies

Germany and Korea shared a number of features in international politics. The two countries were divided by the interventions of external powers. During the Cold War they came to represent the competition between ideologies and were potential flash points of intense armed hostility as pillars of bipolar military systems. Therefore their policies have been directed towards the overcoming of these problems through detente. Unification has also been a central element of their national objectives. These German-Korean analogues evidence the possibility for the applicability of German arms control policies to Korea.

The Design for Peaceful Co-existence of the Two Regimes

The CSCE and MBFR were convened with the completion of the FRG's Eastern treaties for solving the border problems through the implementation of 'Ostpolitik'. The FRG's policy was to accept officially the division of Germany, the existence of the GDR and further to confirm peaceful co-existence with the GDR and crucial neighbour countries. The legal initiatives gave a momentum to the convening of the CSCE and MBFR.

The inter-Korean dialogue of the early 1970s was crucially influenced by the inter-German rapprochement at the time. Notwithstanding the attempt to learn from the German model, the early 1970s dialogue suffered from the absence of a legal framework which would normalize relations. Both sides failed to formally recognize the other regime and establish practical methods of peaceful co-existence. Furthermore they neglected the cross-normalization with hostile neighbour powers. Two decades later Koreans were once again attempting to follow the German experiences. They declared the non-use of force and continued respect of the present border through the 1991 Non-Aggression Agreement. South Korea has been pursuing a 'Nordpolitik' similar to the German Ostpolitik. Its objective is to guarantee peace in Korea through normalization with hostile countries. The policy was very successful in establishing diplomatic relations with the Soviet Union and Communist China. In response to the South's initiatives, the North is carefully attempting a 'Southern Politik' to open diplomatic relations with Japan and the US though it has not produced such successful results.[33]

In the light of the experiences of failure in the 1970s dialogue it is now important to build up confidence through the development of social links and contacts, and political and economic cooperation. It is crucial to reduce distrust and threat perception even in the area of military confrontation. The North seems to believe that such social contact and cooperation will result in North Korea following the example of the collapse of the GDR and the Eastern communist regimes.[34] However, despite the improvement of contacts and cooperation between the East and the West from the early 1970s the Eastern Regimes continued in existence for two decades. There is no doubt that the crucial reason for their collapse was not the development of relations with the West, but the failure of the economic structure. Western Countries including US and Japan have to regulate the North's unpredictable behaviour in the international arena through the establishment of diplomatic relations, not diplomatic isolation. This may produce an arms control dialogue through the peaceful co-existence of the two Korean regimes.

Political Detente through Arms Control

The Germans saw arms control negotiations as a means of political detente. The arms control negotiations were an important component of their security policies. The FRG made major efforts to reduce forces in the MBFR negotiations. However, its approach was based upon the perceived political advantages produced through negotiation rather than from the expected value of reduction itself. The MBFR negotiation was believed to guarantee the continuation of political detente in Europe and bring about an improvement of relations with the GDR.[35]

The German view has not however found favour in Korea. The Korean governments have made arms control an end in itself rather than emphasising the political detente that might result from arms control negotiations. Arms control has been understood as simply a means for force reduction. The North has placed more emphasis on the unilateral withdrawal of USFK than on the achievement of stability and tension reduction through the inter-Korean arms control talks. South Korea has also maintained the position that it would have no arms reduction negotiation with the North without possessing concomitant military equality. In fact the term "military superiority" or "balance" is not so much a military as a political term, defined by its usefulness for securing political objectives rather than for expressing the relative strength of military capabilities.[36]

Nevertheless, a number of political advantages might be expected to result from the North-South arms reduction talks. The arm reduction talks can lead to exchanges of military information and greater military transparency through verification and further can produce a rational reassessment of military requirements, aims and strategies. Furthermore, the beginning of arms reduction negotiations may not only eliminate a source of the North's political propaganda, but reconcile the North-South military imbalance through political cooperation and alter policy objectives likely to require the use of force. Initially such talks could fasten the North to the continuation of political detente.

Linkage of Arms Control to Unification

Given the present Korean arms control attitudes the most important lesson from the German arms control policies is that there should not be direct linkage of arms control and unification. The West Germans did not use arms control and security negotiations as an instrument of unification. Their efforts in the negotiation concentrated on reducing tension and devising measures to prevent surprise attack. The European experience provided no guidance on how to manage a process of confidence building towards the unification of Germany.[37]

Unlike the Germans, Koreans have seen arms control as a means of unification. The North Korean arms control proposals are not primarily aimed at the arms control itself, but focussed on obtaining an upper hand in the politics of unification. South Korea also attempts to devise measures conducive to unification in their arms control proposals. Thus, both sides overload arms control negotiations with tasks of a quite different nature. The basic objective of arms control is to reduce tensions and to prevent war. In this way arms control is indirectly helpful to the fundamental goal of reunification. The separation of the unification and arms control tasks is a pre-requisite to the successful achievement of arms control.

Korean Compliance with International Arms Control Agreements

The sincerity of the German attitude towards arms control is evidenced from their participation in international multilateral arms agreements. Like Germany, South Korea has normally been a reliable member of such arms control agreements. On the other hand, North Korean participation is

252 *Ending the Last Cold War*

limited to a small number of agreements. Most notably the North, despite the recently accepted IAEA safeguards agreement, and agreement with the USA, has not taken a positive attitude toward treaties related to nuclear weapons even in the context of the Nuclear Free Zone. This attitude is in contrast with that of the GDR. As seen in table 8-7, the GDR always acceded to multilateral treaties in advance of the FRG.

Table 9-2   Korean and German Accession to Major Multilateral Arms Control Agreements

	Geneva Protocol	Antarctic Treaty	PTBT	Outer Space	NPT Treaty	Sea-bed
Korea	S, N:1988	S:1986 N: 1987	S:1964 N: ---	S:1967 N: ---	S:1975 N:1985	S:1987 N:---
Germany	F:1919 D: 1959	F:1979 S:1974	F:1964 D:1963	F:1975 D:1967	F:1975 D:1969	F:1983 D:1975

	BW	Enmond	Inhumane weapons
Korea	S, N:1987	S:1986 N:1984	S,N:---
Germany	F: 1975 D: 1972	F: 1983 D:1978	F:S D:1982

North Korea: N, South Korea:S, FRG: F, GDR: D, Source: *SIPRI Yearbook 1990*, p.644, 647.

The GDR's arguments towards the nuclear free zone were made on joining the multilateral nuclear treaties. The arms control environment would benefit greatly if North Korea adopted the East German approach of compliance with international arms control regimes. The North's active participation in international multilateral arms control agreements would increase its credibility regarding Korean arms control.

Priorities for the Model's Application

The Elimination of the Perceived Threat

One of major aims pursued by arms control is to influence perception of threat or actual threats by applying specific measures. A perceived threat is created out of the fears and images that are influenced by the intention and the military behaviour patterns of an enemy. Western threat perceptions were caused by the Soviet Union's immense offensive capability and its frequent uses of military power in Eastern Europe. NATO, in addition to the WTO's physical threat, made efforts to prevent the outcome of an accidental or preemptive war which could have arisen from misperception of the real threat. CBMs were a useful design for the reduction of threat perception. The threat perception of Koreans is higher than that of the Europeans. The Korean mutual threat perception might therefore bring about an unintended war by misunderstanding. Korean apprehensions and threat perceptions are primarily formed by the Korean War experience and by offensive military postures, rather than simply the huge military capabilities themselves. South Korean threat perception is based upon the North's primary objective of "liberating the southern half" of the Korean Peninsula.[38] South Koreans believe that the North aims to communize the South. The 1989 South Korean Defence White Paper argued that "without showing any sign of change in its basic objective and strategy, North Korea pursues merely tactical adjustments on the changing international and internal situations".[39]

The policies and proposals of the North have been interpreted as a means of achieving such an objective. The North is responsible for the formation of this threat perception. Notwithstanding the memory of the Korean War, the North has made a number of military provocations against the South since the cease-fire.

Table 9-3 The Number of Major North Korean Military Provocations against South Korea

	1958-60	1961-70	1971-80	1981-90	Total
Violations along MDL	2	16	28	26	72
Infiltration	35	37	10	82	164
Bomb Terror in the ROK	4	4	8		16
Shooting of Aircraft	2	4	2	8	16
Hijacking	1	1	1	3	6
Kidnapping boat	7	32	11	4	54
(people)	(76)	(494)	(29)	(36)	(635)

Source: These numbers were arranged from the *Korean Defence White Paper 1991-1992*, pp.429-436.

As seen in table 9-4, a number of northern guerrillas and commandos have carried out subversive activities in the ROK. The North's objectives have been to encourage an uprising in the South and construct revolutionary bases as a prelude to an eventual reunification.

The North has likewise derived a very strong threat perception from the presence of US forces and nuclear weapons and the T.S. exercise.[40] This threat perception was demonstrated in a statement by Kim Il-sung in an interview with Representative Solarz in 1980:

> Even if I said here that we will not invade the South, you would not believe me. If you said you would not invade us, we would not believe you ... if we continue to suspect each other, there will be no end to it (confrontation).[41]

The three factors influencing the North's threat perception are its own responsibility. The withdrawal plans of USFK have been reevaluated in the light of the military build up and offensive postures of the North. The T.S. exercise and American nuclear weapons existed to maintain the credibility of deterrent strategy by the South.

However, even though such measures have been produced in response to the North's intensive military provocations, there is no reason to doubt that they have been perceived as a serious threat by the Northern regime. If it were the case that in the absence of USFK in the South, Russian or Chinese forces were stationed near the MDL under a combined command system with the North and further annual a joint exercise of a similar size to the T.S. between them were operated in the North, the South would also consider these as deeply threatening.[42] Thus the two Koreas have perceived each other as having offensive forces and aggressive intentions. The "perceived threat" has constituted a more crucial obstacle to Korean stability than the "physical threat" itself. Therefore as in Europe, the application of CBMs are an important agenda for Korean arms control.

In recent years the factors historically perceived as threatening by the North have been eliminated by the suspension of T.S., withdrawal of nuclear weapons and the reduction plan of USFK. The symbolic size of a minimum deterrent cannot be perceived as a cause of threat to the North. Therefore it is time for DPRK to begin reciprocal reduction towards the South's threat perception. Given the South's traditional position, the North should firstly give up attempts to establish Korean unification on its own terms. An expression of such a change might be the revision of its constitution which seeks the communization of the Korean Peninsula. More practical evidence could be demonstrated through a halt to military provocations and infiltration of armed agents which have been employed as a means of subverting the ROK government. In fact such subversive activities have resulted in encouraging the South's anti-communism and military build-up rather than in weakening the Government. Moreover, such activities now seem redundant given the international demise of communism. Notwithstanding the above, the North continues its military provocations. It attempted the infiltration of three armed agents in the DMZ as recently as in May 1992.[43] The incident was a substantial violation of the spirit of the 1991 non-aggression agreement. As long as North Korea continues this military provocation, the South's perceived threat will not be reduced. Neither will North Korea's arms control gestures provide the South with any confidence.

Prevention of Surprise Attack

The establishment of a buffer zone is a typical case for arms control between actual enemies. A buffer zone plays a major role in preventing the possibility of accidental war through the separation of their armed forces. The DMZ was created by the 1953 Armistice Agreement as a buffer zone between the North and the South with the end of the Korean War. In order to prevent military clashes both sides withdrew 2 km from the MDL. The Agreement also defines limitations on military activities in the DMZ. Only 1,000 soldiers were allowed on each side for the management of the zone. The entry of equipment such as machine guns and heavy combat weapons was prohibited within the zone. The supervision of the Agreement was also specified by the establishment of the NNSC and Joint Observer Teams. However, in violation of the Agreement the zone has become heavily militarized as an area of forward defence. There have been frequent slight military clashes and exchanges of fire.[44] Supervision by the NNSC was stopped as a consequence. At present the zone is an area of high tension and has lost its original buffer function.

Both sides have sought to recover the DMZ as a mechanism for reduction of tension. The conversion of the DMZ into a peaceful area has been recognized as essential for the prevention of a surprise attack. As a result, ideas have concentrated on the demilitarization of the zone. It is an accepted point between North and South Korea that all military forces, equipment and supplies should be withdrawn from the DMZ and the region should be converted to a transparency zone. In recent years practical ideas have been offered which open the DMZ to civilians. A number of prominent proposals came from the South. Good examples of these were the creation of sports facilities for friendly matches between the North and the South, the conducting of a joint academic survey of the ecological system and the construction of a 'Peace City' inside the DMZ.[45]

The "peaceful utilization of the demilitarized zone" was obliged in the 1991 Agreement. The recovering of its original purpose would be the first indication for substantial arms control intentions. The work does not need any asymmetrical application nor does it disadvantage either side. Therefore both sides could easily reach an agreement. Both sides must recognize that the buffer zone between Israel and Egypt in the Sinai which completely duplicated the Korean Armistice case after the October 1973 War has been successful for stability and as a mechanism for the improvement of relations, while the Korean buffer zone has signally failed and become a source of high tension through the violation of the agreement.

A number of ideas about arms reduction zones were proposed during the European arms control talks on the grounds that it would be difficult to implement arms control measures in Europe as a whole. In 1987 Poland presented the "Jaruzelski Plan" which sought to apply CBMs and reduce weapons in Central Europe. The plan's focus was the limitation of the size and intensity of the specified types of military activities and heavy equipment and the reduction of offensive weapons from the forward area.[46] This proposal accorded with the ideas held by the Warsaw Pact which attempted to restrict arms reduction to the region of direct contact between the alliances.

The ideas about sub-zones and sub-limits were also supported by some Western analysts. Zbigniew Brzezinski proposed a "tanks-free zone" in Central Europe in order to prevent surprise attack by the WTO. Jonathan Dean also envisaged an asymmetrical exclusive zone of 50km west and 100km east of the inner-German border for offensive equipment such as tanks, helicopters and self-propelled artillery including major ammunition and fuel supply sites.[47] These zonal applications of CBMs and arms reduction were advocated by the Germans. The West German SPD supported the model of a "300km corridor free of offensive weapons". The SPD and SED put forward an initiative about the creation of a CBMs zone which forbade manoeuvres within a 50km wide belt along the line of contact between the two alliances.[48] Although these ideas were not accepted on the grounds that they could not bring substantial stability to the whole of Europe because they concentrated on particular countries in the context of the multilateral talks, they are noteworthy ideas in that the CBMs and thinning out of offensive weapons could be speedily applied in the heavily armed Korea forward area.

Outside the European theatre, practical experience for a zonal arms control can be sought from the "Sinai Model" between Israel and Egypt. The Sinai Agreement provided for a number of measures to reduce the risk of military clashes between the two closely deployed forces. Their forward area was divided into three zones: UN buffer, Egyptian limited forces and Israeli limited forces zone. The specific weapons and equipment were restricted in the respective limited forces zone. The range of fire power permitted each zone was to be incapable of reaching the opposite zone. The phased withdrawal and formats of disengagement were also established by subsequent negotiations.[49] This model has a specific application to Korea in that a buffer zone under the supervision of the UN was established in the forward area between actual enemies which had experienced war.

One of the important lessons of the European proposals and Sinai experiences applicable to the Korean Peninsula is the establishment of zonal CBMs and the thinning out of offensive weapons and equipment in the forward area. It might present serious psychological difficulties with regard to security and procedure for Koreans without previous arms control experience - to apply arms control to the whole peninsula at one time. Therefore, the establishment of sub-zones for arms control could be a very useful approach. Sub-division provides the advantages of easier verification and phased CBMs and arms reduction. The phased arms control by sub-zone would reduce not only the risk of some cheating of the treaty but also limit the complexities of procedures and administration. The first step reduction within a sub-zone would be an important test with which to examine the wills towards arms control by both sides and indicate the possibility for the achievement of the treaty. Successful implementation might provide the crucial momentum for the next sub-zones and further for the whole country with a build-up of mutual confidence.

As one step, the region between Seoul and Pyongyang could be divided into several sub-zones. One Korean analyst from the Korean Institution of Defence Analysis of MOD, following the example of the CFE treaty, suggests five sub-zones including the DMZ:

. the DMZ: a truly demilitarized area.
. zone 1 (0-50km from DMZ): defensive-necessity forces.
. zone 2 (50-100km from DMZ): 50 percent of the zone 1 forces.
. zone 3 (100-300km from DMZ): 20 percent of the zone 1 forces.
. zone 4 (beyond 300km from DMZ): remaining forces.[50]

Some positive elements are evident in the idea which focusses upon the prevention of a surprise attack and includes a step-by-step reduction. However, it lacks consideration of the geographic asymmetry condition between the two capital cities. From the South's point of view, symmetrical application is not a viable military option because of the vulnerability of the capital city. Seoul is 48km from the DMZ whilst Pyongyang is 150km away. The terrain between the MDL and Seoul is a plain and makes for easy movement. It was here that the North put the weight of its tanks in the Korean War. South Korea would need to have enough time to deploy its in-place, active forces and prepare defensive positions, especially in the western forward area. Because of the closer proximity of Seoul to the MDL, the South cannot accept any symmetrical adjustment of sub-zones. Taking into account this geographic asymmetry and the forward deployment of the North's forces, the South suggests that the DPRK forces should be redeployed 50km behind the DMZ, whereas the ROK forces would be deployed only 10km to the rear of it.[51] A positive proposal was suggested by Soviet scholar Alexei Arbatov. His idea, in the light of geographic asymmetry, is to make a total controlled demilitarization of the belt of 20km to the South and 60km to the North from the DMZ.[52]

Except for the geographic condition that Seoul and Pyongyang are a very short distance from the MDL, they are political and economic centres with a dense concentration of population. They can be assumed as the first important targets of surprise attack. Evidence for this can be drawn from the Korean War. In particular, South Koreans keep in mind the bitter experience that Seoul was lost to the North only three days after the beginning of the Korean War. The priority for Korean arms control is to minimize the possibilities of a surprise attack upon capital cities. Therefore the region between Seoul and Pyongyang should be considered first for the establishment of the sub-zones.

CBMs give some advantages to the defender rather than to the attacker. Given the basic objectives of CBMs for the build-up of mutual confidence and stability, ROK and DPRK should not gain any advantages or disadvantages through the application of CBMs in the region. Therefore the Seoul-Pyongyang region can be established as only one CBMs zone. The European CBMs adopted in Stockholm and Vienna can be generally applied to the region, focussing on transparency and verification measures. In the light of short combat depth, the scope and size of manoeuvres and exercises should be more limited than in Europe, and include the prohibition of exercises along the MDL. The time and kinds of application of notification measures should be advanced and detailed. Unlike Europe, and given the particular Korean situation of direct contact at sea and the short flight time to the heart of each country, the activities of naval and air forces should be included in the subject of CBMs. The measures for consideration must include restrictions on the deployment of attack ships and a ban on operation of combat aircraft over a certain latitude between Seoul and Pyongyang.[53]

Unlike CBMs, the implementation of arms reduction may introduce a psychological impact, fears of cheating and technical complexities. Therefore the phased arms reductions should be made in several sub-zones. Taking into account the geographic asymmetry from the DMZ, the distance ratio of Seoul and Pyongyang from the DMZ could be applied to the establishment of four reduction zones:

. the first zone; DMZ
. the second zone; South: 0-10km, North: 0-40km
. the third zone; South; 0-20km, North; 0-80km
. the fourth zone; South: 0-30km, North: 0-120km

The North will be very reluctant to give up its geographic advantages which are a real military asset. The proposed zones would certainly reduce some Northern advantages for an attack against Seoul. But, it can maintain an advantage for defence of Pyongyang because of the greater combat-depth enjoyed over Seoul. Thus, the North can demonstrate a defensive will through the acceptance of the proposals described. The priority must be given to the reduction of forces and the attenuation of offensive weapons such as tanks, armoured vehicles, artillery, and attack helicopters. The implementation of the CBMs for transparency and verification in the zones must take place in advance of the phased arms reduction. Forces and equipment can be allocated equal ceilings in each zone.

The removal of ballistic surface to surface missiles, with ranges that include both capital cities as targets, should constitute an early item for negotiation. The North would dismantle and eliminate its FROG and SCUD missiles. The Honest John and Nike-Hercules missiles of South Korea would have to go. This would reduce possibilities of surprise attack or pre-emptive strike with no warning time, as a crisis outcome.[54] Further this would contribute to the denuclearization of the Korean Peninsula.

Creation of Crisis Management Centre

A number of ideas for the creation of consultative mechanisms for crisis management were offered in the European arms control talks. They included various elements from hot-line systems to consultative boards. The Jaruzelski Plan envisaged the establishment of procedures for resolving military disputes and the establishment of a hot line between NATO and the WTO. On the basis of the Gorbachev proposal, in October 1988 the WTO put forward the establishment of a centre for diminishing the threat of war and prevention of surprise attack in the CDE. A joint working group of the German SPD and SED designed a "confidence-building centre" as a permanent organ for dealing with military information and observations between the two German states and Czechoslovakia. Jonathan Dean also called for the establishment of a NATO-WTO "risk reduction centre" similar to the WTO proposals.[55] The "conflict centre" was achieved as a mechanism for consultation and cooperation as regards unusual military activities and hazardous incidents of a military nature, through the 1990 Vienna CBMs Agreement.

In fact the idea of a confidence-building centre or conflict prevention centre was offered not so much for the resolution of crisis situations but rather for the prevention of surprise attack or accidental war by misunderstanding through uncertainty over military information and activities. Hereby a distinction might be needed between the function of crisis prevention and that of crisis management. Crisis prevention means the reduction of the possibilities of war prior to crisis occurrence and is achieved through the application of CBMs. On the other hand, crisis management is designed to prevent crisis from escalating to war. The two European blocs did not meet any actual crises by managing them through the application of CBMs.

Unlike Europeans, Koreans have been faced with a number of crises. Many brought the two Koreas to the verge of war. The crises were caused by the North's provocative belligerence. The two regimes came close to another war on 21 January, 1968, when a 31-member commando group attempted to assassinate ROK President Park Chung Hee. They were stopped only a few hundred meters from his residence. The South considered retaliation against the attack in the recognition that "preemptive strikes against one or several of North Korean staging bases would be better than coping with future aggression".[56] The attempt was deterred by the US Government which was reluctant to risk another war in Asia while the Vietnam War was underway.

As seen in table 9-5, a number of crises led to the edge of war in consequence of the North's provocations against the US and the South. The US considered imposing military sanctions or taking other retaliatory measures against the North by deploying "Task Forces" with heavy combat equipment to the North Korean coast. In the Pueblo incident, "Task Force 77" comprised 25 ships including the attack carriers 'Enterprise', 'Kearsage' and 'Coral Sea'. Two fighter-bomber squadrons and 'Strategic Air Command Bombers' were additionally deployed with the reinforcement of the Fifth Air Force in Korea. The US Eighth Army in ROK and the ROK forces were put on alert.[57] In the shooting down of the EC-121, the deployment of "Task Force 71" was larger than in the Pueblo incident. About 40 ships and 256 planes were present with six aircraft carriers'. The forces had more firepower than the US Sixth Fleet.[58] Similar military actions were also ordered after the Poplar Tree Incident in 1976.

Table 9-4   Some Major Crises in the Korean Peninsula after the Korean War

21 Jan. 1968	The attempt to attack president's residence: 31 armed agents.
23 Jan. 1968	The capture of the US Pueblo intelligence ship: 6 officers & 77 sailors.
15 Apr. 1969	The shooting down of US EC-121 aircraft: 31 crew members killed.
26 Feb. 1975	85 fighters' violate the South's airspace:
24. March 1975	30 fighters do so.
18 Aug. 1976	The Poplar Tree incident in the DMZ: 2 US officers killed & 8 soldiers wounded.
1 Aug. 1981	Launching of SA-2 Missile against US SR-71 surveillance plane: no damage.
9 Oct. 1983	Bomb attack on Korean President & his officials in Rangoon: 16 high rank officials killed.

29 Nov. 1987   Bomb attack on the KAL 858:115 passenger's killed.

The killings of a number of high officials and civilians by the North's 1983 and 1987 terror bombings were also serious enough to have triggered the South's military retaliation and further escalate tension to a condition of war. Notwithstanding these numerous crises, the crucial reason that they did not escalate to war was because the US feared the military response from hostile powers in alliance with the North. For the US military sanctions would cause the involvement of North Korea's northern allies and thereby internationalise war in Korea under the condition of Cold War confrontation. The other important reason derives from the fact of the South's inferiority in military strength to the North. Moreover, for the South to independently retaliate separately from the US was very difficult because its forces were under the operational control of USFK. Such crisis management by tacit agreement between regional powers and the South's self-control may not continue in the post-1991 security situation. US military sanctions against the North's provocations would be an option after the collapse of the Soviet Union. The increasing tilt of the military balance towards the South might also induce military retaliation against the DPRK.

Under the situation of direct military contact an accidental or misunderstood action may lead to crisis. Although the North's past provocations against the South were certainly intentional, it is difficult to distinguish whether incidents such as the EC-121 or the Poplar Tree were provoked by intended plans or accidents which arose from mistakes or over-offensive actions of forward commanders out of control of central headquarters. The EC-121 incident coming shortly after the Pueblo might well have been very risky to the North. The 1976 murder of two US officers also seemed to be an accidental event which was caused by the trouble between guard officers of the North and the US during the supervision of the pruning of a giant poplar tree in the Joint Security Area (JSA) of the Military Armistice Commission (MAC) Headquarters.[59] On 30 June, 1975 a similar incident, where a US officer was seriously injured by the North's guards, also took place in the JSA.

The communication links between actual disputants may make an important contribution to the prevention of escalation to war during a crisis. Seoul and Pyongyang have proposed the connection of a hot-line in recognition of the importance of crisis management. The establishment of the hot-line may be of value given the lack of direct communication for the solution of a crisis between them. The usefulness of the hot-line system in a conventional crisis situation between the two Koreas may be limited, although it symbolizes security cooperation. Crisis termination can be achieved through joint efforts between actual adversaries. It may be more urgent to establish a North-South joint crisis management centre. Such joint efforts and experiences for the deterrence of crisis escalation may be helpful in preventing or decreasing crisis situations.

Linkage of Korean Arms Control and USFK

The Western allies were concerned that a unilateral reduction of US forces would have a destabilizing effect on European security, making the East perceive a weak US commitment to the West. They linked as a bargaining chip the US force withdrawals in Western Europe with Soviet force withdrawal from the East. The Soviet Union also used force withdrawals as a means of putting a legal ceiling on the Bundeswehr after the US withdrawal. Thus, the linkage of US and Soviet forces withdrawal was a principal subject of arms reduction negotiations in Europe.

North Korea in 1958 tried to link the withdrawal of Chinese troops from its territory with US force withdrawal from the South.[60] However, the times were hardly ripe. China relinquished an important lever for promoting the US withdrawal because the US forces had been gradually reduced unilaterally after the Korean War. North Korea failed to eliminate the US forces through the Chinese withdrawal, but did not feel strongly a need to have foreign forces on its soil because of a geographical proximity to the USSR and China. In contrast South Korea is separated from the US by approximately 9,000 miles.

The beginning of the MBFR negotiation dealing with a withdrawal of US forces gave North Korea a motive to link its force reduction to that of the US forces. In 1973 North Korea proposed that if the US forces were withdrawn, it would reduce its own troop strength voluntarily to less than 200,000.[61] The idea was unrealistic because the South possessed about 600,000 forces at the time. Furthermore, the North's reductions were to be made after the unilateral withdrawal of the US forces. The DPRK position has not subsequently changed. In fact it has opposed simultaneous linkage of the US forces with the reduction of Korean forces. The arms reduction question between the North and the South has been defined as a Korean problem which must be resolved by North-South talks after the US withdrawal.

As a counterproposal, South Korea suggested the withdrawal of foreign troops as a mechanism for the withdrawal of Chinese troops. An attempt to link the US withdrawal with the conclusion of the North-South nonaggression treaty was made in 1977 in relation to the unilateral American force withdrawal.[62] Fundamentally, however, South Korea could not apply the American and European precedents. The US withdrawal could not be assumed as a bargaining chip for Korean security because of the belief that the withdrawal would be perceived by the North as a weakening US security commitment to the South. The result might induce the North's forces to move Southward. South Koreans feared a replication of the event that led the North to begin the Korean War a year after the US forces were withdrawn in 1949. Therefore for the ROK, the linkage of the US withdrawal with Korean arms reduction would merely lose the advantage of the security umbrella provided by the US, because there were no foreign troops in the North which would threaten the South.

The United States likewise did not use the reduction of USFK as a bargaining chip for arms control and tension-reduction on the Korean Peninsula. Although it stated the threat and military build-up of the North as the reasons for the presence of the USFK, the US troop reductions were always unilaterally decided without reciprocal reduction by North Korean forces. However, there is a new approach which links the cuts of American forces to those of Northern forces. The US planned a three-phase adjustment on its forces during the 1990s:

- phase I (1991-3):7,000 men reduction; Air forces-2,000, ground forces-5,000
- phase II (3-5 years): restructuring of the 2nd Infantry Division and re-examination of the North threat
- phase III (5-10 years): a minimum size of forces for deterrence conversion of US role; from leading to supporting.[63]

A particular point is that the US plans to re-examine the North Korean threat and response to the first phase before implementing the second phase. This was well demonstrated by the postponing of further reduction. At the 23rd Security consultative meeting (SCM: 20-22 Nov.,1991) between the US and the South, both defence Ministers agreed that "US Nunn-Warner phase II troop reductions would be postponed until the danger and uncertainties surrounding the North Korean nuclear program and security in the region have been thoroughly addressed".[64] The postponement was to affect the second phase that was intended to reduce troop numbers by about 6,000.

Both Korean governments have begun to attempt to link the US force cuts with the North-South arms talks. South Korea feels that the reduction

The Application of the European Arms Control Model to Korea 265

of US forces in Korea is inevitable because of the changed global strategic environment. However, it is believed the reduction may give the wrong signal to the North. South Korean central thinking is that any adjustment of the USFK should be made without undermining deterrence. Lim Dong-won, President of the Institute of Foreign Affairs and National Security said that the government is obliged to use the US forces reduction as a bargaining chip in arms control negotiation with the North.[65] This idea is shared with numerous Korean scholars. One South Korean analyst suggests several ways of using a bargaining leverage; linking the southward redeployment of American forces to northward redeployment of North Korean offensive forces; predicating gradual reduction of American forces on the reduction of DPRK offensive forces; and inviting North Korea as an observer in US-South Korean bilateral troop reduction talks.[66]

The possibility can be found in a recent change to the North's policy. It had previously required the US force withdrawal as a precondition of all the negotiations between the North and South. However, unlike the past the 1988 proposal suggested a phased withdrawal:

. the first phase: withdrawal of ground forces to the line Pusan and Jinha (35 degrees 30 minutes North latitude).
. the Second phase: withdrawal of all ground forces.
. the third phase: withdrawal of naval and air forces.[67]

Further the 1990 proposal suggested a phased withdrawal in keeping with the arms reduction of the North and the South. North Korean scholars emphasised the simultaneous reductions of USFK and the two Korean forces in talks with US former officials.[68] However, in fact, the North's proposals are a linkage for unilateral advantage not negotiation. The idea of a linkage between the Korean and the US forces lacks the potential for any negotiation. The North's proposal had no linkage between mutual Korean reduction and US withdrawal. It is very unrealistic that the proposed US withdrawal and mutual reductions to the level of 100,000 men could be made in the three years of the negotiation. The North's intention of no linkage is more evident from the May 1990 proposal. The linkage was made after the US unilateral reduction officially was declared in April of 1990.

The American ploy for bargaining leverage might be a very realistic catalyst for Korean arms control negotiation, because the mainstay of the North's ultimate objective is to eliminate American forces. However, the US also seems to have less concern for a negotiated withdrawal based upon Korean mutual force reduction. The US unilaterally removed nuclear forces in the South without considering any bargaining for Korean security. It relinquished the chance to use it as a means to halt the North's nuclear program through secret negotiations or other channels. The US also voluntarily implemented the first phase reduction. The Second phase is not based upon negotiation, but the North's response and improved relations between the two Koreas. The option of the linkage in the second phase may reflect the US intention of the initial MBFR negotiation in that it hopes to maintain necessary forces for regional stability by imposing burden sharing on Korea.

Previous unilateral reductions gave the South an incentive for military build-up and the North encouragement for use of force. North Korea must recognize that the previous unilateral US withdrawals did not present advantages to the DPRK. Such withdrawals were always compensated by massive US military assistance to the South or the reinforcement of the US-ROK combined forces systems. Under the present situation of a swing of the military balance towards the South, the encouragement of the ROK forces build-up and the compensation of the US would constitute a heavy burden for the North. South Korea could use the withdrawal as a bargaining chip for substantially reducing the North's forces and changing the North's attitude in the arms control negotiation. Moreover, taking into account the European wisdom in the MBFR talks, the linkage of the US withdrawal and the Korean force reduction could be a very useful alternative for the prevention of the unilateral US withdrawal without devising tension reduction. Furthermore, the linkage may be a rationale for the continuous presence of USFK as a trip-wire of the Korean security umbrella in the future.

The True Denuclearization of the Korean Peninsula

The issue of the DPRK's nuclear programme remains a highly problematic one, even following the conclusion of the 'agreed framework' between the United States and North Korea in October 1994. The agreement was designed to resolve the dispute over North Korea's nuclear capabilities.

Under the agreement the United States agreed to create an international consortium to provide light-water nuclear power reactors to replace North Korea's graphite moderated reactors. While the replacements were being built the USA would guarantee oil supplies to North Korea. In return North Korea agreed to suspend its nuclear programme under international inspection. North Korea also committed itself to remaining fully within the

Nuclear Non-Proliferation Treaty (NPT), regime and to allow International Atomic Energy Agency, (IAEA) inspections of its nuclear facilities.

The North's acceptance of the IAEA safeguard inspection has reduced suspicions about its nuclear weapon program. But, this is insufficient to demonstrate its complete innocence. Despite its adherence to the NPT safeguards in 1969, Iraq has made continued efforts to acquire nuclear weapons secretly.[69] In the context of the Iraqi case, the IAEA did not uncover the Iraqi military nuclear programme. Therefore, the framework agreement provides no absolute certainty that the North has given up manufacturing nuclear weapons or stockpiling plutonium. The safeguard operation could not exclude the possibility that the North was already in possession of substantial stockpiles of highly enriched materials needed for nuclear weapons or had moved the experimental apparatus below ground or to another secret place to circumvent the agreement.[70] The North's refusal of special inspection by the South would make this question a likely possibility.

From the North's point of view, the risk of a military strike on its nuclear facility has been largely eliminated through the IAEA inspection regime. Therefore the reluctance to allow inspection by the South could be a political bargaining chip in negotiations for the improvement of relations with Japan and the US.[71] For the North, the US nuclear umbrella for the South may continue to present a heavy psychological burden even after the US tactical nuclear withdrawal, because the North has no nuclear umbrella from its allied powers. Moreover, allowing total transparency on the nuclear arms issue by permitting ROK inspection would dispel the North's security leverage for the maintenance of a military balance with the South. The North could be attempting to duplicate the Israeli ambiguous nuclear policy. The North's nuclear ambiguity may cause the South to believe in the possibility of a substantial stock of nuclear weapons, or the ability to produce them over the short term. For the North, it could bring a stable, credible guarantee against the gradual shift in the military balance towards the South, effectively copying the former US ROK "NCND policy" against the North's conventional threat.

The second major problem regarding full denuclearization derives from the continued dependence of the ROK upon the nuclear umbrella of the US even after the withdrawal of US tactical nuclear weapons. The ROK's Vice Foreign Minister has insisted that the South would remain under the nuclear umbrella of the US through its long-range ballistic missiles, nuclear-armed submarines and warplanes.[72] However, it may be unrealistic to expect the US umbrella over the South to include long-range or inter-mediate missiles.

Even deterrence by tactical weapons is highly questionable. Some US analysts such as Taylor and Mazarr argue that "a major lesson of the US post-1945 military operations, from Korea to Vietnam and now the Middle East, is that moral and pragmatic concerns largely preclude the US from using nuclear weapons against inferior foes".[73] In fact, nuclear threats have not deterred a number of previous DPRK provocations against the US and the South nor the DPRK's military build-up for invasion of the South. During the 1991 Gulf War the US acted through conventional weapons, excluding the possibility of the use of tactical weapons even at the risk of a great number of casualties.

In theory the nuclear umbrella, particularly in Korea, might not possess a "defensive" but a "deterrent" function. The US umbrella may have to some extent contributed to the deterrence of the North's full-scale attack upon the South because of its military inferiority. But, given the present situation of the narrowness of the military gap between the North and the South, it is difficult to envisage a repeat of the outcome of the 1950 Korean War whereby the South was easily occupied by the North. Furthermore, in the light of the present regional security situation, there is no possibility of the North's engaging in war with the full support of Russia and China as happened in the Korean War. Unlike the 1950 War when large US forces were not present in South Korea, the presence of USFK would decisively prevent the North's early occupation of Seoul through the swift reinforcement of US forces from home and Pacific bases. Therefore, even though another Korean War could occur, fighting would be likely to occur in the forward area without an easy, swift or decisive conclusion.

Under this situation, it is doubtful whether the South would call for nuclear strikes by the US on strategic points such as Pyongyang or tactical bases which would necessitate the killing of numerous solders and civilians. Such strikes might also involve the South in damage because of the short combat depth of the zone of operations. Moreover, it is highly unlikely that the US would employ nuclear weapons for the conclusion of protracted war in the forward area given that such an action would generate enormous criticism from world opinion. Consequently, the absence of the nuclear option for defence will probably negate the usefulness of its value as a deterrent. Thus, after the removal of the tactical nuclear forces the US umbrella remains as an essentially symbolic security commitment.[74]

An alternative strategy for the effective denuclearization of the Peninsula might be to work for the establishment of a nuclear free zone. The question of the nuclear free zone has historically been strongly opposed by the South, because the North has proposed the removal of the US nuclear weapons and the nuclear umbrella. However, regional security conditions are favourable for the deterrent of a DPRK invasion. Furthermore the South's expectation of an implementation of the US nuclear umbrella against other regional nuclear powers like Russia and China could be seen as very wishful thinking. Moreover, it is difficult to assume that Russia and China would employ nuclear blackmail diplomacy against non-nuclear Korea.

For the South, the prevention of the North's nuclearization must constitute the first agenda for Korean security. Thus the bargaining between the abandonment of the North's nuclear development program and the relinquishment of the US nuclear umbrella probably remains the most useful leverage for a fully nuclear free Korea. However, because the North refuses any inspection by the South unless the US umbrella over the ROK is withdrawn, an active acceptance of the North's proposal might facilitate inspection in diplomatic terms.

The South would feel a security burden in the event of the removal of the umbrella. This is a psychological fear rather than a physical threat, brought about by the long dependence upon the US guarantee. Even though the symbolic umbrella is removed, the practical umbrella would remain in the event of a DPRK invasion given the continuing presence of USFK. Despite the absence of an actual nuclear umbrella declaration the US considered a nuclear option against the involvement of Chinese troops at the time of the Korean War. Conversely, it cannot be said that the exclusion of the option for use of the tactical nuclear weapons in the 1991 Gulf War was because of the absence of a prior US nuclear umbrella declaration in support of Kuwait.

Because of the lack of credibility of the US umbrella, the North's nuclear weapon flirtation could escalate the South's insecurity and encourage it to develop its own nuclear weapons. The nuclearization of the Korean Peninsula would be likely to result in the nuclearization of Japan. This would give both Koreas irrecoverable security burdens from Japan. As long as the nuclear problem of the North is not solved, tension reduction or conventional arms control cannot be expected on the Korean Peninsula. The continuation of tension and arms race may increase the North's security burden given the changing of military balance. The North's total abandonment of its nuclear weapon program would be a very useful incentive for the resumption of the USFK withdrawal and the North-South arms reduction, following the substantial removal of the US nuclear threat. Clear evidence of the North's abandonment would be signalled by the granting of permission for regular and special inspections by ROK officials.

The doubts about the North's nuclear program would be eliminated if inspections were carried out by the South rather than just by the IAEA.

Conclusion

The Korean Peninsula has the necessary conditions for the application of the European arms control model for Korean security. Despite the substantial difference of strategic environment between Europe and Korea (multilateral blocs confrontation as distinct from bilateral small states confrontation) the Korean Peninsula is very similar to Europe in the structure of confrontation and in the objectives of arms control which require to be implemented: the array of enormous ground forces along the land frontiers, high levels of distrust, vulnerability to surprise attack and accidental war, and external powers' deep involvement in the divisions and confrontation of Germany and Korea. The crucial condition for the successful emulation of the European arms control model is that North and South Korea introduce European arms control measures for Korean security and follow the respective approaches and negotiation strategies of both NATO and WTO. Furthermore, like the past European experience, the present North-South high level talks for conventional arms control remain deadlocked because of the problem of nuclear weapons. The defence cultures of North and South Korea are similar to those of WTO and NATO because the Soviet Union and the United States played leading roles in alliances which previously encompassed the Korean states. The two Korean states' arms control proposals have each been based upon the ideas of NATO and WTO in the early phases of CSCE and MBFR; the South following NATO and the North emulating the WTO.

The first lesson learnt from the European experience for Korean security is the necessity for maintaining the momentum of arms control talks by institutionalization of the negotiation mechanisms. Although the two blocs proposals were initially very divergent and propagandistic, they gradually converged through the continuation of negotiations. Institutionalized discussion bodies have played a crucial role in dealing with and solving all the European security problems through political dialogue and diplomacy as opposed to military force. In the light of the failure of the 1970s Korean arms control, the institutionalization of an arms control body should be a crucial first step for the application of CBMs and arms reduction.

CBMs may well be the most useful arms control measures in the Korean security situation. Through the application of CBMs Europeans reduced deep-rooted mistrust and intensive tension in their relationship and further maintained stability without causing any crises despite the presence of a massive level of military forces. The European CBMs were very effective security measures which neutralized some advantages of the WTO's military superiority by limiting and notifying force activities within an overall structure of military imbalance. In the light of the Korean security situation these measures could easily contribute to tension reduction and stability without requiring a different phase of arms reduction or defence structure. Though the implementation of CBMs need not be strictly phased, their application could be extended from relatively easy notification and information measures to transparency, constraint and verification measures.

North and South Korea both emphasise different priorities in the application of CBMs and arms reduction. However, the Europeans did not negotiate arms control according to specific priorities. CBMs and arms reduction talks were simultaneously begun, but CBMs were applied in advance of arms reduction. Taking into account the particular Korean security burden arising from the maintenance of massive military forces, arms reduction talks should occur in parallel with CBMs negotiations. During the reduction talks it may well be recognized that CBMs must occur first for the effective implementation of arms reduction.

Like the German arms control policy, Korean arms control should be based on the premise of peaceful co-existence. Arms control can overcome military obstacles and further advance or consolidate political detente. In fact arms control talks themselves may be a form of political behaviour which neutralizes the question of the military imbalance and alters the will regarding the use of force. In the process of arms control talks another important lesson from the German wisdom is the separation of arms control talks from the unification problem. Unification would constitute a major change of the status quo, whilst arms control is essentially designed to support the maintenance of the status quo. Therefore the overloading of arms control with unification objectives can distort the basic of purpose of arms control.

The application of the European arms control model, though not a phased application, may well provide not only the fundamental solution for the Korean security problem, but also procedural reliability and other benefits from application. Given the bitter experience of the Korean War and the long period of tense military confrontation lasting over 20 years, the removal of the perceived threat and recovery of identity are the first priority. No physical and hardware arms control can be expected without the development of mutual confidence between North and South Korea. Therefore the European CBMs constitute an important agenda for Korean arms control.

The prevention of a surprise attack remains an urgent problem. The first alternative is to actually demilitarize the so-called DMZ and establish it as a true buffer zone. Taking into account the difficulty of procedure and the lack of experience of arms control, a phased zonal arms control would provide a very useful and practical method. As a first step the creation of several CBMs and an arms reduction zone in the forward area could be applied out of consideration for the asymmetrical distance of Seoul and Pyongyang from the MDL. Because of frequent crises the establishment of a crisis management centre would be an important development in Korea. Given the past crisis cases, continued close arrays of forces in the forward area and deep-rooted distrust and mutual perception of threat, there are risks of a number of crises in the future. Therefore a joint North-South crisis management centre could prevent the escalation of crises into a total war and furthermore, continue to produce useful measures for its preclusion.

The problem of the USFK is the most controversial issue in the North-South arms control talks. Until now the unilateral withdrawal of USFK has been implemented without any reduction in military tension between the Korean states. In fact it has resulted in an increase in the arms build-up. The withdrawal of more US forces must be assumed in the context of the existing regional and international strategic environment. The future reduction of the forces should be made in conjunction with Korean arms control. This linkage could be extended to the realm of the true denuclearization of the Korean Peninsula. The bargaining which introduces the North's termination of its nuclear weapons program and the South's relinquishment of the US nuclear umbrella is in doubt because of the questionable validity of the latter. Verification of nuclear programmes would establish a very good precedent for conventional arms control and a chance to accumulate the techniques of verification.

NOTES

1. *Arms Control on the Korean Peninsula: what lessons can we learn from European experience?* (Seoul: Institute of Foreign Affairs & National Security, 1990), p. 71.
2. John Jorgen Holst, "Confidence and Security Building in Europe: Achievements and Lessons" in the above book, p. 18.
3. *Arms Control on the Korean Peninsula: what lessons,* p. 65

4. Byung Chul Koh, *The Foreign Policy Systems of North and South Korea* (Berkely : University of California Press, 1984), p. 79.
5. Tomas P. Bernstein & Andrew J. Natham, "The Soviet Union, China and Korea", *Journal of Asiatic Studies*, Vol. 25, No. 1 (1982), p. 107.
6. "Amb. Hyun Suggests Application of CSCE Model on the Korean Peninsula", *The Korea Herald*, 7 April, 1991.
7. "The Asian Problems must be solved by Asians", *The Pyongyang Times*, 2 February, 1991.
8. "North Korea's Objection on Two-Plus-Four German Unification", *The Choong Ahang Il-bo,* 14 July, 1990
9. Korean Defense Ministry, *Arms Control on the Korean Peninsula, Arms Control Material Sources* (3 November , 1990, in Korean), pp. 239-242.
10. Jong-Mahn Hong, "Korean Arms Control: Ideal and Reality", *Korea and World Affairs,* Vol 12, No 3, (1988), p. 487.
11. Address by President Roh Tae-Woo of the Republic of Korea at the 43rd session of General Assembly of the United Nation, *Korea and World Affairs* (October 18, 1988), vol. XII, No. 4, Winter 1988, p. 844.
12. The Ministry of Defence of ROK, *Korean Defence White Paper 1991-1992* (in Korean), p. 154.
13. Young-Sun Ha, "The Korean Military Balance: Myth and Reality", a paper presented at CSIS/KIDA International Conference on the Future of ROK-US Security Relations (Seoul: 12-13 September, 1988), p. 21.
14. Ibid.
15. The Minister of Defence of ROK, *The 1989 Korean Defence White Paper,* p. 22.
16. Tong Whan Park, "Political Economy of the Arms Race in Korea", *Asian Survey,* Vol.26, No. 8 (August 1986), p. 840.
17. Jin Young Sa, "Economic Development and Military Expenditure, in Ho Jae Lee (ed), *Arms Control on the Korean Peninsula* (Seoul: Bapmoonsa, 1989, in Korean), p. 161.
18. Yook Jin Whi, "Security Burden and Socio-Economic Progress in South Korea", a paper presented in the Conference of the Korean Political Science Association (25-27 July, 1991), p. 12.
19, *Arms Control on the Korean Peninsula: What Lessons*, p. 63.
20. The Joint Military Commission is composed of a chairman and of vice minister or higher rank and six members each side. The subcommittee comprises of a chairman who is a member of the delegation to the North-South high level talks and six members. *The Korea Herald,* 13 December, and 8 May.
21. For a detailed explanation of Comprehensive CBMs, see Falk Bomsdorf, "the Extension of Confidence-Building Measures: European Experiences, Third World Choice", in Jack Child (ed), *Conflict in Central American: Approaches to Peace and Security* (New York: the International Peace Academy, 1986), pp. 88-110
22. James Goodby, "Operational Arms Control in Europe: Implications for Security Negotiation in Korea", in William J,Taylor, Jr., and Cha Young-Koo (eds), *The Korean Peninsula: Prospects for Arms Reduction under Global Detente*

(Washington Press, 1990), p. 217. He divided all the Korean proposals into political measures: 'confidence' & 'improving relations' and arms control measures: 'operational' & 'structural steps'.
23. These measures were arranged in Thomas J. Hirschfield, "Building Confidence in Korea: The Arms Control Confidence", a paper presented for the 4th KIDA/CSIS International Conference (November 4-5, 1991), pp. 8-15.
24. Michael Sheehan, *Arms Control: Theory & Practice* (Oxford, Basil Blackwell, 1988), p. 145.
25. In the CBMs proposal in 1984, the Western proposal specified adequate verification; national technical means and on-site-inspection. But the Eastern proposal did not specified any verification measures and merely mentioned "developing the practice of inviting observers to notified manoeuvres". John Borawski, *From the Atlantic to the Urals: negotiating arms control at the Stockholm conference* (Pergamon-Brasseys: 1988), p. 60.
26. Dong-Won Lim, "An Urgent Need for Arms Control on the Korean Peninsula: a Framework for Implementation," *The Korean Journal of Defence Analysis,* Vol III, No.1, (Summer, 1991), p. 64.
27. Edward A. Olsen, "The Arms Race on the Korean Peninsula", *Asian Survey*, Vol. XXVI, No.8, (August, 1986) p. 866.
28.The 1990 Vienna CSBM Agreement laid out provisions which can effectively evaluate military information (Article 112). *SIPRI Yearbook 1991,* p. 485.
29. For the mobilization of reserve forces of the two Korean states, see *Korean Defense White Paper 1989,* p. 143, pp. 195-214.
30. James E. Goodby, "Confidence and Security", in Arms control on the Korean Peninsula: What Lessons", p. 111. He suggests in an article that a common ceiling of 1500 tanks and 1500 armoured vehicles, is proper for North and South. On the other hand Alexi G. Abratov mentioned a common ceiling of 1,000 tanks, 2,000 artillery pieces, 400 APC for each side.
31. *The Pyongyang Times*, 16 March, 1991. The newspaper reported that in 1986 150,000 soldiers were demobilized for civilian construction.
32. The Ministry of Defence of ROK, *Korean Defence Whiter Paper 1991* (in Korean), p. 251. The 1991 Korean Defence budget allocated for personnel maintenance: 42.6 percent, investment in force improvement: 34.9 percent, training and education: 3.8 percent, maintenance of facilities and unit: 9.1 percent and maintenance of equipment: 9.6 percent.
33. *The Pyongyang Times,* 27 April, 1991. Kim Il-Sung expressed the need of the normalization of the DPRK-Japan diplomatic relations through an interview with a Japanese newspaper. In 1990 the Workers' Party of Korea and the Liberal-Democratic Party of Japan had the joint declaration for improvement of DPRK-Japan relations. *The Korea Herald,* 14 May 1992. As a signal for the improvement with the U.S., North Korea has three times handed over the remains of American service men of the Korean War to the US since 1990.
34. North Korea is now very cautious about the German style reunification in which the FRG absorbed the GDR . *FBIS-EAS-90-219,* 13 November, 1990, p. 26.

35. For a detailed reference on the political advantage of arms reduction negotiation see, Christoph Bertram, "Mutual Force Reduction in Europe: the Political Aspect", *Adelphi Paper* 84 (London IISS, 1972), p. 12-13.
36. Ibid, p. 12.
37. Holsti, "Confidence and Security Building", p. 22.
38. National unification was declared as a basic objective in the preamble of the regulation of the Workers Party and the article of the constitution of DPRK.
39. *The 1989 Korean Defence White Paper,* p. 57.
40. For an explanation for Korean psychological threat, see Koh, *The Foreign Policy Systems of North and South Korea,* pp. 70-121.
41. US Congressman, Stephen J. Solarz, *The Korean Conundrum: A Conversation with Kim Il-Sung,* p. 8. Report of a study mission to South Korea, Japan, the People's Republic of China (Washing D.C.: GPO, 1980).
42. Andrew Mack, "Nuclear Issues and Arms Control on the Korean Peninsula", *Working Paper,* No. 96 (Canberra: Peace Research Centre, 1991), p. 22.
43. "DMZ Shootout Disturbs Mood of Talks", *The Korea Herald,* 24 May, 1992.
44. According to a report of "UNCURK" to the UN in 1970 and 1972 (25th Session, Supplement No. 26:A/8026, p. 29. and 27th, Session, Supplement No. 27: A/8727, pp. 16-17). There were 1,200 significant incidents and 375 exchanges of fire between 1965 and 1972 in the DMZ. Jong-Chun Baek, *Prob for Korean Unification: Conflict and Security* (Seoul: Research Centre for Peace and Unification of Korea, 1988), p. 182.
45. These are included in the "Twenty Pilot Projects" for peaceful unification proposed by the ROK Minister of National Unification (1 February, 1982).
46. *SIPRI Yearbook 1989,* pp. 329-330. Adam-Daniel Rotfeld, "CBMs in Europe: A future-Oriented Concept", in Robert D. Blackwill and F. Stephen Larrabee (eds) *Conventional Arms Control and East-West Security* (Duke University Press: London & Durham, 1989), p. 368.
47. Klaus Wittmann, "Challenges of Conventional Arms Control", *Adelphipaper* 239 (London: IISS, 1989), p.45. See Jonathan Dean, "Will Negotiated Force Reduction Build Down the NATO-Warsaw Pact Confrontation?", *The Washington Quarterly,* Spring 1988, pp. 75-78.
48. Manfred Muller, "Constraints" in *Conventional Arms Control and East-West Security,* p. 410.
49. Trevor Findlay, "The Non-European Experience of CBMs: Models for the Asia-Pacific Regions", in *Disarmament: Confidence and Security Building Measures in Asia* (New York: United Nations, 1990), pp. 57-58.
50. Man-Kwan Nam, "Enhancing Military Stability Through Operational Arms Control on the Korean Peninsula", A paper presented for the 6th ROK-US Defence Analysis Seminar Proceedings (Seoul:, 9-13 September, 1991), p. 17.
51. Chung Min Lee, "The Future of Arms Control in the Korean Peninsula", *The Washington Quarterly,* Summer 1991, p. 190.
52. Alexei G. Arbatov, "Sheathing the Korean Dagger", in *Arms Control on the Korean Peninsula: What Lessons,* p. 103.

53. South Korean naval forces operate 'the North Limited Line' in the Yellow Sea and 'the Northern Boundary' in the East Sea. Its air forces also operate the flight limited line in the forward area. *Korean Defence White Paper 1990*, pp. 122-123.

54. The North Korean long range Scud Missile which can be targeted anywhere in South Korea may be to some extent deterred by the South's possession of the "Patriot Missile" which proved an effective interceptor of the Iraqi Scud attack during the Gulf War. South Korea considered the purchase of Patriot Missiles from the US Brian Bridges, "South Korea and the Gulf Crisis", *The Pacific Review*, Vol. 5. No. 2. 1992, p. 146. *The Korea Times*, 6 December, 1991.

55. For detailed reference for consultative mechanism proposals, see Timothy E. Wirth, "Confidence-and Security-Building Measures", pp. 350-352. Rotfeld, "CBMs in Europe", pp. 370-372. in *Conventional Arms Control and East-West Security*.

56. Jong-Chun Baek, op. cit., p. 181. This was quoted in Soon Sung Cho, "North and South Korea: Stepped-up Aggression and the Search for New Security", *Asian Survey*, Vol. 9, No. 1, (January, 1969), p. 30.

57. Donald S. Zagoria and Janet D. Zagoria, "Crises on the Korean Peninsula", in Stephen S. Kaplan and Others, *Diplomacy of Power: Soviet Armed Forces as a Political Instrument* (Washington D.C.: Brookings Institution, 1979). pp. 359-400.

58. Ibid. pp. 382-383.

59. Richard G. Head, Frisco W. Short and Robert C. McFarlane(eds), *Crisis Resolution: Presidential Decision Making in the Mayaguez and Korean Confrontations* (Colorado: Westview Press, 1978), pp. 149-215. Donald S. Zagoria and Janet D. Zagoria, op. cit. pp. 9: 72-74. The incident had been staged during the Conference of Non-Aligned Countries in Sri Lanka which began on August 16.

60. Chin W. Chung, *Pyongyang between Peking and Moscow* (The University of Alabama Press, 1978), p. 36.

61. Ohn Chang-il, "Military Talks in Korea; an Overview" in *The Korean Peninsula: Prospects for Arms Reduction under Global Detente*, p. 182.

62. Choi Young, "The Arms Race and Arms Control in Korea", *Korea and World Affairs*, Vol.10, No.2, (Summer 1986), p. 419.

63. *A strategic framework for the Asian Pacific Rim: Looking toward the 21st Century*, Hearings before the Committee on Armed Services United States Senate, One Hundred First Congress, Second Session, April, 19, 1990, (Washington D.C.: GPO, 1990) pp. 44-46.

64. "Full Text of Joint Statement on Korea", *The Korea Herald*, 22 Oct, 1991

65. "US Troop Cuts should be used as a Bargaining Chip for S-N Dialogue", *The Korea Herald*, 15 March, 1990.

66. Chin-in Moon, "Managing the Inter-Korean Conflict and Confidence Building Measures", *Korea Observer*, Spring 1991, p. 62.

67. Communique on the Joint Meeting of the Central People's Committee, Standing Committee of the Supreme People's Assembly and Administration Council of the Democratic People's Republic of Korea, *The Pyongyang Times*, Number 7, 1988.

Dialogue with North Korea (Washington DC: Carnegie Endowment for International Peace, 1989), p. 47.

68 "Proposal of North Korea for a phased reduction of forces of July 23, 1987", in *Dialogue with North Korea*, pp. 1-26.

69. James Leonard, "Steps Toward a Middle East Free of Nuclear Weapons", *Arms Control Today,* Vol. 21, No. 3, (April 1991), p. 13.

70. *The Korea Herald,* 23 February, 1992. US intelligence officials said that North Korea was digging tunnels to hide its nuclear arms program from outside inspection or to protect it from possible attack.

71. Tae-Hwan Kwak, "Designing the Non-Nuclear Korean Peninsula: Problems and Prospects", *The Korean Journal of Defence Analysis,* Vol. IV, No. 1, (Summer, 1992), pp. 224-225.

72. "South Korea to Remain N-umbrella", *The Korea Herald,* 10 October, 1991.

73. William J. Taylor, Jr and Michael J. Mazarr, "ROK-US Defence Cooperation in the Context of Arms Control", a paper presented at the 3rd KIDA/CSIS International Defence Conference (Seoul, 5-6 November, 1991), p. 15.

74. *The New York Times*, 9 November, 1991. The US even withdrew the air delivered bombs deployed on F-16 aircraft from the South.

10. Conclusion

Arms control has become a reality which the two Korean states cannot avoid, as a consequence of the transformation of the regional and world order. Therefore the two Korean states should adapt to the new security environment. The application of the European arms control experience to Korea would provide a useful framework for reducing tension, increasing stability and further arms reduction. In order to provide a theoretical framework for "Koreanization" of the European arms control model the following propositions relating to selective issues can be advanced and answered.

1: The utility of European arms control as a universal security model

Proposition 1: The European conventional arms control model in the Cold War era can be a universal security formula for tension and arms reduction between individual or regional actual and potential enemies beyond Europe.

European arms control suggests itself as a universal security model in that European security or stability has been achieved by political means which could be generally applied by any country or region, rather than by military means based on a particular European security situation. Security management through political negotiation or diplomacy could be a universal measure with a practical application even in a security situation different from Europe. In the European arms control process the beginning and end of the arms control talks was determined not by military but by political considerations. NATO and WTO functioned as military security systems that resulted in mounting threat, confrontation and arms build-up. On the other hand CSCE operated as a political security dialogue and cooperation window for maintenance of the status quo between the two antagonistic political regimes and the solution of disputes without resorting to military means. A number of arms control measures directed at stability and a reduction of the risks of war have been devised through such political means and approaches. The effort towards arms reduction, which began as political considerations for prevention of unilateral US and Soviet force withdrawal and as a vehicle of detente, was subsequently succeeded by the collapse of Eastern communist regimes and WTO. Thus European arms control models could be applied to other countries and regions in that they were dependent upon political considerations and mechanisms more than upon a particular military security situation.

The other rationale for the applicability of the European arms control mechanisms, as a generalized security model, can be sought from the universality of confidence building measures which have been the core of European arms control. Prior to the application of CBMs in Europe, Egypt and Israel utilized CBMs as a means of increasing mutual confidence and thus demonstrated the importance of CBMs as a new paradigm of military security regimes between countries in dispute. The Contadora process of Central America is an example of a similar approach outside of Europe. The Contadora Group has sought the settlement of conflict in Central America through the application of Stockholm-type CBMs. The 1991 Sino-Soviet border treaty was also based upon the CBMs framework. Thus the European CBMs model provides a theoretical framework for build-up of confidence and stability, and advances the development of arms reduction between hostile states or in regions of conflict.

Another rationale for the universalization of the European arms control model derives from the fact that with the collapse of the Cold War security system it has necessarily evolved from collective application to an individual or bilateral ones or from an application between actual enemies to merely potential enemies. The CFE treaty attempted to regulate military activities posing a threat to neighbours by providing countries with the right of "active inspection" even within the same alliance. Because most regions outside of Europe have been involved in conflicts between individual countries, the European collective arms control measures may present a good precedent as a security mechanism for regions or states different from the European collective security situation.

2: Political will is the most crucial key to the success of arms control

Proposition 2: *Detente or political reconciliation precedes arms control talks. The success and failure for arms control is determined by the political will to achieve it.*

Arms control talks in Europe were preceded by political reconciliation between the two blocs. The solution of political problems through the border treaties between the FRG and its neighbours and the convention of CSCE provided a crucial momentum for political compromise between East and West. In fact the declaration of the 1975 Helsinki CSCE confirmed the principle of status quo or co-existence between East and West and consequently reduced the political threat produced by denial of recognition of other political regimes by either side. The application of CBMs in Europe was an outcome of the military confirmation of the CSCE declaration which sought to limit political will towards a use of force through transparency and constraints on military activities. The failure of the MBFR talks was in fact a result of a lack of political will towards substantial arms reduction. Reductions of small size were considered as a symbol of political detente rather than rectifications of the military balance. Because of this the MBFR talks neglected the development of solutions necessary for success. The talks continued to be deadlocked due to the problems of data and verification. Such problems might be a diplomatic pretext for the prevention of arms reductions. The military problems in the talks could not be solved by primarily military means.

However, such technical problems were eventually overcome by the political will to achieve substantial arms reduction. Unlike previous leaders, Gorbachev's new thinking emphasised the security of political means more than military technical means such as arms build-up and the maintenance of secrecy. By such new thinking the problems of data and verification, the largest obstacles to the arms reduction talks, were eliminated through the separation of nuclear weapons problems from the conventional arms control talks. Further it resulted in the change of defence doctrine on the basis of the notion of "reasonable sufficiency".

In conclusion, the pattern of European arms control history, saw the MBFR talks begin with the advent of the detente era between East and West. CBMs helped to advance greater political reconciliation. Finally the CFE talks succeeded with the emergence of a new detente following the collapse of the Eastern communist regimes.

3: The application of German arms control policies to Korea

Proposition 3: *German arms control policies were a means of overcoming the security problems of the NATO and Warsaw Pact front line and achieving unification of the divided state in the long run. Such policies present the most suitable alternative for Korean security and arms control.*

The application of German arms control policies as a model for the Korean security and arms control concerns derives from a number of similarities of security situations between Germany and Korea. Those are the division of nations as a legacy of World War II, ideological and political confrontation sharpened by the structure of bipolar systems, the front line of the Cold War in Europe and Asia, a deep involvement by the four major powers in the German and Korean questions (Germany; US, USSR, UK, France; Korea US, USSR, China, Japan) and the pursuit of unification as a central element of their national objectives.

A decisive point for the success of the FRG's security policy during the Cold War was the combination of deterrence-defence and detente-arms control as a dual security policy. Faced with the Soviet and WTO threat, the basic line of FRG security policy was the pursuit of a strong deterrence-defence strategy through the maintenance of a strong alliance system. However, such a defence strategy "spelled risk not only of genocide but of suicide" because of a geographical location at the centre of the East-West conflict.[1] If a war occurred, the consequence would be unavoidable disaster for the FRG. Thus the ultimate rationale of a security policy drawn from the reality and sense of such vulnerability was the prevention of war. Germans believed that their security could be most effectively achieved through political rather than military means. Ostpolitik for political reconciliation and stability with the GDR and the East were important instruments. Arms control was the core issue for war prevention, tension reduction and stability operating as an imperative for political detente between East and West.

The CSCE was the most suitable consultative body through which the FRG could achieve political security by multilateral negotiations. Therefore the CSCE was a very important anchor of its foreign policy directed at security. A number of arms control measures including CBMs and arms reductions were based on German ideas and security problems. The negotiation subjects were almost always concerned with the reality of the security problem between NATO and WTO along the German division line and involved questions such as the prevention of surprise attack and accidental war and the imposition of a ceiling on the German and foreign forces on its territory. The CFE Treaty itself was finally concluded with the solution of the German question by unification and the imposition of a ceiling upon unified German forces by the "two plus four negotiation" of the involved major powers. Thus Germany played a leading role in the European multilateral arms control talks.

The German policy of separation between arms control and unification problems constitutes an important lesson to Koreans who think direct linkage is necessary in the arms control talks. The pursuit of national unification in the modality of military confrontation would result in the escalation of tension and arms build-up with a necessary increment of the security burden. The Germans recognized that their neighbours and major powers would have reservations about their unification and a military build-up beyond defence requirements. Their belief was that in the long run national unification could be achieved through tension reduction and arms control on the basis of the co-existence of the two German states. Therefore priority was given to the creation of an environment conducive to this process rather than to the goal of unity itself.

The arms control dialogues and proposals between the two German states could also provide Koreans with practical arms control application measures based on the reality of a divided state, common national identity and close array of enormous military forces along the division line. The various arms control proposals of the SPD-SED parties in particular, such as the establishment of nuclear and chemical free-zones, CBMs zone and centres, a hotline and inspections aimed at the prevention of surprise attack and crisis management are among the most significant measures that reflect the reality of Korean security problems.

4: The application of European arms control mechanisms for regional stability and environment conducive to Korean arms control

Proposition 4: An Asian security conference could be a mechanism for the arrest of the arms race and potential conflict between rival major powers or further arms reductions to a low level of forces in Northeast Asia. Korean arms control should be made in the context of security cooperation and arms control between the regional powers.

During the Cold War, on the basis of the dissimilarity of strategic environments, the Northeast Asian countries did not pay attention to the establishment of a European style multilateral security conference in the region. Moreover the monopoly of US power and their dependence for security on the US in the region left little room for a highly institutionalized and interdependent security system modelled upon the CSCE.

However, changes in the security situation in the region after the Cold War demonstrated the need for a regional-wide security forum. Unlike the INF Treaty, the CFE Treaty has resulted in negative effects for Northeast Asian Security. The Soviet combat aircraft and other military equipment withdrawn from Europe were redeployed in the Northeast Asian region. As a result the Russian armed forces in the region were significantly upgraded after the CFE Treaty.[2] In order to prohibit the redeployment of former Cold War armaments and a consequent imbalance in security, an Asian security conference should be held for the participation of the countries which have a dependence for security upon America, Russia and other regional powers.

The other rationale for the security conference derives from the need to halt the arms race and negotiate arms reduction. Even after the ending of the Cold War, the regional countries are now acquiring advanced weapons systems with the upgrading of their defence capabilities.[3] The Chinese arms build-up is shifting from quantity to quality with the construction of a "blue water navy" with a greater reach. Japan also continues to pursue that course, upon the basis of the protection of sea lanes by laying emphasis on the build-up of forces through a multiplication of high technology weapons. Though the Russian military manpower levels have significantly diminished in the region, its naval and air forces still remain a potential threat to neighbour countries as a regional military superpower.

The continuation of such an arms build-up is caused by the rivalry between the regional powers and the absence of arms control mechanisms. They are cautious about respective potential threats and the military strength of the other powers. The multilateral management of the military forces of rival countries through the establishment of a security conference and arms control mechanism might reduce the potential threat perception caused by the arms race and thereby limit armaments to a low level with a build-up of political and military confidence. Until now unilateral arms reduction by some countries in the region has not substantially contributed to regional stability and the arrest of the arms race. In fact informal arms control which is not institutionalized and verifiable might lack credibility and result in a voluntary arms build-up again during a situation of political confrontation or a change of security environment and the repudiation of a tacit agreement. Such possibilities might be eliminated through negotiated arms control between the regional countries.

The prospect of a reduced US presence, in contrast with the arms build-up of the regional states, also demonstrates the need for arms control mechanisms. Under the circumstances of the post Cold War era, the US is seeking the role of regional balancer through the continued presence of reduced forces. During this century its periodic military alignment with the weaker powers might have been successful for preventing the emergence of a dominant power free from US influence in the region.[4] However, it is doubtful whether the US could effectively implement the role of regional policeman with a small military presence in the face of an arms build-up by the regional powers. In fact, its effort towards such a role based solely upon military means may be a high risk strategy. Therefore the role of stabilizer based on political means might be more effective and economic than attempting to do so by force of arms.

Because of the divergence of security situations and the breadth of the region, a sub-regional security forum and arms control mechanism would be more realistic than a region-wide one. In order to mediate disputes and divert hostile confrontation, a number of sub-regional organizations and agreements have been established in Asia with the exception of the Northeast Asian region. A number of CSBMs are also already being practised at both the regional or sub-regional levels; ASEAN, SAARC, Treaty of Rarotonaga etc.[5] Due to the potential conflict through arms build-up and rivalry between the regional powers, Northeast Asia is now in a position to apply a security forum or arms control as a contribution to maintaining regional stability.

Given the geographic location of the Korean Peninsula with its potential for invasion and threat from the regional powers, regional arms control is an essential precondition for Korean security and arms control. Nowadays South Korea is very cautious about the arms build up of neighbouring powers. The South simultaneously considers both the actual northern threat and the potential threat from its neighbours. Evidence of this is well demonstrated by the words of the director of the arms control bureau of the Korean Defence Ministry:

> They (South Koreans) should not limit the scope of their security perspectives to Korea. The threats from evolving regional military environments are likely to be more serious than those from North Korea. Therefore, they have to consider their national defence posture, military force structure, defence expenditure level and foreign military cooperation in terms of these forward-looking attitudes rather than in terms of North-South Korean problems.[6]

Koreans in particular have a very negative attitude towards Japan's regional role as a substitute for the US Whilst Korea admitted the need for a military build-up against Soviet expansion by Japan, within the framework of the US - Japan security cooperation system, a continued Japanese military build-up in a situation of diminished Russian threat raises Korean fears about the revival of Japanese militarism. Thus the threat perception from the Japanese military build-up makes the North-South arms reduction more difficult. The South is obliged to calculate the necessary size of its armed forces on the basis of potential threats from all the regional powers.[7]

As a small state it is very unrealistic to believe that Korea could counter the potential threat of the neighbouring powers through its own military means. Therefore it is very desirable that Korean security is guaranteed through the regional security forum and arms control mechanism on the basis of the US-ROK alliance, following the experience of European small states outside NATO and WTO, who attempted to enhance their security through the CSCE.

5: A consideration of the contribution of the USFK to Korean arms control together with the role of regional stabilizer

Proposition 5: *The USFK will contribute to Korean arms control with a buffer role between the two Korean states and fulfil a regional stabilization role between the rival powers.*

The problem of the USFK has become one of the central issues in the North-South arms control talks. North Korea has called for the withdrawal of American forces as the first step for arms control, while South Korea has excluded it from the negotiating agenda. However, it is time for the North to change its inflexible thinking about the problem. From the North's point of view, the USFK have been the largest barrier to national unification on its own terms whilst posing a very negative function to its security. Due to the strategic significance of the Korean Peninsula, the emergence of a unified Korea may give the regional rival powers an additional burden in maintaining a balance of power in the region. Taking into consideration the fact that the regional situation is unfavourable to the North, there is no evidence that Russia and China would support a unification policy based upon the use of force. Moreover strong doubts are growing as to whether they would remain physical security guarantors. In the days of the Cold War the US was prepared to bear a heavy burden in defending the South on the assumption that the North would get strong support from socialist states if a second Korean war occurred. However the present situation suggests that the US would not hesitate to retaliate against North Korean provocation.[8] In the light of the process of German unification, history demonstrated that foreign troops would not be an obstacle to unification if it proceeded by peaceful means. The North's demand for the withdrawal of the USFK reveals that its unification policy depends upon the use of force.

From the standpoint of North Korea, a positive rationale for the presence of the USFK derives from the aspect of its security maintenance. The previous reduction by the US forces resulted in negative rather than positive outcomes for the DPRK. The reduction gave the South an incentive for military build-up. It always resulted in an increment of the US military assistance to the South and the reinforcement of the US - ROK combined forces system. Moreover, the gradual shift in the military balance in favour of the South means that the real threat for North Korea comes from the ROK. The US might have reservations that Korean unification would weaken justification for the presence of its forces for the balance of power in Asian regional politics. The unification of Korea by military means, which could conceivably be realized through military superiority of the ROK, would shatter political stability in the region. It might be expected that the presence of US forces and the US - ROK Army combined defence system would reduce the likelyhood of the South's independent military intervention in the domestic turmoil which could occur during a leadership crisis, if the North established a relationship with the US. Thus the USFK may be more concerned with the prevention of military conflict between the two Korean states. In fact the American buffer could be a welcome source of relief from the fear of a possible South Korean attack in the long run.[9]

The presence of the USFK has a role of security guarantor for the whole Korean Peninsula from the potential threat of the neighbouring powers. In particular it has functioned as a check on Japan's militarism. The withdrawal of the USFK that the North seeks would require that the South build-up its military strength against the Japanese potential threat. Consequently such a situation would make the South Korean attempts towards arms reduction in Korea more difficult and result in an increase of its security burden in order to balance the Japanese threat. Most Asian states expect American forces to remain as the regional stabilizer or as a necessary counterweight to the revival of Japanese militarism.[10] Given the Korean geopolitical overlap with its neighbours' interests, and its bitter historical experiences, the Korean Peninsula may be made more secure by a continued security commitment from a remote superpower whose home territory lies outside of the region. The geographic remoteness of US may be a more significant consideration than the professions made by the other regional powers because the US is less likely to have territorial ambitions.[11] Consequently, in the light of the US buffer or stabilization role in the region, the presence of the USFK would contribute to Korean arms control.[12]

6: An alternative for the true denuclearization of the Korean Peninsula

Proposition 6: *The true denuclearization of the Korean Peninsula can be achieved through the approach towards the nuclear free Korean zone with the North-South military balance at a low level in the framework of security cooperation between the major powers.*

North and South Korea signed the agreement for the denuclearization of the Korean Peninsula, but talks for implementation of the agreement have reached an impasse. The basic background for the failure of the real denuclearization until now has been caused by the dependence of the ROK's national security on nuclear weapons: the absence of certain evidence of a halt in the North's nuclear weapon program and the adherence of the South to the US nuclear umbrella. The nuclear policies of both sides have been operated as the complementary way to overcome the vulnerability of respective conventional defence. Because of these, they have focussed on the removal of the other side's nuclear commitment, rather than the end of denuclearization itself through an agreement. Therefore true denuclearization might be achieved simultaneously by an escape from dependence on nuclear weapons for defence. Thus bargaining directed towards the abandonment of the North's nuclear program and the South's dependence on the nuclear umbrella could be the most useful leverage for a nuclear free Korea.

Given the lack of credibility of the US nuclear umbrella in practice and the risk of nuclear proliferation through a neighbouring regional power from the North's acquisition of nuclear weapons, such bargaining might be a very desirable option for Korean security in the long run. The nuclearization of the Korean Peninsula would present Japan with the option of nuclearization. Under circumstances where all the surrounding countries have nuclear weapons, Japan will no longer remain sheltered by the nuclear umbrella of the US Japan, though scarred by her history, has the capability to become a nuclear power. Japan possesses plutonium sufficient to make several hundred atomic weapons and the capacity to deliver them. Therefore Japan's technical capacity to become one of the nuclear club quickly is not in doubt.[13]

The true denuclearization of the Korean Peninsula could be achieved through cessation of the arms race and the maintenance of a balance of conventional forces at a low level between the North and the South. The South's adherence to the nuclear umbrella is caused by the North's superiority in conventional forces. The North's attempt to join the nuclear club may be understood as the desire for a sufficient deterrent against threats from the South now tilting the conventional balance in its favour. Moreover the possession of nuclear weapons is perceived as an alternative for survival in a situation where neither the former USSR nor China are reliable guarantors of security. From one point of view denuclearization could be also achieved by the limitation of the major powers' arms supplies to the Korean Peninsula. As demonstrated in the history of Korean arms build-up, the competitive arms supplies of the powers have been a major reason for the North-South arms race. Now the two Korean states are major clients of the powers' arms exports and heavily dependent upon their weapons systems. Therefore a limitation of the powers' arms supplies through formal cooperation between them could constitute the most specific and tangible behind-the-scenes role for Korean arms control.

7: The applicability of the European arms control model to Korean arms control

Proposition: *European arms control measures provide a theoretical framework and model for Korean arms control. Priorities in Korean arms control must be given to the elimination of threat perception, transparency of military capabilities and intentions and prevention of surprise attack through the application of CBMs and finally change from offensive posture into defensive posture through the reduction and redeployment of armed forces.*

It is said that European arms control is more instructive as a theoretical explanation of how the progress works than as a universal pattern or model.[13] This thesis may be not persuasive in that the European case was concerned with bloc to bloc multilateral arms control for application to the whole of Europe, while the Korean case is bilateral talks between small states. However, given the number of similarities between the security situations in the two regions with the same expectations and predictions of the likely results, a number of factors demonstrate the possibility that the European arms control experiences could be applied to the Korean Peninsula as a small-scale case, even though the application would not be mechanical.

The high military tension in the European continent and the Northeast Asian region arose out of the sharp ideological confrontation between capitalism and communism in the structure of the Cold War. In particular Germany and Korea were divided because of ideology and constituted the frontlines of the Cold War through arrays of enormous armed forces along the division lines caused by the deep involvement of the two superpowers. The two regimes also instituted the same defence cultures. The Soviet Union and the US were respectively guarantors of their security with strong conventional and nuclear forces. The communist regimes adopted an offensive doctrine with forward-deployment of forces based on a superiority of conventional forces, while capitalist states countered their conventional inferiority with the nuclear deterrence strategy.

The two antagonistic regimes produced detente and political stability through the adoption of the co-existence principle and respect for borders with a non-aggression agreement. Arms control talks were a process for confirming political stability by military means. It was required initially to eliminate a perceived threat coming from ideologically and militarily deep-rooted distrust between the antagonistic regimes. A surprise attack or accidental war in the European and Korean theatres was regarded as most threatening to their securities. Because of the identity of the Korean security reality and defence culture with Europe, the arms control approaches of the two Korean states have been almost identical to those of the European blocs. Therefore the arms control proposals of the Korean states have been based upon the European ideas and synchronised themselves on NATO-South Korea and WTO-North Korea lines. Like the early European arms control talks the present North-South conventional arms control talks have been deadlocked because of the nuclear problem. Without the solution of the nuclear problem conventional arms control is not likely to proceed. In the light of these similarities of security situations, arms control approaches and proposals, and the likely benefits from the application, Korean arms control would be the most suitable small-scale case for the application of the European model.

Following the European model, the first priority for an application must be given to the removal of the deep-rooted distrust and perceived threat which have been accumulated for four decades after the Korean War. This distrust and threat perception arises from the respective fear of the military capabilities of the opposing Korean state. Arms reductions in Europe have been reached after Europe went through the Helsinki and Stockholm CBMs phase. The Korean arms control must begin with the application of CBMs. Korean fears arising out of the high level of forces might be treated by diminishing the possibility for the use of force and reducing the effective capabilities of forces themselves through constraints on their military activities. Taking into account the arrays of heavy dense military forces along the MDL, the priority for the application of CBM's should be given to the establishment of crisis management arrangements and to the prevention of accidental war. The transparency of military activities and capabilities would be an important part of the agenda for the removal of threat perception and would provide a basis for arms control through an exact comparison of the military balance between the two states.

It is perhaps only realistic to initiate a gradual phased arms control at this stage because of the lack of confidence and practical experience. As an alternative to this, a zonal arms control could be applied in the forward area between Seoul and Pyongyang. This could introduce practical methods and procedures, reducing the psychological and physical impact which might follow from the sudden application of this approach to the whole Korean Peninsula. However even this phased and zonal arms control would not easily be arrived at through negotiation because of the long period of eyeball to eyeball military confrontation. In the light of the experience gained from Gorbachev's unilateral arms reduction and new thinking which gave a decisive momentum to the establishment of the present arms control regime in Europe, "new thinking" in Korea might invite a turning point towards Korean security and arms control. As a first step for implementation of a zonal arms control, South Korea could consider some parts of the eastern region of the DMZ and the original purpose of the 1953 Armistice Agreement, by unilaterally evacuating its armed forces from the demilitarised zone. This unilateral action should not result in serious security problems for the South because this region, with its range of high mountains is far away from Seoul and invulnerable to a surprise attack from the North. This would demonstrate in practical terms the South's political commitment to arms control and further push North Korea to follow up the South's action because the North has in the past strongly demanded the conversion of the DMZ into a buffer zone in accordance with its original purpose. As a consequence the establishment of such zones could give a momentous precedent to that of a zonal arms control in the western DMZ or between Seoul and Pyongyang and the redeployment of the heavily armed forces from the forward area to the rear area.

The two Korean states have already taken a first step towards arms control by concluding the non-aggression agreement and establishing the North-South Joint Military Commission to discuss the reduction of tension and armed forces. As in the case of the early 1970s North-South dialogue in the era of the East-West detente, the present arms control dialogue should not be used only as a means of adjustment to a new international security environment and arms reduction mood. The implementation of the North-South Non-Aggression Agreement can be guaranteed through the transformation of respective military doctrines and strategies into those of a defence posture and structure. The ultimate objective and direction of the Korean Arms Control suggests itself through a consideration of Hans-Dietrich Genscher's comments:

Affirmation of nonaggression and pledge of no-use alone offer no adequate assurance of security and stability. The defensive character of a strategy and a military doctrine is determined mainly by the size, deployment, structure, logistics and training of the armed forces. There must not be a discrepancy between defence policy rhetoric on one side and the actual forces structures and employments concepts on the other.[15]

It is time for the Korean states to consider sincerely arms control. In fact, in North Korean eyes, the real threat from the South is perhaps not military, but rather the economic strength and the wealth of South Korea and the similarity to the situation previously existing between the East and the West of Europe. The most serious threat to the North is domestic unrest and uprising resulting from serious economic problems and respective conflicts between elites about the leadership success in the post-Kim Il-sung era.[16] Moreover, North Korea must truly recognize that because the military balance is moving towards the South, it will be faced with serious security problems in the near future if it misses the opportunity of using arms control to freeze the South's military build-up. The present Southern military preparedness against the North's threats has imposed a large burden on its economy. The reason why the South has succeeded in both the North-South regime competition and "Northern Policy" towards China and Russia is not because of military strength but because of economic strength. Therefore the South must pursue "economic defence" through arms control. For the South the achievement of tension and arms reduction may pave the way for Korean unification.

North Korea is a garrison state. The military has existed as the central pillar of political power. Its present leadership has continued to be hostage to the politics of the North-South confrontation. The implementation of tension and arms reduction might weaken the influence of the military in politics. Beyond these needs an absolute rationale for arms control can be based upon the two Korean states homogeneous identity which has maintained itself over a long history as one nation. The prospect for Korean arms control appears more promising when the Korean peoples are reminded of Jean Monnet's words:

> It was important for the negotiating parties to consider themselves on one side of the table with the problem on the other - with the negotiators acting not as adversaries but as people trying to solve problems together.[17]

NOTES

1. Gert Krell, "Ostpolitik Dimensions of West German Security Policy", *PRIF Report*, English No. 1 (Frankfurt: Peace Research Institute. 1988), p. 3.
2. Defence Agency of Japan, *The Defence of Japan, 1990*, p. 41 & 47.
3. Gerald Segal, "Managing New Arms Races in the Asia/Pacific Region", *The Washington Quarterly*, Vol. 15, No. 3 (Summer, 1992), pp. 83-98.
4. Jonathan D. Pollack and James A. Winnefeld, *US Strategic Alternatives in a Changing Pacific* (RAND Cooperation, R-3933-US-CINPAC, 1990), p. 14. The US contained Russian southward policy in support of Japan in the 1904 Russian-Japan War. Later it sought to limit Japanese capabilities in the Washington Naval Treaty with Britain. With the advent of the Cold War the policy was implemented to limit Soviet penetration of Asia in the US - Japan security framework. The decline of Soviet power returned the US policy to that of a century ago. The US believes that the remaining US forces - ultimately deployed for the containment of Soviet expansion - serve to check and channel Japanese political-military ambitions.
5. Douglas M. Johnston, "Anticipating Instability in the Asia-Pacific Regions", *The Washington Quarterly*, Vol. 15, No. 3 (Summer, 1991), pp. 105-112.
6. Young-ok Park, "Japan's Defence Build-up and Regional Balance", *The Korean Journal of Defence Analysis*, Vol. 3, No .1 (Summer 1991), p. 100.
7. *The Korea Herald*, 25 September, 1991.
8. *The Korea Herald*, 7 March, 1992.
9. Park Tong Whan, "Security Dilemma and the Politics of Arms Control between the Two Koreas", Paper presented at the International Conference of the Korean Political Science Association (Seoul, 25-27 July, 1991), p. 18.
10. Pollack and Winnefeld, op. cit., pp. 1-43. Michael W. Chinworth and Dean Cheng, "The United States and Asia in the Post Cold World", *SAIS Review*, (Winter-Spring 1991), pp. 73-91.
11. Donald S. Macdonald, "The Role of the Major Powers in the Reunification of Korea", *The Washington Quarterly*, Vol.15, No.3 (Summer, 1992), p. 138.
12. *The Korea Herald*, 25 June, 1992. Li Sam-ro, an adviser to the Pyongyang Disarmament and Peace Institute, suggested at an international seminar held in Holonlulu, Hawaii in June 1992 that South and North Korea would after unification have to abide by all the treaties they concluded with foreign countries before unification and if necessary, recognize the continued presence of American fores in Korea.
13. Jeffrey T. Bergner, *The New Superpowers: Germany, Japan, the US and the New World Order* (New York: St. Martin's Press, 1991), pp. 190-193.
14. Adam D. Rotfeld, "Applicability of European Arms Control Model to the Korean Peninsula" in *Arms Control on the Korean Peninsula: What lessons Can We Learn European Experience* (Seoul: Institute of Foreign Affairs & National Security, 1990), p. 40.
15. Manfred R. Hamm and Hartmut Pohlman, "Military Strategy and Doctrine: Why they matter to Conventional Arms Control", *The Washington Quarterly*, Vol. 13, No. 1, (Winter 1990), p. 196.
16. Aidan Foster-Carter, *Korea's Coming Reunification: Another East Asian Superpower* (London: The Economist Intelligence Unit, 1990), Special Report, No. M212, p. 90. The Economist Intelligence Unit reported that there have been about 10 domestic riots and coup attempts between September 1981 and February 1992.
17. Michael Sheehan, *Arms Control: Theory and Practice* (Oxford: Basil Blackwell, 1988), p. 159.

Select Bibliography

Books

Auer, James E. *The Postwar Rearmament of Japanese Maritime Forces: 1945-71*, New York: Praeger Publishers, 1973.

Baek, Jong-Chun, *Problems for Korean Unification: Conflict and Security*, Seoul: Research Centre for Peace and Unification of Korea, 1988.

Baker, Philip J. Noel, *Disarmament*, London: Carland Publishing Inc., 1972.

Barnet, Richard J., T*he Root of War*, Baltimore: Penguin, 1972.

Barton, John J. and Imai, Ryukichi (eds), *Arms Control II: A New Approach to International Security,* Cambridge: OGH, 1981.

Baylis, John and Booth, Ken (eds), *Contemporary Strategy I*, London: Croom Helm, 1987.

Ben-Horin, Y., *Building Confidence and Security in Europe: the Potential Role of Confidence and Security-Building Measures*, RAND Corporation, 1986.

Berg, Rolf and Rotfeld, Adam-Daniel (eds), *Building Security in Europe,* New York: the Institute for East-West Security Studies, 1986.

Bergner, Jeffrey, T., *The New Superpowers: Germany, Japan, the US and the New World Order,* New: York: St. Martin's Press, 1991.

Betts, Richard K., *Surprise Attack: Lessons for Defence Planing,* Washington D.C.: The Brookings Institution, 1982.

Birnbaum Karl E. and Huldt, Bo (eds), *From Stockholm to Vienna: Building Confidence and Security in Europe*, Stockholm:the Swedish Institute of International Affairs, 1987.

Blackwill, Robert D. and Larrabee, F. Stephen (eds), *Conventional Arms Control and East-West Security*, Durham & London: Duke University Press, 1989.

Blechman, Barry M. and Fisher, Cathleen, *The Silent Partner: West Germany and Arms Control* , Cambridge: Ballinger Publishing Company, 1988.

Booth, Ken (ed), *New Thinking about Strategy and International Security*, London: Harper Collins, 1991.

Brauch, Hans Guenter, and Clarke, Duncan L. (eds), *Decision Marking for Arms Limitation: Assessment and Prospects,* Cambridge: Ballinger Publishing Company, 1983.

Brennan, Donald G. (ed.), *Arms Control and Disarmament,* New York: George Braziler Inc., 1961.

Bull, Hedley, *The Control of the Arms Race*, London: The Bradbury Agnew Press Ltd, 1961.

Carnegie Endowment for International Peace, *Dialogue with North Korea,* Washington D.C., 1989.

Carnesale, Albert and Haas, Richard N. (eds), *Superpower Arms Control: Setting the Record Straight,* Cambridge: Ballinger Publishing Company, 1987.

Carnesale, Albert, *Learning from Experience with Arms Control*, A final report submitted to the US Arms Control and Disarmament Agency September, 1986.

Carter, April, *Success and Failure in Arms Control Negotiations SIPRI*: Oxford University Press, 1988.

Carlton, David and Schaerf, Carlo, *Perspectives on the Arms Race*, London: Macmillan Press, 1989.

Cassidy, Richard P., *Arms Transfer and Security Assistance to the Korean Peninsula 1945-1980: Impact and Implications,* Monterey: Naval Postgraduate School, 1980.

Chung, Chin W. *Pyongyang between Peking and Moscow: North Korea's Involvement in the Sino-Soviet Dispute, 1958-1975,* The University of Alabama Press, 1978.

Chung, Tai Ming, *Growth of Chinese Naval Power: Priorities, Goal, Missions, and Regional Implications,* Singapore: Institute of Southeast Asian Studies, 1990.

Child Jack (ed), *Conflict in Central America: Approaches to Peace and Security,* New York: The International Peace Academy, 1986.

Clough, Ralph N., *Embattled Korea: the Rivalry for International Support,* Colorado: Westview Press, 1987.

Select Bibliography 295

Clough, Ralph N. and Barnet, A. Doak (eds), *The United States, China and Arms Control*, Washington D.C.: The Brookings Institution, 1975.

Coffey, Joseph I., *Arms Control and European Security: A Guide to East-West Negotiations*, New York: Praeger, 1977.

Daugherty, James E. and Pfaltzgraft, Robert L, *Contending Theories of International Relations*, New York: Harper & Row, 1981.

Day, Alan J. (ed), *China and the Soviet Union: 1980-84*, Longman Group Limited, 1985.

Drifte, Reinhard, *Japan's Rise to International Possibilities: the Case of Arms Control*, London: The Athlone Press, 1990.

Dupuy, Trevor N. and Hammerman, Gay M. (eds), *A Documentary History of Arms Control and Disarmament*, London: R. R. Bowker and Company, 1973.

Emmerson, John K. and Holland, Harrison M., *The Eagle and the Rising Sun*, Addison-Wesley Publishing Company, 1988.

Flanagen, Stephen J., *NATO's Conventional Defences: Options for the Central Region*, London: Macmillan Press, 1988.

Forsberg, Randall, Burgoon, Brian and others, *Cutting Conventional Forces: An Analysis of the Official Mandate, Statistics and Proposals in the NATO-WTO Talks on Reducing Conventional Force in Europe*, Massachusetts: Institute for Defence and Disarmament Studies, 1989.

Foster-Carter, Aidan, *Korea's Coming Reunification: Another East Asian Superpower*, London: The Economist Intelligence Unit, 1992.

Freedman, Lawrence, *Evolution of Nuclear Strategy*, London: Macmillan Press, 1981.

Friedman, George and Lebard, Meredith, *The Coming War with Japan*, New York: St. Martin's Press, 1991.

Garthoff, Raymand, *Detente and Confrontation: American-Soviet Relations from Nixon to Reagan*, Washington D.C: Brookings Institution, 1985.

Gelman, Harry, *The Soviet Military Leadership and the Question of Soviet Deployment Retreats*, The RAND Corporation, R-3664, 1988.

_____, *The Soviet Turn Toward Conventional Force Reduction*, The RAND Corporation, R-3876-AF December, 1989.

Gibert, Stephen P. (ed), *Security in Northeast Asia: Approaching Pacific Century*, Colorado: Westview Press, 1988.

Hahn, Walter F., *Between Westpolitik and Ostpolitik: Changing West German Security Views*, London: SAGE Publications, 1975.

Grove Eric (ed), *Global Security: North American, European and Japanese Interdependence in the 1990s*, London: Brassey's, 1991.

Hanning Hugh (ed), *Peacekeeping and Confidence-Building Measures in the Third World*, New York: The International Peace Academy, Report No.20, 1985

Hanrieder, Wolfram F. (ed), *West German Foreign Policy: 1949-79*, Colorado: Westview Press, 1980.

_____, Arms Control, *the FRG and the Future of East-West Relations*, London: Westview Press, 1987.

Holsti, Kalevi J, *Peace and War: Armed Conflicts and International Order 1648-1689*, Cambridge: Cambridge University Press, 1991.

Institute of Foreign Affairs & National Security, *Arms Control on the Korean Peninsula: What lessons can we learn from European experiences?*, Seoul: Ut Ko Printing Company, 1990.

Johnston, Alastair I., *China and Arms Control: Emerging Issues and Interests in the 1980s*, The Canadian Centre for Arms Control and Disarmament, Aurora Papers 3, 1986.

Kaiser, Karl, and Roper, John (eds), *British-German Defence Co-operation: Partners Within the Alliance*, London: RIIA, 1988.

Kanet, Roger E. and Kolodziej, T*he Cold War as Co-operation: Superpower Co-operation in Regional Conflict Management*, London: Macmillan, 1991.

Kaplan, Stephen S. and Others, *Diplomacy of Power: Soviet Armed Forces as a Political Instrument*, Washington D.C.: The Brooking Institution, 1981.

Keliher, John G., *The Negotiations on Mutual and Balanced Force Reductions: The Search for Arms Control in Europe*, New York: Pergamon Press, 1980.

_____, *Eastern Arms Control Proposals for Central Europe*, Ph.D Dissertation of Georgetown University, Xerox University Microfilms, 1977.

Katz, Joshua D. and Frieman-Lichtschein (eds), *Japan's New World Role*, London: Westview Press, 1983.

Kim, Young C. and Halperin, Abraham M., *The Future of the Korean Peninsula*, New York: Fredrick A Praeger, 1977.

Klaiber, Wolfgang and Hadik, Laszlo, *Era of Negotiations: European Security and Force Reductions,* London: Lexington Books, 1973.

Koh, Byung Chul, *The Foreign Policy Systems of North and South Korea*, Berkeley and London: University of California Press, 1984.

Korean Unification: Source Materials with Introduction, Seoul: Research Centre for Peace and Unification of Korea, 1986.

Krehbiel, Carl C., *Confidence-and Security-Building Measures in Europe: The Stockholm Conference,* New York: Praeger, 1989.

Krell, Gert, *The Federal Republic of Germany and Arms Control,* Frankfurt: Peace Research Institute, PRIF Reports English No. 10, 1990.

_____, *Ostpolitik Dimensions of West German Security Policy,* Frankfurt: Peace Research Institute, PRIF Report English No.1, 1988.

Kruzel, Joseph J. *The Preconditions and Consequence of Arms Control Agreements*, Harvard University Press: Ph.D thesis, Microfilm, 1975.

_____, Kwak, Tae-Hwan and Kim, Chonghan (eds), *Korean Reunification: New Perspectives and Approaches,* Seoul: the Institution for Far Eastern Studies, 1984.

Langdon, Frank C. and Ross, Douglas A. (eds), *Superpower Maritime Strategy in the Pacific,* London: Routledge, 1990.

Larrabee, Stephen F. (ed), *The Two German States and European Security,* New York: Institute for East-West Security Studies, The Macmillan Press, 1989.

Larrabee, Stephen F. and Stobbe, *Confidence Building Measures in Europe,* New York: Institute for East-West Security Studies, 1983.

Lawrence, Marillee F., *A Game Worth the Candle: The Confidence-and Security-Building Process in Europe - An Analysis of US and Soviet Negotiating Strategies,* The RAND Corporation, P-7264-RGS, 1986.

Lee, Ho-Jae (ed), *Arms Control on the Korean Peninsula,* Bupmoonsa: Seoul, 1989. (in Korean)

Lider, Julian, *Origins and Development of West German Military Thought: 1966-1988,* Gower Publishing Company, 1988.

Lunn, John, *The Conventional Forces in Europe Talks,* London: House of Commons Library: Background Paper No. 241 February 1990.

Maccain, Morris, *Understanding Arms Control: The Options,* London: W. W. Morton & Company, 1989.

Mack, A. and Keal, P. (eds), *Security and Arms Control in the North Pacific,* Sydney: Allen & Unwin, 1988.

Mandell, Brian S., *The Sinai Experience: Lessons in Multimethod Arms Control Verification and Risk Management,* Ottawa: Arms Control Verification Studies, No.3, 1987.

Maresca, John J., *To Helsinki: The Conference on Security and Cooperation in Europe 1973-1975,* London: Duke University Press, 1987.

Mayntz, Renate and Scharpf, Fritz W., *Policy Making in the German Federal Bureaucracy,* New York: Elsevier, 1975.

McGeehan, Robert, *The German Rearmament Question: American Diplomacy and European Defence After World II,* University of Illinois Press, 1971.

McLauin Ronald D. and Moon, Chung-in, *The United States and the Defence of the Pacific,* Colorado: Westview Press, 1989.

Morrison, Charles E., *Asia-Pacific Report: Trends, Issues and Challenges,* Honolulu: the East-West Centre, 1987.

Nerlich, Uwe and Tomas, James A., *Conventional Arms Control and European Security,* London: Westview Press, 1988.

Nolan, Jane E., *Trappings of Power: Ballistic Missiles in the Third World,* Washington D.C.:The Brookings Institution, 1991.

Park, Jae Kya and Byung Chul Koh (eds), *The Foreign Relations of North Korea: New Perspectives,* Seoul: Kyungnam University Press, 1987.

Pollack, Jonathan D. and Winnefeld, James A., *U.S Strategic Alternatives in a Changing Pacific,* The RAND Corporation, R-3933-US-CINCPAC, 1990.

Pugh, Michael C., *European Security towards 2000,* Manchester: Manchester University Press, 1992.

Record, Jeffrey, *Force Reductions in Europe: Starting Over,* Cambridge and Massachusetts, Institute for Foreign Policy Analysis, Inc., 1980.

Reed Jr., John A., *Germany and NATO,* Washington D.C.: National Defence University Press, 1987.

Rees, David, *Soviet Border Problems: China and Japan,* London: Institute for the Study of Conflict, 1982.

Richardson, James L., *Germany and the Atlantic Alliance,* Harvard University Press, 1966.

Rohn, Laurinda L., *Conventional Force Reductions in Europe: A New Approach to Balance, Stability and Arms Control,* The RAND Corporation: R-3732USDP/AF, 1990

Rowell, William F., *Arms Control Verification: A Guide to Policy Issues for the 1980s,* Cambridge: Ballinger Publishing Company, 1986

Scalapino, Robert A., *Major Power Relations in Northeast Asia,* New York: University Press of America, 1987.

Schelling, Thomas C. and Halperin, Morton H., *Strategy and Arms Control,* New York:, 1961.

Schmidt, Helmut, *Defence and Retaliation,* New York: Praeger, 1972.

Segal, Gerald (ed), *Arms Control in Asia, London*: The Macmillan Press, 1987.

_____, *Normalizing Soviet-Japanese Relations*, London: RIIA, 1991.

Sheehan, Michael, *The Arms Race*, Oxford: Martin Robertson Ltd., 1983.

___, *Arms Control: Theory and Practice,* London: Basil Blackwell, 1988.

SIPRI, *The Arms Trade Registers: The Arms Trade with the Third World*, London: MIT Press, 1975.

SIPRI Yearbook 1985, 1987, 1989, 1990, 1991: World Armaments and Disarmament, Oxford: Oxford University Press.

Sizoo, Jan and Jurrejens, Rudolf T, *CSCE Decision-Making: the Madrid Experience*, Lancaster: Martinus Nijhoff, 1984.

Solomon, Richard H., *American Security in the 1980s: Problems and Policies for a Time of Transition*, Cambridge MA: Oegeshlager, Gunn & Hains, 1979.

Solomon, Richard H. and Kosaka Mastaka (eds), *The Soviet Far East Military-up: Nuclear Dilemmas and Asian Security*, Massachusetts: Auburn House Publishing Company, 1986.

South-North Dialogue in Korea 051 (February, 1991), 052 (May 1991), No.3 (December 1991), No.54 (May 1992), Seoul: International Cultural Society of Korea,

Stares, Paul B, *Allied Rights and Legal Constraints on German Military Power*, Washington D.C.: The Brookings Institution, 1990.

Sulliban John and Foss, Robert (eds), *Two Koreas-one Future*, Boston and London: University Press of America, 1987.

Szabo, Stephen F., *The Bundeswehr and Western Security*, London: MacMillan Press, 1990.

___, *The Changing Politics of German Security*, London: Pinter Publishers,1990.

Taylor, Jr., William J. and Cha, Young-Koo (eds), *The Korean Peninsula: Prospects for Arms Reduction under Global Detente*, Oxford: Westview Press, 1990.

The Military Balance 1985-86, 1988-1989, 1990-1991, 1991-1992, London ,IISS.

Thee, Marek (ed), *Armaments, Arms Control and Disarmament*, the UNESCO Press, 1981.

_____, *Armaments and Disarmament: SIPRI Finding*, Oxford University Press, 1986.

Thakur, Ramesh and Thayer, Carlyle A. (ed), *The Soviet Union as an Asian Power,* London: Westview Press, 1987.

Towle, Philip, *Arms Control and East-West Relations,* New York: St. Martin's Press, 1983.

United Nations, *Disarmament: Confidence and Security-building Measures in Asia,* New York, 1990.

White, Yolanda Simmons, *The New Arms Control-Mindedness of the Chinese,* University Microfilms International, 1982.

Wolfers, Armold, *Alliance Policy in the Cold War,* Balltimore: The Johns Hopkins Press, 1959.

Wyllie, James H., *European Security: in the Nuclear Age,* Oxford: Basil Blackwell, Ltd, 1986.

Zinner, Paul E., *East-West Relations in Europe: Observation and Advice from the Sidelines, 1971-1982,* Westview Press, 1984.

Yang Richard (ed), *China's Military: The PLA in 1990/1991,* Colorado.: Westview Press, 1991.

Journals and Periodicals

Abramowith, Morton, "Moving the Glacier: the two Koreas and the Powers", London, IISS, *Adelphi Paper* 80, 1971.

Adragna, Steven P., "Doctrine and Strategy", *Orbis,* Vol. 33, No. 2, Spring 1989.

Alford, Jonathan (ed), "The Future of Arms Control Part III: Confidence Building Measures in Europe", London: IISS, *Adelphi Paper* 149, 1979.

Asda, Masahiko, "Confidence-Building Measures in East Asia: A Japanese Perspective", *Asian Survey,* Vol. XXXVIII, No. 5. May 1988.

Asmus, Donald D., "West Germany Faces Nuclear Modernization", *Survival,* Vol.30, No.6, November/December, 1988.

Bermudez Jr., Joseph S. and Carus, W. Seth, "The North Korean Scud B Programme", *Jane's Soviet Intelligence Review,* April, 1989.

Bertram, Christoph, "Mutual Force Reduction in Europe: the Political Aspect", London, IISS, Adelphi Paper, No. 84, 1972.

Blacker, Coit D., "Negotiating Security: The MBFR Experience", *Arms Control*, Vol.7, No.3, December, 1986.

Blackwill, Robert D., "Conceptual Problems of Conventional Arms Control", *International Security*, Vol. 12, No. 4. Spring 1988.

Blank, Stephen, "Soviet Perspectives on Arms Control in the Korean Peninsula", *The Korean Journal of Defence Analysis*, Vol. III, No. 1, September, 1991.

Bomsdorf, Falk, "The Confidence-Building Offensive in the United Nations", *Aussen Politik*, Vol. 33, No. 4, 1982.

Borwaski, John, "Mutual Force Reduction in Europe from a Soviet Perspective", *Orbis*, Vol.22, No.4, 1979.

_____, "Accord at Stockholm", *Bulletin of the Atomic Scientists*, Vol.42 No.10, December, 1986.

_____, "The Stockholm Agreement of September 1986", *Orbis*, Vol. 30, No. 4, Winter, 1987.

_____, "The Vienna Negotiations on Confidence and Security-Building Measures", *RUSI Journal*, Autumn 1990.

Brodie, Barnard, "On Clarifying the Objective of Arms Control", *International Security*, Vol. 1, No. 1, Summer, 1976.

Brauch, Hans Gunter, "Confidence Building Measure and Disarmament Strategy", *Current Research on Peace and Violence*, 3-4/1979.

Brown, Stuart, "CSBM - The Other Negotiations", *NATO's Sixteen Nations*, Vol.34, No.4, August 1989.

Burt, Richard, "A Glass Half Empty", *Foreign Policy*, No.36, Fall 1979.

Cha, Young Koo, "Northeast Asian Security: A Korean Perspective", *Significant Issues Series*, Vol. X, No. 1, 1988.

Cheung, Tai Ming, "Disarmament and Development in China", *Asian Survey*, Vol. XXXVIII, No. 7, July, 1988.

Chinworth, Michael W. and Cheng, Dean, "United States and Asia in the Post-Cold War World", *SAIS Review*, Winter-Spring, 1991.

Choi, Young, "The Arms Race and Arms Control in Korea", *Korea and World Affairs*, Vol. 10, NO. 2, Summer, 1986.

Chung, In-Moon, "Managing the Inter-Korean Conflict and Confidence Building Measures", *Korea Observer*, Spring 1991.

Cotton, James, "North-South Korean Relations: Another False Start?", *The World Today*, Vol. 45, June, 1989.

Crowe, William Jr., William J. and Rombert D., "Rethinking Security in the Pacific", *Foreign Affairs,* Vol.70, No.2, 1991.

Darilek, Richard E., "Building Confidence and Security in Europe: The Road to and from Stockholm", *Washington Quarterly*, Vol. 8, No. 1, 1985.

Dean, Jonathan, "Directions in Inner-German Relations", *Orbis*, Vol. 29, No. 3, Fall, 1985.

Diehl, Paul, "Arms Race and Escalation: A Closer Look", *Journal of Peace Research,* Vol.20, No.3, 1983.

Feinstein, Lee, "The Case of CFE", *Arms Control Today,* Vol.21, No.1, January /February 1991.

Findlay, Trevor, "Sinai and Contadora: Non-European Models for Asia /Pacific Confidence", Canberra: Peace Research Centre, *Working Paper 79,* April, 1990.

____,"Asia-Pacific CSBM: A Prospectus", Working Paper, No. 90, 1990.

Forray, d'Armee Gilvert, "France-German Co-operation - beyond Hardy Sparrow", *The NATO's Sixteen Nations*, Feb-March, 1990.

Foot, Rosemary J., "Coercion and the Ending of the Korean Conflict", *International Security,* Vol.13, No.3, Winter, 1988/1989.

Freedman Lawerence, "The Politics of Conventional Arms Control", *Survival*, Vol.31, No.5, September/October, 1989.

Galvin, John R., "Some Thoughts on Conventional Arms Control", *Survival*, Vol.31, No.2, March/April, 1983.

Ghebli, Victo-Yves and Tanner, Fred, "Confidence-Building Measures in Arms Control: the Mouse that Roared?", *International Defence Review*, Vol.21, No. 10/1988.

___, *"*CFE First Years Status Report*"*, *International Defence Review*, Vol.23. No.4, 1990.

Giblin, James F, "National Strategies and Japan's Northern Territories", *Naval War College Review*, Winter, 1987.

Glaser, Bonnie S., "Soviet, Chinese and American Perspectives on Arms Control in Northeast Asia", Canberra: Peace Research Centre, *Working Paper*, No. 28., 1988.

Graham, Thomas, Jr. "The CFE Story: Tales from the Negotiating Table", *Arms Control Today,* Vol. 21, No.1, January/February, 1991.

Gong, Gerrit W. and Grant, Richard L., "Security and Economics in the Asian Pacific Region", *Significant Issues Series,* (Washington D.C.: CSIS), Vol.XIII, No.9 1991

Hamm, Mnfred R. and Pohlman, Hartmut, "Military Doctrines and Strategies-The Missing Keys to Success in Conventional Arms Control?", *Aussen Politik,* Vol.41, 1/1990.

Hartmann, Rudiger, "The CFE Negotiations-A Promising Start", *NATO Review,* Vol.37, No.3, June 1989.

Hasegawa, Tsuyoshi, "Soviet Arms Control Policy in Asia and the Japan-US Alliance", *Japan Review of International Affairs*, Fall/Winter, 1988.

Hayes, Peter, "American Nuclear Hegemony in Korea", *Journal of Peace Reserach,* Vol. 25, No. 4 (December, 1988)

Hirschfeld, Tomas J., "MBFR in Eclipse", *Arms Control Today*, Vol.16, No.7, October, 1986.

___, "Arms Control in Europe and Now the Conventional Stability", *Arms Control Today,* Vol.18, No.2, March, 1988.

Holder, Kate and Hunter, Robert E.(eds), "Confidence on Security and Cooperation in Europe: The Next Phase", *Significant Issues Series* (Washington D.C.: CSIS,) Vol.III, No.7, 1991.

Holst, Johan J., "Arms Control and European Political Process", *Survival*, Vol.XV, No.5, September/October, 1973.

____, "Confidence Building Measures: A Conceptual Framework", *Survival*, Vol. XXX, No. 1, January/February, 1983.

Hunter, Helen-Louise, "North Korea and the Myth of Equidistance", *Korea and World Affairs*, Vol.34, No.2, Summer 1980.

Janes, David T, "Post-INF Treaty Attitude in East Asia", *Asian Survey*, Vol. XXX, No. 5, May, 1990.

Johnston, Douglas M., "Anticipating Instability in the Asia-Pacific Regions", *The Washington Quarterly*, Vol.15, No.3, Summer, 1992.

Jung, Ernst F., "Conventional Arms Control in Europe in Light of the MBFR Experience", *Aussen Politik*, Vol. 39, No.2, February, 1988.

Kim, Yong Nam, "A View from Pyongyang", *International Affairs* (Moscow), January 1990.

Kim, Myung-Ki, "Some Legal Problems Concerning Withdrawal of the United Nations Forces", *The Journal of East Asian Affairs*, Vol. IV, No. 2 Summer/Fall, 1990.

Kim, Young C., "The Politics of Arms Control in Korea", *The Korean Journal of Defense Analysis*, No.1, Summer 1989.

Kimura, Hiroshi, "Soviet Focus on the Pacific", *Problems of Communisms*, May-June, 1987.

Kirby, Stephen, "Linking European and Pacific Strategies", *The Pacific Review*, Vol.1, No. 3, 1988.

Klintworth, Gary, "Arms Control and Great-Power Interests in the Korean Peninsula", *The Korean Journal of Defence Analysis*, Vol. III, No. 1, Summer, 1991.

Kwak, Tae-Whanm, "Designing the Non-nuclear Korean Peninsula: Problems and Prospects", *The Korean Journal of Defence Analysis*, Vol. IV, No.1, Summer, 1992.

Kruzel, Joseph J. "From Rush-Bargot to Start: The Lessons of Arms Control", *Orbis*, Vol. 28, No. 4, Winter, 1985.

Leavitt, Robert, "Next Steps for European Conventional Arms Reduction", *Arms Control Today*, Vol.21, No. 1, Jan./Feb. 1991,

Lee, Min Yong, "The Feasibility of the Arms Control Discussion in the Korean Peninsula", *Korea Observer*, Spring, 1990.

Lee, Jung Min, "The Future of Arms Control in the Korean Peninsula", *The Washington Quarterly,* Vol.14. No.3, Summer 1991.

Lewis, Kevin N. and Lorell, Mark A. "Confidence-Building Measures and Crisis Resolution: Historical Perspectives", *Orbis,* Vol. 28, No. 2, Summer, 1984.

Lemon, F., "The Maritime Strategy", *Proceedings,* February, 1986.

Lightburn, David T., "Enhancing Security-Arms Transfers under CFE Ceilings", *NATO's Sixteen Nations*, Vol.36, No.3, May/June, 1991.

Lim, Dong-Won, "An Urgent Need for Arms Control on the Korean Peninsula: A framework for Implementation", *The Korean Journal of Defence Analysis,* Vol.III, No.1, Summer, 1991.

Lincoln, Edward J., "Japan's Role in Asia-Pacific Cooperation: Dimensions, Prospects and Problems", *Journal of Northeast Asian Studies,* Vol.VIII, No.4, Winter, 1989.

Listhaug, Ola, "War and Defence Attitudes: A First Look at Survey Data from 14 Countries", *Journal of Peace Reserach*, Vol.23, No.1, 1986.

Mack, Andrew, "Arms Control in the North Pacific: Problems and Prospects", Canberra: Peace Reserach Centre, *Working Paper*, No.36, 1989.

_____, "Arms Control in the Pacific: the Naval Dimension", Canberra: *Working Paper,* No.88, 1990.

_____ , "Nuclear Issues and Arms Control on the Korean Peninsula", Canberra:*Working Paper*, 96, 1990.

Mack, A. and McClean A., "The Growing Interests in Asia-Pacific Arms Control Issues", Canberra: *Working Paper*, No.75, 1989.

Macdonald, Donald S., "The Role of the Major Powers in the Reunification of Korea", *The Washington Quarterly,* Vol.15, No.3, Summer, 1992.

Mack, A. and O'Hare, Martin, "Moscow-Tokyo and the Northern Territories Dispute", *Asian Survey,* Vol.XXX, No.4, April, 1990.

Menon, Rajan, "New Thinking and Northeast Asian Security", *Problems of Communism,* March-June. 1989.

Meyer, Stephen M., "The Sources and Prospects of Gorbachev's New Political Thinking on Security", *International Security,* Vol.13, No.2, Fall, 1988. Fall

Miller, Steven E., "Politics over Promises: the Domestic Impediments to Arms Control", *International Security*, Vol.8, No.4, Spring, 1986.

Moon, Jung-in, "Managing the Inter-Korean Conflict and Confidence Building Measures", *Korea Observer,* Spring, 1991.

Mueller, Herald and Rissen-Kappen, Thomas, "Origins of Estrangement: the Peace Movement and the Changed Unique of America in West Germany", *International Security,* Vol. 12, No. 1, Summer, 1987.

Olsen, Edward A, "The Arms Race on the Korean Peninsula", *Asian Survey,* Vol. XXVI, NO. 8, August, 1986.

Overholt, William H., "Nuclear Proliferation in Eastern Asia", *Pacific Community*, Vol.8, No.1, October, 1976.

Park, Tong Whan, "Political Economy of the Arms Race in Korea", *Asian Survey,* Vol.26, No.8, August, 1986.

Park, Young-ok, "Japan's Defence Build-up and Regional Balance", *The Korean Journal of Defense Analysis*, Vol. III, No. 1, Summer, 1991.

Rittberger, Volker, Finger, Manfred E. and Mendler, Martin, "Toward an East-West Security Regime: the Case of Confidence-and Security-Building Measures", *Journal of Peace Research*, Vol. 27, No. 1, 1990.

Ruehl, Lothar, "MBFR: Lessons and Problems", London, IISS, *Adelphi Paper*, No. 176, 1982.

Sauerwein, Brigitte, "Military Doctrine: The Software of Defense", *International Defence Review,* Vol.23, 5/1990.

Schandler, Herbert Y., "Arms Control in Northeast Asia", *The Washington Quarterly,* Winter, 1987.

Schelling, Thomas C., "What Went Wrong with Arms Control?", *Foreign Affairs,* Vol.64, No.2, Winter, 1985-1986.

Schmidt, Peter, "Public Opinion and Security Policy in Federal Republic of Germany", *Orbis*, Vol. 28, No. 4, Winter, 1985.

Segal, Gerald, "Informal Arms Control: The Asian Road to Conventional Reductions", *Arms Control Today*, Vol.19, No.4, May, 1989.

____, "A New Order in Northeast Asia", *The Washington Quarterly*, Vol.21, No.7, Winter 1987.

____, "Managing New Arms Race in the Asia Pacific", *The Washington Quarterly*, Vol.15, No.3, Summer, 1992.

Sheehan, Michael, "A More Inane Congress: Twelve Years of MBFR", *Arms Control*, Vol.6, No. 2, September, 1985.

Silverman, Wendy, "Taking Sufficiency in the Hofburg Palace: The Second Seminar on Military Doctrine", *Arms Control Today*, Vol.20, No.10, December, 1990.

Sloan, Stan, "Breaking with Convention: The Start of New European Force Talks", *Arms Control Today*, Vol.19, No.3, April, 1989.

Solomon, Richard H., "The Pacific Basin: Dilemmas and Choices for American Security", *Naval War College Review*, Vol. XXXX, No.1, Winter, 1987.

Spanger, Hans-Joachim, "The GDR in East-West Relations", London, IISS, *Adelphi Paper* 240, 1989.

Spector, Leonard S. and Smith, Jacqueline R., "North Korea: the Next Nuclear Nightmare?", *Arms Control Today*, Vol.21, No.2 March, 1991.

Speight, John, "CFE 1990: Achievements and Prospects", *Faraday Discussion Paper*, No.15, London: the Council for Arms Control, 1990.

Strode, Dan L., "Arms Control and Sino-Soviet Relations", *Orbis*, Vol. 28, No. 1, Spring 1984.

Taylor, William J. and Mazarr, Michael J., and Smith, Jennifer A., "US Troop Reduction from Korea, 1970-1990", *The Journal of East Asian Affairs*, Vol.IV, No.2, Summer/Fall, 1990.

Tretiak, Daniel, "The Sino-Japanese Treaty of 1978: the Senkaku Incident Prelude", *Asian Survey*, Vol. XVIII No.12. December, 1978.

Weiller, Matthew A. "SPD Security Policy", *Survival,* Vol.30, No.6, November/December, 1988.

Wellershof, Dieter C., "First Successful in CSBM Negotiations: the Military Doctrine Seminar", *NATO Review,* Vol.38, No.2 April, 1990.

Wishmick, Elizabeth, "Soviet Asian Collective Security Policy from Brezhnev", *Journal of Northeast Asian Studies,* Fall 1988.

Whiting, Allen S., "New Perspectives in Asia: Arms Control in Northeast Asia", *Pacific Community,* Vol.3, No.2, January, 1972.

Witmann, Klaus, "Challenges of Conventional Arms Control", London, IISS, *Adelphi Paper* 239, Summer, 1989.

Zargorski, Alexei V., "Confidence-Building Measures: An Alternative for Asian-Pacific Security", *The Pacific Review,* 1991, Vol.3, No.4, 1991.

US Congressional Hearings

House, Committee on Armed Services, *Review of the Policy Decision to Withdraw United States Ground Forces from Korea,* A Report of the investigations subcommittee, 95th Congress, 2nd Session, April, 1978.

House, Committee on Foreign Affairs, *The Korean Conundrum: A Conversation with Kim Il Sung,* A Report of a Study Mission to South Korea, Japan, The People's Republic of China and North Korea, 97th Congress, 1st Session, 1981.

House, Committee on Foreign Affairs, *Arms Control in Asia and US Interests in the Region,* Hearings before subcommittee on Asian and Pacific Affairs, 101th Congress, 2nd Session, Washington D:C. GPO., January/March, 1990.

House, Subcommittee on Asian and Pacific Affairs of Committee on Foreign Affairs, *Overview of Recent Events in the East Asian and Pacific Region 1990,* 101th Congress, 2nd Session, February 22, 1990.

House, Subcommittee on Asian and Pacific Affairs of Committee on Foreign Affairs, *Development in the United States-Republic of Korean Relations,* 101th Congress, 2nd Session, July 26, 1990.

Senate, Committee on Foreign Relations, *US Troop Withdrawal From the ROK,* A Report to the Committee by Senators Hubert Humphrey and John Glenn, 95th Congress, 2nd Session, 1978.

Senate, Committee on Armed Services, *The President's Report on the US Military Presence in East Asia,* 101th Congress, 2nd Session, April 19, 1989.

Official Documents

Ministry of Foreign Affairs of GDR, "SED-SPD Working Group in Favour of Continuing Process of Disarmament", *Foreign Affairs Bulletin,* February 1987.

NATO Press Service, "Financial and Economic Data Relating to NATO Defence", November 28, 1989.

ROK, National Unification Board, *A White Paper on South-North Dialogue in Korea,* Seoul, 1988.

The Federal German Minister of Defence, *White Paper 1976, 1985.*

The Japanese Defence Agency, *Defence of Japan, 1989, 1990, 1991.*

The Ministry of National Defence of the Republic of Korea, *Korean Defence White Paper 1989, 1990, 1991-1992.*